Frederick Chopin as
A Man And Musician
Vol. 2

by

Frederick Niecks

Frederick Chopin as
A Man And Musician
Vol. 2
by Frederick Niecks

Copyright © 2023

All Rights reserved.

ISBN: 978-93-59325-25-5

Published by

DOUBLE 9 BOOKS

2/13-B, Ansari Road
Daryaganj, New Delhi – 110002
info@double9books.com
www.double9books.com
Tel. 011-40042856

ABOUT THE AUTHOR

Frederick Niecks (3 February 1845 – 24 June 1924) was a German musical scholar and author who spent much of his life in Scotland. His most famous works are biographies of Frédéric Chopin and Robert Schumann. Friedrich Maternus Niecks was born in Düsseldorf, the son of a conductor and instructor, and the grandson of a professional musician. His father taught him music, and he later studied violin with Leopold Auer and others, as well as piano and composition with Julius Tausch. He made his debut at the age of 13 with Charles Auguste de Bériot's Violin Concerto No. 2, then joined the Musikverein orchestra, where he remained until the age of 21. In 1868, he expressed a wish to go to the United Kingdom, and Alexander Mackenzie persuaded him to reside in Scotland, where he worked as a violist in Mackenzie's string quartet in Edinburgh and as an organist and teacher in Dumfries. In 1879, he began contributing to The Musical Times on a regular basis. He wrote a Concise Dictionary of Musical Terms in two editions in 1884. Frédéric Chopin as Man and Musician, his magnum work, was released in 1888, with a German version following in 1889. This was Chopin's first full biography.

CONTENTS

CHAPTER XX

1836—1838.

THE LOVES OF CELEBRITIES.—VARIOUS ACCOUNTS OF CHOPIN AND GEORGE SAND'S FIRST MEETING.—CHOPIN'S FIRST IMPRESSION OF HER.—A COMPARISON OF THE TWO CHARACTERS.— PORTRAYALS OF CHOPIN AND GEORGE SAND.—HER POWER OF PLEASING.—CHOPIN'S PUBLICATIONS IN 1837 AND 1838.—HE PLAYS AT COURT AND AT CONCERTS IN PARIS AND ROUEN.—CRITICISM.

THE loves of famous men and women, especially of those connected with literature and the fine arts, have always excited much curiosity. In the majority of cases the poet's and artist's choice of a partner falls on a person who is incapable of comprehending his aims and sometimes even of sympathising with his striving. The question "why poets are so apt to choose their mates, not for any similarity of poetical endowment, but for qualities which might make the happiness of the rudest handicrafts-man as well as that of the ideal craftsman" has perhaps never been better answered than by Nathaniel Hawthorne, who remarks that "at his highest elevation the poet needs no human intercourse; but he finds it dreary to descend, and be a stranger." Still, this is by no means a complete solution of the problem which again and again presents itself and challenges our ingenuity. Chopin and George Sand's case belongs to the small minority of loves where both parties are distinguished practitioners of ideal crafts. Great would be the mistake, however, were we to assume that the elective affinities of such lovers are easily discoverable On the contrary, we have here another problem, one which, owing to the higher, finer, and more varied factors that come into play, is much more difficult to solve than the first. But before we can engage in solving the problem, it must be properly propounded. Now, to ascertain facts about the love-affairs of poets and artists is the very reverse of an easy task; and this is so partly because the parties naturally do not let outsiders into all their secrets, and partly because romantic minds and imaginative litterateurs are always busy developing plain facts and unfounded rumours into wonderful myths. The picturesqueness of the story, the piquancy of the anecdote, is generally in inverse proportion to the narrator's knowledge of the matter in question. In short, truth is only too often most unconsciously sacrificed to effect. Accounts, for instance, such as L. Enault and Karasowski have given of Chopin's first meeting with George Sand can be recommended only to those who care for amusing gossip about the world of art, and do not mind whether what they read is the simple truth or not, nay, do not mind even whether it has any verisimilitude. Nevertheless, we will give these gentlemen a hearing, and then try if we cannot find some firmer ground to stand on.

L. Enault relates that Chopin and George Sand met for the first time at one of the fetes of the Marquis de C., where the aristocracy of Europe assembled—the aristocracy of genius, of birth, of wealth, of beauty, &c.:—

The last knots of the chaine anglaise had already been untied, the brilliant crowd had left the ball-room, the murmur of discreet conversation was heard in the boudoirs: the fetes of the intimate friends began. Chopin seated himself at the piano. He played one of those ballads whose words are written by no poet, but whose subjects, floating in the dreamy soul of nations, belong to the artist who likes to take them. I believe it was the Adieux du Cavalier...Suddenly, in the middle of the ballad, he perceived, close to the door, immovable and pale, the beautiful face of Lelia. [FOOTNOTE: This name of the heroine of one of her romances is often given to George Sand. See Vol. I., p. 338.] She fixed her passionate and sombre eyes upon him; the impressionable artist felt at the same time pain and pleasure... others might listen to him: he played only for her.

They met again.

From this moment fears vanished, and these two noble souls understood each other... or believed they understood each other.

Karasowski labours hard to surpass Enault, but is not like him a master of the ars artem celare. The weather, he tells us, was dull and damp, and had a depressing effect on the mind of Chopin. No friend had visited him during the day, no book entertained him, no musical idea gladdened him. It was nearly ten o'clock at night (the circumstantiality of the account ought to inspire confidence) when he bethought himself of paying a visit to the Countess C. (the Marquis, by some means, magical or natural, has been transformed into a Countess), this being her jour fixe, on which an intellectual and agreeable company was always assembled at her house.

When he ascended the carpet-covered stairs [Unfortunately we are not informed whether the carpet was Turkey, Brussels, or Kidderminster], it seemed to him as if he were followed by a shadow that diffused a fragrance of violets [Ah!], and a presentiment as if something strange and wonderful were going to happen to him flashed through his soul. He was on the point of turning back and going home, but, laughing at his own superstition, he bounded lightly and cheerfully over the last steps.

Skipping the fine description of the brilliant company assembled in the salon, the enumeration of the topics on which the conversation ran, and the observation that Chopin, being disinclined to talk, seated himself in a corner and watched the beautiful ladies as they glided hither and thither, we will join Karasowski again where, after the departure of the greater number of the guests, Chopin goes to the piano and begins to improvise.

His auditors, whom he, absorbed in his own thoughts and looking only at the keys, had entirely forgotten, listened with breathless attention. When he had concluded his improvisation, he raised his eyes, and noticed a plainly-dressed lady who, leaning on the instrument, seemed to wish to read his soul with her dark fiery eyes. [Although a severe critic might object to the attitude of a lady leaning on a piano as socially and pictorially awkward, he must admit that from a literary point of view it is unquestionably more effective than sitting or standing by the door.] Chopin felt he was blushing under the fascinating glances of the lady [Bravo! This is a master-touch]; she smiled [Exquisite!], and when the artist was about to withdraw from the company behind a group of camellias, he heard the peculiar rustling of a silk dress, which exhaled a fragrance of violets [Camellias, rustling silks, fragrance of violets! What a profusion of beauty and sweetness!], and the same lady who had watched him so inquiringly at the piano approached him accompanied by Liszt. Speaking to him with a deep, sweet voice, she made some remarks on his playing, and more especially on the contents of his improvisation. Frederick listened to her with pleasure and emotion, and while words full of sparkling wit and indescribable poetry flowed from the lady's eloquent lips [Quite a novel representation of her powers of conversation], he felt that he was understood as he had never been.

All this is undoubtedly very pretty, and would be invaluable in a novel, but I am afraid we should embarrass Karasowski were we to ask him to name his authorities.

Of this meeting at the house of the Marquis de C.—i.e., the Marquis de Custine—I was furnished with a third version by an eye-witness—namely, by Chopin's pupil Adolph Gutmann. From him I learned that the occasion was neither a full-dress ball nor a chance gathering of a jour fixe, but a musical matinee. Gutmann, Vidal (Jean Joseph), and Franchomme opened the proceedings with a trio by Mayseder, a composer the very existence of whose once popular chamber-music is unknown to the present generation. Chopin played a great deal, and George Sand devoured him with her eyes. Afterwards the musician and the novelist walked together a long time in the garden. Gutmann was sure that this matinee took place either in 1836 or in 1837, and was inclined to think that it was in the first-mentioned year.

Franchomme, whom I questioned about the matinee at the Marquis de Custine's, had no recollection of it. Nor did he remember the circumstance of having on this or any other occasion played a trio of Mayseder's with Gutmann and Vidal. But this friend of the Polish pianist—composer, while confessing his ignorance as to the place where the latter met the great novelist for the first time, was quite certain as to the year when he met her. Chopin, Franchomme informed me, made George Sand's acquaintance in 1837, their connection was broken in 1847, and he died, as everyone knows, on October 17, 1849. In each of these dates appears the number which Chopin regarded with a superstitious dread, which he avoided whenever he could-for instance, he would not at any price take lodgings in a house the number of which contained a seven—and which may be thought by some to have really exercised a fatal influence over him. It is hardly necessary to point out that it was this fatal number which fixed the date in Franchomme's memory.

But supposing Chopin and George Sand to have really met at the Marquis de Custine's, was this their first meeting?

[FOONOTE: That they were on one occasion both present at a party given by the Marquis de Custine may be gathered from Freiherr von Flotow's Reminiscences of his life in Paris (published in the "Deutsche Revue" of January, 1883, p. 65); but not that this was their first meeting, nor the time when it took place. As to the character of this dish of reminiscences, I may say that it is sauced and seasoned for the consumption of the blase magazine reader, and has no nutritive substance whatever.]

I put the question to Liszt in the course of a conversation I had with him some years ago in Weimar. His answer was most positive, and to the effect that the first meeting took place at Chopin's own apartments. "I ought to know best," he added, "seeing that I was instrumental in bringing the two together." Indeed, it would be difficult to find a more trustworthy witness in this matter than Liszt, who at that time not only was one of the chief comrades of Chopin, but also of George Sand. According to him, then, the meeting came about in this way. George Sand, whose curiosity had been excited both by the Polish musician's compositions and by the accounts she had heard of him, expressed to Liszt the wish to make the acquaintance of his friend. Liszt thereupon spoke about her to Chopin, but the latter was averse to having any intercourse with her. He said he did not like literary women, and was not made for their society; it was different with his friend, who there found himself in his element. George Sand, however, did not cease to remind Liszt of his promise to introduce her to Chopin. One morning in the early part of 1837 Liszt called on his friend and brother-artist, and found him in high spirits on account of some compositions he had lately finished. As Chopin was anxious to play them to his friends, it was arranged to have in the evening a little party at his rooms.

This seemed to Liszt an excellent opportunity to redeem the promise which he had given George Sand when she asked for an introduction; and, without telling Chopin what he was going to do, he brought her with him along with the Comtesse d'Agoult. The success of the soiree was such that it was soon followed by a second and many more.

In the foregoing accounts the reader will find contradictions enough to exercise his ingenuity upon. But the involuntary tricks of memory and the voluntary ones of imagination make always such terrible havoc of facts that truth, be it ever so much sought and cared for, appears in history, and biography only in a more or less disfigured condition. George Sand's own allusion to the commencement of the acquaintance agrees best with Liszt's account. After passing in the latter part of 1836 some months in Switzerland with Liszt and the Comtesse d'Agoult, she meets them again at Paris in the December of the same year:—

At the Hôtel de France, where Madame d'Agoult had persuaded me to take quarters near her, the conditions of existence were charming for a few days. She received many litterateurs, artists, and some clever men of fashion. It was at Madame d'Agoult's, or through her, that I made the acquaintance of Eugene Sue, Baron d'Eckstein, Chopin, Mickiewicz, Nourrit, Victor Schoelcher, &c. My friends became also hers. Through me she got acquainted with M. Lamennais, Pierre-Leroux, Henri Heine, &c. Her salon, improvised in an inn, was therefore a reunion d'elite over which she presided with exquisite grace, and where she found herself the equal of all the eminent specialists by reason of the extent of her mind and the variety of her faculties, which were at once poetic and serious. Admirable music was performed there, and in the intervals one could instruct one's self by listening to the conversation.

To reconcile Liszt's account with George Sand's remark that Chopin was one of those whose acquaintance she made at Madame d'Agoult's or through her, we have only to remember the intimate relation in which Liszt stood to this lady (subsequently known in literature under the nom de plume of Daniel Stern), who had left her husband, the Comte d'Agoult, in 1835.

And now at last we can step again from the treacherous quicksand of reminiscences on the terra firma of documents. The following extracts from some letters of George Sand's throw light on her relation to Chopin in the early part of 1837:—

Nohant, March 28, 1837.

[To Franz Liszt.]...Come and see us as soon as possible. Love, esteem, and friendship claim you at Nohant. Love (Marie [FOOTNOTE: The Comtesse d'Agoult.]) is some what ailing, esteem (Maurice and Pelletan [FOOTNOTE: The former, George Sand's son; the latter, Eugene Pelletan, Maurice's tutor.]) pretty well, and friendship (myself) obese and in excellent health.

Marie told me that there was some hope of Chopin. Tell Chopin that I beg of him to accompany you; that Marie cannot live without him, and that I adore him.

I shall write to Grzymala personally in order to induce him also, if I can, to come and see us. I should like to be able to surround Marie with all her friends, in order that she also may live in the bosom of love, esteem, and friendship.

[FOOTNOTE: Albert Grzymala, a man of note among the Polish refugees. He was a native of Dunajowce in Podolia, had held various military and other posts—those of maitre des requites, director of the Bank of Poland, attache to the staff of Prince Poniatowski, General Sebastiani, and Lefebvre, &c.—and was in 1830 sent by the Polish Government on a diplomatic mission to Berlin, Paris, and London. (See L'Amanach de L'Emigration polonaise, published at Paris some forty years ago.) He must not be confounded with the publicist Francis Grzymala, who at Warsaw was considered one of the marechaux de plume, and at Paris was connected with the Polish publication Sybilla. With one exception (Vol. I., p. 3), the Grzymala spoken of in these volumes is Albert Grzymala, sometimes also called Count Grzymala. This title, however, was, if I am rightly informed, only a courtesy title. The Polish nobility as such was untitled, titles being of foreign origin and not legally recognised. But many Polish noblemen when abroad assume the prefix de or von, or the title "Count," in order to make known their rank.]

Nohant, April 5, 1837.

[To the Comtesse d'Agoult.]...Tell Mick....[FOOTNOTE: Mickiewicz, the poet.] (non-compromising manner of writing Polish names) that my pen and my house are at his service, and are only too happy to be so; tell Grzy...., [FOOTNOTE: Gryzmala] whom I adore, Chopin, whom I idolatrise, and all those whom you love that I love them, and that, brought by you, they will be welcome. Berry in a body watches for the maestro's [FOOTNOTE: Liszt's] return in order to hear him play the piano. I believe we shall be obliged to place le garde- champetre and la garde nationals of Nohant under arms in order to defend ourselves against the dilettanti berrichoni. Nohant, April 10, 1837.

[To the Comtesse d'Agoult.] I want the fellows, [FOOTNOTE: "Fellows" (English) was the nickname which Liszt gave to himself and his pupil Hermann Cohen.] I want them as soon and as LONG as possible. I want them a mort. I want also Chopin and all the Mickiewiczs and Grzymalas in the world. I want even Sue if you want him. What more would I not want if that were your fancy? For instance, M. de Suzannet or Victor Schoelcher! Everything, a lover excepted. Nohant, April 21, 1837.

[To the Comtesse d'Agoult.] Nobody has permitted himself to breathe the air of your room since you left it. Arrangements will be made to put up all those you may bring with you. I count on the maestro, on Chopin, on the Rat, [FOOTNOTE: Liszt's pupil, Hermann Cohen.] if he does not weary you too much, and all the others at your choice.

Chopin's love for George Sand was not instantaneous like that of Romeo for Juliet. Karasowski remembers having read in one of those letters of the composer which perished in 1863: "Yesterday I met George Sand...; she made a very disagreeable impression upon me." Hiller in his Open Letter to Franz Liszt writes:—

One evening you had assembled in your apartments the aristocracy of the French literary world—George Sand was of course one of the company. On the way home Chopin said to me "What a repellent [antipathische] woman the Sand is! But is she really a woman? I am inclined to doubt it."

Liszt, in discussing this matter with me, spoke only of Chopin's "reserve" towards George Sand, but said nothing of his "aversion" to her. And according to this authority the novelist's extraordinary mind and attractive conversation soon overcame the musician's reserve. Alfred de Musset's experience had been of a similar nature. George Sand did not particularly please him at first, but a few visits which he paid her sufficed to inflame his heart with a violent passion. The liaisons of the poet and musician with the novelist offer other points of resemblance besides the one just mentioned: both Musset and Chopin were younger than George Sand— the one six, the other five years; and both, notwithstanding the dissimilarity of their characters, occupied the position of a weaker half. In the case of Chopin I am reminded of a saying of Sydney Smith, who, in speaking of his friends the historian Grote and his wife, remarked: "I do like them both so much, for he is so lady-like, and she is such a perfect gentleman." Indeed, Chopin was described to me by his pupil Gutmann as feminine in looks, gestures, and taste; as to George Sand, although many may be unwilling to admit her perfect gentlemanliness, no one can doubt her manliness:—

Dark and olive-complexioned Lelia! [writes Liszt] thou hast walked in solitary places, sombre as Lara, distracted as Manfred, rebellious as Cain, but more fierce [farouche], more pitiless, more inconsolable than they, because thou hast found among the hearts of men none feminine enough to love thee as they have been loved, to pay to thy virile charms the tribute of a confiding and blind submission, of a silent and ardent devotion, to suffer his allegiance to be protected by thy Amazonian strength!

The enthusiasm with which the Poles of her acquaintance spoke of their countrywomen, and the amorous suavity, fulness of feeling, and spotless nobleness which she admired in the Polish composer's inspirations, seem to have made her anticipate, even before meeting Chopin, that she would find in him her ideal lover, one whose love takes the form of worship. To quote Liszt's words: "She believed that there, free from all dependence, secure against all inferiority, her role would rise to the fairy-like power of some being at once the superior and the friend of man." Were it not unreasonable to regard spontaneous utterances—expressions of passing moods and fancies, perhaps mere flights of rhetoric—as well-considered expositions of stable principles, one might be tempted to ask: Had George Sand found in Chopin the man who was "bold or vile enough" to accept her "hard and clear" conditions? [FOOTNOTE: See extract from one of her letters in the preceding chapter, Vol. I., p. 334.]

While the ordinary position of man and woman was entirely reversed in this alliance, the qualities which characterised them can nevertheless hardly ever have been more nearly diametrically opposed. Chopin was weak and undecided; George Sand strong and energetic. The former shrank from inquiry and controversy; the latter threw herself eagerly into them. [FOOTNOTE: George Sand talks much of the indolence of her temperament: we may admit this fact, but must not overlook another one— namely, that she was in possession of an immense fund of energy, and was always ready to draw upon it whenever speech or action served her purpose or fancy.] The one was a strict observer of the laws of propriety and an almost exclusive frequenter of fashionable society; the other, on the contrary, had an unmitigated scorn for the so-called proprieties and so-called good society. Chopin's manners exhibited a studied refinement, and no woman could be more particular in the matter of dress than he was. It is characteristic of the man that he was so discerning a judge of the elegance and perfection of a female toilette as to be able to tell at a glance whether a dress had been made in a first-class establishment or in an inferior one. The great composer is said to have had an unlimited admiration for a well-made and well-carried (bien porte) dress. Now what a totally different picture presents itself when we turn to George Sand, who says of herself, in speaking of her girlhood, that although never boorish or importunate, she was always brusque in her movements and natural in her manners, and had a horror of gloves and profound bows. Her fondness for male garments is as characteristic as Chopin's connoisseurship of the female toilette; it did not end with her student life, for she donned them again in 1836 when travelling in Switzerland.

The whole of Chopin's person was harmonious. "His appearance," says Moscheles, who saw him in 1839, "is exactly like his music [ist identificirt mit seiner Musik], both are tender and schwarmerisch."

[FOOTNOTE: I shall not attempt to translate this word, but I will give the reader a recipe. Take the notions "fanciful," "dreamy," and "enthusiastic" (in their poetic sense), mix them well, and you have a conception of schwarmerisck.]

A slim frame of middle height; fragile but wonderfully flexible limbs; delicately-formed hands; very small feet; an oval, softly-outlined head; a pale, transparent complexion; long silken hair of a light chestnut colour, parted on one side; tender brown eyes, intelligent rather than dreamy; a finely-curved aquiline nose; a sweet subtle smile; graceful and varied gestures: such was the outward presence of Chopin. As to the colour of the eyes and hair, the authorities contradict each other most thoroughly. Liszt describes the eyes as blue, Karasowski as dark brown, and M. Mathias as "couleur de biere." [FOOTNOTE: This strange expression we find again in Count Wodzinski's Les trois Romans de Frederic Chopin, where the author says: "His large limpid, expressive, and soft eyes had that tint which the English call auburn, which the Poles, his compatriots, describe as piwne (beer colour), and which the French would denominate brown."] Of the hair Liszt says that it was blonde, Madame Dubois and others that it was cendre, Miss L. Ramann that it was dark blonde, and a Scotch lady that it was dark brown. [FOOTNOTE: Count Wodzinski writes: "It was not blonde, but of a shade similar to that of his eyes: ash-coloured (cendre), with golden reflections in the light."] Happily the matter is settled for us by an authority to which all others must yield—namely, by M. T. Kwiatkowski, the friend and countryman of Chopin, an artist who has drawn and painted the latter frequently. Well, the information I received from him is to the effect that

Chopin had des yeux bruns tendres (eyes of a tender brown), and les cheveux blonds chatains (chestnut-blonde hair). Liszt, from whose book some of the above details are derived, completes his portrayal of Chopin by some characteristic touches. The timbre of his voice, he says, was subdued and often muffled; and his movements had such a distinction and his manners such an impress of good society that one treated him unconsciously like a prince. His whole appearance made one think of that of the convolvuli, which on incredibly slender stems balance divinely-coloured chalices of such vapourous tissue that the slightest touch destroys them.

And whilst Liszt attributes to Chopin all sorts of feminine graces and beauties, he speaks of George Sand as an Amazon, a femme-heros, who is not afraid to expose her masculine countenance to all suns and winds. Merimee says of George Sand that he has known her "maigre comme un clou et noire comme une taupe." Musset, after their first meeting, describes her, to whom he at a subsequent period alludes as femme a l'oeil sombre, thus:—

She is very beautiful; she is the kind of woman I like—brown, pale, dull-complexioned with reflections as of bronze, and strikingly large-eyed like an Indian. I have never been able to contemplate such a countenance without inward emotion. Her physiognomy is rather torpid, but when it becomes animated it assumes a remarkably independent and proud expression.

The most complete literary portrayal of George Sand that has been handed down to us, however, is by Heine. He represents her as Chopin knew her, for although he published the portrait as late as 1854 he did not represent her as she then looked; indeed, at that time he had probably no intercourse with her, and therefore was obliged to draw from memory. The truthfulness of Heine's delineation is testified by the approval of many who knew George Sand, and also by Couture's portrait of her:—

George Sand, the great writer, is at the same time a beautiful woman. She is even a distinguished beauty. Like the genius which manifests itself in her works, her face is rather to be called beautiful than interesting. The interesting is always a graceful or ingenious deviation from the type of the beautiful, and the features of George Sand bear rather the impress of a Greek regularity. Their form, however, is not hard, but softened by the sentimentality which is suffused over them like a veil of sorrow. The forehead is not high, and the delicious chestnut-brown curly hair falls parted down to the shoulders. Her eyes are somewhat dim, at least they are not bright, and their fire may have been extinguished by many tears, or may have passed into her works, which have spread their flaming brands over the whole world, illumined many a comfortless prison, but perhaps also fatally set on fire many a temple of innocence. The authoress of "Lelia" has quiet, soft eyes, which remind one neither of Sodom nor of Gomorrah. She has neither an emancipated aquiline nose nor a witty little snub nose. It is just an ordinary straight nose. A good-natured smile plays usually around her mouth, but it is not very attractive; the somewhat hanging under-lip betrays fatigued sensuality. The chin is full and plump, but nevertheless beautifully proportioned. Also her shoulders are beautiful, nay, magnificent. Likewise her arms and hands, which, like her feet, are small. Let other contemporaries describe the charms of her bosom, I confess my incompetence. The rest of her bodily frame seems to be somewhat too stout, at least too short. Only her head bears the impress of ideality; it reminds one of the noblest remains of Greek art, and in this respect one of our friends could compare the beautiful woman to the marble statue of the Venus of Milo, which stands in one of the lower rooms of the Louvre. Yes, she is as beautiful as the Venus of Milo; she even surpasses the latter in many respects: she is, for instance, very much younger. The physiognomists who maintain that the voice of man reveals his character most unmistakably would be much at a loss if they were called upon to detect George Sand's extraordinary depth of feeling [Innigkeit] in her voice. The latter is dull and faded, without sonority, but soft and agreeable. The naturalness of her speaking lends it some charm. Of vocal talent she exhibits not a trace! George Sand sings at best with the bravura of a beautiful grisette who has not yet breakfasted or happens not to be in good voice. The organ of George Sand has as little brilliancy as what she says. She has nothing whatever of the sparkling esprit of her countrywomen, but also nothing of their talkativeness. The cause of this taciturnity, however, is neither modesty nor sympathetic absorption in the discourse of another. She is taciturn rather from haughtiness, because she does not think you worth squandering her cleverness [Geist] upon, or even from selfishness, because she endeavours to absorb the best of your discourse in order to work it up afterwards in her works. That out of avarice George Sand knows how never to give anything and always to take something in conversation, is a trait to which Alfred de Musset drew my attention. "This gives her a great advantage over us," said Musset, who, as he had for many years occupied the post of cavaliere servente to the lady, had had the best opportunity to learn to know her thoroughly. George Sand never says anything witty; she is indeed one of the most unwitty Frenchwomen I know.

While admiring the clever drawing and the life-like appearance of the portrait, we must, however, not overlook the exaggerations and inaccuracies. The reader cannot have failed to detect the limner tripping with regard to Musset, who occupied not many years but less than a year the post of cavaliere servente. But who would expect religious adherence to fact from Heine, who at all times distinguishes himself rather by wit than conscientiousness? What he says of George Sand's taciturnity in company and want of wit, however, must be true; for she herself tells us of these negative qualities in the Histoire de ma Vie.

The musical accomplishments of Chopin's beloved one have, of course, a peculiar interest for us. Liszt, who knew her so well, informed me that she was not musical, but possessed taste and judgment. By "not musical" he meant no doubt that she was not in the habit of exhibiting her practical musical acquirements, or did not possess these latter to any appreciable extent. She herself seems to me to make too much of her musical talents, studies, and knowledge. Indeed, her writings show that, whatever her talents may have been, her taste was vague and her knowledge very limited.

When we consider the diversity of character, it is not a matter for wonder that Chopin was at first rather repelled than attracted by the personality of George Sand. Nor is it, on the other hand, a matter for wonder that her beauty and power of pleasing proved too strong for his antipathy. How great this power of pleasing was when she wished to exercise it, the reader may judge from the incident I shall now relate. Musset's mother, having been informed of her son's projected tour to Italy, begged him to give it up. The poet promised to comply with her request: "If one must weep, it shall not be you," he said. In the evening George Sand came in a carriage to the door and asked for Madame Musset; the latter came out, and after a short interview gave her consent to her son's departure. Chopin's unsuccessful wooing of Miss Wodzinska and her marriage with Count Skarbek in this year (1837) may not have been without effect on the composer. His heart being left bruised and empty was as it were sensitised (if I may use this photographic term) for the reception of a new impression by the action of love. In short, the intimacy between Chopin and George Sand grew steadily and continued to grow till it reached its climax in the autumn of 1838, when they went together to Majorca. Other matters, however, have to be adverted to before we come to this passage of Chopin's life. First I shall have to say a few words about his artistic activity during the years 1837 and 1838.

Among the works composed by Chopin in 1837 was one of the Variations on the March from I Puritani, which were published under the title Hexameron: Morceau de Concert. Grandes variations de bravoure sur la marche des Puritains de Bellini, composees pour le concert de Madame la Princesse Belgiojoso au benefice des pauvres, par M.M. Liszt, Thalberg, Pixis, H. Herz, Czerny, et Chopin. This co-operative undertaking was set on foot by the Princess, and was one of her many schemes to procure money for her poor exiled countrymen. Liszt played these Variations often at his concerts, and even wrote orchestral accompaniments to them, which, however, were never published.

Chopin's publications of the year 1837 are: in October, Op. 25, Douze Etudes, dedicated to Madame la Comtesse d'Agoult; and in December, Op. 29, Impromptu (in A flat major), dedicated to Mdlle. la Comtesse de Lobau; Op. 30, Quatre Mazurkas, dedicated to Madame la Princesse de Wurtemberg, nee Princesse Czartoryska; Op. 31, Deuxieme Scherzo (B flat minor), dedicated to Mdlle. la Comtesse Adele de Furstenstein; and Op. 32, Deux Nocturnes (B major and A flat major), dedicated to Madame la Baronne de Billing. His publications of the year 1838 are: in October, Op. 33, Quatre Mazurkas, dedicated to Mdlle. la Comtesse Mostowska; and, in December, Op. 34, Trois Valses brillantes (A flat major, A minor, and F major), respectively dedicated to Mdlle. de Thun-Hohenstein, Madame G. d'Ivri, and Mdlle. A. d'Eichthal. This last work appeared at Paris first in an Album des Pianistes, a collection of unpublished pieces by Thalberg, Chopin, Doehler, Osborne, Liszt, and Mereaux. Two things in connection with this album may yet be mentioned—namely, that Mereaux contributed to it a Fantasia on a mazurka by Chopin, and that Stephen Heller reviewed it in the Gazette musicale. Chopin was by no means pleased with the insertion of the waltzes in Schlesinger's Album des Pianistes. But more of this and his labours and grievances as a composer in the next chapter.

There are also to be recorded some public and semi-public appearances of Chopin as a virtuoso. On February 25, 1838, the Gazette musicale informs its readers that Chopin, "that equally extraordinary and modest pianist," had lately been summoned to Court to be heard there en cercle intime. His inexhaustible improvisations, which almost made up the whole of the evening's entertainment, were particularly admired by the audience, which knew as well as a gathering of artists how to appreciate the composer's merits. At a concert given by Valentin Alkan on March 3, 1838, Chopin performed with Zimmermann, Gutmann, and the concert-giver, the latter's arrangement of Beethoven's A major Symphony (or rather some movements from it) for two pianos and eight hands. And in the Gazette musicale of March 25, 1838, there is a report by M. Legouve of Chopin's appearance at a concert given by his countryman Orlowski at Rouen, where the latter had settled after some years stay in Paris. From a writer in the Journal de Rouen (December 1, 1849) we learn that ever since this concert, which was held in the town-hall, and at which the composer played his E minor Concerto with incomparable perfection, the name of Chopin had in the musical world of Rouen a popularity which secured to his memory an honourable and cordial sympathy. But here is what Legouve says about this concert. I transcribe the notice in full, because it shows us both how completely Chopin had retired from the noise and strife of publicity, and how high he stood in the estimation of his contemporaries.

Here is an event which is not without importance in the musical world. Chopin, who has not been heard in public for several years; Chopin, who imprisons his charming genius in an audience of five or six persons; Chopin, who resembles those enchanted isles where so many marvels are said to abound that one regards them as fabulous; Chopin, whom one can never forget after having once heard him; Chopin has just given a grand concert at Rouen before 500 people for the benefit of a Polish professor. Nothing less than a good action to be done and the remembrance of his country could have overcome his repugnance to playing in public. Well! the success was immense! immense! All these enchanting melodies, these ineffable delicacies of execution, these melancholy and impassioned inspirations, and all that poesy of playing and of composition which takes hold at once of your imagination and heart, have penetrated, moved, enraptured 500 auditors, as they do the eight or ten privileged persons who listen to him religiously for whole hours; every moment there were in the hall those electric fremissements, those murmurs of ecstasy and astonishment which are the bravos of the soul. Forward then, Chopin! forward! let this triumph decide you; do not be selfish, give your beautiful talent to all; consent to pass for what you are; put an end to the great debate which divides the artists; and when it shall be asked who is the first pianist of Europe, Liszt or Thalberg, let all the world reply, like those who have heard you..."It is Chopin."

Chopin's artistic achievements, however, were not unanimously received with such enthusiastic approval. A writer in the less friendly La France musicale goes even so far as to stultify himself by ridiculing, a propos of the A flat Impromptu, the composer's style. This jackanapes—who belongs to that numerous class of critics whose smartness of verbiage combined with obtuseness of judgment is so well-known to the serious musical reader and so thoroughly despised by him—ignores the spiritual contents of the work under discussion altogether, and condemns without hesitation every means of expression which in the slightest degree deviates from the time-honoured standards. We are told that Chopin's mode of procedure in composing is this. He goes in quest of an idea, writes, writes, modulates through all the twenty-four keys, and, if the idea fails to come, does without it and concludes the little piece very nicely (tres-bien). And now, gentle reader, ponder on this momentous and immeasurably sad fact: of such a nature was, is, and ever will be the great mass of criticism.

CHAPTER XXI

CHOPIN'S VISITS TO NOHANT IN 1837 AND 1838.—HIS ILL HEALTH.—HE DECIDES TO GO WITH MADAME SAND AND HER CHILDREN TO MAJORCA.—MADAME SAND'S ACCOUNT OF THIS MATTER AND WHAT OTHERS THOUGHT ABOUT IT.—CHOPIN AND HIS FELLOW—TRAVELLERS MEET AT PERPIGNAN IN THE BEGINNING OF NOVEMBER, 1838, AND PROCEED BY PORT-VENDRES AND BARCELONA TO PALMA.—THEIR LIFE AND EXPERIENCES IN THE TOWN, AT THE VILLA SON-VENT, AND AT THE MONASTERY OF VALDEMOSA, AS DESCRIBED IN CHOPIN'S AND GEORGE SAND'S LETTERS, AND THE LATTER'S "MA VIE" AND "UN HIVER A MAJORQUE."—THE PRELUDES.—RETURN TO FRANCE BY BARCELONA AND MARSEILLES IN THE END OF FEBRUARY, 1839.

In a letter written in 1837, and quoted on p. 313 of Vol. I., Chopin said: "I may perhaps go for a few days to George Sand's." How heartily she invited him through their common friends Liszt and the Comtesse d'Agoult, we saw in the preceding chapter. We may safely assume, I think, that Chopin went to Nohant in the summer of 1837, and may be sure that he did so in the summer of 1838, although with regard to neither visit reliable information of any kind is discoverable. Karasowski, it is true, quotes four letters of Chopin to Fontana as written from Nohant in 1838, but internal evidence shows that they must have been written three years later.

We know from Mendelssohn's and Moscheles' allusions to Chopin's visit to London that he was at that time ailing. He himself wrote in the same year (1837) to Anthony Wodzinski that during the winter he had been again ill with influenza, and that the doctors had wanted to send him to Ems. As time went on the state of his health seems to have got worse, and this led to his going to Majorca in the winter of 1838-1839. The circumstance that he had the company of Madame Sand on this occasion has given rise to much discussion. According to Liszt, Chopin was forced by the alarming state of his health to go to the south in order to avoid the severities of the Paris winter; and Madame Sand, who always watched sympathetically over her friends, would not let him depart alone, but resolved to accompany him. Karasowski, on the other hand, maintains that it was not Madame Sand who was induced to accompany Chopin, but that Madame Sand induced Chopin to accompany her. Neither of these statements tallies with Madame Sand's own account. She tells us that when in 1838 her son Maurice, who had been in the custody of his father, was definitively entrusted to her care, she resolved to take him to a milder climate, hoping thus to prevent a return of the rheumatism from which he had suffered so much in the preceding year. Besides, she wished to live for some time in a quiet place where she could make her children work, and could work herself, undisturbed by the claims of society.

As I was making my plans and preparations for departure [she goes on to say], Chopin, whom I saw every day and whose genius and character I tenderly loved, said to me that if he were in Maurice's place he would soon recover. I believed it, and I was mistaken. I did not put him in the place of Maurice on the journey, but beside Maurice. His friends had for long urged him to go and spend some time in the south of Europe. People believed that he was consumptive. Gaubert examined him and declared to me that he was not. "You will save him, in fact," he said to me, "if you give him air, exercise, and rest." Others, knowing well that Chopin would never make up his mind to leave the society and life of Paris without being carried off by a person whom he loved and who was devoted to him, urged me strongly not to oppose the desire he showed so a propos and in a quite unhoped-for way.

As time showed, I was wrong in yielding to their hopes and my own solicitude. It was indeed enough to go abroad alone with two children, one already ill, the other full of exuberant health and spirits, without taking upon myself also a terrible anxiety and a physician's responsibility.

But Chopin was just then in a state of health that reassured everybody. With the exception of Grzymala, who saw more clearly how matters stood, we were all hopeful. I nevertheless begged Chopin to consider well his moral strength, because for several years he had never contemplated without dread the idea of leaving Paris, his physician, his acquaintances, his room even, and his piano. He was a man of imperious habits, and every change, however small it might be, was a terrible event in his life.

Seeing that Liszt—who was at the time in Italy—and Karasowski speak only from hearsay, we cannot do better than accept George Sand's account, which contains nothing improbable. In connection with this migration to the south, I must, however, not omit to mention certain statements of Adolph Gutmann, one of Chopin's pupils. Here is the substance of what Gutmann told me. Chopin was anxious to go to Majorca, but for some time was kept in suspense by the scantiness of his funds. This threatening obstacle, however, disappeared when his friend the pianoforte-maker and publisher, Camille Pleyel, paid him 2,000 francs for the copyright of the Preludes, Op.

28. Chopin remarked of this transaction to Gutmann, or in his hearing: "I sold the Preludes to Pleyel because he liked them [parcequ'il les aimait]." And Pleyel exclaimed on one occasion: "These are my Preludes [Ce sont mes Preludes]." Gutmann thought that Pleyel, who was indebted to Chopin for playing on his instruments and recommending them, wished to assist his friend in a delicate way with some money, and therefore pretended to be greatly taken with these compositions and bent upon possessing them. This, however, cannot be quite correct; for from Chopin's letters, which I shall quote I presently, it appears that he had indeed promised Pleyel the Preludes, but before his departure received from him only 500 francs, the remaining 1,500 being paid months afterwards, on the delivery of the manuscript. These letters show, on the other hand, that when Chopin was in Majorca he owed to Leo 1,000 francs, which very likely he borrowed from him to defray part of the expenses of his sojourn in the south.

[FOOTNOTE: August Leo, a Paris banker, "the friend and patron of many artists," as he is called by Moscheles, who was related to him through his wife Charlotte Embden, of Hamburg. The name of Leo occurs often in the letters and conversations of musicians, especially German musicians, who visited Paris or lived there in the second quarter of this century. Leo kept house together with his brother-in-law Valentin. (See Vol. I., p. 254.)]

Chopin kept his intention of going with Madame Sand to Majorca secret from all but a privileged few. According to Franchomme, he did not speak of it even to his friends. There seem to have been only three exceptions—Fontana, Matuszynski, and Grzymala, and in his letters to the first he repeatedly entreats his friend not to talk about him. Nor does he seem to have been much more communicative after his return, for none of Chopin's acquaintances whom I questioned was able to tell me whether the composer looked back on this migration with satisfaction or with regret; still less did they remember any remark made by him that would throw a more searching light on this period of his life.

Until recently the only sources of information bearing on Chopin's stay in Majorca were George Sand's "Un Hiver a Majorque" and "Histoire de ma Vie." But now we have also Chopin's letters to Fontana (in the Polish edition of Karasowski's "Chopin") and George Sand's "Correspondance," which supplement and correct the two publications of the novelist. Remembering the latter's tendency to idealise everything, and her disinclination to descend to the prose of her subject, I shall make the letters the backbone of my narrative, and for the rest select my material cautiously.

Telling Chopin that she would stay some days at Perpignan if he were not there on her arrival, but would proceed without him if he failed to make his appearance within a certain time, Madame Sand set out with her two children and a maid in the month of November, 1838, for the south of France, and, travelling for travelling's sake, visited Lyons, Avignon, Vaucluse, Nimes, and other places. The distinguished financier and well-known Spanish statesman Mendizabal, their friend, who was going to Madrid, was to accompany Chopin to the Spanish frontier. Madame Sand was not long left in doubt as to whether Chopin would realise his reve de voyage or not, for he put in his appearance at Perpignan the very next day after her arrival there. Madame Sand to Madame Marliani, [FOOTNOTE: The wife of the Spanish politician and author, Manuel Marliani. We shall hear more of her farther on.]

November, 1838:— Chopin arrived at Perpignan last night, fresh as a rose, and rosy as a turnip; moreover, in good health, having stood his four nights of the mail-coach heroically. As to ourselves, we travelled slowly, quietly, and surrounded at all stations by our friends, who overwhelmed us with kindness.

As the weather was fine and the sea calm Chopin did not suffer much on the passage from Port-Vendres to Barcelona. At the latter town the party halted for a while-spending some busy days within its walls, and making an excursion into the country-and then took ship for Palma, the capital of Majorca and the Balearic Isles generally. Again the voyagers were favoured by the elements.

The night was warm and dark, illumined only by an extraordinary phosphorescence in the wake of the ship; everybody was asleep on board except the steersman, who, in order to keep himself awake, sang all night, but in a voice so soft and so subdued that one might have thought that he feared to awake the men of the watch, or that he himself was half asleep. We did not weary of listening to him, for his singing was of the strangest kind. He observed a rhythm and modulations totally different from those we are accustomed to, and seemed to allow his voice to go at random, like the smoke of the vessel carried away and swayed by the breeze. It was a reverie rather than a song, a kind of careless divagation of the voice, with which the mind had little to do, but which kept time with the swaying of the ship, the faint sound of the dead water, and resembled a vague improvisation, restrained, nevertheless, by sweet and monotonous forms.

When night had passed into day, the steep coasts of Majorca, dentelees au soleil du matin par les aloes et les palmiers, came in sight, and soon after El Mallorquin landed its passengers at Palma. Madame Sand had left Paris a fortnight before in extremely cold weather, and here she found in the first half of November summer heat. The newcomers derived much pleasure from their rambles through the town, which has a strongly-pronounced character of its own and is rich in fine and interesting buildings, among which are most prominent the magnificent Cathedral, the elegant Exchange (la lonja), the stately Town-Hall, and the picturesque Royal Palace (palacio real). Indeed, in Majorca everything is picturesque,

from the hut of the peasant, who in his most insignificant buildings has preserved the tradition of the Arabic style, to the infant clothed in rags and triumphant in his "malproprete grandiose," as Heine said a propos of the market-women of Verona. The character of the landscape, whose vegetation is richer than that of Africa is in general, has quite as much breadth, calm, and simplicity. It is green Switzerland under the sky of Calabria, with the solemnity and silence of the East.

But picturesqueness alone does not make man's happiness, and Palma seems to have afforded little else. If we may believe Madame Sand, there was not a single hotel in the town, and the only accommodation her party could get consisted of two small rooms, unfurnished rather than furnished, in some wretched place where travellers are happy to find "a folding-bed, a straw-bottomed chair, and, as regards food, pepper and garlic a discretion." Still, however great their discomfort and disgust might be, they had to do their utmost to hide their feelings; for, if they had made faces on discovering vermin in their beds and scorpions in their soup, they would certainly have hurt the susceptibilities of the natives, and would probably have exposed themselves to unpleasant consequences. No inhabitable apartments were to be had in the town itself, but in its neighbourhood a villa chanced to be vacant, and this our party rented at once.

Madame Sand to Madame Marliani; Palma, November 14, 1838:—

I am leaving the town, and shall establish myself in the country: I have a pretty furnished house, with a garden and a magnificent view, for fifty francs per month. Besides, two leagues from there I have a cell, that is to say, three rooms and a garden full of oranges and lemons, for thirty-five francs PER YEAR, in the large monastery of Valdemosa.

The furniture of the villa was indeed of the most primitive kind, and the walls were only whitewashed, but the house was otherwise convenient, well ventilated—in fact, too well ventilated—and above all beautifully situated at the foot of rounded, fertile mountains, in the bosom of a rich valley which was terminated by the yellow walls of Palma, the mass of the cathedral, and the sparkling sea on the horizon.

Chopin to Fontana; Palma, November 15, 1838:—

[FOOTNOTE: Julius Fontana, born at Warsaw in 1810, studied music (at the Warsaw Conservatoire under Elsner) as an amateur and law for his profession; joined in 1830 the Polish insurrectionary army; left his country after the failure of the insurrection; taught the piano in London; played in 1835 several times with success in Paris; resided there for some years; went in 1841 to Havannah; on account of the climate, removed to New York; gave there concerts with Sivori; and returned to Paris in 1850. This at least is the account we get of him in Sowinski's "Les Musiciens polonais et slaves." Mr. A. J. Hipkins, who became acquainted with Fontana during a stay which the latter made in London in 1856 (May and early part of June), described him to me as "an honourable and gentlemanly man." From the same informant I learned that Fontana married a lady who had an income for life, and that by this marriage he was enabled to retire from the active exercise of his profession. Later on he became very deaf, and this great trouble was followed by a still greater one, the death of his wife. Thus left deaf and poor, he despaired, and, putting a pistol to one of his ears, blew out his brains. According to Karasowski he died at Paris in 1870. The compositions he published (dances, fantasias, studies, &c.) are of no importance. He is said to have published also two books, one on Polish orthography in 1866 and one on popular astronomy in 1869. The above and all the following letters of Chopin to Fontana are in the possession of Madame Johanna Lilpop, of Warsaw, and are here translated from Karasowski's Polish edition of his biography of Chopin. Many of the letters are undated, and the dates suggested by Karasowski generally wrong. There are, moreover, two letters which are given as if dated by Chopin; but as the contents point to Nohant and 1841 rather than to Majorca and 1838 and 1839, I shall place them in Chapter XXIV., where also my reasons for doing so will be more particularly stated. A third letter, supposed by Karasowski to be written at Valdemosa in February, I hold to be written at Marseilles in April. It will be found in the next chapter.]

My dear friend,—I am at Palma, among palms, cedars, cactuses, aloes, and olive, orange, lemon, fig, and pomegranate trees, &c., which the Jardin des Plantes possesses only thanks to its stoves. The sky is like a turquoise, the sea is like lazuli, and the mountains are like emeralds. The air? The air is just as in heaven. During the day there is sunshine, and consequently it is warm—everybody wears summer clothes. During the night guitars and songs are heard everywhere and at all hours. Enormous balconies with vines overhead, Moorish walls...The town, like everything here, looks towards

Africa...In one word, a charming life! Dear Julius, go to Pleyel—the piano has not yet arrived—and ask him by what route they have sent it. The Preludes you shall have soon. I shall probably take up my quarters in a delightful monastery in one of the most beautiful sites in the world: sea, mountains, palm trees, cemetery, church of the Knights of the Cross, ruins of mosques, thousand-year-old olive trees!...Ah, my dear friend, I am now enjoying life a little more; I am near what is most beautiful—I am a better man. Letters from my parents and whatever you have to send me give to Grzymala; he knows the safest address. Embrace Johnnie. [FOOTNOTE: The Johnnie so frequently mentioned in the letters to Fontana is John Matuszynski.] How soon he would recover here! Tell Schlesinger that before long he will receive MS. To acquaintances speak little of me. Should anybody ask, say that I shall be back in spring. The mail goes once a week; I write through the French Consulate here. Send the enclosed letter as it is to my parents; leave it at the postoffice yourself. Yours, CHOPIN.

George Sand relates in "Un Hiver a Majorque" that the first days which her party passed at the Son-Vent (House of the Wind)—this was the name of the villa they had rented—were pretty well taken up with promenading and pleasant lounging, to which the delicious climate and novel scenery invited. But this paradisaic condition was suddenly changed as if by magic when at the end of two or three weeks the wet season began and the Son-Vent became uninhabitable.

The walls of it were so thin that the lime with which our rooms were plastered swelled like a sponge. For my part I never suffered so much from cold, although it was in reality not very cold; but for us, who are accustomed to warm ourselves in winter, this house without a chimney was like a mantle of ice on our shoulders, and I felt paralysed. Chopin, delicate as he was and subject to violent irritation of the larynx, soon felt the effects of the damp. We could not accustom ourselves to the stifling odour of the brasiers, and our invalid began to ail and to cough. From this moment we became an object of dread and horror to the population. We were accused and convicted of pulmonary phthisis, which is equivalent to the plague in the prejudices regarding contagion entertained by Spanish physicians. A rich doctor, who for the moderate remuneration of forty-five francs deigned to come and pay us a visit, declared, nevertheless, that there was nothing the matter, and prescribed nothing. Another physician came obligingly to our assistance; but the pharmacy at Palma was in such a miserable state that we could only procure detestable drugs. Moreover, the illness was to be aggravated by causes which no science and no devotion could efficiently battle against. One morning, when we were given up to serious fears on account of the duration of these rains and these sufferings which were bound up together, we received a letter from the fierce Gomez [the landlord], who declared, in the Spanish style, that we held a person who held a disease which carried contagion into his house, and threatened prematurely the life of his family; in consequence of which he requested us to leave his palace with the shortest delay possible. This did not cause us much regret, for we could no longer stay there without fear of being drowned in our rooms; but our invalid was not in a condition to be moved without danger, especially by such means of transport as are available in Majorca, and in the weather then obtaining. And then the difficulty was to know where to go, for the rumour of our phthisis had spread instantaneously, and we could no longer hope to find a shelter anywhere, not even at a very high price for a night. We knew that the obliging persons who offered to take us in were themselves not free from prejudices, and that, moreover, we should draw upon them, in going near them, the reprobation which weighed upon us. Without the hospitality of the French consul, who did wonders in order to gather us all under his roof, we were threatened with the prospect of camping in some cavern like veritable Bohemians. Another miracle came to pass, and we found an asylum for the winter. At the Carthusian monastery of Valdemosa there was a Spanish refugee, who had hidden himself there for I don't know what political reason. Visiting the monastery, we were struck with the gentility of his manners, the melancholy beauty of his wife, and the rustic and yet comfortable furniture of their cell. The poesy of this monastery had turned my head. It happened that the mysterious couple wished to leave the country precipitately, and—that they were as delighted to dispose to us of their furniture and cell as we were to acquire them. For the moderate sum of a thousand francs we had then a complete establishment, but such a one as we could have procured in France for 300 francs, so rare, costly, and difficult to get are the most necessary things in Majorca.

The outcasts decamped speedily from the Son-Vent. But before Senor Gomez had done with his tenants, he made them pay for the whitewashing and the replastering of the whole house, which he held to have been infected by Chopin.

And now let us turn once more from George Sand's poetical inventions, distortions, and exaggerations, to the comparative sobriety and trustworthiness of letters.

Chopin to Fontana; Palma, December 3, 1838:— I cannot send you the MSS. as they are not yet finished. During the last two weeks I have been as ill as a dog, in spite of eighteen degrees of heat, [FOOTNOTE: That is, eighteen degrees Centigrade, which are equal to about sixty-four degrees Fahrenheit.] and of roses, and orange, palm, and fig trees in blossom. I caught a severe cold. Three doctors, the most renowned in the island, were called in for consultation. One smelt what I spat, the second knocked whence I spat, the third sounded and listened when I spat. The first said that I would die, the second that I was dying, the third that I had died already; and in the meantime I live as I was living. I cannot forgive Johnnie that in the case of bronchite aigue, which he could always notice in me, he gave me no advice. I had a narrow escape from their bleedings, cataplasms, and such like operations. Thanks to Providence, I am now myself again. My illness has nevertheless a pernicious effect on the Preludes, which you will receive God knows when. In a few days I shall live in the most beautiful part of the world. Sea, mountains... whatever you wish. We are to have our quarters in an old, vast, abandoned and ruined monastery of Carthusians whom Mend [FOOTNOTE: Mendizabal] drove away as it were for me. Near Palma—nothing more wonderful: cloisters, most poetic cemeteries. In short, I feel that there it will be well with me. Only the piano has not yet come! I wrote to Pleyel. Ask there and tell him that on the day after my arrival here I was taken very ill, and that I am well again. On the whole, speak little about me and my manuscripts. Write to me. As yet I have not received a letter from you. Tell Leo that I have not as yet sent the Preludes to the Albrechts, but that I still love them sincerely, and shall write to them shortly. Post the enclosed letter to my parents yourself, and write as soon as possible. My love to Johnnie. Do not tell anyone that I was ill, they would only gossip about it.

[FOOTNOTE: to Madame Dubois I owe the information that Albrecht, an attache to the Saxon legation (a post which gave him a good standing in society) and at the same time a wine-merchant (with offices in the Place Vendome—his specialty being "vins de Bordeaux"), was one of Chopin's "fanatic friends." In the letters there are allusions to two Albrechts, father and son; the foregoing information refers to the son, who, I think, is the T. Albrecht to whom the Premier Scherzo, Chopin's Op. 20, is dedicated.]

Chopin to Fontana; Palma, December 14, 1838:— As yet not a word from you, and this is my third or fourth letter. Did you prepay? Perhaps my parents did not write. Maybe some misfortune has befallen them. Or are you so lazy? But no, you are not lazy, you are so obliging. No doubt you sent my two letters to my people (both from Palma). And you must have written to me, only the post of this place, which is the most irregular in the world, has not yet delivered your letters. Only to-day I was informed that on the ist of December my piano was embarked at Marseilles on a merchant vessel. The letter took fourteen days to come from that town. Thus there is some hope that the piano may pass the winter in the port, as here nobody stirs when it rains. The idea of my getting it just at my departure pleases me, for in addition to the 500 francs for freight and duty which I must pay, I shall have the pleasure of packing it and sending it back. Meanwhile my manuscripts are sleeping, whereas I cannot sleep, but cough, and am covered with plasters, waiting anxiously for spring or something else. To-morrow I start for this delightful monastery of Valdemosa.

I shall live, muse, and write in the cell of some old monk who may have had more fire in his heart than I, and was obliged to hide and smother it, not being able to make use of it. I think that shortly I shall be able to send you my Preludes and my Ballade. Go and see Leo; do not mention that I am ill, he would fear for his 1,000 francs.

Give my kind remembrances to Johnnie and Pleyel. Madame Sand to Madame Marliani; Palma, December 14, 1838:— ...What is really beautiful here is the country, the sky, the mountains, the good health of Maurice, and the radoucissement of Solange. The good Chopin is not in equally brilliant health. He misses his piano very much. We received news of it to-day. It has left Marseilles, and we shall perhaps have it in a fortnight. Mon Dieu, how hard, difficult, and miserable the physical life is here! It is beyond what one can imagine. By a stroke of fortune I have found for sale a clean suite of furniture, charming for this country, but which a French peasant would not have. Unheard-of trouble was required to get a stove, wood, linen, and who knows what else. Though for a month I have believed myself established, I am always on the eve of being so. Here a cart takes five hours to go three leagues; judge of the rest. They require two months to manufacture a pair of tongs. There is no exaggeration in what I say. Guess about this country all I do not tell you. For my part I do not mind it, but I have suffered a little from it in the fear of seeing my children suffer much from it. Happily, my ambulance is doing well. To-morrow we depart for the Carthusian monastery of Valdemosa, the most poetic residence on earth. We shall pass there the winter, which has hardly begun and will soon end. This is the sole happiness of this country. I have never in my life met with a nature so delicious as that of Majorca. ...The people of this country are generally very gracious, very obliging; but all this in words... I shall write to Leroux from the monastery at leisure. If you knew what I have to do! I have almost to cook. Here, another amenity, one cannot get served. The domestic is a brute: bigoted, lazy, and gluttonous; a veritable son of a monk (I think that all are that). It requires ten to do the work which your brave Mary does. Happily, the maid whom I have brought with me from Paris is very devoted, and resigns herself to do heavy work; but she is not strong, and I must help her. Besides, everything is dear, and proper nourishment is difficult to get when the stomach cannot stand either rancid oil or pig's grease. I begin to get accustomed to it; but Chopin is ill every time that we do not prepare his food ourselves. In short, our expedition here is, in many respects, a frightful fiasco.

On December 15, 1838, then, the Sand party took possession of their quarters in the monastery of Valdemosa, and thence the next letters are dated.

Chopin to Fontana; "Palma, December 28, 1838, or rather Valdemosa, a few miles distant from Palma":—

Between rocks and the sea, in a great abandoned Carthusian monastery, in one of the cells with doors bigger than the gates in Paris, you may imagine me with my hair uncurled, without white gloves, pale as usual. The cell is in the shape of a coffin, high, and full of dust on the vault. The window small, before the window orange, palm, and cypress trees. Opposite the window, under a Moorish filigree rosette, stands my bed. By its side an old square thing like a table for writing, scarcely serviceable; on it a leaden candlestick (a great luxury) with a little tallow-candle, Works of Bach, my jottings, and old scrawls that are not mine, this is all I possess. Quietness... one may shout and nobody will hear... in short, I am writing to you from a strange place.

Your letter of the 9th of December I received the day before yesterday; as on account of the holidays the express mail does not leave till next week, I write to you in no great hurry. It will be a Russian month before you get the bill of exchange which I send you.

Sublime nature is a fine thing, but one should have nothing to do with men—nor with roads and posts. Many a time I came here from Palma, always with the same driver and always by another road. Streams of water make roads, violent rains destroy them; to-day it is impossible to pass, for what was a road is ploughed; next day only mules can pass where you were driving yesterday. And what carriages here! That is the reason, Julius, why you do not see a single Englishman, not even an English consul.

Leo is a Jew, a rogue! I was at his house the day before my departure, and I told him not to send me anything here. I cannot send you the Preludes, they are not yet finished. At present I am better and shall push on the work. I shall write and thank him in a way that will make him wince.

But Schlesinger is a still worse dog to put my Waltzes [FOOTNOTE: "Trois Valses brillantes," Op. 34.] in the Album, and to sell them to Probst [FOOTNOTE: Heinrich Albert Probst founded in 1823 a music-shop and publishing-house at Leipzig. In 1831 Fr. Kistner entered the business (Probst-Kistner), which under his name has existed from 1836 down to this day. In the Chopin letters we meet Probst in the character of Breitkopf and Hartel's agent.] when I gave him them because he begged them for his father in Berlin. [FOOTNOTE: Adolf Martin Schlesinger, a music-publisher like his son Maurice Adolph of Paris, so frequently mentioned in these letters.] All this irritates me. I am only sorry for you; but in one month at the latest you will be clear of Leo and my landlord. With the money which you receive on the bill of exchange, do what is necessary. And my servant, what is he doing? Give the portier twenty francs as a New Year's present.

I do not remember whether I left any debts of importance. At all events, as I promised you, we shall be clear in a month at the latest.

To-day the moon is wonderful, I never saw it more beautiful.

By the way, you write that you sent me a letter from my people. I neither saw nor heard of one, and I am longing so much for one! Did you prepay when you sent them the letter?

Your letter, the only one I have hitherto received, was very badly addressed. Here nature is benevolent, but the people are thievish. They never see any strangers, and therefore do not know what to ask of them. For instance, an orange they will give you for nothing, but ask a fabulous sum for a coat- button.

Under this sky you are penetrated with a kind of poetical feeling which everything seems to exhale. Eagles alarmed by no one soar every day majestically over our heads.

For God's sake write, always prepay, and to Palma add always Valdemosa.

I love Johnnie, and I think it is a pity that he did not altogether qualify himself as director of the children of some benevolent institution in some Nuremberg or Bamberg. Get him to write to me, were it only a few words.

I enclose you a letter to my people...I think it is already the third or fourth that I send you for my parents. My love to Albrecht, but speak very little about me. Chopin to Fontana; Valdemosa, January 12, 1839:— I send you the Preludes, make a copy of them, you and Wolf; [FOOTNOTE: Edouard Wolff] I think there are no mistakes. You will give the transcript to Probst, but my manuscript to Pleyel. When you get the money from Probst, for whom I enclose a receipt, you will take it at once to Leo. I do not write and thank him just now, for I have no time. Out of the money which Pleyel will give you, that is 1,500 francs, you will pay the rent of my rooms till the New Year, 450 francs and you will give notice of my giving them up if you have a chance to get others from April. If not it will be necessary to keep them for a quarter longer. The rest of the amount, or 1,000 francs, you will return from me to Nougi. Where he lives you will learn from Johnnie, but don't tell the latter of the money, for he might attack Nougi, and I do not wish that anyone but you and I should know of it. Should you succeed in finding rooms, you could send one part of the furniture to Johnnie and another to Grzymala. You will tell Pleyel to send letters through you.

I sent you before the New Year a bill of exchange for Wessel; tell Pleyel that I have settled with Wessel.

[FOOTNOTE: The music-publisher Christian Rudolph Wessel, of Bremen, who came to London in 1825. Up to 1838 he had Stodart, and from 1839 to 1845 Stapleton, as partner. He retired in 1860, Messrs. Edwin Ashdown and Henry Parry being his successors. Since the retirement of Mr. Parry, in 1882, Mr. Ashdown is the sole proprietor. Mr. Ashdown, whom I have to thank for the latter part of this note, informs me that Wessel died in 1885.]

In a few weeks you will receive a Ballade, a Polonaise, and a Scherzo. Until now I have not yet received any letters from my parents. I embrace you. Sometimes I have Arabian balls, African sun, and always before my eyes the Mediterranean Sea. I do not know when I shall be back, perhaps as late as May, perhaps even later. Madame Sand to Madame Marliani; Valdemosa, January 15, 1839:— ...We inhabit the Carthusian monastery of Valdemosa, a really sublime place, which I have hardly the time to admire, so many occupations have I with my children, their lessons, and my work.

There are rains here of which one has elsewhere no idea: it is a frightful deluge! The air is on account of it so relaxing, so soft, that one cannot drag one's self along; one is really ill. Happily, Maurice is in admirable health; his constitution is only afraid of frost, a thing unknown here. But the little Chopin [FOOTNOTE: Madame Marliani seems to have been in the habit of calling Chopin "le petit." In another letter to her (April 28, 1839) George Sand writes of Chopin as votre petit. This reminds one of Mendelssohn's Chopinetto.] is very depressed and always coughs much. For his sake I await with impatience the return of fine weather, which will not be long in coming. His piano has at last arrived at Palma; but it is in the clutches of the custom-house officers, who demand from five to six hundred francs duty, and show themselves intractable.

...I am plunged with Maurice in Thucydides and company; with Solange in the indirect object and the agreement of the participle. Chopin plays on a poor Majorcan piano which reminds me of that of Bouffe in "Pauvre Jacques." I pass my nights generally in scrawling. When I raise my nose, it is to see through the sky-light of my cell the moon which shines in the midst of the rain on the orange trees, and I think no more of it than she.

Madame Sand to M. A. M. Duteil; Valdemosa, January 20, 1839:— ...This [the slowness and irregularity of the post] is not the only inconvenience of the country. There are innumerable ones, and yet this is the most beautiful country. The climate is delicious. At the time I am writing, Maurice is gardening in his shirt-sleeves, and Solange, seated under an orange tree loaded with fruit, studies her lesson with a grave air. We have bushes covered with roses, and spring is coming in. Our winter lasted six weeks, not cold, but rainy to a degree to frighten us. It is a deluge! The rain uproots the mountains; all the waters of the mountain rush into the plain; the roads become torrents. We found ourselves caught in them, Maurice and I. We had been at Palma in superb weather. When we returned in the evening, there were no fields, no roads, but only trees to indicate approximately the way which we had to go. I was really very frightened, especially as the horse refused to proceed, and we were obliged to traverse the mountain on foot in the night, with torrents across our legs. Madame Sand to Madame Marliani; Valdemosa, February 22, 1839:— ...You see me at my Carthusian monastery, still sedentary, and occupied during the day with my children, at night with my work. In the midst of all this, the warbling of Chopin, who goes his usual pretty way, and whom the walls of the cell are much astonished to hear.

The only remarkable event since my last letter is the arrival of the so much-expected piano. After a fortnight of applications and waiting we have been able to get it out of the custom-house by paying three hundred francs of duty. Pretty country this! After all, it has been disembarked without accident, and the vaults of the monastery are delighted with it. And all this is not profaned by the admiration of fools-we do not see a cat.

Our retreat in the mountains, three leagues from the town, has freed us from the politeness of idlers. Nevertheless, we have had one visitor, and a visitor from Paris!—namely, M. Dembowski, an Italian Pole whom Chopin knew, and who calls himself a cousin of Marliani—I don't know in what degree.

...The fact is, that we are very much pleased with the freedom which this gives us, because we have work to do; but we understand very well that these poetic intervals which one introduces into one's life are only times of transition and rest allowed to the mind before it resumes the exercise of the emotions. I mean this in the purely intellectual sense; for, as regards the life of the heart, it cannot cease for a moment...

This brings us to the end of the known letters written by Chopin and Madame Sand from Majorca. And now let us see what we can find in George Sand's books to complete the picture of the life of her and her party at Valdemosa, of which the letters give only more or less disconnected indications. I shall use the materials at my disposal freely and cautiously, quoting some passages in full, regrouping and summing-up others, and keeping always in mind—which the reader should likewise do—the authoress's tendency to emphasise, colour, and embellish, for the sake of literary and moral effect.

Not to extend this chapter too much, I refer the curious to George Sand's "Un Hiver a Majorque" for a description of the "admirable, grandiose, and wild nature" in the midst of which the "poetic abode" of her and her party was situated—of the grandly and beautifully-varied surface of the earth, the luxuriant southern vegetation, and the marvellous phenomena of light and air; of the sea stretching out on two sides and meeting the horizon; of the surrounding formidable peaks, and the more distant round-swelling hills; of the eagles descending in the pursuit of their prey down to the orange trees of the monastery gardens; of the avenue of cypresses serpentining from the top of the mountain to the bottom of the gorge; of the torrents covered with myrtles; in short, of the immense ensemble, the infinite details, which overwhelm the imagination and outvie the poet's and painter's dreams. Here it will be advisable to confine ourselves to the investigation of a more limited sphere, to inspect rather narrow interiors than vast landscapes.

As the reader has gathered from the preceding letters, there was no longer a monastic community at Valdemosa. The monks had been dispersed some time before, and the monastery had become the property of the state. During the hot summer months it was in great part occupied by small burghers from Palma who came in quest of fresh air. The only permanent inhabitants of the monastery, and the only fellow-tenants of George Sand's party, were two men and one woman, called by the novelist respectively the Apothecary, the Sacristan, and Maria Antonia. The first, a remnant of the dispersed community, sold mallows and couch-grass, the only specifics he had; the second was the person in whose keeping were the keys of the monastery; and the third was a kind of housekeeper who, for the love of God and out of neighbourly friendship, offered her help to new-comers, and, if it was accepted, did not fail to levy heavy contributions.

The monastery was a complex of strongly-constructed, buildings without any architectural beauty, and such was, its circumference and mass of stones that it would have been easy to house an army corps. Besides the dwelling of the superior, the cells of the lay-brothers, the lodgings for visitors, the stables, and other structures, there were three cloisters, each consisting of twelve cells and twelve chapels. The most ancient of these cloisters, which is also the smallest, dates from the 15th century.

It presents a charming coup d'oeil. The court which it encloses with its broken-down walls is the ancient cemetery of the monks. No inscription distinguishes these tombs...The graves are scarcely indicated by the swellings of the turf.

In the cells were stored up the remains of all sorts of fine old furniture and sculpture, but these could only be seen through the chinks, for the cells were carefully locked, and the sacristan would not open them to anyone. The second cloister, although of more recent date, was likewise in a dilapidated state, which, however, gave it character. In stormy weather it was not at all safe to pass through it on account of the falling fragments of walls and vaults.

I never heard the wind sound so like mournful voices and utter such despairing howls as in these empty and sonorous galleries. The noise of the torrents, the swift motion of the clouds, the grand, monotonous sound of the sea, interrupted by the whistling of the storm and the plaintive cries of sea- birds which passed, quite terrified and bewildered, in the squalls; then thick fogs which fell suddenly like a shroud and which, penetrating into the cloisters through the broken arcades, rendered us invisible, and made the little lamp we carried to guide us appear like a will-o'-the-wisp wandering under the galleries; and a thousand other details of this monastic life which crowd all at once into my memory: all combined made indeed this monastery the most romantic abode in the world.

I was not sorry to see for once fully and in reality what I had seen only in a dream, or in the fashionable ballads, and in the nuns' scene in Robert le Diable at the Opera. Even fantastic apparitions were not wanting to us. [FOOTNOTE: "Un Hiver a Majorque," pp. 116 and 117.]

In the same book from which the above passage is extracted we find also a minute description of the new cloister; the chapels, variously ornamented, covered with gilding, decorated with rude paintings and horrible statues of saints in coloured wood, paved in the Arabic style with enamelled faience laid out in various mosaic designs, and provided with a fountain or marble conch; the pretty church, unfortunately without an organ, but with wainscot, confessionals, and doors of most excellent workmanship, a floor of finely-painted faience, and a remarkable statue in painted wood of St. Bruno; the little meadow in the centre of the cloister, symmetrically planted with box-trees, &c., &c.

George Sand's party occupied one of the spacious, well-ventilated, and well-lighted cells in this part of the monastery. I shall let her describe it herself.

The three rooms of which it was composed were spacious, elegantly vaulted, and ventilated at the back by open rosettes, all different and very prettily designed. These three rooms were separated from the cloister by a dark passage at the end of which was a strong door of oak. The wall was three feet thick. The middle room was destined for reading, prayer, and meditation; all its furniture consisted of a large chair with a praying-desk and a back, from six to eight feet high, let into and fixed in the wall. The room to the right of this was the friar's bed-room; at the farther end of it was situated the alcove, very low, and paved above with flags like a tomb. The room to the left was the workshop, the refectory, the store-room of the recluse. A press at the far end of the room had a wooden compartment with a window opening on the cloister, through which his provisions were passed in. His kitchen consisted of two little stoves placed outside, but not, as was the strict rule, in the open air; a vault, opening on the garden, protected the culinary labours of the monk from the rain, and allowed him to give himself up to this occupation a little more than the founder would have wished. Moreover, a fire-place introduced into this third room indicated many other relaxations, although the science of the architect had not gone so far as to make this fire-place serviceable.

Running along the back of the rooms, on a level with the rosettes, was a long channel, narrow and dark, intended for the ventilation of the cell, and above was a loft in which the maize, onions, beans, and other simple winter provisions were kept. On the south the three rooms opened on a flower garden, exactly the size of the cell itself, which was separated from the neighbouring gardens by walls ten feet high, and was supported by a strongly-built terrace above a little orange grove which occupied this ledge of the mountain. The lower ledge was covered with a beautiful arbour of vines, the third with almond and palm trees, and so on to the bottom of the little valley, which, as I have said, was an immense garden.

The flower garden of each cell had all along its right side a reservoir, made of freestone, from three to four feet in width and the same in depth, receiving through conduits placed in the balustrade of the terrace the waters of the mountain, and distributing them in the flower garden by means of a stone cross, which divided it into four equal squares.

As to this flower garden, planted with pomegranate, lemon, and orange trees, surrounded by raised walks made of bricks which, like the reservoir, were shaded by perfumed arbours, it was like a pretty salon of flowers and verdure, where the monk could walk dry-footed on wet days.

Even without being told, we should have known that the artists who had now become inmates of the monastery were charmed with their surroundings. Moreover, George Sand did her utmost to make life within doors comfortable. When the furniture bought from the Spanish refugee had been supplemented by further purchases, they were, considering the circumstances, not at all badly off in this respect. The tables and straw-bottomed chairs were indeed no better than those one finds in the cottages of peasants; the sofa of white wood with cushions of mattress cloth stuffed with wool could only ironically be called "voluptuous"; and the large yellow leather trunks, whatever their ornamental properties might be, must have made but poor substitutes for wardrobes. The folding-beds, on the other hand, proved irreproachable; the mattresses, though not very soft, were new and clean, and the padded and quilted chintz coverlets left nothing to be desired. Nor does this enumeration exhaust the comforts and adornments of which the establishment could boast. Feathers, a rare article in Majorca, had been got from a French lady to make pillows for Chopin; Valenciennes matting and long-fleeced sheep skins covered the dusty floor; a large tartan shawl did duty as an alcove curtain; a stove of somewhat eccentric habits, and consisting simply of an iron cylinder with a pipe that passed through the window, had been manufactured for them at Palma; a charming clay vase surrounded with a garland of ivy displayed its beauty on the top of the stove; a beautiful large Gothic carved oak chair with a small chest convenient as a book-case had, with the consent of the sacristan, been brought from the monks' chapel; and last, but not least, there was, as we have already read in the letters, a piano, in the first weeks only a miserable Majorcan instrument, which, however, in the second half of January, after much waiting, was replaced by one of Pleyel's excellent cottage pianos.

[FOOTNOTE: By the way, among the many important and unimportant doubtful points which Chopin's and George Sand's letters settle, is also that of the amount of duty paid for the piano. The sum originally asked by the Palma custom-house officers seems to have been from 500 to 600 francs, and this demand was after a fortnight's negotiations reduced to 300 francs. That the imaginative novelist did not long remember the exact particulars of this transaction need not surprise us. In Un Hiver a Majorque she states tha the original demand was 700 francs, and the sum ultimately paid about 400 francs.]

These various items collectively and in conjunction with the rooms in which they were gathered together form a tout-ensemble picturesque and homely withal. As regards the supply of provisions, the situation of our Carthusians was decidedly less brilliant. Indeed, the water and the juicy raisins, Malaga potatoes, fried Valencia pumpkins, &c., which they had for dessert, were the only things that gave them unmixed satisfaction. With anything but pleasure they made the discovery that the chief ingredient of Majorcan cookery, an ingredient appearing in all imaginable and unimaginable guises and disguises, was pork. Fowl was all skin and bones, fish dry and tasteless, sugar of so bad a quality that it made them sick, and butter could not be procured at all. Indeed, they found it difficult to get anything of any kind. On account of their non-attendance at church they were disliked by the villagers of Valdemosa, who sold their produce to such heretics only at twice or thrice the usual price. Still, thanks to the good offices of the French consul's cook, they might have done fairly well had not wet weather been against them. But, alas, their eagerly-awaited provisions often arrived spoiled with rain, oftener still they did not arrive at all. Many a time they had to eat bread as hard as ship-biscuits, and content themselves with real Carthusian dinners. The wine was good and cheap, but, unfortunately, it had the objectionable quality of being heady.

These discomforts and wants were not painfully felt by George Sand and her children, nay, they gave, for a time at least, a new zest to life. It was otherwise with Chopin. "With his feeling for details and the wants of a refined well-being, he naturally took an intense dislike to Majorca after a few days of illness." We have already seen what a bad effect the wet weather and the damp of Son-Vent had on Chopin's health. But, according to George Sand, [FOOTNOTE: "Un Hiver a Marjorque," pp. 161-168. I suspect that she mixes up matters in a very unhistorical manner; I have, however, no means of checking her statements, her and her companion's letters being insufficient for the purpose. Chopin certainly was not likely to tell his friend the worst about his health.] it was not till later, although still in the early days of their sojourn in Majorca, that his disease declared itself in a really alarming manner. The cause of this change for the worse was over-fatigue incurred on an excursion which he made with his friends to a hermitage three miles [FOOTNOTE: George Sand does not say what kind of miles] distant from Valdemosa; the length and badness of the road alone would have been more than enough to exhaust his fund of strength, but in addition to these hardships they had, on returning, to encounter a violent wind which threw them down repeatedly. Bronchitis, from which he had previously suffered, was now followed by a nervous excitement that produced several symptoms of laryngeal phthisis. [FOOTNOTE: In the Histoire de ma Vie George Sand Bays: "From the beginning of winter, which set in all at once with a diluvian rain, Chopin showed, suddenly also, all the symptoms of pulmonary affection."] The physician, judging of the disease by the symptoms that presented themselves at the time of his visits, mistook its real nature, and prescribed bleeding, milk diet, &c. Chopin felt instinctively that all this would be injurious to him, that bleeding would even be fatal. George Sand, who was an experienced nurse, and whose opportunities for observing were less limited than those of the physician, had the same presentiment. After a long and anxious struggle she decided to disregard the strongly-urged advice of the physician and to obey the voice that said to her, even in her sleep: "Bleeding will kill him; but if you save him from it, he will not die," She was persuaded that this voice was the voice of Providence, and that by obeying it she saved her friend's life. What Chopin stood most in need of in his weakness and languor was a strengthening diet, and that, unfortunately, was impossible to procure:—

What would I not have given to have had some beef-tea and a glass of Bordeaux wine to offer to our invalid every day! The Majorcan food, and especially the manner in which it was prepared when we were not there with eye and hand, caused him an invincible disgust. Shall I tell you how well founded this disgust was? One day when a lean chicken was put on the table we saw jumping on its steaming back enormous Mattres Floh, [FOOTNOTE: Anglice "fleas."] of which Hoffmann would have made as many evil spirits, but which he certainly would not have eaten in gravy. My children laughed so heartily that they nearly fell under the table.

Chopin's most ardent wish was to get away from Majorca and back to France. But for some time he was too weak to travel, and when he had got a little stronger, contrary winds prevented the steamer from leaving the port. The following words of George Sand depict vividly our poor Carthusian friends' situation in all its gloom:—

As the winter advanced, sadness more and more paralysed my efforts at gaiety and cheerfulness. The state of our invalid grew always worse; the wind wailed in the ravines, the rain beat against our windows, the voice of the thunder penetrated through our thick walls and mingled its mournful sounds with the laughter and sports of the children. The eagles and vultures, emboldened by the fog, came to devour our poor sparrows, even on the pomegranate tree which shaded my window.

The raging sea kept the ships in the harbours; we felt ourselves prisoners, far from all enlightened help and from all efficacious sympathy. Death seemed to hover over our heads to seize one of us, and we were alone in contending with him for his prey.

If George Sand's serenity and gaiety succumbed to these influences, we may easily imagine how much more they oppressed Chopin, of whom she tells us that—

The mournful cry of the famished eagle and the gloomy desolation of the yew trees covered with snow saddened him much longer and more keenly than the perfume of the orange trees, the gracefulness of the vines, and the Moorish song of the labourers gladdened him.

The above-quoted letters have already given us some hints of how the prisoners of Valdemosa passed their time. In the morning there were first the day's provisions to be procured and the rooms to be tidied—which latter business could not be entrusted to Maria Antonia without the sacrifice of their night's rest. [FOOTNOTE: George Sand's share of the household work was not so great as she wished to make the readers of Un Hiver a Majorque believe, for it consisted, as we gather from her letters, only in giving a helping hand to her maid, who had undertaken to cook and clean up, but found that her strength fell short of the requirements.] Then George Sand would teach her children for some hours. These lessons over, the young ones ran about and amused themselves for the rest of the day, while their mother sat down to her literary studies and labours. In the evening they either strolled together through the moonlit cloisters or read in their cell, half of the night being generally devoted by the novelist to writing. George Sand says in the "Histoire de ma Vie" that she wrote a good deal and read beautiful philosophical and historical works when she was not nursing her friend. The latter, however, took up much of her time, and prevented her from getting out much, for he did not like to be left alone, nor, indeed, could he safely be left long alone. Sometimes she and her children would set out on an expedition of discovery, and satisfy their curiosity and pleasantly while away an hour or two in examining the various parts of the vast aggregation of buildings; or the whole party would sit round the stove and laugh over the rehearsal of the morning's transactions with the villagers. Once they witnessed even a ball in this sanctuary. It was on Shrove-Tuesday, after dark, that their attention was roused by a strange, crackling noise. On going to the door of their cell they could see nothing, but they heard the noise approaching. After a little there appeared at the opposite end of the cloister a faint glimmer of white light, then the red glare of torches, and at last a crew the sight of which made their flesh creep and their hair stand on end—he-devils with birds' heads, horses' tails, and tinsel of all colours; she-devils or abducted shepherdesses in white and pink dresses; and at the head of them Lucifer himself, horned and, except the blood-red face, all black. The strange noise, however, turned out to be the rattling of castanets, and the terrible-looking figures a merry company of rich farmers and well-to-do villagers who were going to have a dance in Maria Antonia's cell. The orchestra, which consisted of a large and a small guitar, a kind of high-pitched violin, and from three to four pairs of castanets, began to play indigenous jotas and fandangos which, George Sand tells us, resemble those of Spain, but have an even bolder form and more original rhythm. The critical spectators thought that the dancing of the Majorcans was not any gayer than their singing, which was not gay at all, and that their boleros had "la gravite des ancetres, et point de ces graces profanes qu'on admire en Andalousie." Much of the music of these islanders was rather interesting than pleasing to their visitors. The clicking of the castanets with which they accompany their festal processions, and which, unlike the broken and measured rhythm of the Spaniards, consists of a continuous roll like that of a drum "battant aux champs," is from time to time suddenly interrupted in order to sing in unison a coplita on a phrase which always recommences but never finishes. George Sand shares the opinion of M. Tastu that the principal Majorcan rhythms and favourite fioriture are Arabic in type and origin.

Of quite another nature was the music that might be heard in those winter months in one of the cells of the monastery of Valdemosa. "With what poesy did his music fill this sanctuary, even in the midst of his most grievous troubles!" exclaims George Sand. I like to picture to myself the vaulted cell, in which Pleyel's piano sounded so magnificently, illumined by a lamp, the rich traceries of the Gothic chair shadowed on the wall, George Sand absorbed in her studies, her children at play, and Chopin pouring out his soul in music.

It would be a mistake to think that those months which the friends spent in Majorca were for them a time of unintermittent or even largely-predominating wretchedness. Indeed, George Sand herself admits that, in spite of the wildness of the country and the pilfering habits of the people, their existence might have been an agreeable one in this romantic solitude had it not been for the sad spectacle of her companion's sufferings and certain days of serious anxiety about his life. And now I must quote a. long but very important passage from the "Histoire de ma Vie":—

The poor great artist was a detestable patient. What I had feared, but unfortunately not enough, happened. He became completely demoralised. Bearing pain courageously enough, he could not overcome the disquietude of his imagination. The monastery was for him full of terrors and phantoms, even when he was well. He did not say so, and I had to guess it. On returning from my nocturnal explorations in the ruins with my children, I found him at ten o'clock at night before his piano, his face pale, his eyes wild, and his hair almost standing on end. It was some moments before he could recognise us.

He then made an attempt to laugh, and played to us sublime things he had just composed, or rather, to be more accurate, terrible or heartrending ideas which had taken possession of him, as it were without his knowledge, in that hour of solitude, sadness, and terror.

It was there that he composed the most beautiful of those short pages he modestly entitled "Preludes." They are masterpieces. Several present to the mind visions of deceased monks and the sounds of the funeral chants which beset his imagination; others are melancholy and sweet—they occurred to him in the hours of sunshine and of health, with the noise of the children's laughter under the window, the distant sound of guitars, the warbling of the birds among the humid foliage, and the sight of the pale little full-blown roses on the snow.

Others again are of a mournful sadness, and, while charming the ear, rend the heart. There is one of them which occurred to him on a dismal rainy evening which produces a terrible mental depression. We had left him well that day, Maurice and I, and had gone to Palma to buy things we required for our encampment. The rain had come on, the torrents had overflowed, we had travelled three leagues in six hours to return in the midst of the inundation, and we arrived in the dead of night, without boots, abandoned by our driver, having passed through unheard-of dangers. We made haste, anticipating the anxiety of our invalid. It had been indeed great, but it had become as it were congealed into a kind of calm despair, and he played his wonderful prelude weeping. On seeing us enter he rose, uttering a great cry, then he said to us, with a wild look and in a strange tone: "Ah! I knew well that you were dead!"

When he had come to himself again, and saw the state in which we were, he was ill at the retrospective spectacle of our dangers; but he confessed to me afterwards that while waiting for our return he had seen all this in a dream and that, no longer distinguishing this dream from reality, he had grown calm and been almost lulled to sleep while playing the piano, believing that he was dead himself. He saw himself drowned in a lake; heavy and ice-cold drops of water fell at regular intervals upon his breast, and when I drew his attention to those drops of water which were actually falling at regular intervals upon the roof, he denied having heard them. He was even vexed at what I translated by the term imitative harmony. He protested with all his might, and he was right, against the puerility of these imitations for the ear. His genius was full of mysterious harmonies of nature, translated by sublime equivalents into his musical thought, and not by a servile repetition of external sounds. His composition of this evening was indeed full of the drops of rain which resounded on the sonorous tiles of the monastery, but they were transformed in his imagination and his music into tears falling from heaven on his heart.

Although George Sand cannot be acquitted of the charge of exaggerating the weak points in her lover's character, what she says about his being a detestable patient seems to have a good foundation in fact. Gutmann, who nursed him often, told me that his master was very irritable and difficult to manage in sickness. On the other hand, Gutmann contradicted George Sand's remarks about the Preludes, saying that Chopin composed them before starting on his journey. When I mentioned to him that Fontana had made a statement irreconcilable with his, and suggested that Chopin might have composed some of the Preludes in Majorca, Gutmann maintained firmly that every one of them was composed previously, and that he himself had copied them. Now with Chopin's letters to Fontana before us we must come to the conclusion that Gutmann was either under a false impression or confirmed a rash statement by a bold assertion, unless we prefer to assume that Chopin's labours on the Preludes in Majorca were confined to selecting, [FOOTNOTE: Internal evidence suggests that the Preludes consist (to a great extent at least) of pickings from the composer's portfolios, of pieces, sketches, and memoranda written at various times and kept to be utilised when occasion might offer.] filing, and polishing. My opinion—which not only has probability but also the low opus number (28) and the letters in its favour—is that most of the Preludes, if not all, were finished or sketched before Chopin went to the south, and that a few, if any, were composed and the whole revised at Palma and Valdemosa. Chopin cannot have composed many in Majorca, because a few days after his arrival there he wrote: from Palma (Nov. 15, 1838) to Fontana that he would send the Preludes soon; and it was only his illness that prevented him from doing so. There is one statement in George Sand's above-quoted narrative which it is difficult to reconcile with other statements in "Un Hiver a Majorque" and in her and Chopin's letters. In the just-mentioned book (p. 177) she says that the journey in question was made for the purpose of rescuing the piano from the hands of the custom-house officers; and in a letter of January 15, 1839, to her friend Madame Marliani (quoted on p. 31), which does not contain a word about adventures on a stormy night, [They are first mentioned in the letter of January 20, 1839, quoted on p. 32.] she writes that the piano is still in the clutches of the custom-house officers. From this, I think, we may conclude that it must have taken place after January 15. But, then, how could Chopin have composed on that occasion a Prelude included in a work the manuscript of which he sent away on the 1ath? Still, this does not quite settle the question. Is it not possible that Chopin may have afterwards substituted the new Prelude for one of those already forwarded to France? To this our answer must be that it is possible, but that the letters do not give any support to such an assumption. Another and stronger objection would be the uncertainty as to the correctness of the date of the letter. Seeing that so many of Chopin's letters have been published with wrong dates, why not also that of January 12? Unfortunately, we cannot in this case prove or disprove the point by internal evidence. There is, however, one factor we must be especially careful not to forget in our calculations—namely, George Sand's habitual unconscientious inaccuracy; but the nature of her narrative will indeed be a sufficient warning to the reader, for nobody can read it without at once perceiving that it is not a plain, unvarnished recital of facts.

It would be interesting to know which were the compositions that Chopin produced at Valdemosa. As to the Prelude particularly referred to by George Sand, it is generally and reasonably believed to be No. 6 (in B minor). [FOOTNOTE: Liszt, who tells the story differently, brings in the F sharp minor Prelude. (See Liszt's Chopin, new edition, pp. 273 and 274.)] The only compositions besides the Preludes which Chopin mentions in his letters from Majorca are the Ballade, Op, 38, the Scherzo, Op. 39, and the two Polonaises, Op. 40. The peevish, fretful, and fiercely-scornful Scherzo and the despairingly-melancholy second Polonaise (in C minor) are quite in keeping with the moods one imagines the composer to have been in at the time. Nor is there anything discrepant in the Ballade. But if the sadly-ailing composer really created, and not merely elaborated and finished, in Majorca the superlatively-healthy, vigorously-martial, brilliantly-chivalrous Polonaise in A major, we have here a remarkable instance of the mind's ascendency over the body, of its independence of it. This piece, however, may have been conceived under happier circumstances, just as the gloomy Sonata, Op. 35 (the one in B flat minor, with the funeral march), and the two Nocturnes, Op. 37—the one (in G minor) plaintive, longing, and prayerful; the other (in G major) sunny and perfume-laden—may have had their origin in the days of Chopin's sojourn in the Balearic island. A letter of Chopin's, written from Nohant in the summer of 1839, leaves, as regards the Nocturnes, scarcely room for such a conjecture. On the other hand, we learn from the same letter that he composed at Palma the sad, yearning Mazurka in E minor (No. 2 of Op. 41).

As soon as fair weather set in and the steamer resumed its weekly courses to Barcelona, George Sand and her party hastened to leave the island. The delightful prospects of spring could not detain them.

Our invalid (she says) did not seem to be in a state to stand the passage, but he seemed equally incapable of enduring another week in Majorca. The situation was frightful; there were days when I lost hope and courage. To console us, Maria Antonia and her village gossips repeated to us in chorus the most edifying discourses on the future life. "This consumptive person," they said, "is going to hell, first because he is consumptive, secondly, because he does not confess. If he is in this condition when he dies, we shall not bury him in consecrated ground, and as nobody will be willing to give him a grave, his friends will have to manage matters as well as they can. It remains to be seen how they will get out of the difficulty; as for me, I will have Inothing to do with it,— Nor I—Nor I: and Amen!"

In fact, Valdemosa, which at first was enchanting to them, lost afterwards much of its poesy in their eyes. George Sand, as we have seen, said that their sojourn was I in many respects a frightful fiasco; it was so certainly as far as Chopin was concerned, for he arrived with a cough and left the place spitting blood.

The passage from Palma to Barcelona was not so pleasant as that from Barcelona to Palma had been. Chopin suffered much from sleeplessness, which was caused by the noise and bad smell of the most favoured class of passengers on board the Mallorquin—i.e., pigs. "The captain showed us no other attention than that of begging us not to let the invalid lie down on the best bed of the cabin, because according to Spanish prejudice every illness is contagious; and as our man thought already of burning the couch on which the invalid reposed, he wished it should be the worst." [FOOTNOTE: "Un Hiver a Majorque," pp. 24—25.]

On arriving at Barcelona George Sand wrote from the Mallorquin and sent by boat a note to M. Belves, the officer in command at the station, who at once came in his cutter to take her and her party to the Meleagre, where they were well received by the officers, doctor, and all the crew. It seemed to them as if they had left the Polynesian savages and were once more in civilised society. When they shook hands with the French consul they could contain themselves no longer, but jumped for joy and cried "Vive La France!"

A fortnight after their leaving Palma the Phenicien landed them at Marseilles. The treatment Chopin received from the French captain of this steamer differed widely from that he had met with at the hands of the captain of the Mallorquin; for fearing that the invalid was not quite comfortable in a common berth, he gave him his own bed. [FOOTNOTE: "Un Hiver a Majorque," p. 183.]

An extract from a letter written by George Sand from Marseilles on March 8, 1839, to her friend Francois Rollinat, which contains interesting details concerning Chopin in the last scenes of the Majorca intermezzo, may fitly conclude this chapter.

Chopin got worse and worse, and in spite of all offers of service which were made to us in the Spanish manner, we should not have found a hospitable house in all the island. At last we resolved to depart at any price, although Chopin had not the strength to drag himself along. We asked only one—a first and a last service—a carriage to convey him to Palma, where we wished to embark. This service was refused to us, although our FRIENDS had all equipages and fortunes to correspond. We were obliged to travel three leagues on the worst roads in a birlocho [FOOTNOTE: A cabriolet. In a Spainish Dictionary I find a birlocho defined as a vehicle open in front, with two seats, and two or four wheels. A more detailed description is to be found on p. 101 of George Sand's "Un Hiver a Marjorque."] that is to say, a brouette.

On arriving at Palma, Chopin had a frightful spitting of blood; we embarked the following day on the only steamboat of the island, which serves to transport pigs to Barcelona. There is no other way of leaving this cursed country. We were in company of 100 pigs, whose continual cries and foul odour left our patient no rest and no respirable air. He arrived at Barcelona still spitting basins full of blood, and crawling along like a ghost. There, happily, our misfortunes were mitigated! The French consul and the commandant of the French maritime station received us with a hospitality and grace which one does not know in Spain. We were brought on board a fine brig of war, the doctor of which, an honest and worthy man, came at once to the assistance of the invalid, and stopped the hemorrhage of the lung within twenty-four hours.

From that moment he got better and better. The consul had us driven in his carriage to an hotel. Chopin rested there a week, at the end of which the same vessel which had conveyed us to Spain brought us back to France. When we left the hotel at Barcelona the landlord wished to make us pay for the bed in which Chopin had slept, under the pretext that it had been infected, and that the police regulations obliged him to burn it.

CHAPTER XXII

STAY AT MARSEILLES (FROM MARCH TO MAY, 1839) AS DESCRIBED IN CHOPIN'S AND MADAME SAND'S LETTERS.—HIS STATE OF HEALTH.—COMPOSITIONS AND THEIR PUBLICATION.— PLAYING THE ORGAN AT A FUNERAL SERVICE FOR NOURRIT.—AN EXCURSION TO GENOA.—DEPARTURE FOR NOHANT.

As George Sand and her party were obliged to stop at Marseilles, she had Chopin examined by Dr. Cauviere. This celebrated physician thought him in great danger, but, on seeing him recover rapidly, augured that with proper care his patient might nevertheless live a long time. Their stay at Marseilles was more protracted than they intended and desired; in fact, they did not start for Nohant till the 22nd of May. Dr. Cauviere would not permit Chopin to leave Marseilles before summer; but whether this was the only cause of the long sojourn of the Sand party in the great commercial city, or whether there were others, I have not been able to discover. Happily, we have first-hand information—namely, letters of Chopin and George Sand—to throw a little light on these months of the pianist-composer's life. As to his letters, their main contents consist of business matters—wranglings about terms, abuse of publishers, &c. Here and there, however, we find also a few words about his health, characteristic remarks about friends and acquaintances, interesting hints about domestic arrangements and the like—the allusion (in the letter of March 2, 1839) to a will made by him some time before, and which he wishes to be burned, will be read with some curiosity.

An extract or two from the letter which George Sand wrote on March 8, 1839, to Francois Rollinat, launches us at once in medias res.

At last we are in Marseilles. Chopin has stood the passage very well. He is very weak here, but is doing infinitely better in all respects, and is in the hands of Dr. Cauviere, an excellent man and excellent physician, who takes a paternal care of him, and who answers for his recovery. We breathe at last, but after how many troubles and anxieties!...Write to me here to the address of Dr. Cauviere, Rue de Rome, 71. Chopin charges me to shake you heartily by the hand for him. Maurice and Solange embrace you. They are wonderfully well. Maurice has completely recovered.

Chopin to Fontana; Marseilles, March 2, 1839:— You no doubt learned from Grzymala of the state of my health and my manuscripts. Two months ago I sent you from Palma my Preludes. After making a copy of them for Probst and getting the money from him, you were to give to Leo 1,000 francs; and out of the 1,500 francs which Pleyel was to give you for the Preludes I wrote you to pay Nougi and one term to the landlord. In the same letter, if I am not mistaken, I asked you to give notice of my leaving the apartments; for were this not done before April, I should be obliged to retain them for the next quarter, till July.

The second batch of manuscripts may have now reached you; for it must have remained a long time at the custom-house, on the sea, and again at the custom-house.

I also wrote to Pleyel with the Preludes that I give him the Ballade (which I sold to Probst for Germany) for 1,000 francs. For the two Polonaises I asked 1,500 francs for France, England, and Germany (the right of Probst is confined to the Ballade). It seems to me that this is not too dear.

In this way you ought to get, on receiving the second batch of manuscripts, from Pleyel 2,500 francs, and from Probst, for the Ballade, 500 or 600 francs, I do not quite remember, which makes altogether 3,000 francs.

I asked Grzymala if he could send me immediately at least 500 francs, which need not prevent him from sending me soon the rest. Thus much for business.

Now if, which I doubt, you succeed in getting apartments from next month, divide my furniture amongst you three: Grzymala, Johnnie, and you. Johnnie has the most room, although not the most sense, judging from the childish letter he wrote to me. For his telling me that I should become a Camaldolite, let him take all the shabby things. Do not overload Grzymala too much, and take to your house what you judge necessary and serviceable to you, as I do not know whether I shall return to Paris in summer (keep this to yourself). At all events, we will always write one another, and if, as I expect, it be necessary to keep my apartments till July, I beg of you to look after them and pay the quarterly rent.

For your sincere and truly affectionate letter you have an answer in the second Polonaise. [FOOTNOTE: See next foot- note.] It is not my fault that I am like a mushroom that poisons when you unearth and taste it. I know I have never in anything been of service to anyone, but also not of much to myself.

I told you that in the first drawer of my writing-desk near the door there was a paper which you or Grzymala or Johnnie might unseal on a certain occasion. Now I beg of you to take it out and, WITHOUT READING IT,

BURN IT. Do this, I entreat you, for friendship's sake. This paper is now of no use. If Anthony leaves without sending you the money, it is very much in the Polish style; nota bene, do not say to him a word about it. Try to see Pleyel; tell him I have received no word from him, and that his pianino is entrusted to safe hands. Does he agree to the transaction I proposed to him?

The letters from home reached me all three together, with yours, before going on board the vessel. I again send you one.

I thank you for the friendly help you give me, who am not strong. My love to Johnnie, tell him that I did not allow them, or rather that they were not permitted, to bleed me; that I wear vesicatories, that I am coughing a very little in the morning, and that I am not yet at all looked upon as a consumptive person. I drink neither coffee nor wine, but milk. Lastly, I keep myself warm, and look like a girl. Chopin to Fontana; Marseilles, March 6, 1839:— My health is still improving; I begin to play, eat, walk, and speak, like other men; and when you receive these few words from me you will see that I again write with ease. But once more of business. I would like very much that my Preludes should be dedicated to Pleyel (surely there is still time, for they are not yet printed) and the Ballade to Robert Schumann. The Polonaises, as they are, to you and to Kessler. If Pleyel does not like to give up the dedication of the Ballade, you will dedicate the Preludes to Schumann.

[FOOTNOTE: The final arrangement was that Op. 38, the "Deuxieme Ballade," was dedicated to Robert Schumann; Op. 40, the "Deux Polonaises," to Julius Fontana; the French and the English edition of Op. 28, "Vingt-quatre Preludes," to Camille Pleyel, and the German editon to J. C. Kessler.]

Garczynski called upon me yesterday on his way back from Aix; he is the only person that I have received, for I keep the door well shut to all amateurs of music and literature.

Of the change of dedication you will inform Probst as soon as you have arranged with Pleyel.

From the money obtained you will give Grzymala 500 francs, the rest, 2,500 francs, you will send me as soon as possible.

Love me and write.

Pardon me if I overwhelm you too much with commissions, but do not be afraid, these are not the last. I think you do willingly what I ask you.

My love to Johnnie.

Chopin to Fontana; Marseilles, March 10, 1839:—

Thanks for your trouble. I did not expect Jewish tricks from Pleyel; but if it is so, I beg of you to give him the enclosed letter, unless he makes no difficulties about the Ballade and the Polonaises. On the other hand, on receiving for the Ballade 500 francs from Probst, you will take it to Schlesinger. If one has to deal with Jews, let it at least be with orthodox ones. Probst may cheat me still worse; he is a bird you will not catch. Schlesinger used to cheat me, he gained enough by me, and he will not reject new profit, only be polite to him. Though a Jew, he nevertheless wishes to pass for something better.

Thus, should Pleyel make the least difficulties, you will go to Schlesinger, and tell him that I give him the Ballade for France and England for 800 francs, and the Polonaises for Germany, England, and France for 1,500 francs (should he not be inclined to give so much, give them for 1,400, 1,300, and even for 1,200 francs). If he mentions the Preludes, you may say that it is a thing long ago promised to Pleyel—he wished to be the publisher of them; that he asked them from me as a favour before my departure from Paris—as was really the case. You see, my very dear friend, for Pleyel I could break with Schlesinger, but for Probst I cannot. What is it to me if Schlesinger makes Probst pay dearer for my manuscripts? If Probst pays dear for them to Schlesinger, it shows that the latter cheats me, paying me too little. After all, Probst has no establishment in Paris. For all my printed things Schlesinger paid me at once, and Probst very often made me wait for money. If he will not have them all, give him the Ballade separately, and the Polonaises separately, but at the latest within two weeks. If he does not accept the offer, then apply to Probst. Being such an admirer of mine, he must not pay less than Pleyel. You will deliver my letter to Pleyel only if he makes any difficulties.

Dear me! this Pleyel who is such an adorer of mine! He thinks, perhaps, that I shall never return to Paris alive. I shall come back, and shall pay him a visit, and thank him as well as Leo.

I enclose a note to Schlesinger, in which I give you full authority to act in this matter. I feel better every day; nevertheless, you will pay the portier these fifty francs, to which I completely agree, for my doctor does not permit me to move from here before summer. Mickiewicz's "Dziady" I received yesterday. What shall you do with my papers?

The letters you will leave in the writing-desk, and send the music to Johnnie, or take it to your own house. In the little table that stands in the anteroom there are also letters; you must lock it well.

My love to Johnnie, I am glad he is better. Chopin to Fontana; March 17, 1839:— I thank you for all your efforts. Pleyel is a scoundrel, Probst a scape-grace. He never gave me 1,000 francs for three manuscripts. Very likely you have received my long letter about Schlesinger, therefore I wish you and beg of you to give that letter of mine to Pleyel, who thinks my manuscripts too dear. If I have to sell them cheap, I would rather do so to Schlesinger than look for new and improbable connections. For Schlesinger can always count upon England, and as I am square with Wessel, he may sell them to whomsoever he likes. The same with the Polonaises in Germany, for Probst is a bird whom I have known a long time. As regards the money, you must make an unequivocal agreement, and do not give the manuscripts except for cash. I send you a reconnaissance for Pleyel, it astonishes me that he absolutely wants it, as if he could not trust me and you.

Dear me, this Pleyel who said that Schlesinger paid me badly! 500 francs for a manuscript for all the countries seems to him too dear! I assure you I prefer to deal with a real Jew. And Probst, that good-for-nothing fellow, who pays me 300 francs for my mazurkas! You see, the last mazurkas brought me with ease 800 francs—namely, Probst 300 francs, Schlesinger 400, and Wessel 100. I prefer giving my manuscripts as formerly at a very low price to stooping before these...I prefer being submissive to one Jew to being so to three. Therefore go to Schlesinger, but perhaps you settled with Pleyel.

Oh, men, men! But this Mrs. Migneron, she too is a good one! However, Fortune turns round, I may yet live and hear that this lady will come and ask you for some leather; if, as you say, you are aiming at being a shoemaker. I beg of you to make shoes neither for Pleyel nor for Probst.

Do not yet speak to anyone of the Scherzo [Op. 39]. I do not know when I shall finish it, for I am still weak and cannot write.

As yet I have no idea when I shall see you. My love to Grzymala; and give him such furniture as he will like, and let Johnnie take the rest from the apartments. I do not write to him, but I love him always. Tell him this, and give him my love. Wodzinski still astonishes me.

When you receive the money from Pleyel, pay first the landlord's rent, and send me immediately 500 francs. I left on the receipt for Pleyel the Op. blank, for I do not remember the following number.

Madame Sand to Madame Marliani; Marseilles, April 22, 1839:— ...I was also occupied with the removal from one hotel to another. Notwithstanding all his efforts and inquiries, the good doctor was not able to find me a corner in the country where to pass the month of April.

I am pretty tired of this town of merchants and shopkeepers, where the intellectual life is wholly unknown; but here I am still shut up for the month of April.

Further on in the letter, after inviting Madame Marliani and her husband to come to Nohant in May, she proceeds thus:—

He [M. Marliani] loves the country, and I shall be a match for him as regards rural pleasures, while you [Madame Marliani] will philosophise at the piano with Chopin. It can hardly be said that he enjoys himself in Marseilles; but he resigns himself to recover patiently.

The following letter of Chopin to Fontana, which Karasowski thinks was written at Valdemosa in the middle of February, ought to be dated Marseilles, April, 1839:—

As they are such Jews, keep everything till my return. The Preludes I have sold to Pleyel (I received from him 500 francs). He is entitled to do with them what he likes. But as to the Ballades and Polonaises, sell them neither to Schlesinger nor to Probst. But whatever may happen, with no Schonenberger [FOOTNOTE: A Paris music-publisher] will I have anything to do. Therefore, if you gave the Ballade to Probst, take it back, even though he offered a thousand. You may tell him that I have asked you to keep it till my return, that when I am back we shall see.

Enough of these...Enough for me and for you. My very life, I beg of you to forgive me all the trouble; you have really been busying yourself like a friend, and now you will have still on your shoulders my removal. I beg Grzymala to pay the cost of the removal. As to the portier, he very likely tells lies, but who will prove it? You must give, in order to stop his barking.

My love to Johnnie, I will write to him when I am in better spirits. My health is improved, but I am in a rage. Tell Johnnie that from Anthony as well as from me he will have neither word nor money.

Yesterday I received your letter, together with letters from

Pleyel and Johnnie.

If Clara Wieck pleased you, that is good, for nobody can play better than she does. When you see her give her my compliments, and also to her father.

Did I happen to lend you Witwicki's songs? I cannot find them.

I only ask for them in case you should chance to have them.

Chopin to Fontana; Marseilles, March 25 [should no doubt be April 25], 1839:—

I received your letter, in which you let me know the particulars of the removal. I have no words to thank you for your true, friendly help. The particulars were very interesting to me. But I am sorry that you complain, and that Johnnie is spitting blood. Yesterday I played for Nourrit on the organ, you see by this that I am better. Sometimes I play to myself at home, but as yet I can neither sing nor dance. Although the news of my mother is welcome, its having been originated by Plat... is enough to make one consider it a falsehood. The warm weather has set in here, and I shall certainly not leave Marseilles before May, and then go somewhere else in the south of France.

It is not likely that we shall soon have news from Anthony.

Why should he write? Perhaps to pay his debts? But this is not customary in Poland. The reason Raciborski appreciates you so much is that you have no Polish habits, nota bene, not those Polish habits you know and I mean.

You are staying at No. 26 [Chaussee d'Antin]. Are you comfortable? On what floor, and how much do you pay? I take more and more interest in these matters, for I also shall be obliged to think of new apartments, but not till after my return to Paris.

I had only that letter from Pleyel which he sent through you —

it is a month ago or more. Write to the same address, Rue etHotel Beauveau.

Perhaps you did not understand what I said above about my having played for Nourrit. His body was brought from Italy and carried to Paris. There was a Requiem Mass for his soul. I was asked by his friends to play on the organ during the Elevation.

Did Miss Wieck play my Etude well? Could she not select something better than just this etude, the least interesting for those who do not know that it is written for the black keys? It would have been far better to do nothing at all. [FOOTNOTE: Clara Wieck gave a concert in Paris on April 16, 1839. The study in question is No. 5 of Op. 10 (G flat major). Only the right hand plays throughout on black keys.]

In conclusion, I have nothing more to write, except to wish you good luck in the new house. Hide my manuscripts, that they may not appear printed before the time. If the Prelude is printed, that is Pleyel's trick. But I do not care. Mischievous Germans, rascally Jews...! Finish the litany, for you know them as well as I do.

Give my love to Johnnie and Grzymaia if you see them. — Your

FREDERICK.

One subject mentioned in this letter deserves a fuller explanation than Chopin vouchsafes. Adolphe Nourrit, the celebrated tenor singer, had in a state of despondency, caused by the idea that since the appearance of his rival Duprez his popularity was on the wane, put an end to his life by throwing himself out of a window at Naples on the 8th of March, 1839. [FOOTNOTE: This is the generally-accepted account of Nourrit's death. But Madame Garcia, the mother of the famous Malibran, who at the time was staying in the same house, thought it might have been an accident, the unfortuante artist having in the dark opened a window on a level with the floor instead of a door. (See Fetis: Biographie universelle des Musiciens.)] Madame Nourrit brought her husband's body to Paris, and it was on the way thither that a funeral service was held at Marseilles for the much-lamented man and singer.

Le Sud, Journal de la Mediterranee of April 25, 1839, [FOOTNOTE: Quoted in L. M. Quicherat's Adolphe Nourrit, sa vie, son talent, son caractere] shall tell us of Chopin's part in this service:—

At the Elevation of the Host were heard the melancholy tones of the organ. It was M. Chopin, the celebrated pianist, who came to place a souvenir on the coffin of Nourrit; and what a souvenir! a simple melody of Schubert, but the same which had so filled us with enthusiasm when Nourrit revealed it to us at Marseilles—the melody of Les Astres. [FOOTNOTE: Die gestirne is the original German title of this song.]

A less colourless account, one full of interesting facts and free from conventional newspaper sentiment and enthusiasm, we find in a letter of Chopin's companion.

Madame Sand to Madame Marliani; Marseilles, April 28, 1839:— The day before yesterday I saw Madame Nourrit with her six children, and the seventh coming shortly...Poor unfortunate woman! what a return to France! accompanying this corpse, and she herself super-intending the packing, transporting, and unpacking [charger, voiturer, deballer] of it like a parcel!

They held here a very meagre service for the poor deceased, the bishop being ill-disposed. This was in the little church of Notre-Dame-du-Mont. I do not know if the singers did so intentionally, but I never heard such false singing. Chopin devoted himself to playing the organ at the Elevation, what an organ! A false, screaming instrument, which had no wind except for the purpose of being out of tune. Nevertheless, YOUR LITTLE ONE [votre petit] made the most of it. He took the least shrill stops, and played Les Astres, not in a proud and enthusiastic style as Nourrit used to sing it, but in a plaintive and soft style, like the far-off echo from another world. Two, at the most three, were there who deeply felt this, and our eyes filled with tears.

The rest of the audience, who had gone there en masse, and had been led by curiosity to pay as much as fifty centimes for a chair (an unheard-of price for Marseilles), were very much disappointed; for it was expected that he would make a tremendous noise and break at least two or three stops. They expected also to see me, in full dress, in the very middle of the choir; what not? They did not see me at all; I was hidden in the organ-loft, and through the balustrade I descried the coffin of poor Nourrit.

Thanks to the revivifying influences of spring and Dr. Cauviere's attention and happy treatment, Chopin was able to accompany George

Sand on a trip to Genoa, that vaga gemma del mar, fior delta terra. It gave George Sand much pleasure to see again, now with her son Maurice by her side, the beautiful edifices and pictures of the city which six years before she had visited with Musset. Chopin was probably not strong enough to join his friends in all their sight-seeing, but if he saw Genoa as it presents itself on being approached from the sea, passed along the Via Nuova between the double row of magnificent palaces, and viewed from the cupola of S. Maria in Carignano the city, its port, the sea beyond, and the stretches of the Riviera di Levante and Riviera di Ponente, he did not travel to Italy in vain. Thus Chopin got at last a glimpse of the land where nine years before he had contemplated taking up his abode for some time.

On returning to Marseilles, after a stormy passage, on which Chopin suffered much from sea-sickness, George Sand and her party rested for a few days at the house of Dr. Cauviere, and then set out, on the 22nd of May, for Nohant.

Madame Sand to Madame Marliani; Marseilles, May 20, 1839:— We have just arrived from Genoa, in a terrible storm. The bad weather kept us on sea double the ordinary time; forty hours of rolling such as I have not seen for a long time. It was a fine spectacle, and if everybody had not been ill, I would have greatly enjoyed it...

We shall depart the day after to-morrow for Nohant. Address your next letter to me there, we shall be there in eight days. My carriage has arrived from Chalon at Arles by boat, and we shall post home very quietly, sleeping at the inns like good bourgeois.

CHAPTER XXIII

JUNE TO OCTOBER, 1839.

GEORGE SAND AND CHOPIN'S RETURN TO NOHANT.—STATE OF HIS HEALTH.—HIS POSITION IN HIS FRIEND'S HOUSE.—HER ACCOUNT OF THEIR RELATIONSHIP.—HIS LETTERS TO FONTANA, WHICH, AMONG MANY OTHER MATTERS, TREAT OF HIS COMPOSITIONS AND OF PREPARATIONS TO BE MADE FOR HIS AND GEORGE SAND'S ARRIVAL IN PARIS.

The date of one of George Sand's letters shows that the travellers were settled again at Nohant on the 3rd of June, 1839. Dr. Papet, a rich friend of George Sand's, who practised his art only for the benefit of the poor and his friends, took the convalescent Chopin at once under his care. He declared that his patient showed no longer any symptoms of pulmonary affection, but was suffering merely from a slight chronic laryngeal affection which, although he did not expect to be able to cure it, need not cause any serious alarm.

On returning to Nohant, George Sand had her mind much exercised by the question how to teach her children. She resolved to undertake the task herself, but found she was not suited for it, at any rate, could not acquit herself of it satisfactorily without giving up writing. This question, however, was not the only one that troubled her.

In the irresolution in which I was for a time regarding the arrangement of my life with a view to what would be best for my dear children, a serious question was debated in my conscience. I asked myself if I ought to entertain the idea which Chopin had formed of taking up his abode near me. I should not have hesitated to say "no," had I known then for how short a time the retired life and the solemnity of the country suited his moral and physical health. I still attributed his despair and horror of Majorca to the excitement of fever and the exces de caractere of that place. Nohant offered pleasanter conditions, a less austere retreat, congenial society, and resources in case of illness. Papet was to him an enlightened and kind physician. Fleury, Duteil, Duvernet, and their families, Planet, and especially Rollinat, were dear to him at first sight. All of them loved him also, and felt disposed to spoil him as I did.

Among those with whom the family at Nohant had much intercourse, and who were frequent guests at the chateau, was also an old acquaintance of ours, one who had not grown in wisdom as in age, I mean George Sand's half-brother, Hippolyte Chatiron, who was now again living in Berry, his wife having inherited the estate of Montgivray, situated only half a league from Nohant.

His warmth of manner, his inexhaustible gaiety, the originality of his sallies, his enthusiastic and naive effusions of admiration for the genius of Chopin, the always respectful deference which he showed to him alone, even in the inevitable and terrible apres-boire, found favour with the eminently-aristocratic artist. All, then, went very well at first, and I entertained eventually the idea that Chopin might rest and regain his health by spending a few summers with us, his work necessarily calling him back to Paris in the winter.

However, the prospect of this kind of family union with a newly-made friend caused me to reflect. I felt alarmed at the task which I was about to undertake, and which I had believed would be limited to the journey in Spain.

In short, George Sand presents herself as a sister of mercy, who, prompted by charity, sacrifices her own happiness for that of another. Contemplating the possibility of her son falling ill and herself being thereby deprived of the joys of her work, she exclaims: "What hours of my calm and invigorating life should I be able to devote to another patient, much more difficult to nurse and comfort than Maurice?"

The discussion of this matter by George Sand is so characteristic of her that, lengthy as it is, I cannot refrain from giving it in full.

A kind of terror seized me in presence of a new duty which I was to take upon me. I was not under the illusion of passion. I had for the artist a kind of maternal adoration which was very warm, very real, but which could not for a moment contend with maternal love, the only chaste feeling which may be passionate.

I was still young enough to have perhaps to contend with love, with passion properly so called. This contingency of my age, of my situation, and of the destiny of artistic women, especially when they have a horror of passing diversions, alarmed me much, and, resolved as I was never to submit to any influence which might divert me from my children, I saw a less, but still possible danger in the tender friendship with which Chopin inspired me.

Well, after reflection, this danger disappeared and even assumed an opposite character—that of a preservative against emotions which I no longer wished to know. One duty more in my life, already so full of and so overburdened with work, appeared to me one chance more to attain the austerity towards which I felt myself attracted with a kind of religious enthusiasm.

If this is a sincere confession, we can only wonder at the height of self-deception attainable by the human mind; if, however, it is meant as a justification, we cannot but be surprised at the want of skill displayed by the generally so clever advocate. In fact, George Sand has in no instance been less happy in defending her conduct and in setting forth her immaculate virtuousness. The great words "chastity" and "maternity" are of course not absent. George Sand could as little leave off using them as some people can leave off using oaths. In either case the words imply much more than is intended by those from whose mouths or pens they come. A chaste woman speculating on "real love" and "passing diversions," as George Sand does here, seems to me a strange phenomenon. And how charmingly naive is the remark she makes regarding her relations with Chopin as a "PRESERVATIVE against emotions which she no longer wished to know"! I am afraid the concluding sentence, which in its unction is worthy of Pecksniff, and where she exhibits herself as an ascetic and martyr in all the radiance of saintliness, will not have the desired effect, but will make the reader laugh as loud as Musset is said to have done when she upbraided him with his ungratefulness to her, who had been devoted to him to the utmost bounds of self-abnegation, to the sacrifice of her noblest impulses, to the degradation of her chaste nature.

George Sand, looking back in later years on this period of her life, thought that if she had put into execution her project of becoming the teacher of her children, and of shutting herself up all the year round at Nohant, she would have saved Chopin from the danger which, unknown to her, threatened him—namely, the danger of attaching himself too absolutely to her. At that time, she says, his love was not so great but that absence would have diverted him from it. Nor did she consider his affection exclusive. In fact, she had no doubt that the six months which his profession obliged him to pass every year in Paris would, "after a few days of malaise and tears," have given him back to "his habits of elegance, exquisite success, and intellectual coquetry." The correctness of the facts and the probability of the supposition may be doubted. At any rate, the reasons which led her to assume the non-exclusiveness of Chopin's affection are simply childish. That he spoke to her of a romantic love-affair he had had in Poland, and of sweet attractions he had afterwards experienced in Paris, proves nothing. What she says about his mother having been his only passion is still less to the point. But reasoning avails little, and the strength of Chopin's love was not put to the test. He went, indeed, in the autumn of 1839 to Paris, but not alone; George Sand, professedly for the sake of her children's education, went there likewise. "We were driven by fate," she says, "into the bonds of a long connection, and both of us entered into it unawares." The words "driven by fate," and "entered into it unawares," sound strange, if we remember that they apply not to a young girl who, inexperienced and confiding, had lost herself in the mazes of life, but to a novelist skilled in the reading of human hearts, to a constantly-reasoning and calculating woman, aged 35, who had better reasons than poor Amelia in Schiller's play for saying "I have lived and loved."

After all this reasoning, moralising, and sentimentalising, it is pleasant to be once more face to face with facts, of which the following letters, written by Chopin to Fontana during the months from June to October, 1839, contain a goodly number. The rather monotonous publishing transactions play here and there again a prominent part, but these Nohant letters are on the whole more interesting than the Majorca letters, and decidedly more varied as regards contents than those he wrote from Marseilles—they tell us much more of the writer's tastes and requirements, and even reveal something of his relationship to George Sand. Chopin, it appears to me, did not take exactly the same view of this relationship as the novelist. What will be read with most interest are Chopin's directions as to the decoration and furnishing of his rooms, the engagement of a valet, the ordering of clothes and a hat, the taking of a house for George Sand, and certain remarks made en passant on composers and other less-known people.

[I.]

...The best part of your letter is your address, which I had already forgotten, and without which I do not know if I would have answered you so soon; but the worst is the death of Albrecht. [FOOTNOTE: See p.27 foot-note 7.]

You wish to know when I shall be back. When the misty and rainy weather begins, for I must breathe fresh air.

Johnnie has left. I don't know if he asked you to forward to me the letters from my parents should any arrive during his absence and be sent to his usual address. Perhaps he thought of it, perhaps not. I should be very sorry if any of them miscarried. It is not long since I had a letter from home, they will not write soon, and by this time he, who is so kind and good, will be in good health and return.

I am composing here a Sonata in B flat minor, in which will be the Funeral March which you have already. There is an allegro, then a "Scherzo" in E flat minor, the "March," and a short "Finale" of about three pages. The left hand unisono with the right hand are gossiping [FOOTNOTE: "Lewa reka unisono z prawa, ogaduja po Marszu."] after the March. I have a new "Nocturne" in G major, which will go along with the Nocturne in G minor, [FOOTNOTE: "Deux Nocturnes," Op.37.] if you remember such a one.

You know that I have four new mazurkas: one from Palma in E minor, three from here in B major, A flat major, and C sharp minor. [FOOTNOTE: Quatre mazurkas, Op. 41.] They seem to me pretty, as the youngest children usually do when the parents grow old.

Otherwise I do nothing; I correct for myself the Parisian edition of Bach; not only the stroke-makers' [FOOTNOTE: In Polish strycharz, the usual meaning of which is "brickmaker." Chopin may have played upon the word. A mistake, however, is likewise possible, as the Polish for engraver is sztycharz.] (engravers') errors, but, I think, the harmonic errors committed by those who pretend to understand Bach. I do not do it with the pretension that I understand him better than they, but from a conviction that I sometimes guess how it ought to be.

You see I have praised myself enough to you.
Now, if Grzymata will visit me (which is doubtful), send me through him Weber for four hands. Also the last of my Ballade in manuscript, as I wish to change something in it. I should like very much to have your copy of the last mazurkas, if you have such a thing, for I do not know if my gallantry went so far as to give you a copy.

Pleyel wrote to me that you were very obliging, and have corrected the Preludes. Do you know how much Wessel paid him for them? It would be well to know this for the future.

My father has written to me that my old sonata has been published by Haslinger, and that the Germans praise it. [FOOTNOTE: There must have been some misunderstanding; the Sonata, Op. 4, was not published till 1851.]

I have now, counting those you have, six manuscripts; the devil take them if they get them for nothing. Pleyel did not do me any service with his offers, for he thereby made

Schlesinger indifferent about me. But I hope this will be set right, f wrote to ask him to let me know if he had been paid for the piano sent to Palma, and I did so because the French consul in Majorca, whom I know very well, was to be changed, and had he not been paid, it would have been very difficult for me to settle this affair at such a distance. Fortunately, he is paid, and very liberally, as he wrote to me only last week.

Write to me what sort of lodgings you have. Do you board at the club?

Woyciechowski wrote to me to compose an oratorio. I answered him in the letter to my parents. Why does he build a sugar-refinery and not a monastery of Camaldolites or a nunnery of Dominican sisters!
[2.]

I give you my most hearty thanks for your upright, friendly, not English but Polish soul.

Select paper (wall-paper) such as I had formerly, tourterelle (dove colour), only bright and glossy, for the two rooms, also dark green with not too broad stripes. For the anteroom something else, but still respectable. Nevertheless, if there are any nicer and more fashionable papers that are to your liking, and you think that I also will like them, then take them. I prefer the plain, unpretending, and neat ones to the common shopkeeper's staring colours. Therefore, pearl colour pleases me, for it is neither loud nor does it look vulgar. I thank you for the servant's room, for it is much needed.

Now, as to the furniture: you will make the best of it if you look to it yourself. I did not dare to trouble you with it, but if you will be so kind, take it and arrange it as it ought to be. I shall ask Grzymala to give money for the removal. I shall write to him about it at once. As to the bed and writing-desk, it may be necessary to give them to the cabinet-maker to be renewed. In this case you will take the papers out of the writing-desk, and lock them up somewhere else. I need not tell you what you ought to do. Act as you like and judge what is necessary. Whatever you may do will be well done. You have my full confidence: this is one thing.

Now the second.

You must write to Wessel—doubtless you have already written about the Preludes. Let him know that I have six new manuscripts, for which I want 300 francs each (how many pounds is that?). If you think he would not give so much, let me know first. Inform me also if Probst is in Paris. Further look out for a servant. I should prefer a respectable honest Pole. Tell also Grzymala of it. Stipulate that he is to board himself; no more than 80 francs. I shall not be in Paris before the end of October—keep this, however, to yourself.

My dear friend, the state of Johnnie's health weighs sometimes strangely on my heart. May God give him what he stands in need of, but he should not allow himself to be cheated...However, this is neither here nor there. The greatest truth in the world is that I shall always love you as a most honest and kind man and Johnnie as another.

I embrace you both, write each of you and soon, were it of nothing more than the weather.—Your old more than ever long-nosed

FREDERICK.

[3.]

According to your description and that of Grzymala you have found such capital rooms that we are now thinking you have a lucky hand, and for this reason a man—and he is a great man, being the portier of George's house—who will run about to find a house for her, is ordered to apply to you when he has found a few; and you with your elegant tact (you see how I flatter you) will also examine what he has found, and give your opinion thereon. The main point is that it should be detached, if possible; for instance, a little hotel. Or something in a courtyard, with a view into a garden, or, if there be no garden, into a large court-yard; nota bene, very few lodgers—elegant—not higher than the second story. Perhaps some corps de logis, but small, or something like Perthuis's house, or even smaller. Lastly, should it be in front, the street must not be noisy. In one word, something you judge would be good for her. If it could be near me, so much the better; but if it cannot be, this consideration need not prevent you.

It seems to me that a little hotel in the new streets—such as Clichy, Blanche, or Notre-Dame-de-Lorette, as far as Rue des Martyrs—would be most suitable. Moreover, I send you a list of the streets where Mr. Mardelle—the portier of the Hotel Narbonne, Rue de la Harpe, No. 89, which belongs to George— will look for a house. If in your leisure time you also looked out for something in our part of the town, it would be very nice. Fancy, I don't know why, but we think that you will find something wonderfully good, although it is already late.

The price she wishes to pay is from 2,000 to 2,500 francs, you might also give a couple of hundred francs more if anything extra fine should turn up. Grzymala and Arago promised to look out for something, but in spite of Grzymala's efforts nothing acceptable has thus far been found. I have written to him that he should employ you also in this business of mine (I say of MINE, for it is just the same as if it were mine). I shall write to him again to-day and tell him that I have asked you to give your help and use all your talents. It is necessary that there should be three bedrooms, two of which must be beside each other and one separated, for instance, by the drawing-room. Adjoining the third there will be required a well-lighted cabinet for her study. The other two may be small, this one, the third, also not very large. Besides this a drawing-room and dining-room in proportion. A pretty large kitchen. Two rooms for the servants, and a coal-cellar. The rooms must of course have inlaid floors, be newly laid, if possible, and require no repairs. But a little hotel or a separate part of a house in a court-yard looking into a garden would be most desirable. There must be tranquillity, quietness, no blacksmith in the neighbourhood. Respectable stairs. The windows exposed to the sun, absolutely to the south. Further, there must be no smoke, no bad odour, but a fine view, a garden, or at least a large court. A garden would be best. In the Faubourg St. Germain are many gardens, also in the Faubourg St. Honore. Find something quickly, something splendid, and near me. As soon as you have any chance, write immediately, don't be lazy; or get hold of Grzymala, go and see, both of you, take et que cela finisse. I send you a plan of the arrangement of the apartments. If you find something like this, draw the plan, or take it at once, which will be better than letting it slip out of your hands.

Mr. Mardelle is a decent man, and no fool, he was not always a portier. He is ordered to go and see you whenever he finds anything. You must also on your part be on the look-out, but

let us keep that between us. I embrace you and Johnnie also.
You will have our true gratitude when you find a house.

[a diagram of the apartments is inserted here in the letter.]

```
+— — — — — — — — — — — — — — — — — — — — — — — — — — — — — — — +
| | | | | | | Study | Bedroom. | Drawing room. | Bedroom. | Servants' room. | | |
| | | |
| — — — — — — — — — — — — — — — — — — — — — — — — — — — — — — — |
| | | | | | | Dining room | | | | | |
| — — — — — — — — — — — — — — — — — — — — — — — — — — — — — — — |
| | | | | | | Lobby | | | | | |
+— — — — — — — — — — — — — — — — — — — — — — — — — — — — — — — +
```

Pas de voisinage, surtout blacksmith, nor anything that
belongs to him. For God's sake I beg of you take an active
interest in the matter, my dear friend!
[4.]

I thank you for all your kind actions.

In the anteroom you will direct the grey curtains to be hung
which were in my cabinet with the piano, and in the bedroom
the same that were in the bedroom, only under them the white
muslin ones which were under the grey ones.

I should like to have a little press in my bedroom, unless
there be not room enough, or the drawing-room be too bare
between the windows.

If the little sofa, the same which stood in the dining-room,
could be covered with red, with the same stuff with which the
chairs are covered, it might be placed in the drawing-room;
but as it would be necessary to call in the upholsterer for

that, it may be difficult.

It is a good thing that Domaradzki is going to be married, for surely he will give me back the 80 francs after the wedding. I should like also to see Podczaski married, and Nakw. (Nakwaska), and Anthony also. Let this remain between this paper, myself, and you.

Find me a valet. Kiss Madame Leo (surely the first commission will be the more pleasant to you, wherefore I relieve you of the second if you will do the first).

Let me know about Probst, whether he is in Paris or not. Do not forget Wessel. Tell Gutmann that I was much pleased that he asked for me at least once. To Moscheles, should he be in Paris, order to be given an injection of Neukomm's oratorios, prepared with Berlioz's "Cellini" and Doehler's Concerto. Give Johnnie from me for his breakfast moustaches of sphinxes and kidneys of parrots, with tomato sauce powdered with little eggs of the microscopic world. You yourself take a bath in whale's infusion as a rest from all the commissions I give you, for I know that you will do willingly as much as time will permit, and I shall do the same for you when you are married—of which Johnnie will very likely inform me soon. Only not to Ox, for that is my party.
[5.]

My dear friend,—In five, six, or seven days I shall be in Paris. Get things prepared as quickly as possible; if not all, let me find at least the rooms papered and the bed ready.

I am hastening my arrival as the presence of George Sand is necessary on account of a piece to be played. [FOOTNOTE: "Cosima." The first representation, at the Comedie Francaise, did not take place until April, 1840.] But this remains between us. We have fixed our departure for the day after to-morrow; thus, counting a few days for delay, we shall see each other on Wednesday or Thursday.

Besides the different commissions I gave you, especially that in the last letter about her house, which after our arrival will be off your shoulders—but till then, for God's sake, be obliging—besides all this, I say, I forgot to ask you to order for me a hat from my Duport in your street, Chaussee d'Antin. He has my measure, and knows how light I want it and of what kind. Let him give the hat of this year's shape, not too much exaggerated, for I do not know how you are dressing yourself just now. Again, besides this, call in passing at Dautremont's, my tailor's, on the Boulevards, and order him to make me at once a pair of grey trousers. You will yourself select a dark-grey colour for winter trousers; something respectable, not striped, but plain and elastic. You are an Englishman, so you know what I require. Dautremont will be glad to hear that I am coming. Also a quiet black velvet waistcoat, but with very little and no loud pattern, something very quiet but very elegant. Should he not have the best velvet of this kind, let him make a quiet, fine silk waistcoat, but not too much open. If the servant could be got for less than 80 francs, I should prefer it; but as you have already found one, let the matter rest.

My very dear friend, pardon me once more for troubling you, but I must. In a few days we shall see each other, and embrace for all this.

I beg of you, for God's sake, do not say to any Poles that I am coming so soon, nor to any Jewess either, as I should like to reserve myself during the first few days only for you,

Grzymala, and Johnnie. Give them my love; to the latter I
shall write once more.

I expect that the rooms will be ready. Write constantly to me,
three times a day if you like, whether you have anything to
say or not. Before leaving here I shall once more write to
you.
Monday.

You are inappreciable! Take Rue Pigal [Pigalle], both houses,
without asking anybody. Make haste. If by taking both houses
you can diminish a little the price, well; if not, take them
for 2,500 francs. Do not let them slip out of your hands, for
we think them the best and most excellent. SHE regards you as
my most logical and best—and I would add: the most splenetic,
Anglo-Polish, from my soul beloved—friend.
[6.]

The day after to-morrow, Thursday, at five o'clock in the
morning, we start, and on Friday at three, four, certainly at
five o'clock, I shall be in Rue Tronchet, No. 5. I beg of you
to inform the people there of this, I wrote to Johnnie to-day
to retain for me that valet, and order him to wait for me at
Rue Tronchet on Friday from noon. Should you have time to call
upon me at that time, we would most heartily embrace each
other. Once more my and my companion's most sincere thanks for
Rue Pigalle.

Now, keep a sharp look-out on the tailor, he must have the
clothes ready by Friday morning, so that I can change my
clothes as soon as I come. Order him to take them to Rue
Tronchet, and deliver them there to the valet Tineau—if I
mistake not, that is his name. Likewise the hat from Dupont,
[FOOTNOTE: In the preceding letter it was Duport] and for that

I shall alter for you the second part of the Polonaise till the last moment of my life. Yesterday's version also may not please you, although I racked my brains with it for at least eighty seconds.

I have written out my manuscripts in good order. There are six with your Polonaises, not counting the seventh, an impromptu, which may perhaps be worthless—I do not know myself, it is too new. But it would be well if it be not too much in the style of Orlowski, Zimmermann, or Karsko-Konski, [FOOTNOTE: Chopin's countryman, the pianist and composer Antoine Kontski] or Sowinski, or other similar animals. For, according to my reckoning, it might fetch me about 800 francs. That will be seen afterwards.

As you are such a clever man, you might also arrange that no black thoughts and suffocating coughs shall annoy me in the new rooms. Try to make me good. Change, if you can, many episodes of my past. It would also not be a bad thing if I should find a few years of great work accomplished. By this you will greatly oblige me, also if you would make yourself younger or bring about that we had never been born.—Your old

FREDERICK.

CHAPTER XXIV

1839-1842.

RETURN OF GEORGE SAND AND CHOPIN TO PARIS.—GEORGE SAND IN THE RUE PIGALLE.—CHOPIN IN THE RUE TRONCHET: REMINISCENCES OF BRINLEY RICHARDS AND MOSCHELES.— SOIREES AT LEO'S AND ST. CLOUD.—CHOPIN JOINS MADAME SAND IN THE RUE PIGALLE.—EXTRACTS FROM GEORGE SAND'S CORRESPONDANCE; A LETTER OF MADAME SAND'S TO CHOPIN; BALZAC ANECDOTES.—MADAME SAND AND CHOPIN DO NOT GO TO NOHANT IN 1840.—COMPOSITIONS OF THIS PERIOD.—ABOUT CHOPIN AS A PIANIST.—LETTERS WRITTEN TO FONTANA IN THE SUMMER AND AUTUMN OF 1841.

Although Chopin and George Sand came to Paris towards the end of October, 1839, months passed before the latter got into the house which Fontana had taken for her. This we learn from a letter written by her to her friend Gustave Papet, and dated Paris, January, 1840, wherein we read:—

At last I am installed in the Rue Pigalle, 16, only since the

last two days, after having fumed, raged, stormed, and sworn

at the upholsterers, locksmith, &c., &c. What a long,

horrible, unbearable business it is to lodge one's self here!

[FOOTNOTE: In the letter, dated Paris, October, 1839,

preceding, in the George Sand "Correspondance," the one from

which the above passage is extracted, occur the following

words: "Je suis enfin installee chez moi a Paris." Where this

chez moi was, I do not know.]

How greatly the interiors of George Sand's pavilions in the Rue Pigalle differed from those of Senor Gomez's villa and the cells in the monastery of Valdemosa, may be gathered from Gutmann's description of two of the apartments.

[FOOTNOTE: I do not guarantee the correctness of all the following details, although I found them in a sketch of Gutmann's life inspired by himself ("Der Lieblings-schuler Chopin's", No. 3 of "Schone Geister," by Bernhard Stavenow, Bremen, 1879), and which he assured me was trustworthy. The reasons of my scepticism are—1, Gutmann's imaginative memory and tendency to show himself off to advantage; 2, Stavenow's love of fine writing and a good story; 3, innumerable misstatements that can be indisputably proved by documents.]

Regarding the small salon, he gives only the general information that it was quaintly fitted up with antique furniture. But of George Sand's own room, which made a deeper impression upon him, he mentions so many particulars—the brown carpet covering the whole floor, the walls hung with a dark-brown ribbed cloth (Ripsstoff), the fine paintings, the carved furniture of dark oak, the brown velvet seats of the chairs, the large square bed, rising but little above the floor, and covered with a Persian rug (Teppich)—that it is easy to picture to ourselves the tout-ensemble of its appearance. Gutmann tells us that he had an early opportunity of making these observations, for Chopin visited his pupil the very day after his arrival (?), and invited him at once to call on George Sand in order to be introduced to her. When Gutmann presented himself in the small salon above alluded to, he found George Sand seated on an ottoman smoking a cigarette. She received the young man with great cordiality, telling him that his master had often spoken to her of him most lovingly. Chopin entered soon after from an adjoining apartment, and then they all went into the dining-room to have dinner. When they were seated again in the cosy salon, and George Sand had lit another cigarette, the conversation, which had touched on a variety of topics, among the rest on Majorca, turned on art. It was then that the authoress said to her friend: "Chop, Chop, show Gutmann my room that he may see the pictures which Eugene Delacroix painted for me."

Chopin on arriving in Paris had taken up his lodgings in the Rue Tronchet, No. 5, and resumed teaching. One of his pupils there was Brinley Richards, who practised under him one of the books of studies. Chopin also assisted the British musician in the publication, by Troupenas, of his first composition, having previously looked over and corrected it. Brinley Richards informed me that Chopin, who played rarely in these lessons, making his corrections and suggestions rather by word of mouth than by example, was very languid, indeed so much so that he looked as if he felt inclined to lie down, and seemed to say: "I wish you would come another time."

About this time, that is in the autumn or early in the winter of 1839, Moscheles came to Paris. We learn from his diary that at Leo's, where he liked best to play, he met for the first time Chopin, who had just returned from the country, and whose acquaintance he was impatient to make. I have already quoted what Moscheles said of Chopin's appearance—namely, that it was exactly like [identificirt mit] his music, both being delicate and dreamy [schwarmerisch]. His remarks on his great contemporary's musical performances are, of course, still more interesting to us.

> He played to me at my request, and now for the first time I understand his music, and can also explain to myself the enthusiasm of the ladies. His ad libitum playing, which with the interpreters of his music degenerates into disregard of time, is with him only the most charming originality of execution; the dilettantish harsh modulations which strike me disagreeably when I am playing his compositions no longer shock me, because he glides lightly over them in a fairy-like way with his delicate fingers; his piano is so softly breathed forth that he does not need any strong forte in order to produce the wished-for contrasts; it is for this reason that one does not miss the orchestral-like effects which the German school demands from a pianoforte-player, but allows one's self to be carried away, as by a singer who, little concerned about the accompaniment, entirely follows his feeling. In short, he is an unicum in the world of pianists. He declares that he loves my music very much, and at all events he knows it very well. He played me some studies and his latest work, the "Preludes," and I played him many of my compositions.

In addition to this characterisation of the artist Chopin, Moscheles' notes afford us also some glimpses of the man. "Chopin was lively, merry, nay, exceedingly comical in his imitations of Pixis, Liszt, and a hunchbacked pianoforte-player." Some days afterwards, when Moscheles saw him at his own house, he found him an altogether different Chopin:—

> I called on him according to agreement with Ch. and E., who are also quite enthusiastic about him, and who were particularly struck with the "Prelude" in A flat major in 6/8 time with the ever-recurring pedal A flat. Only the Countess O. [Obreskoff] from St. Petersburg, who adores us artists en bloc, was there, and some gentlemen. Chopin's excellent pupil Gutmann played his master's manuscript Scherzo in C sharp minor. Chopin himself played his manuscript Sonata in B flat

minor with the Funeral March.

Gutmann relates that Chopin sent for him early in the morning of the day following that on which he paid the above-mentioned visit to George Sand, and said to him:—

Pardon me for disturbing you so early in the morning, but I
have just received a note from Moscheles, wherein he expresses
his joy at my return to Paris, and announces that he will
visit me at five in the afternoon to hear my new compositions.
Now I am unfortunately too weak to play my things to him; so
you must play. I am chiefly concerned about this Scherzo.

Gutmann, who did not yet know the work (Op. 39), thereupon sat down at Chopin's piano, and by dint of hard practising managed to play it at the appointed hour from memory, and to the satisfaction of the composer. Gutmann's account does not tally in several of its details with Moscheles'. As, however, Moscheles does not give us reminiscences, but sober, business-like notes taken down at the time they refer to, and without any attempt at making a nice story, he is the safer authority. Still, thus much at least we may assume to be certain:—Gutmann played the Scherzo, Op. 39, on this occasion, and his rendering of it was such as to induce his master to dedicate it to him.

Comte de Perthuis, the adjutant of King Louis Philippe, who had heard Chopin and Moscheles repeatedly play the latter's Sonata in E flat major for four hands, spoke so much and so enthusiastically about it at Court that the royal family, wishing "to have also the great treat," invited the two artists to come to St. Cloud. The day after this soiree Moscheles wrote in his diary:—

Yesterday was a memorable day... at nine o'clock Chopin and I,
with Perthuis and his amiable wife, who had called for us,
drove out to St. Cloud in the heaviest showers of rain, and
felt so much the more comfortable when we entered the
brilliant, well-lighted palace. We passed through many state-
rooms into a salon carre, where the royal family was assembled
en petit comite. At a round table sat the queen with an
elegant work-basket before her (perhaps to embroider a purse
for me?); near her were Madame Adelaide, the Duchess of
Orleans, and ladies-in-waiting. The noble ladies were as
affable as if we had been old acquaintances...Chopin played
first a number of nocturnes and studies, and was admired and

petted like a favourite. After I also had played some old and new studies, and been honoured with the same applause, we seated ourselves together at the instrument—he again playing the bass, which he always insists on doing. The close attention of the little circle during my E flat major Sonata was interrupted only by the exclamations "divine!" "delicious!" After the Andante the queen whispered to a lady-in-waiting: "Would it not be indiscreet to ask them to play it again?" which naturally was equivalent to a command to repeat it, and so we played it again with increased abandon. In the Finale we gave ourselves up to a musical delirium. Chopin's enthusiasm throughout the whole piece must, I believe, have infected the auditors, who now burst forth into eulogies of us. Chopin played again alone with the same charm, and called forth the same sympathy as before; then I improvised...

[FOOTNOTE: In the "Neue Zeitschrift fur Musik" of November 12, 1839, we read that Chopin improvised on Grisar's "La Folle," Moscheles on themes by Mozart. La Folle is a romance the success of which was so great that a wit called it une folie de salon. It had for some years an extraordinary popularity, and made the composer a reputation.]

To show his gratitude, the king sent the two artists valuable presents: to Chopin a gold cup and saucer, to Moscheles a travelling case. "The king," remarked Chopin, "gave Moscheles a travelling case to get the sooner rid of him." The composer was fond of and had a talent for throwing off sharp and witty sayings; but it is most probable that on this occasion the words were prompted solely by the fancy, and that their ill-nature was only apparent. Or must we assume that the man Moscheles was less congenial to Chopin than the artist? Moscheles was a Jew, and Chopin disliked the Jews. As, however, the tempting opportunity afforded by the nature of the king's present to Moscheles is sufficient to account for Chopin's remark, and no proofs warranting a less creditable explanation are forthcoming, it would be unfair to listen to the suggestions of suspicion.

George Sand tells us in the "Histoire de ma Vie" that Chopin found his rooms in the Rue Tronchet cold and damp, and felt sorely the separation from her. The consequence of this was that the saintly woman, the sister of mercy, took, after some time, pity upon her suffering worshipper, and once more sacrificed herself. Not to misrepresent her account, the only one we have, of this change in the domestic arrangements of the two friends, I shall faithfully transcribe her delicately-worded statements:—

He again began to cough alarmingly, and I saw myself forced either to give in my resignation as nurse, or to pass my life in impossible journeyings to and fro. He, in order to spare me these, came every day to tell me with a troubled face and a feeble voice that he was wonderfully well. He asked if he might dine with us, and he went away in the evening, shivering in his cab. Seeing how he took to heart his exclusion from our family life, I offered to let to him one of the pavilions, a part of which I could give up to him. He joyfully accepted. He had there his room, received there his friends, and gave there his lessons without incommoding me. Maurice had the room above his; I occupied the other pavilion with my daughter.

Let us see if we cannot get some glimpses of the life in the pavilions of the Rue Pigalle, No. 16. In the first months of 1840, George Sand was busy with preparations for the performance of her drama Cosima, moving heaven and earth to bring about the admission of her friend Madame Dorval into the company of the Theatre-Francais, where her piece, in which she wished this lady to take the principal part, was to be performed. Her son Maurice passed his days in the studio of Eugene Delacroix; and Solange gave much time to her lessons, and lost much over her toilet. Of Grzymala we hear that he is always in love with all the beautiful women, and rolls his big eyes at the tall Borgnotte and the little Jacqueline; and that Madame Marliani is always up to her ears in philosophy. This I gathered from George Sand's Correspondance, where, as the reader will see presently, more is to be found.

George Sand to Chopin; Cambrai, August 13, 1840:—
I arrived at noon very tired, for it is 45 and 35 leagues from Paris to this place. We shall relate to you good stories of the bourgeois of Cambrai. They are beaux, they are stupid, they are shopkeepers; they are the sublime of the genre. If the Historical Procession does not console us, we are capable of dying of ennui at the politeness which people show us. We are lodged like princes. But what hosts, what conversations, what dinners! We laugh at them when we are by ourselves, but

when we are before the enemy, what a pitiable figure we
selves, make! I am no longer desirous to see you come; but I
aspire to depart very quickly, and I understand why you do not
wish to give concerts. It is not unlikely that Pauline Viardot
may not sing the day after to-morrow, for want of a hall. We
shall, perhaps, leave a day sooner. I wish I were already far
away from the Cambresians, male and female.

Good night! I am going to bed, I am overcome with fatigue.

Love your old woman [votre vieille] as she loves you.

From a letter written two days later to her son, we learn that Madame
Viardot after all gave two concerts at Cambrai. But amusing as the letter is,
we will pass it over as not concerning us here. Of another letter (September
20,1840), likewise addressed to her son, I shall quote only one passage,
although it contains much interesting matter about the friends and visitors
of the inmates of the pavilions of the Rue Pigalle, No. 16:—

Balzac came to dine here the day before yesterday. He is quite
mad. He has discovered the blue rose, for which the
horticultural societies of London and Belgium have promised a
reward of 500,000 francs (qui dit, dit-il). He will sell,
moreover, every grain at a hundred sous, and for this great
botanic production he will lay out only fifty centimes.
Hereupon Rollinat asked him naively:—

"Well, why, then, do you not set about it at once?"

To which Balzac replied:

"Oh! because I have so many other things to do; but I shall set about it
one of these days."

Stavenow, in Schone Geister (see foot-note, p. 70), tells an anecdote of
Balzac, which may find a place here:—

One day Balzac had invited George Sand, Chopin, and Gutmann to
dinner. On that occasion he related to them that the next day
he would have to meet a bill of 30,000 francs, but that he had
not a sou in his pocket. Gutmann asked what he intended to do?
"Well," replied Balzac, "what shall I do? I wait quietly.
Before to-morrow something unexpected may turn up, and give me

the means to pay the sum." Scarcely had he said this when the door bell rang. The servant entered and announced that a gentleman was there who urgently wished to speak with M. Balzac.

Balzac rose and left the room. After a quarter of an hour he came back in high spirits and said:

"The 30,000 francs are found. My publisher wishes to bring out a new edition of my works, and he offers me just this sum."

George Sand, Chopin, and Gutmann looked at each other with a smile, and thought—"Another one!"
George Sand to her son; Paris, September 4, 1840:—
We have had here great shows of troops. They have fione the gendarme and cuisse the national guardsman. All Paris was in agitation, as if there were to be a revolution. Nothing took place, except that some passers-by were knocked down by the police.

There were places in Paris where it was dangerous to pass, as these gentlemen assassinated right and left for the pleasure of getting their hands into practice. Chopin, who will not believe anything, has at last the proof and certainty of it.

Madame Marliani is back. I dined at her house the day before yesterday with the Abbe de Lamennais. Yesterday Leroux dined here. Chopin embraces you a thousand times. He is always qui, qui, qui, me, me, me. Rollinat smokes like a steam-boat.
Solange has been good for two or three days, but yesterday she had a fit of temper [acces de fureur]. It is the Rebouls, the English neighbours, people and dogs, who turn her head.
In the summer of 1840 George Sand did not go to Nohant, and Chopin seems to have passed most of, if not all, the time in Paris. From a letter addressed to her half-brother, we learn that the reason of her staying away from her country-seat was a wish to economise:—
If you will guarantee my being able to pass the summer at Nohant for 4,000 francs, I will go. But I have never been

there without spending 1,500 francs per month, and as I do not spend here the half of this, it is neither the love of work, nor that of spending, nor that of glory, which makes me stay...

George Sand's fits of economy never lasted very long. At any rate, in the summer of 1841 we find her again at Nohant. But as it is my intention to treat of Chopin's domestic life at Nohant and in Paris with some fulness in special chapters, I shall now turn to his artistic doings.

In 1839 there appeared only one work by Chopin, Op. 28, the "Preludes," but in the two following years as many as sixteen—namely, Op. 35-50. Here is an enumeration of these compositions, with the dates of publication and the dedications.

[FOOTNOTE: Both the absence of dedications in the case of some compositions, and the persons to whom others are dedicated, have a biographical significance. They tell us of the composer's absence from Paris and aristocratic society, and his return to them.]

The "Vingt-quatre Preludes," Op. 28, published in September, 1839, have a twofold dedication, the French and English editions being dedicated a son ami Pleyel, and the German to Mr. J. C. Kessler. The publications of 1840 are: in May—Op. 35, "Sonate" (B flat minor); Op. 36, "Deuxieme Impromptu" (F sharp minor); Op. 37, "Deux Nocturnes" (G minor and G major); in July—Op. 42, "Valse" (A flat major); in September—Op. 38, "Deuxieme Ballade" (F major), dedicated to Mr. R. Schumann; in October— Op. 39, "Troisieme Scherzo" (C sharp minor), dedicated to Mr. A. Gutmann; in November—Op. 40, "Deux Polonaises" (A major and C minor), dedicated to Mr. J. Fontana; and in December—Op. 41, "Quatre Mazurkas" (C sharp and E minor, B and A flat major), dedicated to E. Witwicki. Those of 1841 are: in October—Op. 43, "Tarantelle" (A flat major), without any dedication; and in November—Op. 44, "Polonaise" (F sharp minor), dedicated to Madame la Princesse Charles de Beauvau; Op. 45, "Prelude" (C sharp minor), dedicated to Madame la Princesse Elizabeth Czernicheff; Op. 46, "Allegro de Concert" (A major), dedicated to Mdlle. F. Muller; Op. 47, "Troisieme Ballade" (A flat major), dedicated to Mdlle. P. de Noailles; Op. 48, "Deux Nocturnes" (C minor and F sharp minor), dedicated to Mdlle. L. Duperre; Op. 49, "Fantaisie" (F minor), dedicated to Madame la Princesse C. de Souzzo; and Op. 50, "Trois Mazurkas" (G and A flat major, and C sharp minor), dedicated to Mr. Leon Smitkowski.

Chopin's genius had now reached the most perfect stage of its development, and was radiating with all the intensity of which its nature was capable. Notwithstanding such later creations as the fourth "Ballade,"

Op. 52, the "Barcarolle," Op. 60, and the "Polonaise," Op. 53, it can hardly be said that the composer surpassed in his subsequent works those which he had published in recent years, works among which were the first three ballades, the preludes, and a number of stirring polonaises and charming nocturnes, mazurkas, and other pieces.

However, not only as a creative artist, but also as an executant, Chopin was at the zenith of his power. His bodily frame had indeed suffered from disease, but as yet it was not seriously injured, at least, not so seriously as to disable him to discharge the functions of a musical interpreter. Moreover, the great majority of his compositions demanded from the executant other qualities than physical strength, which was indispensable in only a few of his works. A writer in the "Menestrel" (April 25, 1841) asks himself the question whether Chopin had progressed as a pianist, and answers: "No, for he troubles himself little about the mechanical secrets of the piano; in him there is no charlatanism; heart and genius alone speak, and in these respects his privileged organisation has nothing to learn." Or rather let us say, Chopin troubled himself enough about the mechanical secrets of the piano, but not for their own sakes: he regarded them not as ends, but as means to ends, and although mechanically he may have made no progress, he had done so poetically. Love and sorrow, those most successful teachers of poets and musicians, had not taught him in vain.

It was a fortunate occurrence that at this period of his career Chopin was induced to give a concert, and equally fortunate that men of knowledge, judgment, and literary ability have left us their impressions of the event. The desirability of replenishing an ever-empty purse, and the instigations of George Sand, were no doubt the chief motive powers which helped the composer to overcome his dislike to playing in public.

"Do you practise when the day of the concert approaches?" asked Lenz. [FOOTNOTE: Die grossen Pianoforte-Virtuosen unstrer Zeit, p. 36.] "It is a terrible time for me," was Chopin's answer; "I dislike publicity, but it is part of my position. I shut myself up for a fortnight and play Bach. That is my preparation; I never practise my own compositions." What Gutmann told me confirms these statements. Chopin detested playing in public, and became nervous when the dreaded time approached. He then fidgeted a great deal about his clothes, and felt very unhappy if one or the other article did not quite fit or pinched him a little. On one occasion Chopin, being dissatisfied with his own things, made use of a dress-coat and shirt of his pupil Gutmann. By the way, the latter, who gave me this piece of information, must have been in those days of less bulk, and, I feel inclined to add, of less height, than he was when I became acquainted with him.

Leaving the two concerts given by Chopin in 1841 and 1842 to be discussed in detail in the next chapter, I shall now give a translation of the Polish letters which he wrote in the summer and autumn of 1841 to Fontana. The letters numbered 4 and 5 are those already alluded to on p. 24 (footnote 3) which Karasowski gives as respectively dated by Chopin: "Palma, November 17, 1838"; and "Valdemosa, January 9, 1839." But against these dates militate the contents: the mention of Troupenas, with whom the composer's business connection began only in 1840 (with the Sonata, Op. 35); the mention of the Tarantelle, which was not published until 1841; the mention (contradictory to an earlier inquiry—see p. 30) of the sending back of a valet nowhere else alluded to; the mention of the sending and arrival of a piano, irreconcilable with the circumstances and certain statements in indisputably correctly-dated letters; and, lastly, the absence of all mention of Majorca and the Preludes, those important topics in the letters really from that place and of that time. Karasowski thinks that the letters numbered 1, 2, 3, and 9 were of the year 1838, and those numbered 6, 7, and 8 of the year 1839; but as the "Tarantelle," Op. 43, the "Polonaise," Op. 44, the "Prelude," Op. 45, the "Allegro de Concert," Op. 46, the third "Ballade," Op. 47, the two "Nocturnes," Op. 48, and the "Fantaisie," Op. 49, therein mentioned, were published in 1841, I have no doubt that they are of the year 1841. The mention in the ninth letter of the Rue Pigalle, 16, George Sand's and Chopin's abode in Paris, of Pelletan, the tutor of George Sand's son Maurice, and of the latter's coming to Paris, speaks likewise against 1838 and for 1841, 1840 being out of the question, as neither George Sand nor Chopin was in this year at Nohant. What decides me especially to reject the date 1839 for the seventh letter is that Pauline Garcia had then not yet become the wife of Louis Viardot. There is, moreover, an allusion to a visit of Pauline Viardot to Nohant in the summer of 1841 in one of George Sand's letters (August 13, 1841). In this letter occurs a passage which is important for the dating both of the fifth and the seventh letter. As to the order of succession of the letters, it may be wrong, it certainly does not altogether satisfy me; but it is the result of long and careful weighing of all the pros and cons. I have some doubt about the seventh letter, which, read by the light of George Sand's letter, ought perhaps to be placed after the ninth. But the seventh letter is somewhat of a puzzle. Puzzles, owing to his confused statements and slipshod style, are, however, not a rare thing in Chopin's correspondence. The passage in the above-mentioned letter of George Sand runs thus: "Pauline leaves me on the 16th [of August]; Maurice goes on the 17th to fetch his sister, who should be here on the 23rd."

[I.] 1841.

My very dear friend,—I arrived here yesterday, Thursday. For Schlesinger [FOOTNOTE: The Paris music-publisher.] I have composed a Prelude in C sharp minor [Op. 45], which is short, as he wished it. Seeing that, like Mechetti's [FOOTNOTE: The Vienna music-publisher.] Beethoven, this has to come out at the New Year, do not yet give my Polonaise to Leo (although you have already transcribed it), for to-morrow I shall send you a letter for Mechetti, in which I shall explain to him that, if he wishes something short, I will give him for the Album instead of the mazurka (which is already old) the NEW prelude. It is well modulated, and I can send it without hesitation. He ought to give me 300 francs for it, n'est-ce pas? Par-dessus le marche he may get the mazurka, only he must not print it in the Album.

Should Troupenas, [FOOTNOTE: Eugene Troupenas, the Paris music-publisher.] that is, Masset, [FOOTNOTE: Masset (his daughter, Madame Colombier, informed me) was the partner of Troupenas, and managed almost the whole business, Troupenas being in weak health, which obliged him to pass the last ten winters of his life at Hyeres.] make any difficulties, do not give him the pieces a farthing cheaper, and tell him that if he does not wish to print them all—which I should not like—I could sell them at a better price to others.

Now of something else.

You will find in the right-hand drawer of my writing-desk (in the place where the cash-box always is) a sealed parcel addressed to Madame Sand. Wrap this parcel in wax-cloth, seal it, and send it by post to Madame Sand's address. Sew on the address with a strong thread, that it may not come off the wax-cloth. It is Madame Sand who asks me to do this. I know you will do it perfectly well. The key, I think, is on the top shelf of the little cabinet with the mirror. If it should not be there, get a locksmith to open the drawer.

I love you as an old friend. Embrace Johnnie.—Your

FREDERICK.

[2.] 1841.

Thanks for forwarding the parcel. I send you the Prelude, in large characters for Schlesinger and in small characters for Mechetti. Clip the MS. of the Polonaise to the same size, number the pages, and fold it like the Prelude, add to the whole my letter to Mechetti, and deliver it into Leo's own hands, praying him to send it by the first mail, as Mechetti is waiting for it.

The letter to Haslinger [FOOTNOTE: The Vienna music-publisher.] post yourself; and if you do not find Schlesinger at home leave the letter, but do not give him the MS. until he tells you that he accepts the Prelude as a settlement of the account. If he does not wish to acquire the right of publication for London, tell him to inform me of it by letter. Do not forget to add the opus on the Polonaise and the following number on the Prelude—that is, on the copies that are going to Vienna.

I do not know how Czerniszewowa is spelt. Perhaps you will find under the vase or on the little table near the bronze ornament a note from her, from her daughter, or from the governess; if not, I should be glad if you would go—they know you already as my friend—to the Hotel de Londres in the Place Vendome, and beg in my name the young Princess to give you her name in writing and to say whether it is Tscher or Tcher. Or better still, ask for Mdlle. Krause, the governess; tell her that I wish to give the young Princess a surprise; and inquire of her whether it is usual to write Elisabeth and

Tschernichef, or ff. [FOOTNOTE: Chopin dedicated the Prelude, Op. 45, to Mdlle. la Princesse Elisabeth Czernicheff.]

If you do not wish to do this, don't be bashful with me, and write that you would rather be excused, in which case I shall find it out by some other means. But do not yet direct Schlesinger to print the title. Tell him I don't know how to spell. Nevertheless, I hope that you will find at my house some note from them on which will be the name....

I conclude because it is time for the mail, and I wish that my letter should reach Vienna without fail this week.
[3.] Nohant, Sunday, 1841.

I send you the Tarantella [Op. 43]. Please to copy it. But first go to Schlesinger, or, better still, to Troupenas, and see the collection of Rossini's songs published by Troupenas. In it there is a Tarantella in F. I do not know whether it is written in 6/8 or 12/8 time. As to my composition, it does not matter which way it is written, but I should prefer it to be like Rossini's. Therefore, if the latter be in 12/8 or in C with triplets, make in copying one bar out of two. It will be thus: [here follows one bar of music, bars four and five of the Tarantella as it is printed.] [FOOTNOTE: This is a characteristic instance of Chopin's carelessness in the notation of his music. To write his Tarantella in 12/8 or C would have been an egregious mistake. How Chopin failed to see this is inexplicable to me.]
I beg of you also to write out everything in full, instead of marking repeats. Be quick, and give it to Leo with my letter to Schubert. [FOOTNOTE: Schuberth, the Hamburg music-publisher.] You know he leaves for Hamburg before the 8th of next month, and I should not like to lose 500 francs.

As regards Troupenas, there is no hurry. If the time of my manuscript is not right, do not deliver the latter, but make a

copy of it. Besides this, make a third copy of it for Wessel.
It will weary you to copy this nasty thing so often; but I
hope I shall not compose anything worse for a long time. I
also beg of you to look up the number of the last opus—
namely, the last mazurkas, or rather the waltz published by
Paccini [FOOTNOTE: Pacini, a Paris music-publisher. He
published the Waltz in A flat major, Op. 42, in the summer of
1840, if not earlier.]—and give the following number to the
Tarantella.

I am keeping my mind easy, for I know you are willing and
clever. I trust you will receive from me no more letters
burdened with commissions. Had I not been with only one foot
at home before my departure you would have none of these
unpleasantnesses. Attend to the Tarantella, give it to Leo,
and tell him to keep the money he may receive till I come
back. Once more I beg of you to excuse my troubling you so
much. To-day I received the letter from my people in Poland
you sent me. Tell the portier to give you all the letters
addressed to me.

[4.]

My dear friend,—As you are so good, be so to the end. Go to
the transport commission-office of Mr. Hamberg et Levistal
successeurs de Mr. Corstel fils aine et Cie, rue des Marais
St. Martin, No. 51, a Paris, and direct them to send at once
to Pleyel for the piano I am to have, so that it may go off
the next day. Say at the office that it is to be forwarded par
un envoy [sic] accelere et non ordinaire. Such a transport
costs of course far more, but is incomparably quicker. It will
probably cost five francs per cwt. I shall pay here. Only
direct them to give you a receipt, on which they will write
how many cwts. the piano weighs, when it leaves, and when it
will arrive at Chateauroux. If the piano is conveyed by
roulage [land-transport]—which goes straight to Toulouse and
leaves goods only on the route—the address must not be a la

Chatre, [FOOTNOTE: Instead of "la Chatre" we have in Karasowski's Polish book "la Chatie," which ought to warn us not to attribute all the peculiar French in this letter to Chopin, who surely knew how to spell the name of the town in the neighbourhood of the familiar Nohant.] but Madame Dudevant, a Chateauroux, as I wrote above. [FOOTNOTE: "Address of the piano: Madame Dudevant, a Chateauroux. Bureau Restant chez M. Vollant Patureau." This is what Chopin wrote above.] At the last-mentioned place the agency has been informed, and will forward it at once. You need not send me the receipt, we should require it only in case of some unforeseen reclamation. The correspondent in Chateauroux says that PAR LA VOYE ACCELERE [SIC] it will come from Paris in four days. If this is so, let him bind himself to deliver the piano at Chateauroux in four or five days.

Now to other business.

Should Pleyel make any difficulties, apply to Erard; I think that the latter in all probability ought to be serviceable to you. Only do not act hastily, and first ascertain how the matter really stands.

As to the Tarantella, seal it and send it to Hamburg. To-morrow I shall write you of other affairs, concerning Troupenas, &c.

Embrace Johnnie, and tell him to write.
[5.]

Thanks for all the commissions you have executed so well. To-day, that is on the 9th, I received the piano and the other things. Do not send my little bust to Warsaw, it would frighten them, leave it in the press. Kiss Johnnie for his letter. I shall write him a few lines shortly.

To-morrow I shall very likely send back my old servant, who

loses his wits here. He is an honest man and knows how to
serve, but he is tiresome, and makes one lose one's patience.
I shall send him back, telling him to wait for me in Paris. If
he appears at the house, do not be frightened.

Latterly the weather has been only so-so.

The man in Chateauroux was waiting three days for the piano;
yesterday, after receiving your letter, I gave orders that he
should be recalled. To-day I do not yet know what kind of tone
the piano has, as it is not yet unpacked; this great event is
to take place to-morrow. As to the delay and misunderstanding
in sending it, do not make any inquiries; let the matter rest,
it is not worth a quarrel. You did the best you could. A
little ill-humour and a few days lost in expectation are not
worth a pinch of snuff. Forget, therefore, my commissions and
your transaction; next time, if God permits us to live,
matters will turn out better.

I write you these few words late at night. Once more I thank
you, most obliging of men, for the commissions, which are not
yet ended, for now comes the turn of the Troupenas business,
which will hang on your shoulders. I shall write to you on
this subject more fully some other time, and to-day I wish you
good night. But don't have dreams like Johnnie—that I died;
but rather dream that I am about to be born, or something of
the sort.

In fact, I am feeling now as calm and serene as a baby in
swaddling-clothes; and if somebody wished to put me in leading-
strings, I should be very glad—nota bene, with a cap thickly
lined with wadding on my head, for I feel that at every moment
I should stumble and turn upside down. Unfortunately, instead
of leading-strings there are probably awaiting me crutches, if
I approach old age with my present step. I once dreamt that I
was dying in a hospital, and this is so strongly rooted in my

mind that I cannot forget it—it is as if I had dreamt it yesterday. If you survive me, you will learn whether we may believe in dreams.

And now I often dream with my eyes open what may be said to have neither rhyme nor reason in it.

That is why I write you such a foolish letter, is it?

Send me soon a letter from my people, and love your old

FREDERICK.
[6.] Nohant, 1841.

Thanks for your very kind letter. Unseal all you judge necessary.

Do not give the manuscripts to Troupenas till Schubert has informed you of the day of publication. The answer will very likely come soon through Leo.

What a pity that the Tarantella is gone to Berlin, for, as you know from Schubert's letter, Liszt is mixed up in this monetary affair, and I may have some unpleasantness. He is a thin-skinned Hungarian, and may think that I do not trust him because I directed that the manuscripts should not be given otherwise than for cash. I do not know, but I have a presentiment of a disagreeable mess. Do not say anything about it to the ailing Leo; go and see him if you think it necessary, give him my compliments and thanks (although undeserved), and ask pardon for troubling him so much. After all, it is kind of him to take upon him the forwarding of my things. Give my compliments, also to Pleyel, and ask him to excuse my not writing to him (do not say anything about his sending me a very inferior piano).

I beg of you to put into the letter-box at the Exchange yourself the letter to my parents, but I say do it yourself, and before 4 o'clock. Excuse my troubling you, but you know of what great importance my letter is to my people.

Escudier has very likely sent you that famous album. If you wish you may ask Troupenas to get you a copy as if it were for me; but if you don't wish, say nothing.

[FOOTNOTE: Leon Escudier, I suppose. The brothers Marie and Leon Escudier established a music business in the latter part of the fourth decade of this century; but when soon after both married and divided their common property, Marie got their journal "La France Musicale" and Leon the music-business. They wrote and published together various books on music and musicians.]

Still one more bother.

At your leisure transcribe once more this unlucky Tarantella, which will be sent to Wessel when the day [of publication] is known. If I tire you so much with this Tarentella, you may be sure that it is for the last time. From here, I am sure you will have no more manuscript from me. If there should not be any news from Schubert within a week, please write to me. In that case you would give the manuscript to Troupenas. But I shall write him about it.

[7.] Nohant, 1841, Friday evening.

My dear Julius,—I send you a letter for Bonnet; read, seal, and deliver it. And if in passing through the streets in which you know I can lodge, you find something suitable for me, please write to me. Just now the condition about the staircase exists no longer. [FOOTNOTE: Chopin felt so much stronger that high stairs were no longer any objection to lodgings.] I also send you a letter to Dessauer [FOOTNOTE: Joseph Dessauer, a native of Prague, best known by his songs. He stayed in Paris in 1833, and afterwards settled in Vienna. George Sand numbered him among her friends.] in answer to his letter which Madame Deller sent me from Austria. He must already be back to Paris; be sure and ask Schlesinger, who will be best able to inform you of this.

Do not give Dessauer many particulars about me; do not tell him that you are looking for rooms, nor Anthony either, for he will mention it to Mdlle. de Rozieres, and she is a babbler and makes the least thing a subject for gossip. Some of her gossipings have already reached me here in a strange way. You know how great things sometimes grow out of nothing if they pass through a mouth with a loose tongue. Much could be said on this head.

As to the unlucky Tarantella, you may give it to Troupenas (that is, to Masset); but, if you think otherwise, send it by post to Wessel, only insist on his answering at once that he has received it. The weather has been charming here for the last few days, but my music—is ugly. Madame Viardot spent a fortnight here; we occupied ourselves less with music than with other things.

Please write to me whatever you like, but write.

May Johnnie be in good health!

But remember to write on Troupenas's copy: Hamburg, Schubert; Wessel, London.

In a few days I shall send you a letter for Mechetti in Vienna, to whom I promised to give some compositions. If you see Dessauer or Schlesinger, ask if it is absolutely necessary to pay postage for the letters sent to Vienna.—I embrace you, adieu.

CHOPIN.

[8.]

Nohant, Sunday, 1841.

What you have done you have done well. Strange world! Masset is a fool, so also is Pelletan. Masset knew of Pacini's waltz and that I promised it to the "Gazette" for the Album. I did not wish to make any advances to him. If he does not wish them at 600 francs, with London (the price of my USUAL manuscripts was 300 francs with him)—three times five being fifteen—I should have to give so much labour for 1,500 francs—that cannot be. So much the more as I told him when I had the first conversation with him that it might happen that I could not let him have my things at this price. For instance, he cannot expect that I should give him twelve Etudes or a new Methode de Piano for 300 francs. The Allegro maestoso ["Allegro de Concert," Op. 46] which I send you to-day I cannot give for 300 francs, but only for 600 francs, nor the "Fantasia" [Op. 49], for which I ask 500 francs. Nevertheless, the "Ballade" [the third, Op. 47], the Nocturnes ["Deux Nocturnes," Op. 48], and Polonaise [F sharp minor, Op. 44], I shall let him have at 300 francs, for he has already formerly printed such things. In one word, for Paris I give these five compositions for 2,000 francs. If he does not care for them, so much the better. I say it entre nous—for Schlesinger will most willingly buy them. But I should not like him to take me for a man who does not keep his word in an agreement. "Il n'y avait qu'une convention facile d'honnete homme a honnete homme." therefore, he should not complain of my terms, for they are very easy. I want nothing but to come out of this affair respectably. You know that I do not sell myself. But tell him further that if I were desirous of taking advantage of him or of cheating him, I could write fifteen things per year, but worthless ones, which he would buy at 300 francs and I would have a better income. Would it be an honest action?

My dear friend, tell him that I write seldom, and spend but little. He must not think that I wish to raise the price. But when you yourself see my manuscript flies, [FOOTNOTE: An allusion to his small, fine writing.] you will agree with me that I may ask 600 francs when I was paid 300 francs for the Tarantella and 500 for the Bolero.

For God's sake take good care of the manuscripts, do not squeeze, dirty, or tear them. I know you are not capable of doing anything of the sort, but I love my WRITTEN TEDIOUSNESS [NUDY, tediousness; NUTY, notes] so much that I always fear that something might happen to them.

To-morrow you will receive the Nocturne, and at the end of the week the Ballade and Fantasia; I cannot get my writing done sooner. Each of these things you will transcribe; your copies will remain in Paris. If copying wearies you, console yourself with thinking that you are doing it for THE REMISSION OF YOUR SINS. I should not like to give my little spider-feet to any copyist who would daub coarsely. Once more I make this request, for had I again to write these eighteen pages, I should most certainly go wrong in my mind.

I send you a letter from Hartel.

Try to get another valet instead of the one you have. I shall probably be in Paris during the first days of November. To-morrow I will write to you again.

**Monday
morning.**

On reading your letter attentively, I see that Masset does not

ask for Paris. Leave this point untouched if you can. Mention only 3,000 francs pour les deux pays, and 2,000 francs for Paris itself if he particularly asks about it. Because la condition des deux pays is still easier, and for me also more convenient. If he should not want it, it must be because he seeks an opportunity for breaking with me. In that case, wait for his answer from London. Write to him openly and frankly, but always politely, and act cautiously and coolly, but mind, not to me, for you know how much loves you your...
[9.] Nohant, 1841.

My dear friend,—You would be sure to receive my letters and compositions. You have read the German letters, sealed them, and done everything I asked you, have you not? As to Wessel, he is a fool and a cheat. Write him whatever you like, but tell him that I do not intend to give up my rights to the Tarantella, as he did not send it back in time. If he sustained losses by my compositions, it is most likely owing to the foolish titles he gave them, in spite of my directions. Were I to listen to the voice of my soul, I would not send him anything more after these titles. Say as many sharp things to him as you can.

[FOOTNOTE: Here are some specimens of the publisher's ingenious inventiveness:—"Adieu a Varsovie" (Rondeau, Op. 1), "Hommage a Mozart" (Variations, Op. 2), "La Gaite" (Introduction et Polonaise, Op. 3), "La Posiana" (Rondeau a la Mazur, Op. 5), "Murmures de la Seine" (Nocturnes, Op. 9), "Les Zephirs" (Nocturnes, Op. 15), "Invitation a la Valse" (Valse, Op. 18), "Souvenir d'Andalousie" (Bolero, Op. 19), "Le banquet infernal" (Premier Scherzo, Op. 20), "Ballade ohne Worte" [Ballad without words] (Ballade, Op. 23), "Les Plaintives" (Nocturnes, Op. 27), "La Meditation" (Deuxieme Scherzo, Op. 31), "Il lamento e la consolazione" (Nocturnes, Op. 32), "Les Soupirs" (Nocturnes, Op. 37), and "Les Favorites" (Polonaises, Op. 40). The mazurkas generally received the title of

"Souvenir de la Pologne."]

Madame Sand thanks you for the kind words accompanying the parcel. Give directions that my letters may be delivered to Pelletan, Rue Pigal [i.e., Pigalle], 16, and impress it very strongly on the portier. The son of Madame Sand will be in Paris about the 16th. I shall send you, through him, the MS. of the Concerto ["Allegro de Concert"] and the Nocturnes [Op. 46 and 48].

These letters of the romantic tone-poet to a friend and fellow-artist will probably take the reader by surprise, nay, may even disillusionise him. Their matter is indeed very suggestive of a commercial man writing to one of his agents. Nor is this feature, as the sequel will show, peculiar to the letters just quoted. Trafficking takes up a very large part of Chopin's Parisian correspondence; [FOOTNOTE: I indicate by this phrase comprehensively the whole correspondence since his settling in the French capital, whether written there or elsewhere.] of the ideal within him that made him what he was as an artist we catch, if any, only rare glimmerings and glimpses.

CHAPTER XXV

TWO PUBLIC CONCERTS, ONE IN 1841 AND ANOTHER IN 1842.—CHOPIN'S STYLE OF PLAYING: TECHNICAL QUALITIES; FAVOURABLE PHYSICAL CONDITIONS; VOLUME OF TONE; USE OF THE PEDALS; SPIRITUAL QUALITIES; TEMPO RUBATO; INSTRUMENTS.—HIS MUSICAL SYMPATHIES AND ANTIPATHIES.—OPINIONS ON MUSIC AND MUSICIANS.

The concert which Chopin gave in 1841, after several years of retirement, took place at Pleyel's rooms on Monday, the 26th of April. It was like his subsequent concerts a semi-public rather than a public one, for the audience consisted of a select circle of pupils, friends, and partisans who, as Chopin told Lenz, took the tickets in advance and divided them among themselves. As most of the pupils belonged to the aristocracy, it followed as a matter of course that the concert was emphatically what Liszt calls it, "un concert de fashion." The three chief musical papers of Paris: the "Gazette Musicale," the "France Musicale," and the "Menestrel" were unanimous in their high, unqualified praise of the concert-giver, "the king of the fete, who was overwhelmed with bravos." The pianoforte performances of Chopin took up by far the greater part of the programme, which was varied by two arias from Adam's "La Rose de Peronne," sung by Mdme. Damoreau—Cinti, who was as usual "ravissante de perfection," and by Ernst's "Elegie," played by the composer himself "in a grand style, with passionate feeling and a purity worthy of the great masters." Escudier, the writer of the notice in the "France Musicale," says of Ernst's playing: "If you wish to hear the violin weep, go and hear Ernst; he produces such heart-rending, such passionate sounds, that you fear every moment to see his instrument break to pieces in his hands. It is difficult to carry farther the expression of sadness, of suffering, and of despair."

To give the reader an idea of the character of the concert, I shall quote largely from Liszt's notice, in which he not only sets forth the merits of the artists, but also describes the appearance of the room and the audience. First, however, I must tell a pretty anecdote of which this notice reminds me. When Liszt was moving about among the audience during the intervals of the concert, paying his respects here and there, he came upon M. Ernest Legouve. The latter told him of his intention to give an account of the concert in the "Gazette Musicale." Liszt thereupon said that he had a great wish to write one himself, and M. Legouve, although reluctantly, gave way. When it came to the ears of Chopin that Liszt was going to report on the concert, he remarked: "Il me donnera un petit royaume dans son empire" (He will give me a little kingdom in his empire).

[FOOTNOTE: Since I wrote the above, M. Legouve has published his "Soixante ans de Souvenirs," and in this book gives his version of the story, which, it is to be hoped, is less incorrect than some other statements of his relating to Chopin: "He [Chopin] had asked me to write a report of the concert. Liszt claimed the honour. I hastened to announce this good news to Chopin, who quietly said to me: "I should have liked better if it had been you." "What are you thinking of my dear friend! An article by Liszt, that is a fortunate thing for the public and for you. Trust in his admiration for your talent. I promise you qu'il vous fera un beau royaume.' — 'Oui, me dit-il en souriant, dans son empire!'""]

These few words speak volumes. But here is what Liszt wrote about the concert in the "Gazette musicale" of May 2, 1841:—

Last Monday, at eight o'clock in the evening, M. Pleyel's rooms were brilliantly lighted up; numerous carriages brought incessantly to the foot of a staircase covered with carpet and perfumed with flowers the most elegant women, the most fashionable young men, the most celebrated artists, the richest financiers, the most illustrious noblemen, a whole elite of society, a whole aristocracy of birth, fortune, talent, and beauty.

A grand piano was open on a platform; people crowded round, eager for the seats nearest it; they prepared to listen, they composed them-selves, they said to themselves that they must not lose a chord, a note, an intention, a thought of him who was going to seat himself there. And people were right in being thus eager, attentive, and religiously moved, because he for whom they waited, whom they wished to hear, admire, and applaud, was not only a clever virtuoso, a pianist expert in the art of making notes [de faire des notes], not only an artist of great renown, he was all this and more than all this, he was Chopin...

...If less eclat has gathered round his name, if a less bright aureole has encircled his head, it is not because he had not in him perhaps the same depth of feeling as the illustrious author of "Conrad Wallenrod" and the "Pilgrims," [FOOTNOTE: Adam Mickiewicz.] but his means of expression were too limited, his instrument too imperfect; he could not reveal his whole self by means of a piano. Hence, if we are not mistaken, a dull and continual suffering, a certain repugnance to reveal himself to the outer world, a sadness which shrinks out of sight under apparent gaiety, in short, a whole individuality in the highest degree remarkable and attractive.

...It was only rarely, at very distant intervals, that Chopin played in public; but what would have been for anyone else an almost certain cause of oblivion and obscurity was precisely what assured to him a fame above the caprices of fashion, and kept him from rivalries, jealousies, and injustice. Chopin, who has taken no part in the extreme movement which for several years has thrust one on another and one against another the executive artists from all quarters of the world, has been constantly surrounded by faithful adepts, enthusiastic pupils, and warm friends, all of whom, while guarding him against disagreeable contests and painful collisions, have not ceased to spread abroad his works, and with them admiration for his name. Moreover, this exquisite, altogether lofty, and eminently aristocratic celebrity has remained unattacked. A complete silence of criticism already reigns round it, as if posterity were come; and in the brilliant audience which flocked together to hear the too long silent poet there was neither reticence nor restriction, unanimous praise was on the lips of all.

...He has known how to give to new thoughts a new form. That element of wildness and abruptness which belongs to his country has found its expression in bold dissonances, in strange harmonies, while the delicacy and grace which belong to his personality were revealed in a thousand contours, in a thousand embellishments of an inimitable fancy.

In Monday's concert Chopin had chosen in preference those of his works which swerve more from the classical forms. He played neither concerto, nor sonata, nor fantasia, nor variations, but preludes, studies, nocturnes, and mazurkas. Addressing himself to a society rather than to a public, he could show himself with impunity as he is, an elegiac poet, profound, chaste, and dreamy. He did not need either to astonish or to overwhelm, he sought for delicate sympathy rather than for noisy enthusiasm. Let us say at once that he had no reason to complain of want of sympathy. From the first chords there was established a close communication between him and his audience. Two studies and a ballade were encored, and had it not been for the fear of adding to the already great fatigue which betrayed itself on his pale face, people would have asked for a repetition of the pieces of the programme one by one...

An account of the concert in La France musicale of May 2, 1841, contained a general characterisation of Chopin's artistic position with regard to the public coinciding with that given by Liszt, but the following excerpts from the other parts of the article may not be unacceptable to the reader:—

We spoke of Schubert because there is no other nature which has a more complete analogy with him. The one has done for the piano what the other has done for the voice...Chopin was a composer from conviction. He composes for himself, and what he composes he performs for himself...Chopin is the pianist of sentiment PAR EXCELLENCE. One may say that Chopin is the creator of a school of pianoforte-playing and of a school of composition. Indeed, nothing equals the lightness and sweetness with which the artist preludes on the piano, nothing again can be placed by the side of his works full of originality, distinction, and grace. Chopin is an exceptional pianist who ought not to be, and cannot be, compared with anyone.

The words with which the critic of the Menestrel closes his remarks, describe well the nature of the emotions which the artist excited in his hearers:—

In order to appreciate Chopin rightly, one must love gentle impressions, and have the feeling for poetry: to hear Chopin is to read a strophe of Lamartine....Everyone went away full of sweet joy and deep reverie (recueillement).

The concert, which was beyond a doubt a complete success, must have given Chopin satisfaction in every respect. At any rate, he faced the public again before a year had gone by. In the Gazette Musicale of February 20, 1842, we read that on the following evening, Monday, at Pleyel's rooms, the haute societe de Paris et tous les artistes s'y donneront rendez-vous. The programme of the concert was to be as follows:—

1. Andante suivi de la 3ieme Ballade, par Chopin.

2. Felice Donzella, air de Dessauer.

3. Suite de Nocturnes, Preludes et Etudes, par Chopin.

4. Divers fragments de Handel, chante par Madame Viardot-Garcia.

5. Solo pour Violoncello, par M. Franchomme.

6. Nocturne, Preludes, Mazurkas et Impromptu.

7. Le Chene et le Roseau, chante par Madame Viardot-Garcia, accompagne par Chopin.

Maurice Bourges, who a week later reports on the concert, states more particularly what Chopin played. He mentions three mazurkas in A flat major, B major, and A minor; three studies in A flat major, F minor, and C minor; the Ballade in A flat major; four nocturnes, one of which was that in F sharp minor; a prelude in D flat; and an impromptu in G (G flat major?). Maurice Bourges's account is not altogether free from strictures. He finds Chopin's ornamentations always novel, but sometimes mannered (manierees). He says: "Trop de recherche fine et minutieuse n'est pas quelquefois sans pretention et san froideur." But on the whole the critique is very laudatory. "Liszt and Thalberg excite, as is well known, violent enthusiasm; Chopin also awakens enthusiasm, but of a less energetic, less noisy nature, precisely because he causes the most intimate chords of the heart to vibrate."

From the report in the "France musicale" we see that the audience was not less brilliant than that of the first concert:—

...Chopin has given in Pleyel's hall a charming soiree, a fete peopled with adorable smiles, delicate and rosy faces, small and well-formed white hands; a splendid fete where simplicity was combined with grace and elegance, and where good taste served as a pedestal to wealth. Those ugly black hats which give to men the most unsightly appearance possible were very few in number. The gilded ribbons, the delicate blue gauze, the chaplets of trembling pearls, the freshest roses and mignonettes, in short, a thousand medleys of the prettiest and gayest colours were assembled, and intersected each other in all sorts of ways on the perfumed heads and snowy shoulders of the most charming women for whom the princely salons contend. The first success of the seance was for Madame George Sand. As soon as she appeared with her two charming daughters [daughter and cousin?], she was the observed of all observers. Others would have been disturbed by all those eyes turned on her like so many stars; but George Sand contented herself with lowering her head and smiling...

This description is so graphic that one seems to see the actual scene, and imagines one's self one of the audience. It also points out a very characteristic feature of these concerts—namely, the preponderance of the fair sex. As regards Chopin's playing, the writer remarks that the genre of execution which aims at the imitation of orchestral effects suits neither Chopin's organisation nor his ideas:—

In listening to all these sounds, all these nuances, which follow each other, intermingle, separate, and reunite to arrive at one and the same goal, melody, do you not think you hear little fairy voices sighing under silver bells, or a rain of pearls falling on crystal tables? The fingers of the pianist seem to multiply ad infinitum; it does not appear possible that only two hands can produce effects of rapidity so precise and so natural...

I shall now try to give the reader a clearer idea of what Chopin's style of playing was like than any and all of the criticisms and descriptions I have hitherto quoted can have done. And I do this not only in order to satisfy a natural curiosity, but also, and more especially, to furnish a guide for the better understanding and execution of the master's works. Some, seeing that no music reflects more clearly its author's nature than that of Chopin, may think that it would be wiser to illustrate the style of playing by the style of composition, and not the style of composition by the style of playing. Two reasons determine me to differ from them. Our musical notation is an inadequate exponent of the conceptions of the great masters—visible signs cannot express the subtle shades of the emotional language; and the capabilities of Chopin the composer and of Chopin the executant were by no means coextensive—we cannot draw conclusions as to the character of his playing from the character of his Polonaises in A major (Op. 40) and in A flat (Op. 53), and certain movements of the Sonata in B flat minor (Op. 35). The information contained in the following remarks is derived partly from printed publications, partly from private letters and conversations; nothing is admitted which does not proceed from Chopin's pupils, friends, and such persons as have frequently heard him.

What struck everyone who had the good fortune to hear Chopin was the fact that he was a pianist sui generis. Moscheles calls him an unicum; Mendelssohn describes him as "radically original" (Gruneigentumlich); Meyerbeer said of him that he knew no pianist, no composer for the piano, like him; and thus I could go on quoting ad infinitum. A writer in the "Gazette musicale" (of the year 1835, I think), who, although he places at the head of his article side by side the names of Liszt, Hiller, Chopin, and—Bertini, proved himself in the characterisation of these pianists a man of some insight, remarks of Chopin: "Thought, style, conception, even the fingering, everything, in fact, appears individual, but of a communicative, expansive individuality, an individuality of which superficial organisations alone fail to recognise the magnetic influence." Chopin's place among the great pianists of the second quarter of this century has been felicitously characterised by an anonymous contemporary: Thalberg, he said, is a king, Liszt a prophet, Chopin a poet, Herz an advocate, Kalkbrenner a minstrel, Madame Pleyel a sibyl, and Doehler a pianist.

But if our investigation is to be profitable, we must proceed analytically. It will be best to begin with the fundamental technical qualities. First of all, then, we have to note the suppleness and equality of Chopin's fingers and the perfect independence of his hands. "The evenness of his scales and passages in all kinds of touch," writes Mikuli, "was unsurpassed, nay, prodigious." Gutmann told me that his master's playing was particularly smooth, and his fingering calculated to attain this result. A great lady who was present at Chopin's last concert in Paris (1848), when he played among other works his Valse in D flat (Op. 64, No. 1), wished to know "le secret de Chopin pour que les gammes fussent si COULEES sur le piano." Madame Dubois, who related this incident to me, added that the expression was felicitous, for this "limpidite delicate" had never been equalled. Such indeed were the lightness, delicacy, neatness, elegance, and gracefulness of Chopin's playing that they won for him the name of Ariel of the piano. The reader will remember how much Chopin admired these qualities in other artists, notably in Mdlle. Sontag and in Kalkbrenner.

So high a degree and so peculiar a kind of excellence was of course attainable only under exceptionally favourable conditions, physical as well as mental. The first and chief condition was a suitably formed hand. Now, no one can look at Chopin's hand, of which there exists a cast, without perceiving at once its capabilities. It was indeed small, but at the same time it was thin, light, delicately articulated, and, if I may say so, highly expressive. Chopin's whole body was extraordinarily flexible. According to Gutmann, he could, like a clown, throw his legs over his shoulders. After this we may easily imagine how great must have been the flexibility of his hands, those members of his body which he had specially trained all his life. Indeed, the startlingly wide-spread chords, arpeggios, &c., which constantly occur in his compositions, and which until he introduced them had been undreamt-of and still are far from being common, seemed to offer him no difficulty, for he executed them not only without any visible effort, but even with a pleasing ease and freedom. Stephen Heller told me that it was a wonderful sight to see one of those small hands expand and cover a third of the keyboard. It was like the opening of the mouth of a serpent which is going to swallow a rabbit whole. In fact, Chopin appeared to be made of caoutchouc.

In the criticisms on Chopin's public performances we have met again and again with the statement that he brought little tone out of the piano. Now, although it is no doubt true that Chopin could neither subdue to his sway large audiences nor successfully battle with a full orchestra, it would be a mistake to infer from this that he was always a weak and languid player. Stephen Heller, who declared that Chopin's tone was rich, remembered hearing him play a duet with Moscheles (the latter's duet, of which Chopin was so fond), and on this occasion the Polish pianist, who insisted on playing the bass, drowned the treble of his partner, a virtuoso well known for his vigour and brilliancy. Were we, however, to form our judgment on this single item of evidence, we should again arrive at a wrong conclusion. Where musical matters—i.e., matters generally estimated according to individual taste and momentary impressibility alone—are concerned, there is safety only in the multitude of witnesses. Let us, therefore, hear first what Chopin's pupils have got to say on this point, and then go and inquire further. Gutmann said that Chopin played generally very quietly, and rarely, indeed hardly ever, fortissimo. The A flat major Polonaise (Op. 53), for instance, he could not thunder forth in the way we are accustomed to hear it. As for the famous octave passages which occur in it, he began them pianissimo and continued thus without much increase in loudness. And, then, Chopin never thumped. M. Mathias remarks that his master had extraordinary vigour, but only in flashes. Mikuli's preface to his edition of the works of Chopin affords more explicit information. We read there:—

> The tone which Chopin brought out of the instrument was
>
> always, especially in the cantabiles, immense (riesengross),
>
> only Field could perhaps in this respect be compared to him. A
>
> manly energy gave to appropriate passages overpowering effect—
>
> energy without roughness (Rohheit); but, on the other hand,
>
> he knew how by delicacy—delicacy without affectation—to
>
> captivate the hearer.

We may summarise these various depositions by saying with Lenz that, being deficient in physical strength, Chopin put his all in the cantabile style, in the connections and combinations, in the detail. But two things are evident, and they ought to be noted: (1) The volume of tone, of pure tone, which Chopin was capable of producing was by no means inconsiderable; (2) he had learnt the art of economising his means so as to cover his shortcomings. This last statement is confirmed by some remarks of Moscheles which have already been quoted—namely, that Chopin's piano was breathed forth so softly that he required no vigorous forte to produce the desired contrasts; and that one did not miss the orchestral effects which the German school demanded from a pianist, but allowed one's self to be carried away as by a singer who takes little heed of the accompaniment and follows his own feelings.

In listening to accounts of Chopin's style of playing, we must not leave out of consideration the time to which they refer. What is true of the Chopin of 1848 is not true of the Chopin of 1831 nor of 1841. In the last years of his life he became so weak that sometimes, as Stephen Heller told me, his playing was hardly audible. He then made use of all sorts of devices to hide the want of vigour, often modifying the original conception of his compositions, but always producing beautiful effects. Thus, to give only one example (for which and much other interesting information I am indebted to Mr. Charles Halle), Chopin played at his last concert in Paris (February, 1848) the two forte passages towards the end of the Barcarole, not as they are printed, but pianissimo and with all sorts of dynamic finesses. Having possessed himself of the most recondite mysteries of touch, and mastered as no other pianist had done the subtlest gradations of tone, he even then, reduced by disease as he was, did not give the hearer the impression of weakness. At least this is what Mr. Otto Goldschmidt relates, who likewise was present at this concert. There can be no doubt that what Chopin aimed at chiefly, or rather, let us say, what his physical constitution permitted him to aim at, was quality not quantity of tone. A writer in the "Menestrel" (October 21, 1849) remarks that for Chopin, who in this was unlike all other pianists, the piano had always too much tone; and that his constant endeavour was to SENTIMENTALISE the timbre, his greatest care to avoid everything which approached the fracas pianistique of the time.

Of course, a true artist's touch has besides its mechanical also its spiritual aspect. With regard to this it is impossible to overlook the personal element which pervaded and characterised Chopin's touch. M. Marmontel does not forget to note it in his "Pianistes Celebres." He writes:—

In the marvellous art of carrying and modulating the tone, in the expressive, melancholy manner of shading it off, Chopin was entirely himself. He had quite an individual way of attacking the keyboard, a supple, mellow touch, sonorous effects of a vaporous fluidity of which only he knew the secret.

In connection with Chopin's production of tone, I must not omit to mention his felicitous utilisation of the loud and soft pedals. It was not till the time of Liszt, Thalberg, and Chopin that the pedals became a power in pianoforte-playing. Hummel did not understand their importance, and failed to take advantage of them. The few indications we find in Beethoven's works prove that this genius began to see some of the as yet latent possibilities. Of the virtuosi,

Moscheles was the first who made a more extensive and artistic use of the pedals, although also he employed them sparingly compared with his above-named younger contemporaries. Every pianist of note has, of course, his own style of pedalling. Unfortunately, there are no particulars forthcoming with regard to Chopin's peculiar style; and this is the more to be regretted as the composer was very careless in his notation of the pedals.

Rubinstein declares that most of the pedal marks in Chopin's compositions are wrongly placed. If nothing more, we know at least thus much: "No pianist before him [Chopin] has employed the pedals alternately or simultaneously with so much tact and ability," and "in making constantly use of the pedal he obtained des harmonies ravissantes, des bruissements melodiques qui etonnaient et charmaient." [FOOTNOTE: Marmontel: "Les Pianistes celebres."]

The poetical qualities of Chopin's playingare not so easily defined as the technical ones. Indeed, if they are definable at all they are so only by one who, like Liszt, is a poet as well as a great pianist. I shall, therefore, transcribe from his book some of the most important remarks bearing on this matter.

After saying that Chopin idealised the fugitive poesy inspired by fugitive apparitions like "La Fee aux Miettes," "Le Lutin d'Argail," &c., to such an extent as to render its fibres so thin and friable that they seemed no longer to belong to our nature, but to reveal to us the indiscreet confidences of the Undines, Titanias, Ariels, Queen Mabs, and Oberons, Liszt proceeds thus:—

When this kind of inspiration laid hold of Chopin his playing assumed a distinctive character, whatever the kind of music he executed might be—dance-music or dreamy music, mazurkas or nocturnes, preludes or scherzos, waltzes or tarantellas, studies or ballades. He imprinted on them all one knows not what nameless colour, what vague appearance, what pulsations akin to vibration, that had almost no longer anything material about them, and, like the imponderables, seemed to act on one's being without passing through the senses. Sometimes one thought one heard the joyous tripping of some amorously-teasing Peri; sometimes there were modulations velvety and iridescent as the robe of a salamander; sometimes one heard accents of deep despondency, as if souls in torment did not find the loving prayers necessary for their final deliverance. At other times there breathed forth from his fingers a despair so mournful, so inconsolable, that one thought one saw Byron's Jacopo Foscari come to life again, and contemplated the extreme dejection of him who, dying of love for his country, preferred death to exile, being unable to endure the pain of leaving Venezia la bella!

It is interesting to compare this description with that of another poet, a poet who sent forth his poetry daintily dressed in verse as well as carelessly wrapped in prose. Liszt tells us that Chopin had in his imagination and talent something "qui, par la purete de sa diction, par ses accointances avec La Fee aux Miettes et Le Lutin d'Argail, par ses rencon-tres de Seraphine et de Diane, murmurant a son oreille leurs plus confidentielles plaintes, leurs reves les plus innommes," [FOOTNOTE: The allusions are to stories by Charles Nodier. According to Sainte-Beuve, "La Fee aux Miettes" was one of those stories in which the author was influenced by Hoffmann's creations.] reminded him of Nodier. Now, what thoughts did Chopin's playing call up in Heine?

Yes, one must admit that Chopin has genius in the full sense of the word; he is not only a virtuoso, he is also a poet; he can embody for us the poesy which lives within his soul, he is a tone-poet, and nothing can be compared to the pleasure which he gives us when he sits at the piano and improvises. He is then neither a Pole, nor a Frenchman, nor a German, he reveals then a higher origin, one perceives then that he comes from the land of Mozart, Raphael, and Goethe, his true fatherland is the dream-realm of poesy. When he sits at the piano and improvises I feel as though a countryman from my beloved native land were visiting me and telling me the most curious things which have taken place there during my absence...Sometimes I should like to interrupt him with questions: And how is the beautiful little water-nymph who knows how to fasten her silvery veil so coquettishly round her green locks? Does the white-bearded sea-god still persecute her with his foolish, stale love? Are the roses at home still in their flame-hued pride? Do the trees still sing as beautifully in the moonlight?

But to return to Liszt. A little farther on than the passage I quoted above he says:—

In his playing the great artist rendered exquisitely that kind of agitated trepidation, timid or breathless, which seizes the heart when one believes one's self in the vicinity of supernatural beings, in presence of those whom one does not know either how to divine or to lay hold of, to embrace or to charm. He always made the melody undulate like a skiff borne on the bosom of a powerful wave; or he made it move vaguely like an aerial apparition suddenly sprung up in this tangible and palpable world. In his writings he at first indicated this manner which gave so individual an impress to his virtuosity by the term tempo rubato: stolen, broken time—a measure at once supple, abrupt, and languid, vacillating like the flame under the breath which agitates it, like the corn in a field swayed by the soft pressure of a warm air, like the top of trees bent hither and thither by a keen breeze.

But as the term taught nothing to him who knew, said nothing to him who did not know, understand, and feel, Chopin afterwards ceased to add this explanation to his music, being persuaded that if one understood it, it was impossible not to divine this rule of irregularity. Accordingly, all his compositions ought to be played with that kind of accented, rhythmical balancement, that morbidezza, the secret of which it was difficult to seize if one had not often heard him play.

Let us try if it is not possible to obtain a clearer notion of this mysterious tempo rubato. Among instrumentalists the "stolen time" was brought into vogue especially by Chopin and Liszt. But it is not an invention of theirs or their time. Quanz, the great flutist (see Marpurg: "Kritische Beitrage." Vol. I.), said that he heard it for the first time from the celebrated singer Santa Stella Lotti, who was engaged in 1717 at the Dresden Opera, and died in 1759 at Venice. Above all, however, we have to keep in mind that the tempo rubato is a genus which comprehends numerous species. In short, the tempo rubato of Chopin is not that of Liszt, that of Liszt is not that of Henselt, and so on. As for the general definitions we find in dictionaries, they can afford us no particular enlightenment. But help comes to us from elsewhere. Liszt explained Chopin's tempo rubato in a very poetical and graphic manner to his pupil the Russian pianist Neilissow:—"Look at these trees!" he said, "the wind plays in the leaves, stirs up life among them, the tree remains the same, that is Chopinesque rubato." But how did the composer himself describe it? From Madame Dubois and other pupils of

Chopin we learn that he was in the habit of saying to them: "Que votre main gauche soit votre maitre de chapelle et garde toujours la mesure" (Let your left hand be your conductor and always keep time). According to Lenz Chopin taught also: "Angenommen, ein Stuck dauert so und so viel Minuten, wenn das Ganze nur so lange gedauert hat, im Einzelnen kann's anders sein!" (Suppose a piece lasts so and so many minutes, if only the whole lasts so long, the differences in the details do not matter). This is somewhat ambiguous teaching, and seems to be in contradiction to the preceding precept. Mikuli, another pupil of Chopin's, explains his master's tempo rubato thus:—"While the singing hand, either irresolutely lingering or as in passionate speech eagerly anticipating with a certain impatient vehemence, freed the truth of the musical expression from all rhythmical fetters, the other, the accompanying hand, continued to play strictly in time." We get a very lucid description of Chopin's tempo rubato from the critic of the Athenaeum who after hearing the pianist-composer at a London matinee in 1848 wrote:—"He makes free use of tempo rubato; leaning about within his bars more than any player we recollect, but still subject to a presiding measure such as presently habituates the ear to the liberties taken." Often, no doubt, people mistook for tempo rubato what in reality was a suppression or displacement of accent, to which kind of playing the term is indeed sometimes applied. The reader will remember the following passage from a criticism in the "Wiener Theaterzeitung" of 1829:—"There are defects noticeable in the young man's [Chopin's] playing, among which is perhaps especially to be mentioned the non-observance of the indication by accent of the commencement of musical phrases." Mr. Halle related to me an interesting dispute bearing on this matter. The German pianist told Chopin one day that he played in his mazurkas often 4/4 instead of 3/4 time. Chopin would not admit it at first, but when Mr. Halle proved his case by counting to Chopin's playing, the latter admitted the correctness of the observation, and laughing said that this was national. Lenz reports a similar dispute between Chopin and Meyerbeer. In short, we may sum up in Moscheles' words, Chopin's playing did not degenerate into Tactlosigkeit [lit., timelessness], but it was of the most charming originality. Along with the above testimony we have, however, to take note of what Berlioz said on the subject: "Chopin supportait mal le frein de la mesure; il a pousse beaucoup trap loin, selon moi, l'independance rhythmique." Berlioz even went so far as to say that "Chopin could not play strictly in time [ne pouvait pas jouer regulierement]."

Indeed, so strange was Chopin's style that when Mr. Charles Halle first heard him play his compositions he could not imagine how what he heard was represented by musical signs. But strange as Chopin's style of playing was he thinks that its peculiarities are generally exaggerated. The Parisians said of Rubinstein's playing of compositions of Chopin: "Ce n'est pas ca!" Mr. Halle himself thinks that Rubinstein's rendering of Chopin is clever, but not Chopinesque. Nor do Von Bulow's readings come near the original. As for Chopin's pupils, they are even less successful than others in imitating their master's style. The opinion of one who is so distinguished a pianist and at the same time was so well acquainted with Chopin as Mr. Halle is worth having. Hearing Chopin often play his compositions he got so familiar with that master's music and felt so much in sympathy with it that the composer liked to have it played by him, and told him that when he was in the adjoining room he could imagine he was playing himself.

But it is time that we got off the shoals on which we have been lying so long. Well, Lenz shall set us afloat:—

In the undulation of the motion, in that suspension and unrest [Hangen und Bangen], in the rubato as he understood it, Chopin was captivating, every note was the outcome of the best taste in the best sense of the word. If he introduced an embellishment, which happened only rarely, it was always a kind of miracle of good taste. Chopin was by his whole nature unfitted to render Beethoven or Weber, who paint on a large scale and with a big brush. Chopin was an artist in crayons [Pastellmaler], but an INCOMPARABLE one! By the side of Liszt he might pass with honour for that master's well-matched wife [ebenburtige Frau, i.e., wife of equal rank]. Beethoven's B flat major Sonata, Op. 106, and Chopin exclude each other.

One day Chopin took Lenz with him to the Baronne Krudner and her friend the Countess Scheremetjew to whom he had promised to play the variations of Beethoven's Sonata in A flat major (Op. 26). And how did he play them?

Beautifully [says Lenz], but not so beautifully as his own things, not enthrallingly [packend], not en relief, not as a romance increasing in interest from variation to variation. He whispered it mezza voce, but it was incomparable in the cantilena, infinitely perfect in the phrasing of the structure, ideally beautiful, but FEMININE! Beethoven is a man and never ceases to be one!

Chopin played on a Pleyel, he made it a point never to give
lessons on another instrument; they were obliged to get a
Pleyel. All were charmed, I also was charmed, but only with
the tone of Chopin, with his touch, with his sweetness and
grace, with the purity of his style.

Chopin's purity of style, self-command, and aristocratic reserve have
to be quite especially noted by us who are accustomed to hear the master's
compositions played wildly, deliriously, ostentatiously. J. B. Cramer's
remarks on Chopin are significant. The master of a bygone age said of the
master of the then flourishing generation:—

I do not understand him, but he plays beautifully and
correctly, oh! very correctly, he does not give way to his
passion like other young men, but I do not understand him.

What one reads and hears of Chopin's playing agrees with the account
of his pupil Mikuli, who remarks that, with all the warmth which Chopin
possessed in so high a degree, his rendering was nevertheless temperate
[massvoll], chaste, nay, aristocratic, and sometimes even severely reserved.
When, on returning home from the above-mentioned visit to the Russian
ladies, Lenz expressed his sincere opinion of Chopin's playing of Beethoven's
variations, the master replied testily: "I indicate (j'indique); the hearer
must complete (parachever) the picture." And when afterwards, while
Chopin was changing his clothes in an adjoining room, Lenz committed the
impertinence of playing Beethoven's theme as he understood it, the master
came in in his shirt-sleeves, sat down beside him, and at the end of the
theme laid his hand on Lenz's shoulder and said: "I shall tell Liszt of it; this
has never happened to me before; but it is beautiful—well, BUT MUST ONE
THEN ALWAYS SPEAK SO PASSIONATELY (si declamatoirement)?" The
italics in the text, not those in parentheses, are mine. I marked some of
Chopin's words thus that they might get the attention they deserve. "Tell
me with whom you associate, and I will tell you who you are." Parodying
this aphorism one might say, not without a good deal of truth: Tell me what
piano you use, and I will tell you what sort of a pianist you are. Liszt gives
us all the desirable information as to Chopin's predilection in this respect.
But Lenz too has, as we have seen, touched on this point. Liszt writes:—

While Chopin was strong and healthy, as during the first years
of his residence in Paris, he used to play on an Erard piano;
but after his friend Camille Pleyel had made him a present of
one of his splendid instruments, remarkable for their metallic

ring and very light touch, he would play on no other maker's.

If he was engaged for a soiree at the house of one of his Polish or French friends, he would often send his own instrument, if there did not happen to be a Pleyel in the house.

Chopin was very partial to [affectionnait] Pleyel's pianos, particularly on account of their silvery and somewhat veiled sonority, and of the easy touch which permitted him to draw from them sounds which one might have believed to belong to those harmonicas of which romantic Germany has kept the monopoly, and which her ancient masters constructed so ingeniously, marrying crystal to water.

Chopin himself said:—

When I am indisposed, I play on one of Erard's pianos and there I easily find a ready-made tone. But when I feel in the right mood and strong enough to find my own tone for myself, I must have one of Pleyel's pianos.

From the fact that Chopin played during his visit to Great Britain in 1848 at public concerts as well as at private parties on instruments of Broadwood's, we may conclude that he also appreciated the pianos of this firm. In a letter dated London, 48, Dover Street, May 6, 1848, he writes to Gutmann: "Erard a ete charmant, il m'a fait poser un piano. J'ai un de Broadwood et un de Pleyel, ce qui fait 3, et je ne trouve pas encore le temps pour les jouer." And in a letter dated Edinburgh, August 6, and Calder House, August 11, he writes to Franchomme: "I have a Broadwood piano in my room, and the Pleyel of Miss Stirling in the salon."

Here, I think, will be the fittest place to record what I have learnt regarding Chopin's musical taste and opinions on music and musicians, and what will perhaps illustrate better than any other part of this book the character of the man and artist. His opinions of composers and musical works show that he had in a high degree les vices de ses qualites. The delicacy of his constitution and the super-refinement of his breeding, which put within his reach the inimitable beauties of subtlest tenderness and grace that distinguish his compositions and distinguished his playing, were disqualifications as well as qualifications. "Every kind of uncouth roughness [toutes les rudesses sauvages] inspired him with aversion," says Liszt. "In music as in literature and in every-day life everything which bordered on melodrama was torture to him." In short, Chopin was an aristocrat with all the exclusiveness of an aristocrat.

The inability of men of genius to appreciate the merit of one or the other of their great predecessors and more especially of their contemporaries has often been commented on and wondered at, but I doubt very much whether a musician could be instanced whose sympathies were narrower than those of Chopin. Besides being biographically important, the record of the master's likings and dislikings will teach a useful lesson to the critic and furnish some curious material for the psychological student.

Highest among all the composers, living and dead, Chopin esteemed Mozart. Him he regarded as "the ideal type, the poet par excellence." It is related of Chopin—with what truth I do not know—that he never travelled without having either the score of "Don Giovanni" or that of the "Requiem" in his portmanteau. Significant, although not founded on fact, is the story according to which he expressed the wish that the "Requiem" should be performed at his funeral service. Nothing, however, shows his love for the great German master more unmistakably and more touchingly than the words which on his death-bed he addressed to his dear friends the Princess Czartoryska and M. Franchomme: "You will play Mozart together, and I shall hear you." And why did Chopin regard Mozart as the ideal type, the poet par excellence? Liszt answers: "Because Mozart condescended more rarely than any other composer to cross the steps which separate refinement from vulgarity." But what no doubt more especially stirred sympathetic chords in the heart of Chopin, and inspired him with that loving admiration for the earlier master, was the sweetness, the grace, and the harmoniousness which in Mozart's works reign supreme and undisturbed—the unsurpassed and unsurpassable perfect loveliness and lovely perfection which result from a complete absence of everything that is harsh, hard, awkward, unhealthy, and eccentric. And yet, says Liszt of Chopin:—

> His sybaritism of purity, his apprehension of what was
> commonplace, were such that even in "Don Giovanni," even in
> this immortal chef-d'oeuvre, he discovered passages the
> presence of which we have heard him regret. His worship of
> Mozart was not thereby diminished, but as it were saddened.

The composer who next to Mozart stood highest in Chopin's esteem was Bach. "It was difficult to say," remarks Mikuli, "which of the two he loved most." Chopin not only, as has already been mentioned, had works of Bach on his writing-table at Valdemosa, corrected the Parisian edition for his own use, and prepared himself for his concerts by playing Bach, but also set his pupils to study the immortal cantor's suites, partitas, and preludes and fugues. Madame Dubois told me that at her last meeting with him (in 1848) he recommended her "de toujours travailler Bach," adding that that was the best means of making progress.

Hummel, Field, and Moscheles were the pianoforte composers who seem to have given Chopin most satisfaction. Mozart and Bach were his gods, but these were his friends. Gutmann informed me that Chopin was particularly fond of Hummel; Liszt writes that Hummel was one of the composers Chopin played again and again with the greatest pleasure; and from Mikuli we learn that of Hummel's compositions his master liked best the Fantasia, the Septet, and the Concertos. Liszt's statement that the Nocturnes of Field were regarded by Chopin as "insuffisants" seems to me disproved by unexceptionable evidence. Chopin schooled his pupils most assiduously and carefully in the Nocturnes as well as in the Concertos of Field, who was, to use Madame Dubois's words, "an author very sympathetic to him." Mikuli relates that Chopin had a predilection for Field's A flat Concerto and the Nocturnes, and that, when playing the latter, he used to improvise the most charming embellishments. To take liberties with another artist's works and complain when another artist takes liberties with your own works is very inconsistent, is it not? But it is also thoroughly human, and Chopin was not exempt from the common failing. One day when Liszt did with some composition of Chopin's what the latter was in the habit of doing with Field's Nocturnes, the enraged composer is said to have told his friend to play his compositions as they were written or to let them alone. M. Marmontel writes:—

> Either from a profound love of the art or from an excess of conscience personelle, Chopin could not bear any one to touch the text of his works. The slightest modification seemed to him a grave fault which he did not even forgive his intimate friends, his fervent admirers, Liszt not excepted. I have many a time, as well as my master, Zimmermann, caused Chopin's sonatas, concertos, ballades, and allegros to be played as examination pieces; but restricted as I was to a fragment of the work, I was pained by the thought of hurting the composer, who considered these alterations a veritable sacrilege.

This, however, is a digression. Little need be added to what has already been said in another chapter of the third composer of the group we were speaking of. Chopin, the reader will remember, told Moscheles that he loved his music, and Moscheles admitted that he who thus complimented him was intimately acquainted with it. From Mikuli we learn that Moscheles' studies were very sympathetic to his master. As to Moscheles' duets, they were played by Chopin probably more frequently than the works of any other composer, excepting of course his own works. We hear of his playing them not only with his pupils, but with Osborne, with Moscheles himself, and with Liszt, who told me that Chopin was fond of playing with him the duets of Moscheles and Hummel.

Speaking of playing duets reminds me of Schubert, who, Gutmann informed me, was a favourite of Chopin's. The Viennese master's "Divertissement hongrois" he admired without reserve. Also the marches and polonaises a quatre mains he played with his pupils. But his teaching repertoire seems to have contained, with the exception of the waltzes, none of the works a deux mains, neither the sonatas, nor the impromptus, nor the "Moments musicals." This shows that if Schubert was a favourite of Chopin's, he was so only to a certain extent. Indeed, Chopin even found fault with the master where he is universally regarded as facile princeps. Liszt remarks:—

In spite of the charm which he recognised in some of
Schubert's melodies, he did not care to hear those whose
contours were too sharp for his ear, where feeling is as it
were denuded, where one feels, so to speak, the flesh
palpitate and the bones crack under the grasp of anguish. A
propos of Schubert, Chopin is reported to have said: "The
sublime is dimmed when it is followed by the common or the
trivial."

I shall now mention some of those composers with whom Chopin was less
in sympathy. In the case of Weber his approval, however, seems to have
outweighed his censure. At least Mikuli relates that the E minor and
A flat major Sonatas and the "Concertstuck" were among those works for which his master had a predilection, and Madame Dubois says that he made his pupils play the Sonatas in C and in A flat major with extreme care.

Now let us hear Lenz:— He could not appreciate Weber; he spoke of "opera," "unsuitable for the piano" [unklaviermassig]! On the whole,

Chopin was little in sympathy with the GERMAN spirit in music, although I heard him say: "There is only ONE SCHOOL, the German!"

Gutmann informed me that he brought the A flat major Sonata with him from Germany in 1836 or 1837, and that Chopin did not know it then. It is hard enough to believe that Liszt asked Lenz in 1828 if the composer of the "Freischutz" had also written for the piano, but Chopin's ignorance in 1836 is much more startling. Did fame and publications travel so slowly in the earlier part of the century? Had genius to wait so long for recognition? If the statement, for the correctness of which Gutmann alone is responsible, rests on fact and not on some delusion of memory, this most characteristic work of Weber and one of the most important items of the pianoforte literature did not reach Chopin, one of the foremost European pianists, till twenty years after its publication, which took place in December, 1816.

That Chopin had a high opinion of Beethoven may be gathered from a story which Lenz relates in an article written for the "Berliner Musikzeitung" (Vol. XXVI). Little Filtsch—the talented young Hungarian who made Liszt say: "I shall shut my shop when he begins to travel"—having played to a select company invited by his master the latter's Concerto in E minor, Chopin was so pleased with his pupil's performance that he went with him to Schlesinger's music-shop, asked for the score of "Fidelio," and presented it to him with the words:—"I am in your debt, you have given me great pleasure to-day, I wrote the concerto in a happy time, accept, my dear young friend, the great master work! read in it as long as you live and remember me also sometimes." But Chopin's high opinion of Beethoven was neither unlimited nor unqualified. His attitude as regards this master, which Franchomme briefly indicated by saying that his friend loved Beethoven, but had his dislikes in connection with him, is more fully explained by Liszt.

However great his admiration for the works of Beethoven might be, certain parts of them seemed to him too rudely fashioned. Their structure was too athletic to please him; their wraths seemed to him too violent [leurs courroux lui semblaient trop rugissants]. He held that in them passion too closely approaches cataclysm; the lion's marrow which is found in every member of his phrases was in his opinion a too substantial matter, and the seraphic accents, the Raphaelesque profiles, which appear in the midst of the powerful creations of this genius, became at times almost painful to him in so violent a contrast.

I am able to illustrate this most excellent general description by some examples. Chopin said that Beethoven raised him one moment up to the heavens and the next moment precipitated him to the earth, nay, into the very mire. Such a fall Chopin experienced always at the commencement of the last movement of the C minor Symphony. Gutmann, who informed me of this, added that pieces such as the first movement of the Moonlight Sonata (C sharp minor) were most highly appreciated by his master. One day when Mr. Halle played to Chopin one of the three Sonatas, Op. 31 (I am not sure which it was), the latter remarked that he had formerly thought the last movement VULGAR. From this Mr. Halle naturally concluded that Chopin could not have studied the works of Beethoven thoroughly. This conjecture is confirmed by what we learn from Lenz, who in 1842 saw a good deal of Chopin, and thanks to his Boswellian inquisitiveness, persistence, and forwardness, made himself acquainted with a number of interesting facts. Lenz and Chopin spoke a great deal about Beethoven after that visit to the Russian ladies mentioned in a foregoing part of this chapter. They had never spoken of the great master before. Lenz says of Chopin:—

He did not take a very serious interest in Beethoven; he knew only his principal compositions, the last works not at all.

This was in the Paris air! People knew the symphonies, the quartets of the middle period but little, the last ones not at all.

Chopin, on being told by Lenz that Beethoven had in the F minor Quartet anticipated Mendelssohn, Schumann, and him; and that the scherzo prepared the way for his mazurka-fantasias, said: "Bring me this quartet, I do not know it." According to Mikuli Chopin was a regular frequenter of the concerts of the Societe des Concerts du Conservatoire and of the Alard, Franchomme, &c., quartet party. But one of the most distinguished musicians living in Paris, who knew Chopin's opinion of Beethoven, suspects that the music was for him not the greatest attraction of the Conservatoire concerts, that in fact, like most of those who went there, he considered them a fashionable resort. True or not, the suspicion is undeniably significant. "But Mendelssohn," the reader will say, "surely Chopin must have admired and felt in sympathy with this sweet-voiced, well-mannered musician?" Nothing, however, could be farther from the truth. Chopin hated Mendelssohn's D minor Trio, and told Halle that that composer had never written anything better than the first Song without Words. Franchomme, stating the case mildly, says that Chopin did not care much for Mendelssohn's music; Gutmann, however, declared stoutly that his master positively disliked it and thought it COMMON. This word and the mention of the Trio remind me of a passage in Hiller's "Mendelssohn:

Letters and Recollections," in which the author relates how, when his friend played to him the D minor Trio after its completion, he was favourably impressed by the fire, spirit, and flow, in one word, the masterly character of the work, but had some misgivings about certain pianoforte passages, especially those based on broken chords, which, accustomed as he was by his constant intercourse with Liszt and Chopin during his stay of several years in Paris to the rich passage work of the new school, appeared to him old-fashioned. Mendelssohn, who in his letters repeatedly alludes to his sterility in the matter of new pianoforte passages, allowed himself to be persuaded by Hiller to rewrite the pianoforte part, and was pleased with the result. It is clear from the above that if Mendelssohn failed to give Chopin his due, Chopin did more than apply the jus talionis.

Schumann, however, found still less favour in the eyes of Chopin than Mendelssohn; for whilst among the works which, for instance, Madame Dubois, who was Chopin's pupil for five years, studied under her master, Mendelssohn was represented at least by the Songs without Words and the G minor Concerto, Schumann was conspicuous by his total absence. And let it be remarked that this was in the last years of Chopin's life, when Schumann had composed and published almost all his important works for pianoforte alone and many of his finest works for pianoforte with other instruments. M. Mathias, Chopin's pupil during the years 1839-1844, wrote to me: "I think I recollect that he had no great opinion of Schumann. I remember seeing the "Carnaval," Op. 9, on his table; he did not speak very highly of it." In 1838, when Stephen Heller was about to leave Augsburg for Paris, Schumann sent him a copy of his "Carnaval" (published in September, 1837), to be presented to Chopin. This copy had a title-page printed in various colours and was most tastefully bound; for Schumann knew Chopin's love of elegance, and wished to please him. Soon after his arrival in Paris, Heller called on the Polish musician and found him sitting for his portrait. On receiving the copy of the "Carnaval" Chopin said: "How beautifully they get up these things in Germany!" but uttered not a word about the music. However, we shall see presently what his opinion of it was. Some time, perhaps some years, after this first meeting with Chopin, Heller was asked by Schlesinger whether he would advise him to publish Schumann's "Carnaval." Heller answered that it would be a good speculation, for although the work would probably not sell well at first, it was sure to pay in the long run. Thereupon Schlesinger confided to Heller what Chopin had told him—namely, that the "Carnaval" was not music at all. The contemplation of this indifference and more than indifference of a great artist to the creations of one of his most distinguished contemporaries is saddening, especially if we remember how devoted Schumann was to Chopin, how he admired him, loved him, upheld him, and idolised him. Had it not been for Schumann's enthusiastic praise and valiant defence Chopin's fame would have risen and spread, more slowly in Germany.

"Of virtuoso music of any kind I never saw anything on his desk, nor do I think anybody else ever did," says Mikuli.. This, although true in the main, is somewhat too strongly stated. Kalkbrenner, whose "noisy virtuosities [virtuosites tapageuses] and decorative expressivities [expressivites decoratives]" Chopin regarded with antipathy, and Thalberg, whose shallow elegancies and brilliancies he despised, were no doubt altogether banished from his desk; this, however, seems not to have been the case with Liszt, who occasionally made his appearance there. Thus Madame Dubois studied under Chopin Liszt's transcription of Rossini's "Tarantella" and of the Septet from Donizetti's "Lucia di Lammermoor." But the compositions of Liszt that had Chopin's approval were very limited in number. Chopin, who viewed making concessions to bad taste at the cost of true art and for the sake of success with the greatest indignation, found his former friend often guilty of this sin. In 1840 Liszt's transcription of Beethoven's "Adelaide" was published in a supplement to the Gazette musicale. M. Mathias happened to come to Chopin on the day when the latter had received the number of the journal which contained the piece in question, and found his master furious, outre, on account of certain cadenzas which he considered out of place and out of keeping.

We have seen in one of the earlier chapters how little Chopin approved of Berlioz's matter and manner; some of the ultra-romanticist's antipodes did not fare much better. As for Halevy, Chopin had no great opinion of him; Meyerbeer's music he heartily disliked; and, although not insensible to Auber's French esprit and liveliness, he did not prize this master's works very highly. Indeed, at the Italian opera-house he found more that was to his taste than at the French opera-houses. Bellini's music had a particular charm for Chopin, and he was also an admirer of Rossini.

The above notes exemplify and show the truth of Liszt's remark:—

In the great models and the master-works of art Chopin sought only what corresponded with his nature. What resembled it pleased him; what differed from it hardly received justice from him.

CHAPTER XXVI

1843-1847.

CHOPIN'S PECUNIARY CIRCUMSTANCES, AND BUSINESS EXPERIENCES WITH PUBLISHERS.—LETTERS TO FRANCHOMME.— PUBLICATIONS FROM 1842-7.—SOJOURNS AT NOHANT.—LISZT, MATTHEW ARNOLD, GEORGE SAND, CHARLES ROLLINAT, AND EUGENE DELACROIX ON NOHANT AND LIFE AT NOHANT.— CHOPIN'S MODE OF COMPOSITION.—CHOPIN AND GEORGE SAND TAKE UP THEIR PARIS QUARTERS IN THE CITE D'ORLEANS.—THEIR WAY OF LIFE THERE, PARTICULARLY CHOPIN'S, AS DESCRIBED BY HIS PUPILS LINDSAY SLOPER, MATHIAS, AND MADAME DUBOIS, AND MORE ESPECIALLY BY LENZ, MADAME SAND HERSELF, AND PROFESSOR ALEXANDER CHODZKO (DOMESTIC RELATIONS, APARTMENTS, MANNERS, SYMPATHIES, HIS TALENT FOR MIMICRY, GEORGE SAND'S FRIENDS, AND HER ESTIMATE OF CHOPIN'S CHARACTER).

Chopin's life from 1843 to 1847 was too little eventful to lend itself to a chronologically progressive narrative. I shall, therefore, begin this chapter with a number of letters written by the composer during this period to his friend Franchomme, and then endeavour to describe Chopin's mode of life, friends, character, &c.

The following fascicle of letters, although containing less about the writer's thoughts, feelings, and doings than we could wish, affords nevertheless matter of interest. At any rate, much additional light is thrown on Chopin's pecuniary circumstances and his dealings with his publishers.

Impecuniosity seems to have been a chronic state with the artist and sometimes to have pressed hard upon him. On one occasion it even made him write to the father of one of his pupils, and ask for the payment of the fees for five lessons (100 francs). M. Mathias tells me that the letter is still in his possession. One would hardly have expected such a proceeding from a grand seigneur like Chopin, and many will, no doubt, ask, how it was that a teacher so much sought after, who got 20 francs a lesson, and besides had an income from his compositions, was reduced to such straits. The riddle is easily solved. Chopin was open-handed and not much of an economist: he spent a good deal on pretty trifles, assisted liberally his needy countrymen, made handsome presents to his friends, and is said to have had occasionally to pay bills of his likewise often impecunious lady-love. Moreover, his total income was not so large as may be supposed, for although he could have as many pupils as he wished, he never taught more than five hours a day, and lived every year for several months in the country. And then there is one other point to be taken into consideration: he often gave his lessons gratis. From Madame Rubio I learned that on one occasion when she had placed the money for a series of lessons on the mantel-piece, the master declined to take any of it, with the exception of a 20-franc piece, for which sum he put her name down on a subscription list for poor Poles. Lindsay Sloper, too, told me that Chopin declined payment for the lessons he gave him.

Chopin's business experiences were not, for the most part, of a pleasant nature; this is shown as much by the facts he mentions in his letters as by the distrust with which he speaks of the publishers. Here are some more particulars on the same subject. Gutmann says that Chopin on his return from Majorca asked Schlesinger for better terms. But the publisher, whilst professing the highest opinion of the composer's merit, regretted that the sale of the compositions was not such as to allow him to pay more than he had hitherto done. [FOOTNOTE: Chopin's letters show that Gutmann's statement is correct. Troupenas was Chopin's publisher for some time after his return from Majorca.] Stephen Heller remembered hearing that Breitkopf and Hartel, of Leipzig, wrote to their Paris agent informing him that they would go on publishing Chopin's compositions, although, considering their by no means large sale, the terms at which they got them were too high. Ed. Wolff related to me that one day he drove with his countryman to the publisher Troupenas, to whom Chopin wished to sell his Sonata (probably the one in B flat minor). When after his negotiations with the publisher Chopin was seated again in the carriage, he said in Polish: "The pig, he offered me 200 francs for my Sonata!" Chopin's relations with England were even less satisfactory. At a concert at which Filtsch played, Chopin introduced Stephen Heller to Wessel or to a representative ofthat firm, but afterwards remarked: "You won't find them pleasant to deal with." Chopin at any rate did not find them pleasant to deal with. Hearing that Gutmann was going to London he asked his pupil to call at Wessel's and try to renew the contract which had expired. The publisher on being applied to answered that not only would he not renew the contract, but that he would not even print Chopin's compositions if he got them for nothing. Among the pieces offered was the Berceuse. With regard to this story of Gutmann's it has, however, to be stated that, though it may have some foundation of fact, it is not true as he told it; for Wessel certainly had published the Berceuse by

June 26, 1845, and also published in the course of time the five following works. Then, however, the connection was broken off by Wessel. Chopin's grumblings at his English publisher brings before us only one side of the question. The other side comes in view in the following piece of information with which Wessel's successor, Mr. Edwin Ashdown, favoured me:—"In 1847 Mr. Wessel got tired of buying Chopin's works, which at that time had scarcely any sale, and discontinued the agreement, his last assignment from Chopin (of Op. 60, 61, and 62) being dated July 17, 1847." Wessel advertised these works on September 26, 1846.

Although in the first of the following letters the day, month, and year when it was written are not mentioned, and the second and third inform us only of the day and month, but not of the year, internal evidence shows that the first four letters form one group and belong to the year 1844. Chopin places the date sometimes at the head, sometimes at the foot, and sometimes in the middle of his letters; to give it prominence I shall place it always at the head, but indicate where he places it in the middle.

Chateau de Nohant, near La Chatre, Indre [August 1, 1844].

Dearest [Cherissime],—I send you [FOOTNOTE: In addressing Franchomme Chopin makes use of the pronoun of the second person singular.] the letter from Schlesinger and another for him. Read them. He wishes to delay the publication, and I cannot do so. If he says NO, give my manuscripts to Maho [FOOTNOTE: See next letter.] so that he may get M. Meissonnier [FOOTNOTE: A Paris music-publisher. He brought out in the following year (1845) Chopin's Op. 57, Berceuse, and Op. 58, Sonate (B minor). The compositions spoken of in this and the next two letters are Op. 55, Deux Nocturnes, and Op. 56, Trois Mazurkas.] to take them for the same price, 600 francs, I believe that he (Schlesinger) will engrave them. They must be published on the 20th. But you know it is only necessary to register the title on that day. I ask your pardon for troubling you with all these things. I love you, and apply to you as I would to my brother. Embrace your children. My regards to Madame Franchomme.—Your devoted friend,

F. Chopin.

A thousand compliments from Madame Sand.
Chateau de Nohant, Indre, August 2, 1844.

Dearest,—I was in great haste yesterday when I wrote to you
to apply at Meissonnier's through Maho IF SCHLESINGER REFUSES
my compositions. I forgot that Henri Lemoine [FOOTNOTE: A
Paris music-publisher.] paid Schlesinger a very high price for
my studies, and that I had rather have Lemoine engrave my
manuscripts than Meissonnier. I give you much trouble, dear
friend, but here is a letter for H. Lemoine, which I send to
you. Read it, and arrange with him. He must either publish the
compositions or register the titles on the 20th of this month
(August); ask from him only 300 francs for each, which makes
600 francs for the two. Tell him he need not pay me till my
return to Paris if he likes. Give him even the two for 500
francs if you think it necessary. I had rather do that than
give them to Meissonnier for 600 francs, as I wrote to you
yesterday without reflecting. If you have in the meantime
already arranged something with M., it is a different matter.
If not, do not let them go for less than 1,000 francs. For
Maho, who is the correspondent of Haertel (who pays me well)
might, knowing that I sell my compositions for so little in
Paris, make me lower my price in Germany. I torment you much
with my affairs. It is only in case Schlesinger persists in
his intention not to publish this month. If you think Lemoine
would give 800 francs for the two works, ask them. I do not
mention THE PRICE to him so as to leave you complete freedom.
I have no time to lose before the departure of the mail. I
embrace you, dear brother—write me a line.—Yours devotedly,

Chopin.

My regards to Madame. A thousand kisses to your children.
Nohant, Monday, August 4, 1844.

Dearest,—I relied indeed on your friendship—therefore the
celerity with which you have arranged the Schlesinger affair
for me does not surprise me at all. I thank you from the
bottom of my heart, and await the moment when I shall be able
to do as much for you. I imagine all is well in your home—
that Madame Franchomme and your dear children are well—and
that you love me as I love you.—Yours devotedly,

F. CH.

Madame Sand embraces your dear big darling [fanfan], and sends
you a hearty grasp of the hand.
Chateau de Nohant, September 20, 1844.

Dearest,—If I did not write you before, it was because I
thought I should see you again this week in Paris. My
departure being postponed, I send you a line for Schlesinger
so that he may remit to you the price of my last manuscripts,
that is to say, 600 francs (100 of which you will keep for
me). I hope he will do it without making any difficulty about
it—if not, ask him at once for a line in reply (without
getting angry), send it to me, and I shall write immediately
to M. Leo to have the 500 francs you had the kindness to lend
me remitted to you before the end of the month.

What shall I say? I often think of our last evening spent with
my dear sister. [FOOTNOTE: His sister Louise, who had been on
a visit to him.] How glad she was to hear you! She wrote to me
about it since from Strasburg, and asked me to remember her to
you and Madame Franchomme. I hope you are all well, and that I

shall find you so. Write to me, and love me as I love you.
Your old

[A scrawl.]

A thousand compliments to Madame. I embrace your dear
children. A thousand compliments from Madame Sand.
[Date.]

I send you also a receipt for Schlesinger which you will give
up to him for the money only. Once more, do not be vexed if he
makes any difficulties. I embrace you.

C.
August 30, 1845.

Very dear friend,—Here are three manuscripts for Brandus,
[FOOTNOTE: Brandus, whose name here appears for the first time
in Chopin's letters, was the successor of Schlesinger.] and
three for Maho, who will remit to you Haertel's price for them
(1,500 francs). Give the manuscripts only at the moment of
payment. Send a note for 500 francs in your next letter, and
keep the rest for me. I give you much trouble, I should like
to spare you it—but—but——.

Ask Maho not to change the manuscripts destined for Haertel,
because, as I shall not correct the Leipzig proofs, it is
important that my copy should be clear. Also ask Brandus to
send me two proofs, one of which I may keep.

Now, how are you? and Madame Franchomme and her dear children?
I know you are in the country—(if St. Germain may be called
country)—that ought to do you all infinite good in the fine

weather which we continue to have. Look at my erasures! I should not end if I were to launch out into a chat with you, and I have not time to resume my letter, for Eug. Delacroix, who wishes much to take charge of my message for you, leaves immediately. He is the most admirable artist possible—I have spent delightful times with him. He adores Mozart—knows all his operas by heart.

Decidedly I am only making blots to-day—pardon me for them. Au revoir, dear friend, I love you always, and I think of you every day.

Give my kind regards to Madame Franchomme, and embrace the dear children.
September 22, 1845.

Very dear friend,—I thank you with all my heart for all your journeys after Maho, and your letter which I have just received with the money. The day of the publication seems to me good, and I have only to ask you again not to let Brandus fall asleep on my account or over my accounts.
Nohant, July 8, 1846.

Very dear friend,—It was not because I did not think of it that I have not written to you sooner, but because I wished to send you at the same time my poor manuscripts, which are not yet finished. In the meantime here is a letter for M. Brandus. When you deliver it to him, be so kind as to ask him for a line in reply, which you will have the goodness to send to me; because if any unforeseen event occurs, I shall have to apply to Meissonnier, their offers being equal.

My good friend,—I am doing my utmost to work, but I do not

get on; and if this state of things continues, my new productions will no longer remind people either of the WARBLING OF LINNETS [gazouillement des fauvettes] [FOOTNOTE: This is an allusion to a remark which somebody made on his compositions.] or even of BROKEN CHINA [porcelaine cassee]. I must resign myself.

Write to me. I love you as much as ever.

A thousand kind regards to Madame Franchomme, and many compliments from my sister Louise. I embrace your dear children.
[Date.]

Madame Sand begs to be remembered to you and Madame Franchomme.

Chateau de Nohant, near La Chatre, September 17, 1846.

Very dear friend,—I am very sorry that Brandus is away, and that Maho is not yet in a position to receive the manuscripts that he has so often asked me for this winter. One must therefore wait; meanwhile I beg you will be so kind as to go back AS SOON as you judge it possible, for I should not now like this to be a long business, having sent my copy to London at the same time as to you. Do not tell them this—if they are CLEVER tradesmen [marchands habiles] they may cheat me like honest people [en honnetes gens]. As this is all my present fortune I should prefer the affair to turn out differently. Also have the kindness not to consign my manuscripts to them without receiving the money agreed upon, and send me immediately a note for 500 francs in your letter. You will keep the rest for me till my arrival in Paris, which will take place probably in the end of October. I thank you a thousand times, dear friend, for your good heart and friendly offers. Keep your millions for me till another time—is it not already too much to dispose of your time as I do?

[Here follow compliments to and friendly enquiries after Franchomme's family.]

Madame Sand sends you a thousand compliments and desires to be remembered to Madame Franchomme.

[Date.]

I shall answer Madame Rubio. [FOOTNOTE: Nee Vera de Kologriwof, a pupil of Chopin's and teacher of music in Paris; she married Signor Rubio, an artist, and died in the summer of 1880 at Florence.] If Mdlle. Stirling [FOOTNOTE: A Scotch lady and pupil of Chopin's; I shall have to say more about her by-and-by. Madame Erskine was her elder sister.] is at St. Germain, do not forget to remember me to her, also to Madame Erskine.

This will be the proper place to mention the compositions of the years 1842-47, about the publication of many of which we have read so much in the above letters. There is no new publication to be recorded in 1842. The publications of 1843 were: in February—Op. 51, Allegro vivace, Troisieme Impromptu (G flat major), dedicated to Madame la Comtesse Esterhazy; in December—Op. 52, Quatrieme Ballade (F minor), dedicated to Madame la Baronne C. de Rothschild; Op. 53, Huitieme Polonaise (A flat major), dedicated to Mr. A. Leo; and Op. 54, Scherzo, No. 4 (E major), dedicated to Mdlle. J. de Caraman. Those of 1844 were: in August—Op. 55, Deux Nocturnes (F minor and E flat major), dedicated to Mdlle. J. H. Stirling; and Op. 56, Trois Mazurkas (A minor, A flat major, and F sharp minor), dedicated to Mdlle. C. Maberly. Those of 1845: in May—Op. 57, Berceuse (D flat major), dedicated to Mdlle. Elise Gavard; and in June—Op. 58, Sonate (B minor), dedicated to Madame la Comtesse E. de Perthuis. Those of 1846: in April—Op. 59, Trois Mazurkas (A minor, A flat major, and F sharp minor); and in September—Op. 60, Barcarole (F sharp major), dedicated to Madame la Baronne de Stockhausen; Op. 61, Polonaise-Fantaisie (A flat major), dedicated to Madame A. Veyret; and Op. 62, Deux Nocturnes (B major and E major), dedicated to Mdlle. R. de Konneritz. Those of 1847: in September—Op. 63, Trois Mazurkas (B major, F minor, and C sharp minor), dedicated to Madame la Comtesse L. Czosnowska, and Op. 64, Trois Valses (D flat major, C sharp minor, and A flat major), respectively dedicated to Madame la Comtesse Delphine Potocka, Madame la Baronne Nathaniel de Rothschild, and Madame la Baronne Bronicka; and lastly, in October— Op. 65, Sonate (G minor), pour piano et violoncelle, dedicated to Mr. A. Franchomme.

From 1838 to 1846 Chopin passed regularly every year, with the exception of 1840, three or four months at Nohant. The musical papers announced Chopin's return to town sometimes at the beginning of October, sometimes at the beginning of November. In 1844 he must either have made a longer stay at Nohant than usual or paid it a visit during the winter, for in the "Gazette musicale" of January 5, 1845, we read: "Chopin has returned to Paris and brought with him a new grand Sonata and variantes. These two important works will soon be published."

[FOOTNOTE: The new Sonata here mentioned is the one in B minor, Op. 58, which was published in June, 1845. As to the other item mentioned, I am somewhat puzzled. Has the word to be taken in its literal sense of "various readings," i.e., new readings of works already known (the context, however, does not favour this supposition), or does it refer to the ever-varying evolutions of the Berceuse, Op. 57. published in May, 1845, or, lastly, is it simply a misprint?]

George Sand generally prolonged her stay at Nohant till pretty far into the winter, much to the sorrow of her malade ordinaire (thus Chopin used to style himself), who yearned for her return to Paris.

According to Liszt, the country and the vie de chateau pleased Chopin so much that for the sake of enjoying them he put up with company that did not please him at all. George Sand has a different story to tell. She declares that the retired life and the solemnity of the country agreed neither with Chopin's physical nor with his moral health; that he loved the country only for a fortnight, after which he bore it only out of attachment to her; and that he never felt regret on leaving it. Whether Chopin loved country life or not, whether he liked George Sand's Berry friends and her guests from elsewhere or not, we may be sure that he missed Paris and his accustomed Paris society.

"Of all the troubles I had not to endure but to contend against, the sufferings of my malade ordinaire were not the least," says George Sand. "Chopin always wished for Nohant, and never could bear it." And, speaking of the later years, when the havoc made in Chopin's constitution by the inroads of his malady showed itself more and more, she remarks: "Nohant had become repugnant to him. His return in the spring still filled him with ecstatic joy for a short time. But as soon as he began to work everything round him assumed a gloomy aspect."

Before we peep into Chopin's room and watch him at work, let us see what the chateau of Nohant and life there were like. "The railway through the centre of France went in those days [August, 1846] no further than Vierzon," [FOOTNOTE: The opening of the extension of the line to Chateauroux was daily expected at that time.] writes Mr. Matthew Arnold in an account of a visit paid by him to George Sand:—

From Vierzon to Chateauroux one travelled by an ordinary diligence, from Chateauroux to La Chatre by a humbler diligence, from La Chatre to Broussac by the humblest diligence cf. all. At Broussac diligence ended, and PATACHE began. Between Chateauroux and La Chatre, a mile or two before reaching the latter place, the road passes by the village of Nohant. The chateau of Nohant, in which Madame Sand lived, is a plain house by the roadside, with a walled garden. Down in the meadows not far off flows the Indre, bordered by trees.

The Chateau of Nohant is indeed, as Mr. Matthew Arnold says, a plain house, only the roof with its irregularly distributed dormars and chimney-stacks of various size giving to it a touch of picturesqueness. On the other hand, the ground-floor, with its central door flanked on each side by three windows, and the seven windowed story above, impresses one with the sense of spaciousness.

Liszt, speaking of a three months' stay at Nohant made by himself and his friend the Comtesse d'Agoult in the summer of 1837—i.e., before the closer connection of George Sand and Chopin began—relates that the hostess and her guests spent the days in reading good books, receiving letters from absent friends, taking long walks on the banks of the Indre, and in other equally simple occupations and amusements. In the evenings they assembled on the terrace. There, where the light of the lamps cast fantastic shadows on the neighbouring trees, they sat listening to the murmuring of the river and the warbling of the nightingales, and breathing in the sweet perfume of the lime-trees and the stronger scent of the larches till the

Countess would exclaim: "There you are again dreaming, you incorrigible artists! Do you not know that the hour for working has come?" And then George Sand would go and write at the book on which she was engaged, and Liszt would betake himself to the old scores which he was studying with a view to discover some of the great masters' secrets. [FOOTNOTE: Liszt. "Essays and Reisebriefe eines Baccalaureus der Tonkunst." Vol. II., pp. 146 and 147 of the collected works.]

Thus was Nohant in quiet days. But the days at Nohant were by no means always quiet. For George Sand was most hospitable, kept indeed literally open house for her friends, and did so regardless of credit and debit. The following passage from a letter written by her in 1840 from Paris to her half-brother Hippolyte Chatiron gives us a good idea of the state of matters:—

If you will guarantee my being able to pass the summer at Nohant for 4,000 francs, I will go. But I have never been there without spending 1,500 francs per month, and as I do not spend here the half of this, it is neither the love of work, nor that of spending, nor that of GLORY, which makes me stay. I do not know whether I have been pillaged; but I am at a loss how to avoid it with my nonchalance, in so vast a house, and so easy a kind of life as that of Nohant. Here I can see clearly; everything is done under my eyes as I understand and wish it. At Nohant—let this remain between us—you know that before I am up a dozen people have often made themselves at home in the house. What can I do? Were I to pose as a good manager [econome] they would accuse me of stinginess; were I to let things go on, I should not be able to provide for them. Try if you can find a remedy for this.

In George Sand's letters many glimpses may be caught of the life at Nohant. To some of them I have already drawn the reader's attention in preceding chapters; now I shall point out a few more.

George Sand to Madame Marliani; Nohant, August 13, 1841:—

I have had all my nights absorbed by work and fatigue. I have passed all my days with Pauline [Viardot] in walking, playing at billiards, and all this makes me so entirely go out of my indolent character and lazy habits that, at night, instead of working quickly, I fall stupidly asleep at every line....Viardot [Louis Viardot, the husband of Pauline] passes his days in poaching with my brother and Papet; for the shooting season has not yet begun, and they brave the laws, divine and human. Pauline reads with Chopin whole scores at the piano. She is always good-natured and charming, as you know her.

George Sand to Mdlle. Rozieres: Nohant, October 15, 1841:—

Papet is in the depths of the forests; in "Erymanthe" at least, hunting the wild boar. Chopin is in Paris, and he has relapsed, as he says, into his triples croches [demisemiquavers].

George Sand to Mdlle. Rozieres; Nohant, May 9, 1842:—

Quick to work! Your master, the great Chopin, has forgotten (that for which he nevertheless cares a great deal) to buy a beautiful present for Francoise, my faithful servant, whom he adores, and he is very right.

He begs of you therefore to send him, IMMEDIATELY, four yards of lace, two fingers broad at least, within the price of ten francs a yard; further, a shawl of whatever material you like, within the price of forty francs....This, then, is the superb present which your HONOURED MASTER asks you to get for him, with an eagerness worthy of the ardour which he carries into his gifts, and of the impatience which he puts into little things.

Charles Rollinat, a friend of George Sand's, the brother of one of George Sand's most intimate and valued friends, Francois Rollinat, published in "Le Temps" (September 1, 1874) a charming "Souvenir de Nohant," which shows us the the chateau astir with a more numerous company:—

The hospitality there [he writes] was comfortable, and the

freedom absolute. There were guns and dogs for those who loved hunting, boats and nets for those who loved fishing, a splendid garden to walk in. Everyone did as he liked. Liszt and Chopin composed; Pauline Garcia studied her role of the "Prophete"; the mistress of the house wrote a romance or a drama; and it was the same with the others. At six o'clock they assembled again to dine, and did not part company till two or three o'clock in the morning.

Chopin rarely played. He could only be prevailed upon to play when he was sure of perfection. Nothing in the world would have made him consent to play indifferently. Liszt, on the contrary, played always, well or badly.

[FOOTNOTE: Charles Rollinat, a younger brother of Francois, went afterwards to Russia, where, according to George Sand (see letter to Edmond Plauchut, April 8, 1874), he was for twenty-five years "professeur de musique et haut enseignement, avec une bonne place du gouvernement." He made a fortune and lost it, retaining only enough to live upon quietly in Italy. He tried then to supplement his scanty income by literary work (translations from the Russian). George Sand, recalling the days of long ago, says: "Il chantait comme on ne chante plus, excepte Pauline [Viardot-Garcia]!"]

Unfortunately, the greater portion of M. Rollinat's so-called Souvenir consists of "poetry WITHOUT truth." Nevertheless, we will not altogether ignore his pretty stories.

One evening when Liszt played a piece of Chopin's with embellishments of his own, the composer became impatient and at last, unable to restrain himself any longer, walked up to Liszt and said with his ENGLISH PHLEGM:—

"I beg of you, my dear friend, if you do me the honour to play a piece of mine, to play what is written, or to play something else. It is only Chopin who has the right to alter Chopin."

"Well! play yourself!" said Liszt, rising from his seat a little irritated,

"With pleasure," said Chopin.

At that moment a moth extinguished the lamp. Chopin would not have it relighted, and played in the dark. When he had finished his delighted auditors overwhelmed him with compliments, and Liszt said:

"Ah, my friend, you were right! The works of a genius like you are sacred; it is a profanation to meddle with them. You are a true poet, and I am only a mountebank."

Whereupon Chopin replied: "We have each our genre."

M. Rollinat then proceeds to tell his readers that Chopin, believing he had eclipsed Liszt that evening, boasted of it, and said: "How vexed he was!" It seems that the author felt that this part of the story put a dangerously severe strain on the credulity of his readers, for he thinks it necessary to assure them that these were the ipsissima verba of Chopin. Well, the words in question came to the ears of Liszt, and he resolved at once to have his revenge.

Five days afterwards the friends were again assembled in the same place and at the same time. Liszt asked Chopin to play, and had all the lights put out and all the curtains drawn; but when Chopin was going to the piano, Liszt whispered something in his ear and sat down in his stead. He played the same composition which Chopin had played on the previous occasion, and the audience was again enchanted. At the end of the piece Liszt struck a match and lighted the candles which stood on the piano. Of course general stupefaction ensued.

"What do you say to it?" said Liszt to his rival.

"I say what everyone says; I too believed it was Chopin."

"You see," said the virtuoso rising, "that Liszt can be Chopin when he likes; but could Chopin be Liszt?"

Instead of commenting on the improbability of a generous artist thus cruelly taunting his sensitive rival, I shall simply say that Liszt had not the slightest recollection of ever having imitated Chopin's playing in a darkened room. There may be some minute grains of truth mixed up with all this chaff of fancy—Chopin's displeasure at the liberties Liszt took with his compositions was no doubt one of them—but it is impossible to separate them.

M. Rollinat relates also how in 184-, when Chopin, Liszt, the Comtesse d'Agoult, Pauline Garcia, Eugene Delacroix, the actor Bocage, and other celebrities were at Nohant, the piano was one moonlit night carried out to the terrace; how Liszt played the hunting chorus from Weber's Euryanthe, Chopin some bars from an impromptu he was then composing; how Pauline Garcia sang Nel cor piu non mi sento, and a niece of George Sand a popular air; how the echo answered the musicians; and how after the music the company, which included also a number of friends from the neighbouring town, had punch and remained together till dawn. But here again M. Rollinat's veracity is impugned on all sides. Madame Viardot-Garcia declares that she was never at Nohant when Liszt was there; and Liszt did not remember having played on the terrace of the chateau. Moreover, seeing that the first performance of the Prophete took place on April 16, 1849, is it likely that Madame Pauline Garcia was studying her part before or in 1846? And unless she did so she could not meet Chopin at Nohant when she was studying it.

M. Rollinat is more trustworthy when he tells us that there was a pretty theatre and quite an assortment of costumes at the chateau; that the dramas and comedies played there were improvised by the actors, only the subject and the division into scenes being given; and that on two pianos, concealed by curtains, one on the right and one on the left of the stage, Chopin and Liszt improvised the musical part of the entertainment. All this is, however, so much better and so much more fully told by George Sand (in Dernieres Pages: Le Theatre des Marionnettes de Nohant) that we will take our information from her. It was in the long nights of a winter that she conceived the plan of these private theatricals in imitation of the comedia dell' arte—namely, of "pieces the improvised dialogue of which followed a written sketch posted up behind the scenes."

They resembled the charades which are acted in society and which are more or less developed according to the ensemble and the talent of the performers. We had begun with these. By degrees the word of the charade disappeared and we played first mad saynetes, then comedies of intrigues and adventures, and finally dramas of incidents and emotions. The whole thing began by pantomime, and this was of Chopin's invention; he occupied the place at the piano and improvised, while the young people gesticulated scenes and danced comic ballets. I leave you to imagine whether these now wonderful, now charming improvisations quickened the brains and made supple the legs of our performers. He led them as he pleased and made them pass, according to his fancy, from the droll to the severe, from the burlesque to the solemn, from the graceful to the passionate. We improvised costumes in order to play successively several roles. As soon as the artist saw them appear, he adapted his theme and his accent in a marvellous manner to their respective characters. This went on for three evenings, and then the master, setting out for Paris, left us thoroughly stirred up, enthusiastic, and determined not to suffer the spark which had electrified us to be lost.

To get away from the quicksands of Souvenirs—for George Sand's pages, too, were written more than thirty years after the occurrences she describes, and not published till 1877—I shall make some extracts from the contemporaneous correspondence of George Sand's great friend, the celebrated painter Eugene Delacroix. [FOOTNOTE: Lettres de Eugene Delacroix (1815 a 1863) recucillies et publiees par M. Philippe Burty. Paris, 1878.] The reader cannot fail to feel at once the fresh breeze of reality that issues from these letters, which contain vivid sketches full of natural beauties and free from affectation and striving after effect:—

Nohant, June 7, 1842.

...The place is very pleasant, and the hosts do their utmost to please me. When we are not assembled to dine, breakfast, play at billiards, or walk, we are in our rooms, reading, or resting on our sofas. Now and then there come to you through the window opening on the garden, whiffs of the music of Chopin, who is working in his room; this mingles with the song of the nightingales and the odour of the roses. You see that so far I am not much to be pitied, and, nevertheless, work must come to give the grain of salt to all this. This life is too easy, I must purchase it with a little racking of my brains; and like the huntsman who eats with more appetite when he has got his skin torn by bushes, one must strive a little after ideas in order to feel the charm of doing nothing.

Nohant, June 14, 1842.

...Although I am in every respect most agreeably circumstanced, both as regards body and mind, for I am in much better health, I have not been able to prevent myself from thinking of work. How strange! this work is fatiguing, and yet the species of activity it gives to the mind is necessary to the body itself. In vain did I try to get up a passion for billiards, in which I receive a lesson every day, in vain have I good conversations on all the subjects that please me, music that I seize on the wing and by whiffs, I have felt the need of doing something. I have begun a Sainte-Anne for the parish, and I have already set it agoing. Nohant, June 22, 1842.

...Pen and ink certainly become more and more repugnant to me. I have no more than you any event to record. I lead a monastic life, and as monotonous as it well can be. No event varies the course of it. We expected Balzac, who has not come, and I am not sorry. He is a babbler who would have destroyed this harmony of NONCHALANCE which I am enjoying thoroughly; at intervals a little painting, billiards, and walking, that is more than is necessary to fill up the days. There is not even the distraction of neighbours and friends from the environs; in this part of the country everyone remains at home and occupies him self with his oxen and his land. One would become a fossil here in a very short time.

I have interminable private interviews with Chopin, whom I love much, and who is a man of a rare distinction; he is the most true artist I have met. He is one of the few one can admire and esteem. Madame Sand suffers frequently from violent headaches and pains in her eyes, which she tries to master as much as possible and with much strength of will, so as not to weary us with what she suffers.

The greatest event of my stay has been a peasants' ball on the lawn of the chateau with the best bagpipers of the place. The people of this part of the country present a remarkable type of gentleness and good nature; ugliness is rare here, though

beauty is not often seen, but there is not that kind of fever
which is observable in the peasants of the environs of Paris.
All the women have the appearance of those sweet faces one
sees only in the pictures of the old masters. They are all
Saint Annes.

Amidst the affectations, insincerities, and superficialities of Chopin's social intercourse, Delacroix's friendship—we have already seen that the musician reciprocated the painter's sentiments—stands out like a green oasis in a barren desert. When, on October 28, 1849, a few days after Chopin's death, Delacroix sent a friend a ticket for the funeral service of the deceased, he speaks of him as "my poor and dear Chopin." But the sincerity of Delacroix's esteem and the tenderness of his love for Chopin are most fully revealed in some lines of a letter which he wrote on January 7, 1861, to Count Czymala [Grzymala]:—

When I have finished [the labours that took up all his time],
I shall let you know, and shall see you again, with the
pleasure I have always had, and with the feelings your kind
letter has reanimated in me. With whom shall I speak of the
incomparable genius whom heaven has envied the earth, and of
whom I dream often, being no longer able to see him in this
world nor to hear his divine harmonies.

If you see sometimes the charming Princess Marcelline
[Czartoryska], another object of my respect, place at her feet
the homage of a poor man who has not ceased to be full of the
memory of her kindnesses and of admiration for her talent,
another bond of union with the seraph whom we have lost and
who, at this hour, charms the celestial spheres.

The first three of the above extracts from Delacroix's letters enable us to form a clear idea of what the everyday life at Nohant was like, and after reading them we can easily imagine that its monotony must have had a depressing effect on the company-loving Chopin. But the drawback was counterbalanced by an advantage. At Paris most of Chopin's time was occupied with teaching and the pleasures of society, at Nohant he could devote himself undisturbed and undistracted to composition. And there is more than sufficient evidence to prove that in this respect Chopin utilised well the quiet and leisure of his rural retirement.

Few things excite the curiosity of those who have a taste for art and literature so much as an artist's or poet's mode of creation. With what interest, for instance, do we read Schindler's account of how Beethoven composed his Missa Solemnis—of the master's absolute detachment from the terrestrial world during the time he was engaged on this work; of his singing, shouting, and stamping, when he was in the act of giving birth to the fugue of the Credo! But as regards musicians, we know, generally speaking, very little on the subject; and had not George Sand left us her reminiscences, I should not have much to tell the reader about Chopin's mode of creation. From Gutmann I learned that his master worked long before he put a composition to paper, but when it was once in writing did not keep it long in his portfolio. The latter part of this statement is contradicted by a remark of the better-informed Fontana, who, in the preface to Chopin's posthumous works, says that the composer, whether from caprice or nonchalance, had the habit of keeping his manuscripts sometimes a very long time in his portfolio before giving them to the public. As George Sand observed the composer with an artist's eye and interest, and had, of course, better opportunities than anybody else to observe him, her remarks are particularly valuable. She writes:—

His creation was spontaneous and miraculous. He found it without seeking it, without foreseeing it. It came on his piano suddenly, complete, sublime, or it sang in his head during a walk, and he was impatient to play it to himself. But then began the most heart-rending labour I ever saw. It was a series of efforts, of irresolutions, and of frettings to seize again certain details of the theme he had heard; what he had conceived as a whole he analysed too much when wishing to write it, and his regret at not finding it again, in his opinion, clearly defined, threw him into a kind of despair. He shut himself up in his room for whole days, weeping, walking, breaking his pens, repeating and altering a bar a hundred times, writing and effacing it as many times, and recommencing the next day with a minute and desperate perseverance. He spent six weeks over a single page to write it at last as he had noted it down at the very first.

I had for a long time been able to make him consent to trust to this first inspiration. But when he was no longer disposed to believe me, he reproached me gently with having spoiled him and with not being severe enough for him. I tried to amuse him, to take him out for walks. Sometimes, taking away all my brood in a country char a bancs, I dragged him away in spite of himself from this agony. I took him to the banks of the Creuse, and after being for two or three days lost amid sunshine and rain in frightful roads, we arrived, cheerful and famished, at some magnificently-situated place where he seemed to revive. These fatigues knocked him up the first day, but he slept. The last day he was quite revived, quite rejuvenated in returning to Nohant, and he found the solution of his work without too much effort; but it was not always possible to prevail upon him to leave that piano which was much oftener his torment than his joy, and by degrees he showed temper when I disturbed him. I dared not insist. Chopin when angry was alarming, and as, with me, he always restrained himself, he seemed almost to choke and die.

A critic remarks in reference to this account that Chopin's mode of creation does not show genius, but only passion. From which we may conclude that he would not, like Carlyle, have defined genius as the power of taking infinite pains. To be sure, the great Scotchman's definition is inadequate, but nothing is more false than the popular notion that the great authors throw off their works with the pleasantest ease, that creation is an act of pure enjoyment. Beethoven's sketch-books tell a different story; so do also Balzac's proof-sheets and the manuscripts of Pope's version of the Iliad and Odyssey in the British Museum. Dr. Johnson speaking of Milton's MSS. observed truly: "Such reliques show how excellence is acquired." Goethe in writing to Schiller asks him to return certain books of "Wilhelm Meister" that he may go over them A FEW TIMES before sending them to the press. And on re-reading one of these books he cut out one third of its contents. Moreover, if an author writes with ease, this is not necessarily a proof that he labours little, for he may finish the work before bringing it to paper. Mozart is a striking instance. He has himself described his mode of composing— which was a process of accumulation, agglutination, and crystallisation— in a letter to a friend. The constitution of the mind determines the mode of working. Some qualities favour, others obstruct the realisation of a first conception. Among the former are acuteness and quickness of vision, the power of grasping complex subjects, and a good memory. But however varied the mode of creation may be, an almost unvarying characteristic of the production of really precious and lasting artwork is ungrudging painstaking, such as we find described in William Hunt's "Talks about Art":—"If you could see me dig and groan, rub it out and start again, hate myself and feel dreadfully! The people who do things easily, their things you look at easily, and give away easily." Lastly and briefly, it is not the mode of working, but the result of this working which demonstrates genius.

As Chopin disliked the pavilion in the Rue Pigalle, George Sand moved with her household in 1842 to the quiet, aristocratic-looking Cite (Court or Square) d'Orleans, where their friend Madame Marliani arranged for them a vie de famille. To get to the Cite d'Orleans one has to pass through two gateways—the first leads from the Rue Taitbout (close to the Rue St. Lazare), into a small out-court with the lodge of the principal concierge; the second, into the court itself. In the centre is a grass plot with four flower-beds and a fountain; and between this grass plot and the footpath which runs along the houses extends a carriage drive. As to the houses which form the square, they are well and handsomely built, the block opposite the entrance making even some architectural pretensions. Madame Sand's, Madame Marliani's, and Chopin's houses, which bore respectively the numbers 5, 4, and 3, were situated on the right side, the last-mentioned being just in the first right-hand corner on entering from the out-court. On account of the predilection shown for it by artists and literary men as a place of abode, the Court d'Orldans has not inaptly been called a little Athens. Alexander Dumas was one of the many celebrities who lived there at one time or other; and Chopin had for neighbours the famous singer Pauline Viardot-Garcia, the distinguished pianoforte-professor Zimmermann, and the sculptor Dantan, from whose famous gallery of caricatures, or rather charges, the composer's portrait was not absent. Madame Marliani, the friend of George Sand and Chopin, who has already repeatedly been mentioned in this book, was the wife of Manuel Marliani, Spanish Consul in Paris, author, [FOOTNOTE: Especially notable among his political and historical publications in Spanish and French is: "Histoire politique de l'Espagne moderne suivie d'un apercu sur les finances." 2 vols. in 8vo (Paris, 1840).] politician, and subsequently senator. Lenz says that Madame Marliani was a Spanish countess and a fine lady; and George Sand describes her as good-natured and active, endowed with a passionate head and maternal heart, but destined to be unhappy because she wished to make the reality of life yield to the ideal of her imagination and the exigences of her sensibility.

Some excerpts from a letter written by George Sand on November 12, 1842, to her friend Charles Duvernet, and a passage from Ma Vie will bring scene and actors vividly before us:—

We also cultivate billiards; I have a pretty little table, which I hire for twenty francs a month, in my salon, and thanks to kind friendships we approach Nohant life as much as is possible in this melancholy Paris. What makes things country-like also is that I live in the same square as the family Marliani, Chopin in the next pavilion, so that without leaving this large well-lighted and sanded Court d'Orleans, we run in the evening from one to another like good provincial neighbours. We have even contrived to have only one pot [marmite], and eat all together at Madame Marliani's, which is more economical and by far more lively than taking one's meals at home. It is a kind of phalanstery which amuses us, and where mutual liberty is much better guaranteed than in that of the Fourierists...

Solange is at a boarding-school, and comes out every Saturday to Monday morning. Maurice has resumed the studio con furia, and I, I have resumed Consuelo like a dog that is being whipped; for I have idled on account of my removal and the fitting up of my apartments...

Kind regards and shakes of the hand from Viardot, Chopin, and my children.

The passge [sic: passage] from Ma Vie, which contains some repetitions along with a few additional touches, runs as follows:— She [Madame Marliani] had fine apartments between the two we [George Sand and Chopin] occupied. We had only a large planted and sanded and always clean court to cross in order to meet, sometimes, in her rooms, sometimes in mine, sometimes in Chopin's when he was inclined to give us some music. We dined with her at common expense. It was a very good association, economical like all associations, and enabled one to see society at Madame Marliani's, my friends more privately in my apartments, and to take up my work at the hour when it suited me to withdraw. Chopin rejoiced also at having a fine, isolated salon where he could go to compose or to dream. But he loved society, and made little use of his sanctuary except to give lessons in it.

Although George Sand speaks only of a salon, Chopin's official residence, as we may call it, consisted of several rooms. They were elegantly furnished and always adorned with flowers—for he loved le luxe and had the coquetterie des appartements.

[FOOTNOTE: When I visited in 1880 M. Kwiatkowski in Paris, he showed me some Chopin relics: 1, a pastel drawing by Jules Coignet (representing Les Pyramides d'Egypte), which hung always above the composer's piano; 2, a little causeuse which Chopin bought with his first Parisian savings; 3, an embroidered easy-chair worked and presented to him by the Princess Czartoiyska; and 4, an embroidered cushion worked and presented to him by Madame de Rothschild. If we keep in mind Chopin's remarks about his furniture and the papering of his rooms, and add to the above-mentioned articles those which Karasowski mentions as having been bought by Miss Stirling after the composer's death, left by her to his mother, and destroyed by the Russians along with his letters in 1861 when in possession of his sister Isabella Barcinska—his portrait by Ary Scheffer, some Sevres porcelain with the inscription "Offert par Louis Philippe a Frederic Chopin," a fine inlaid box, a present from one of the Rothschild family, carpets, table-cloths, easy-chairs, &c., worked by his pupils—we can form some sort of idea of the internal arrangements of the pianist-composer's rooms.]

Nevertheless, they exhibited none of the splendour which was to be found in the houses of many of the celebrities then living in Paris. "He observed," remarks Liszt, "on this point as well as in the then so fashionable elegancies of walking-sticks, pins, studs, and jewels, the instinctive line of the comme il faut between the too much and the too little." But Chopin's letters written from Nohant in 1839 to Fontana have afforded the reader sufficient opportunities to make himself acquainted with the master's fastidiousness and good taste in matters of furniture and room decoration, above all, his horror of vulgar gaudiness.

Let us try to get some glimpses of Chopin in his new home. Lindsay Sloper, who—owing, no doubt, to a great extent at least, to the letter of recommendation from Moscheles which he brought with him—had got permission from Chopin to come for a lesson as often as he liked at eight o'clock in the morning, found the master at that hour not in deshabille, but dressed with the greatest care. Another early pupil, M. Mathias, always fell in with the daily-attending barber. M. Mathias told me also of Chopin's habit of leaning with his back against the mantel-piece while he was chatting at the end of the lesson. It must have been a pretty sight to see the master in this favourite attitude of his, his coat buttoned up to the chin (this was his usual style), the most elegant shoes on his small feet, faultless exquisiteness characterising the whole of his attire, and his small eyes sparkling with esprit and sometimes with malice.

Of all who came in contact with Chopin, however, no one made so much of his opportunities as Lenz: some of his observations on the pianist have already been quoted, those on the man and his surroundings deserve likewise attention. [FOOTNOTE: W. von Lenz: "Die Grossen Pianoforte-Virtuosen unserer Zeit."] Lenz came to Paris in the summer or autumn of the year 1842; and as he wished to study Chopin's mazurkas with the master himself, he awaited impatiently his return from Nohant. At last, late in October, Lenz heard from Liszt that Chopin had arrived in town; but Liszt told him also that it was by no means an easy thing to get lessons from Chopin, that indeed many had journeyed to Paris for the purpose and failed even to get sight of him. To guard Lenz against such a mishap, Liszt gave him a card with the words "Laissez passer, Franz Liszt" on it, and advised him to call on Chopin at two o'clock. The enthusiastic amateur was not slow in availing himself of his artist friend's card and advice. But on reaching his destination he was met in the anteroom by a male servant—"an article of luxury in Paris, a rarissima avis in the house of an artist," observes Lenz— who informed him that Chopin was not in town. The visitor, however, was not to be put off in this way, and insisted that the card should be taken in to Chopin. Fortune favours the brave. A moment after the servant had left the room the great artist made his appearance holding the card in his hand: "a young man of middle height, slim, thin, with a careworn, speaking face and the finest Parisian tournure." Lenz does not hesitate to declare that he hardly ever met a person so naturally elegant and winning. But here is what took place at this interview.

Chopin did not press me to sit down [says Lenz], I stood as before a reigning sovereign. "What do you wish? a pupil of Liszt's, an artist?" "A friend of Liszt's. I wish to have the happiness of making, under your guidance, acquaintance with your mazurkas, which I regard as a literature. Some of them I have already studied with Liszt." I felt I had been imprudent, but it was too late. "Indeed!" replied Chopin, with a drawl, but in the politest tone, "what do you want me for then? Please play to me what you have played with Liszt, I have still a few minutes at my disposal"—he drew from his fob an elegant, small watch—"I was on the point of going out, I had told my servant to admit nobody, pardon me!"

Lenz sat down at the piano, tried the gue of it—an expression at which Chopin, who was leaning languidly on the piano and looking with his intelligent eyes straight in his visitor's face, smiled—and then struck up the Mazurka in B flat major. When he came to a passage in which Liszt had taught him to introduce a volata through two octaves, Chopin whispered blandly:—

"This TRAIT is not your own; am I right? HE has shown it you—
he must meddle with everything; well! he may do it, he plays
before THOUSANDS, I rarely before ONE. Well, this will do, I
will give you lessons, but only twice a week, I never give
more, it is difficult for me to find three-quarters of an
hour." He again looked at his watch. "What do you read then?
With what do you occupy yourself generally?" This was a
question for which I was well prepared. "George Sand and Jean
Jacques I prefer to all other writers," said I quickly. He
smiled, he was most beautiful at that moment. "Liszt has told
you this. I see, you are initiated, so much the better. Only
be punctual, with me things go by the clock, my house is a
pigeon-house (pigeonnier). I see already we shall become more
intimate, a recommendation from Liszt is worth something, you
are the first pupil whom he has recommended to me; we are
friends, we were comrades."

Lenz had, of course, too imaginative a turn of mind to leave facts in their native nakedness, but this tendency of his is too apparent to need pointing out. What betrays him is the wonderful family likeness of his portraits, a kind of vapid esprit, not distantly related to silliness, with which the limner endows his unfortunate sitters, Chopin as well as Liszt and Tausig. Indeed, the portraits compared with the originals are like Dresden china figures compared with Greek statuary. It seems to me also very improbable that so perfect a gentleman as Chopin was should subject a stranger to an examination as to his reading and general occupation. These questions have very much the appearance of having been invented by the narrator for the sake of the answers. However, notwithstanding the many unmistakable embellishments, Lenz's account was worth quoting, for after all it is not without a basis of fact and truth. The following reminiscences of the lively

Russian councillor, although not wanting in exaggerations, are less open to objections:—

I always made my appearance long before my hour and waited. One lady after another came out, one more beautiful than the other, on one occasion Mdlle. Laure Duperre, the daughter of the admiral, whom Chopin accompanied to the staircase, she was the most beautiful of all, and as straight as a palm; to her Chopin has dedicated two of his most important Nocturnes (in C minor and F sharp minor, Op. 48); she was at that time his favourite pupil. In the anteroom I often met little Filtsch, who, unfortunately, died too young, at the age of thirteen, a Hungarian and a genius. He knew how to play Chopin! Of Filtsch Liszt said in my presence at a soiree of the Comtesse d'Agoult: "When the little one begins to travel, I shall shut up my shop" (Quand le petit voyagera, je fermerai boutique). I was jealous of Filtsch, Chopin had eyes only for him.

How high an opinion the master had of this talented pupil appears from his assertion that the boy played the E minor Concerto better than he himself. Lenz mentions Filtsch and his playing of the E minor Concerto only in passing in "Die grossen Pianoforte-Virtuosen unserer Zeit," but devotes to them more of his leisure in an article which appeared in the Berliner Musikzeitung (Vol. XXVI.), the amusing gossip of which deserves notice here on account of the light thrown by some of its details on Chopin's ways and the company he received in his salon. On one occasion when Filtsch had given his master particular satisfaction by a tasteful rendering of the second solo of the first movement of the E minor Concerto, Chopin said: "You have played this well, my boy (mon garcon), I must try it myself." Lenz relates that what now followed was indescribable: the little one (der Kleine) burst into tears, and Chopin, who indeed had been telling them the story of his artist life, said, as if speaking to himself, "I have loved it! I have already once played it!" Then, turning to Filtsch, he spoke these words: "Yours is a beautiful artist nature (une belle nature d'artiste), you will become a great artist." Whilst the youthful pianist was studying the Concerto with Chopin, he was never allowed to play more than one solo at a time, the work affecting too much the feelings of the composer, who, moreover, thought that the whole was contained in every one of the solos; and when he at last got leave to perform the whole, an event for which he prepared himself by fasting and prayers of the Roman Catholic Church, and by such reading as was pointed out by his master, practising being forbidden for the time,

Chopin said to him: "As you have now mastered the movement so well, we will bring it to a hearing."

The reader must understand that I do not vouch for the strict correctness of Lenz's somewhat melodramatic narrative; and having given this warning I shall, to keep myself free from all responsibility, simply translate the rest of what is yet to be told:—

Chopin invited a party of ladies, George Sand was one of them, and was as quiet as a mouse; moreover, she knew nothing of music. The favoured pupils from the highest aristocracy appeared with modest demeanour and full of the most profound devotion, they glided silently, like gold-fishes in a vase, one after another into the salon, and sat down as far as possible from the piano, as Chopin liked people to do. Nobody spoke, Chopin only nodded, and shook hands with one here and there, not with all of them. The square pianoforte, which stood in his cabinet, he had placed beside the Pleyel concert grand in the salon, not without the most painful embarras to him. The most insignificant trifle affected him; he was a noli me tangere. He had said once, or rather had thought aloud: "If I saw a crack more in the ceiling, I should not be able to bring out a note." Chopin poured the whole dreamy, vaporous instrumentation of the work into his incomparable accompaniment. He played without book. I have never heard anything that could be compared to the first tutti, which he played alone on the piano. The little one did wonders. The whole was an impression for all the rest of one's life. After Chopin had briefly dismissed the ladies (he loved praise neither for himself nor for others, and only George Sand was permitted to embrace Filtsch), he said to the latter, his brother, who always accompanied the little one, and me: "We have yet to take a walk." It was a command which we received with the most respectful bow.

The destination of this walk was Schlesinger's music-shop, where Chopin presented his promising young pupil with the score of Beethoven's "Fidelio":—

"I am in your debt, you have given me much pleasure to-day. I wrote the Concerto in happier days. Receive, my dear little friend, this great master-work; read therein as long as you live, and remember me also sometimes." The little one was as if stunned, and kissed Chopin's hand. We were all deeply moved, Chopin himself was so. He disappeared immediately through the glass door on a level with the Rue Richelieu, into which it leads.

A scene of a very different nature which occurred some years later was described to me by Madame Dubois. This lady, then still Mdlle. O'Meara and a pupil of Chopin's, had in 1847 played, accompanied on a second piano by her master, the latter's Concerto in E minor at a party of Madame de Courbonne's. Madame Girardin, who was among the guests, afterwards wrote most charmingly and eulogistically about the young girl's beauty and talent in one of her Lettres parisiennes, which appeared in La Presse and were subsequently published in a collected form under the title of "Le Vicomte de Launay." Made curious by Madame Girardin's account, and probably also by remarks of Chopin and others, George Sand wished to see the heroine of that much-talked-of letter. Thus it came to pass that one day when Miss O'Meara was having her lesson, George Sand crossed the Square d'Orleans and paid Chopin a visit in his apartments. The master received her with all the grace and amiability he was capable of. Noticing that her pardessus was bespattered with mud, he seemed to be much vexed, and the exquisitely-elegant gentleman (l'homme de toutes les elegances) began to rub off with his small, white hands the stains which on any other person would have caused him disgust. And Mdlle. O'Meara, child as she still was, watched what was going on from the corner of her eye and thought: "Comme il aime cette femme!" [FOOTNOTE: Madame A. Audley gives an altogether incorrect account of this incident in her FREDERIC CHOPIN. Madame Girardin was not one of the actors, and Mdlle. O'Meara did not think the thoughts attributed to her.]

Whenever Chopin's connection with George Sand is mentioned, one hears a great deal of the misery and nothing or little of the happiness which accrued to him out of it. The years of tenderness and devotion are slurred over and her infidelities, growing indifference, and final desertion are dwelt upon with undue emphasis. Whatever those of Chopin's friends who were not also George Sand's friends may say, we may be sure that his joys outweighed his sorrows. Her resoluteness must have been an invaluable support to so vacillating a character as Chopin's was; and, although their natures were in many respects discordant, the poetic element of hers cannot but have found sympathetic chords in his. Every character has many aspects, but the world is little disposed to see more than one side of George Sand's—

namely, that which is most conspicuous by its defiance of law and custom, and finds expression in loud declamation and denunciation. To observe her in one of her more lovable attitudes of mind, we will transport ourselves from Chopin's to her salon.

Louis Enault relates how one evening George Sand, who sometimes thought aloud when with Chopin—this being her way of chatting—spoke of the peacefulness of the country and unfolded a picture of the rural harmonies that had all the charming and negligent grace of a village idyl, bringing, in fact, her beloved Berry to the fireside of the room in the Square d'Orleans.

"How well you have spoken!" said Chopin naively.

"You think so?" she replied. "Well, then, set me to music!"
Hereupon Chopin improvised a veritable pastoral symphony, and
George Sand placing herself beside him and laying her hand
gently on his shoulder said: "Go on, velvet fingers [courage,
doigts de velour]!"

Here is another anecdote of quiet home-life. George Sand had a little dog which was in the habit of turning round and round in the endeavour to catch its tail. One evening when it was thus engaged, she said to Chopin: "If I had your talent, I would compose a pianoforte piece for this dog." Chopin at once sat down at the piano, and improvised the charming Waltz in D flat (Op. 64), which hence has obtained the name of Valse du petit chien. This story is well known among the pupils and friends of the master, but not always told in exactly the same way. According to another version, Chopin improvised the waltz when the little dog was playing with a ball of wool. This variation, however, does not affect the pith of the story.

The following two extracts tell us more about the intimate home-life at Nohant and in the Court d'Orleans than anything we have as yet met with.

Madame Sand to her son; October 17, 1843:—

Tell me if Chopin is ill; his letters are short and sad. Take
care of him if he is ailing. Take a little my place. He would
take my place with so much zeal if you were ill.
Madame Sand to her son; November 16, 1843:—

If you care for the letter which I have written you about her
[Solange], ask Chopin for it. It was for both of you, and it

has not given him much pleasure. He has taken it amiss, and
yet I did not wish to annoy him, God forbid! We shall all see
each other soon again, and hearty embraces [de bonnes
bigeades] [FOOTNOTE: Biger is in the Berry dialect "to kiss."]
all round shall efface all my sermons.

In another of George Sand's letters to her son—it is dated November 28,
1843—we read about Chopin's already often-mentioned valet. Speaking of
the foundation of a provincial journal, "L'Eclaireur de l'Indre," by herself
and a number of her friends, and of their being on the look-out for an editor
who would be content with the modest salary of 2,000 francs, she says:—

This is hardly more than the wages of Chopin's domestic, and
to imagine that for this it is possible to find a man of
talent! First measure of the Committee of Public Safety: we
shall outlaw Chopin if he allows himself to have lackeys
salaried like publicists.

Chopin treated George Sand with the greatest respect and devotion;
he was always aux petits soins with her. It is characteristic of the man and
exemplifies strikingly the delicacy of his taste and feeling that his demeanour
in her house showed in no way the intimate relation in which he stood to
the mistress of it: he seemed to be a guest like any other occasional visitor.
Lenz wishes to make us believe that George Sand's treatment of Chopin
was unworthy of the great artist, but his statements are emphatically
contradicted by Gutmann, who says that her behaviour towards him was
always respectful. If the lively Russian councillor in the passages I am
going to translate describes correctly what he heard and saw, he must have
witnessed an exceptional occurrence; it is, however, more likely that the bad
reception he received from the lady prejudiced him against her.

Lenz relates that one day Chopin took him to the salon of Madame
Marliani, where there was in the evening always a gathering of friends.

George Sand [thus runs his account of his first meeting with
the great novelist] did not say a word when Chopin introduced
me. This was rude. Just for that reason I seated myself beside
her. Chopin fluttered about like a little frightened bird in
its cage, he saw something was going to happen. What had he
not always feared on this terrain? At the first pause in the
conversation, which was led by Madame Sand's friend, Madame
Viardot, the great singer whose acquaintance I was later to
make in St. Petersburg, Chopin put his arm through mine and

led me to the piano. Reader! if you play the piano you will imagine how I felt! It was an upright or cottage piano [Steh- oder Stutzflugel] of Pleyel's, which people in Paris regard as a pianoforte. I played the Invitation in a fragmentary fashion, Chopin gave me his hand in the most friendly manner, George Sand did not say a word. I seated myself once more beside her. I had obviously a purpose. Chopin looked anxiously at us across the table, on which was burning the inevitable carcel.

"Are you not coming sometime to St. Petersburg," said I to George Sand in the most polite tone, "where you are so much read, so highly admired?"

"I shall never lower myself by visiting a country of slaves!" answered George Sand shortly.

This was indecorous [unanstandig] after she had been uncivil.

"After all, you are right NOT to come," I replied in the same tone; "you might find the door closed! I was thinking of the Emperor Nicholas."

George Sand looked at me in astonishment, I plunged boldly into her large, beautiful, brown, cow-like eyes. Chopin did not seem displeased, I knew the movements of his head.

Instead of giving any answer George Sand rose in a theatrical fashion, and strode in the most manly way through the salon to the blazing fire. I followed her closely, and seated myself for the third time beside her, ready for another attack.

She would be obliged at last to say something.

George Sand drew an enormously thick Trabucco cigar out of her apron pocket, and called out "Frederic! un fidibus!"

This offended me for him, that perfect gentleman, my master; I understood Liszt's words: "Pauvre Frederic!" in all their significance.

Chopin immediately came up with a fidibus.

As she was sending forth the first terrible cloud of smoke, George Sand honoured me with a word:

"In St. Petersburg," she began, "I could not even smoke a cigar in a drawing-room?"

"In NO drawing-room have I ever seen anyone smoke a cigar, Madame," I answered, not without emphasis, with a bow!

George Sand fixed her eyes sharply upon me—the thrust had gone home! I looked calmly around me at the good pictures in the salon, each of which was lighted up by a separate lamp. Chopin had probably heard nothing; he had returned to the hostess at the table.

Pauvre Frederic! How sorry I was for him, the great artist! The next day the Suisse [hall-porter] in the hotel, Mr. Armand, said to me: "A gentleman and a lady have been here, I said you were not at home, you had not said you would receive visitors; the gentleman left his name, he had no card with him." I read: Chopin et Madame Sand. After this I quarrelled for two months with Mr. Armand.

George Sand was probably out of humour on the evening in question; that it was not her usual manner of receiving visitors may be gathered from what Chopin said soon after to Lenz when the latter came to him for a lesson. "George Sand," he said, "called with me on you. What a pity you were not at home! I regretted it very much. George Sand thought she had been uncivil to you. You would have seen how amiable she can be. You have pleased her."

Alexander Chodzko, the learned professor of Slavonic literature at the College de France, told me that he was half-a-dozen times at George Sand's house. Her apartments were furnished in a style in favour with young men. First you came into a vestibule where hats, coats, and sticks were left, then into a large salon with a billiard-table. On the mantel-piece were to be found the materials requisite for smoking. George Sand set her guests an example by lighting a cigar. M. Chodzko met there among others the historian and statesman Guizot, the litterateur Francois, and Madame Marliani. If Chopin was not present, George Sand would often ask the servant what he was doing, whether he was working or sleeping, whether he was in good or bad humour. And when he came in all eyes were directed towards him. If he happened to be in good humour George Sand would lead him to the piano, which stood in one of the two smaller apartments adjoining the salon. These smaller apartments were provided with couches for those who wished to talk. Chopin began generally to prelude apathetically and only gradually grew warm, but then his playing was really grand. If, however, he was not in a playing mood, he was often asked to give some of his wonderful mimetic imitations. On such occasions Chopin retired to one of the side-rooms, and when he returned he was irrecognisable. Professor Chodzko remembers seeing him as Frederick the Great.

Chopin's talent for mimicry, which even such distinguished actors as Bocage and Madame Dorval regarded with admiration, is alluded to by Balzac in his novel "Un Homme d'affaires," where he says of one of the characters that "he is endowed with the same talent for imitating people which Chopin, the pianist, possesses in so high a degree; he represents a personage instantly and with astounding truth." Liszt remarks that Chopin displayed in pantomime an inexhaustible verve drolatique, and often amused himself with reproducing in comical improvisations the musical formulas and peculiar ways of certain virtuosos, whose faces and gestures he at the same time imitated in the most striking manner. These statements are corroborated by the accounts of innumerable eye and ear-witnesses of such performances. One of the most illustrative of these accounts is the following very amusing anecdote. When the Polish musician Nowakowski [FOOTNOTE: He visited Paris in 1838, 1841, and 1846, partly for the purpose of making arrangements for the publication of his compositions, among which are Etudes dedicated to Chopin.] visited Paris, he begged his countryman to bring him in contact with Kalkbrenner, Liszt, and Pixis. Chopin, replying that he need not put himself to the trouble of going in search of these artists if he wished to make their acquaintance, forthwith sat down at the piano and assumed the attitude, imitated the style of playing, and mimicked the mien and gestures, first of Liszt and then of Pixis. Next evening Chopin and Nowakowski went together to the theatre. The former having left the box during one of the intervals, the latter looked round after awhile and saw Pixis sitting beside him. Nowakowski, thinking Chopin was at his favourite game, clapped Pixis familiarly on the shoulder and said: "Leave off, don't imitate now!" The surprise of Pixis and the subsequent confusion of Nowakowski may be easily imagined. When Chopin, who at this moment returned, had been made to understand what had taken place, he laughed heartily, and with the grace peculiar to him knew how to make his friend's and his own excuses. One thing in connection with Chopin's mimicry has to be particularly noted—it is very characteristic of the man. Chopin, we learn from Liszt, while subjecting his features to all kinds of metamorphoses and imitating even the ugly and grotesque, never lost his native grace, "la grimace ne parvenait meme pas a l'enlaidir."

We shall see presently what George Sand has to say about her lover's imitative talent; first, however, we will make ourselves acquainted with the friends with whom she especially associated. Besides Pierre Leroux, Balzac, Pauline Viardot-Garcia, and others who have already been mentioned in the foregoing chapters, she numbered among her most intimate friends the Republican politician and historian Louis Blanc, the Republican litterateur Godefroy Cavaignac, the historian Henri Martin, and the litterateur Louis Viardot, the husband of Pauline Garcia.

[FOOTNOTE: This name reminds me of a passage in Louis Blanc's "Histoire de la Revolution de 1840" (p. 210 of Fifth Edition. Paris, 1880). "A short time before his [Godefroy Cavaignac's] end, he was seized by an extraordinary desire to hear music once more. I knew Chopin. I offered to go to him, and to bring him with me, if the doctor did not oppose it. The entreaties thereupon took the character of a supplication. With the consent, or rather at the urgent prayer, of Madame Cavaignac, I betook myself to Chopin. Madame George Sand was there. She expressed in a touching manner the lively interest with which the invalid inspired her; and Chopin placed himself at my service with much readiness and grace. I conducted him then into the chamber of the dying man, where there was a bad piano. The great artist begins...Suddenly he is interrupted by sobs. Godefroy, in a transport of sensibility which gave him a moment's physical strength, had quite unexpectedly raised himself in his bed of suffering, his face bathed in tears. Chopin stopped, much disturbed; Madame Cavaignac, leaning towards her son, anxiously interrogated him with her eyes. He made an effort to become self-possessed; he attempted to smile, and with a feeble voice said, 'Do not be uneasy, mamma, it is nothing; real childishness...Ah! how beautiful music is, understood thus!' His thought was—we had no difficulty in divining it—that he would no longer hear anything like it in this world, but he refrained from saying so."]

Friends not less esteemed by her than these, but with whom she was less intimate, were the Polish poet Mickiewicz, the famous bass singer Lablache, the excellent pianist and composer Alkan aine, the Italian composer and singing-master Soliva (whom we met already in Warsaw), the philosopher and poet Edgar Quinet, General Guglielmo Pepe (commander-in-chief of the Neapolitan insurrectionary army in 1820-21), and likewise the actor Bocage, the litterateur Ferdinand Francois, the German musician Dessauer, the Spanish politician Mendizabal, the dramatist and journalist Etienne Arago, [FOOTNOTE: The name of Etienne Arago is mentioned in "Ma Vie," but it is that of Emmanuel Arago which occurs frequently in the "Corrcspcndance."] and a number of literary and other personages of less note, of whom I shall mention only Agricol Perdiguier and Gilland, the noble artisan and the ecrivain proletaire, as George Sand calls them.

Although some of George Sand's friends were also Chopin's, there can be no doubt that the society which gathered around her was on the whole not congenial to him. Some remarks which Liszt makes with regard to George Sand's salon at Nohant are even more applicable to her salon in Paris.

An author's relations with the representatives of publicity and his dramatic executants, actors and actresses, and with those whom he treats with marked attention on account of their merits or because they please him; the crossing of incidents, the clash and rebound of the infatuations and disagreements which result therefrom; were naturally hateful to him [to Chopin]. For a long time he endeavoured to escape from them by shutting his eyes, by making up his mind not to see anything. There happened, however, such things, such catastrophes [denouements], as, by shocking too much his delicacy, offending too much his habits of the moral and social comme-il-faut, ended in rendering his presence at Nohant impossible, although he seemed at first to have felt more content [plus de repif] there than elsewhere.

These are, of course, only mere surmises, but Liszt, although often wrong as to incidents, is, thanks to his penetrative genius, generally right as to essences. Indeed, if George Sand's surroundings and Chopin's character and tastes are kept in view nothing seems to be more probable than that his over-delicate susceptibilities may have occasionally been shocked by unrestrained vivacity, loud laughter, and perhaps even coarse words; that his uncompromising idealism may have been disturbed by the discordance of literary squabbles, intrigues, and business transactions; that his peaceable, non-speculative, and non-argumentative disposition may have been vexed and wearied by discussions of political, social, religious, literary, and artistic problems. Unless his own art was the subject, Chopin did not take part in discussions. And Liszt tells us that Chopin not only, like most artists, lacked a generalising mind [esprit generalisateur], but showed hardly any inclination for aesthetics, of which he had not even heard much. We may be sure that to Chopin to whom discussions of any kind were distasteful, those of a circle in which, as in that of George Sand, democratic and socialistic, theistic and atheistic views prevailed, were particularly so. For, notwithstanding his bourgeois birth, his sympathies were with the aristocracy; and notwithstanding his neglect of ritual observances, his attachment to the Church of Rome remained unbroken. Chopin does not seem to have concealed his dislike to George Sand's circle; if he did not give audible expression to it, he made it sufficiently manifest by seeking other company. That she was aware of the fact and displeased with it, is evident from what she says of her lover's social habits in Ma Vie. The following excerpt from that work is an important biographical contribution; it is written not without bitterness, but with hardly any exaggeration:—

He was a man of the world par excellence, not of the too formal and too numerous world, but of the intimate world, of the salons of twenty persons, of the hour when the crowd goes away and the habitues crowd round the artist to wrest from him by amiable importunity his purest inspiration. It was then only that he exhibited all his genius and all his talent. It was then also that after having plunged his audience into a profound recueillement or into a painful sadness, for his music sometimes discouraged one's soul terribly, especially when he improvised, he would suddenly, as if to take away the impression and remembrance of his sorrow from others and from himself, turn stealthily to a glass, arrange his hair and his cravat, and show himself suddenly transformed into a phlegmatic Englishman, into an impertinent old man, into a sentimental and ridiculous Englishwoman, into a sordid Jew. The types were always sad, however comical they might be, but perfectly conceived and so delicately rendered that one could not grow weary of admiring them.

All these sublime, charming, or bizarre things that he knew how to evolve out of himself made him the soul of select society, and there was literally a contest for his company, his noble character, his disinterestedness, his self-respect, his proper pride, enemy of every vanity of bad taste and of every insolent reclame, the security of intercourse with him, and the exquisite delicacy of his manners, making him a friend equally serious and agreeable.

To tear Chopin away from so many gdteries, to associate him with a simple, uniform, and constantly studious life, him who had been brought up on the knees of princesses, was to deprive him of that which made him live, of a factitious life, it is true, for, like a painted woman, he laid aside in the evening, in returning to his home, his verve and his energy, to give the night to fever and sleeplessness; but of a life which would have been shorter and more animated than that of the retirement and of the intimacy restricted to the uniform circle of a single family. In Paris he visited several salons every day, or he chose at least every evening a different one as a milieu. He had thus by turns twenty or thirty salons to intoxicate or to charm with his presence.

CHAPTER XXVII

CHOPIN IN HIS SOCIAL RELATIONS: HIS PREDILECTION FOR
THE FASHIONABLE SALON SOCIETY (ACCOUNTS BY MADAME
GIRARDIN AND BERLIOZ); HIS NEGLECT OF THE SOCIETY OF ARTISTS
(ARY SCHEFFER, MARMONTEL, HELLER, SCHULHOFF, THE PARIS
CORRESPONDENT OF THE MUSICAL WORLD); APHORISMS BY LISZT
ON CHOPIN IN HIS SOCIAL ASPECT.—CHOPIN'S FRIENDSHIPS.—
GEORGE SAND, LISZT, LENZ, HELLER, MARMONTEL, AND HILLER
ON HIS CHARACTER (IRRITABILITY, FITS OF ANGER—SCENE WITH
MEYERBEER—GAIETY AND RAILLERY, LOVE OF SOCIETY, AND
LITTLE TASTE FOR READING, PREDILECTION FOR THINGS POLISH).—
HIS POLISH, GERMAN, ENGLISH, AND RUSSIAN FRIENDS.—THE
PARTY MADE FAMOUS BY LISZT'S ACCOUNT.—HIS INTERCOURSE
WITH MUSICIANS (OSBORNE, BERLIOZ, BAILLOT, CHERUBINI,
KALKBRENNER, FONTANA, SOWINSKI, WOLFF, MEYERBEER,
ALKAN, ETC.).—HIS FRIENDSHIP WITH LISZT.—HIS DISLIKE TO
LETTER-WRITING.

George Sand, although one of the cleverest of the literary portrayers
who have tried their hand at Chopin, cannot be regarded as one of the most
impartial; but it must be admitted that in describing her deserted lover as
un homme du monde par excellence, non pas du monde trop officiel, trop
nombreux, she says what is confirmed by all who have known him, by his
friends, foes, and those that are neither. Aristocratic society, with which
he was acquainted from his earliest childhood, had always a great charm
for him. When at the beginning of 1833, a little more than two years after
his arrival in Paris, he informed his friend Dziewanowski that he moved
in the highest society—among ambassadors, princes, and ministers—it is
impossible not to see that the fact gives him much satisfaction. Without
going so far as to say with a great contemporary of Chopin, Stephen Heller,
that the higher you go in society the greater is the ignorance you find, I think
that little if any good for either heart or mind can come from intercourse
with that section of the people which proudly styles itself "society" (le
monde). Many individuals that belong to it possess, no doubt, true nobility,
wisdom, and learning, nay, even the majority may possess one or the other
or all of them in some degree, but these qualities are so out of keeping
with the prevailing frivolity that few have the moral courage to show their

better nature. If Chopin imagined that he was fully understood as an artist by society, he was sadly mistaken. Liszt and Heller certainly held that he was not fully understood, and they did not merely surmise or speak from hearsay, for neither of them was a stranger in that quarter, although the latter avoided it as much as possible. What society could and did appreciate in Chopin was his virtuosity, his elegance, and his delicacy. It is not my intention to attempt an enumeration of Chopin's aristocratic friends and acquaintances, but in the dedications of his works the curious will find the most important of them. There, then, we read the names of the Princess Czartoryska, Countess Plater, Countess Potocka, Princesse de Beauvau, Countess Appony, Countess Esterhazy, Comte and Comtesse de Perthuis, Baroness Bronicka, Princess Czernicheff, Princess Souzzo, Countess Mostowska, Countess Czosnowska, Comtesse de Flahault, Baroness von Billing, Baron and Baroness von Stockhausen, Countess von Lobau, Mdlle. de Noailles, &c. And in addition to these we have representatives of the aristocracy of wealth, Madame C. de Rothschild foremost amongst them. Whether the banker Leo with whom and his family Chopin was on very friendly terms may be mentioned in this connection, I do not know. But we must remember that round many of the above names cluster large families. The names of the sisters Countess Potocka and Princesse de Beauvau call up at once that of their mother, Countess Komar. Many of these here enumerated are repeatedly mentioned in the course of this book, some will receive particular attention in the next chapter. Now we will try to get a glimpse of Chopin in society.

Madame de Girardin, after having described in one of her "Lettres parisiennes" (March 7, 1847) [FOOTNOTE: The full title of the work is: "Le Vicomte de Launay—Lettres parisiennes par Mdme. Emile de Girardin." (Paris: Michel Levy freres.)] with what success Mdlle. O'Meara accompanied by her master played his E minor Concerto at a soiree of Madame de Courbonne, proceeds thus:—

Mdlle. Meara is a pupil of Chopin's. He was there, he was present at the triumph of his pupil, the anxious audience asked itself: "Shall we hear him?"

The fact is that it was for passionate admirers the torment of Tantalus to see Chopin going about a whole evening in a salon and not to hear him. The mistress of the house took pity on us; she was indiscreet, and Chopin played, sang his most delicious songs; we set to these joyous or sad airs the words which came into our heads; we followed with our thoughts his melodious caprices. There were some twenty of us, sincere amateurs, true believers, and not a note was lost, not an intention was misunderstood; it was not a concert, it was intimate, serious music such as we love; he was not a virtuoso who comes and plays the air agreed upon and then disappears; he was a beautiful talent, monopolised, worried, tormented, without consideration and scruples, whom one dared ask for the most beloved airs, and who full of grace and charity repeated to you the favourite phrase, in order that you might carry it away correct and pure in your memory, and for a long time yet feast on it in remembrance. Madame so-and-so said: "Please, play this pretty nocturne dedicated to Mdlle. Stirling." —The nocturne which I called the dangerous one.—He smiled, and played the fatal nocturne. "I," said another lady, "should like to hear once played by you this mazurka, so sad and so charming." He smiled again, and played the delicious mazurka. The most profoundly artful among the ladies sought expedients to attain their end: "I am practising the grand sonata which commences with this beautiful funeral march," and "I should like to know the movement in which the finale ought to be played." He smiled a little at the stratagem, and played the finale, of the grand sonata, one of the most magnificent pieces which he has composed.

Although Madame Girardin's language and opinions are fair specimens of those prevalent in the beatified regions in which Chopin delighted to move, we will not follow her rhapsodic eulogy of his playing. That she cannot be ranked with the connoisseurs is evident from her statement that the sonata BEGINS with the funeral march, and that the FINALE is one of the most magnificent creations of the composer. Notwithstanding Madame Girardin's subsequent remark that Chopin's playing at Madame de Courbonne's was quite an exception, her letter may mislead the reader into the belief that the great pianist was easily induced to sit down at the piano. A more correct idea may be formed of the real state of matters from a passage in an article by Berlioz (Feuilleton du Journal des Debats, October 27, 1849) in which the supremacy of style over matter is a little less absolute than in the lady's elegant chit-chat: —

A small circle of select auditors, whose real desire to hear him was beyond doubt, could alone determine him to approach the piano. What emotions he would then call forth! In what ardent and melancholy reveries he loved to pour out his soul! It was usually towards midnight that he gave himself up with the greatest ABANDON, when the big butterflies of the salon had left, when the political questions of the day had been discussed at length, when all the scandal-mongers were at the end of their anecdotes, when all the snares were laid, all the perfidies consummated, when one was thoroughly tired of prose, then, obedient to the mute petition of some beautiful, intelligent eyes, he became a poet, and sang the Ossianic loves of the heroes of his dreams, their chivalrous joys, and the sorrows of the absent fatherland, his dear Poland always ready to conquer and always defeated. But without these conditions—the exacting of which for his playing all artists must thank him for—it was useless to solicit him. The curiosity excited by his fame seemed even to irritate him, and he shunned as far as possible the nonsympathetic world when chance had led him into it. I remember a cutting saying which he let fly one evening at the master of a house where he had dined. Scarcely had the company taken coffee when the host, approaching Chopin, told him that his fellow-guests who had never heard him hoped that he would be so good as to sit down at the piano and play them some little thing [quelque petite chose]. Chopin excused himself from the very first in a way which left not the slightest doubt as to his inclination. But when the other insisted, in an almost offensive manner, like a man who knows the worth and the object of the dinner which he has given, the artist cut the conversation short by saying with a weak and broken voice and a fit of coughing: "Ah! sir...I have... eaten so little!"

Chopin's predilection for the fashionable salon society led him to neglect the society of artists. That he carried the odi profanum vulgus, et arceo too far cannot for a moment be doubted. For many of those who sought to have intercourse with him were men of no less nobility of sentiment and striving than himself. Chopin offended even Ary Scheffer, the great painter, who admired him and loved him, by promising to spend an evening with him and again and again disappointing him. Musicians, with a few exceptions. Chopin seems always to have been careful to keep at a distance, at least after the first years of his arrival in Paris. This is regrettable especially in the case of the young men who looked up to him with veneration and enthusiasm, and whose feelings were cruelly hurt by the polite but unsympathetic reception he gave them:—

We have had always a profound admiration for Chopin's talent [writes M. Marmontel], and, let us add, a lively sympathy for his person. No artist, the intimate disciples not excepted, has more studied his compositions, and more caused them to be played, and yet our relations with this great musician have only been rare and transient. Chopin was surrounded, fawned upon, closely watched by a small cenacle of enthusiastic friends, who guarded him against importunate visitors and admirers of the second order. It was difficult to get access to him; and it was necessary, as he said himself to that other great artist whose name is Stephen Heller, to try several times before one succeeded in meeting him. These trials ["essais"] being no more to my taste than to Heller's, I could not belong to that little congregation of faithful ones whose cult verged on fanaticism.

As to Stephen Heller—who himself told me that he would have liked to be more with Chopin, but was afraid of being regarded as intrusive—Mr. Heller thinks that Chopin had an antipathy to him, which considering the amiable and truly gentlemanly character of this artist seems rather strange.

If the details of Karasowski's account of Chopin's and Schulhoff's first meeting are correct, the Polish artist was in his aloofness sometimes even deficient in that common civility which good-breeding and consideration for the feelings of others demand. Premising that Fetis in telling the story is less circumstantial and lays the scene of the incident in the pianoforte-saloon of Pleyel, I shall quote Karasowski's version, as he may have had direct information from Schulhoff, who since 1855 has lived much of his time at Dresden, where Karasowski also resides:—

Schulhoff came when quite a young man and as yet completely unknown to Paris. There he learned that Chopin, who was then already very ailing and difficult of access, was coming to the pianoforte-manufactory of Mercier to inspect one of the newly-invented transposing pianofortes. It was in the year 1844. Schulhoff seized the opportunity to become personally acquainted with the master, and made his appearance among the small party which awaited Chopin. The latter came with an old friend, a Russian Capellmeister [Soliva?]. Taking advantage of a propitious moment, Schulhoff got himself introduced by one of the ladies present. On the latter begging Chopin to allow Schulhoff to play him something, the renowned master, who was much bothered by dilettante tormentors, signified, somewhat displeased, his consent by a slight nod of the head. Schulhoff seated himself at the pianoforte, while Chopin, with his back turned to him, was leaning against it. But already during the short prelude he turned his head attentively towards Schulhoff who now performed an Allegro brillant en forme de Senate (Op. I), which he had lately composed. With growing interest Chopin came nearer and nearer the keyboard and listened to the fine, poetic playing of the young Bohemian; his pale features grew animated, and by mien and gesture he showed to all who were present his lively approbation. When Schulhoff had finished, Chopin held out his hand to him with the words: "Vous etes un vrai artiste, un collegue!" Some days after Schulhoff paid the revered master a visit, and asked him to accept the dedication of the composition he had played to him. Chopin thanked him in a heart-winning manner, and said in the presence of several ladies: "Je suis tres flatte de l'honneur que vous me faites."

The behaviour of Chopin during the latter part of this transaction made, no doubt, amends for that of the earlier. But the ungracious manner in which he granted the young musician permission to play to him, and especially his turning his back to Schulhoff when the latter began to play, are not excused by the fact that he was often bothered by dilettante tormentors.

The Paris correspondent of the Musical World, writing immediately after the death of the composer, describes the feeling which existed among the musicians in the French capital, and also suggests an explanation and excuse. In the number of the paper bearing date November 10, 1849, we read as follows:—

Owing to his retired way of living and his habitual reserve, Chopin had few friends in the profession; and, indeed, spoiled from his original nature by the caprice of society, he was too apt to treat his brother-artists with a supercilious hauteur, which many, his equals, and a few, his superiors, were wont to stigmatise as insulting. But from want of sympathy with the man, they overlooked the fact that a pulmonary complaint, which for years had been gradually wasting him to a shadow, rendered him little fit for the enjoyments of society and the relaxations of artistic conviviality. In short, Chopin, in self-defence, was compelled to live in comparative seclusion, but we wholly disbelieve that this isolation had its source in unkindness or egotism. We are the more inclined to this opinion by the fact that the intimate friends whom he possessed in the profession (and some of them were pianists) were as devotedly attached to him as the most romantic of his aristocratic worshippers.

The reasoning does not seem to me quite conclusive. Would it not have been possible to live in retirement without drawing upon himself the accusation of supercilious hauteur? Moreover, as Chopin was strong enough to frequent fashionable salons, he cannot have been altogether unable to hold intercourse with his brother-artists. And, lastly, who are the pianist friends that were as devotedly attached to him as the most romantic of his aristocratic worshippers? The fact that Chopin became subsequently less social and more reticent than he had been in his early Paris days, confined himself to a very limited number of friends and families, and had relations of an intimate nature with only a very few musicians, cannot, therefore, be attributable to ill-health alone, although that too had, no doubt, something to do with it, directly or indirectly. In short, the allegation that Chopin was "spoiled by the caprice of society," as the above-quoted correspondent puts it, is not only probable, but even very likely. Fastidious by nature and education, he became more so, partly in consequence of his growing physical weakness, and still more through the influence of the society with which, in the exercise of his profession and otherwise, he was in constant contact. His pupils and many of his other admirers, mostly of the female sex and the aristocratic class, accustomed him to adulation and adoration to such an extent as to make these to be regarded by him as necessaries of life. Some excerpts from Liszt's book, which I shall quote here in the form of aphorisms, will help to bring Chopin, in his social aspect, clearly before the reader's eyes:—

As he did not confound his time, thought, and ways with those of anyone, the society of women was often more convenient to him in that it involved fewer subsequent relations.

He carried into society the uniformity of temper of people whom no annoyance troubles because they expect no interest.

His conversation dwelt little on stirring subjects. He glided over them; as he was not at all lavish of his time, the talk was easily absorbed by the details of the day.

He loved the unimportant talk [les causeries sans portee] of people whom he esteemed; he delighted in the childish pleasures of young people. He passed readily whole evenings in playing blind-man's-buff with young girls, in telling them amusing or funny little stories, in making them laugh the mad laughter of youth, which it gives even more pleasure to hear than the singing of the warbler. [FOOTNOTE: This, I think, must refer to the earlier years of Chopin's residence in Paris.]

In his relations and conversations he seemed to take an interest in what preoccupied the others; he took care not to draw them out of the circle of their personality inorder to lead them into his. If he gave up little of his time, he, to make up for it, reserved to himself nothing of that which he granted.

The presence of Chopin was, therefore, always heartily welcome [fetee]. Not hoping to be understood [devine], disdaining to speak of himself [de se raconter lui-meme], he occupied himself so much with everything that was not himself that his intimate personality remained aloof, unapproached and unapproachable, under this polite and smooth [glissant] surface where it was impossible to get a footing.

He pleased too much to make people reflect.

He hardly spoke either of love or of friendship.

He was not exacting like those whose rights and just demands surpass by far what one would have to offer them. The most intimate acquaintances did not penetrate to this sacred recess where, withdrawn from all the rest of his life, dwelt the secret motive power of his soul: a recess so concealed that one scarcely suspected its existence.

Ready to give everything, he did not give himself.

The last dictum and part of the last but one were already quoted by me in an earlier chapter, but for the sake of completeness, and also because they form an excellent starting-point for the following additional remarks on Chopin's friendships, I have repeated them here. First of all, I venture to make the sweeping assertion that Chopin had among his non-Polish friends none who could be called intimate in the fullest sense of the word, none to whom he unbosomed himself as he did to Woyciechowski and Matuszynski, the friends of his youth, and Grzymala, a friend of a later time. Long cessation of personal intercourse together with the diverging development of their characters in totally unlike conditions of life cannot but have diminished the intimacy with the first named. [FOOTNOTE: Titus Woyciechowski continued to live on his estate Poturzyn, in the kingdom of Poland.] With Matuszyriski Chopin remained in close connection till this friend's death. [FOOTNOTE: Karasowski says in the first volume of his Polish biography of Chopin that Matuszynski died on April 20, 1842; and in the second that he died after Chopin's father, but in the same year—that is, in 1844.] How he opened his whole heart to Grzymala we shall see in a subsequent chapter. That his friendship with Fontana was of a less intimate character becomes at once apparent on comparing Chopin's letters to him with those he wrote to the three other Polish friends. Of all his connections with non-Poles there seems to be only one which really deserves the name of friendship, and that is his connection with Franchomme. Even here, however, he gave much less than he received. Indeed, we may say—speaking generally, and not only with a view to Franchomme—that Chopin was more loved than loving. But he knew well how to conceal his deficiencies in this respect under the blandness of his manners and the coaxing affectionateness of his language. There is something really tragic, and comic too, in the fact that every friend of Chopin's thought that he had more of the composer's love and confidence than any other friend. Thus, for instance, while Gutmann told me that Franchomme was not so intimate with Chopin that the latter would confide any secrets to him, Franchomme made to me a similar statement with regard to Gutmann. And so we find every friend of Chopin declaring that every other friend was not so much of a friend as himself. Of Chopin's procedures in friendship much may be learned from his letters; in them is to be seen something of his insinuating, cajoling ways, of his endeavours to make the person addressed believe himself a privileged favourite, and of his habit of speaking not only ungenerously and unlovingly, but even unjustly of other persons with whom he was apparently on cordial terms. In fact, it is only too clear that Chopin spoke differently before the faces and behind the backs of people. You remember how in his letters to Fontana he abuses Camille Pleyel in a manner irreconcilable with genuine love and esteem. Well, to this same Camille Pleyel, of whom he thus falls foul when he thinks himself in the slightest aggrieved, he addresses on one occasion the following note. Mark the last sentence:—

Dearest friend [Cherissime],—Here is what Onslow has written to me. I wished to call on you and tell you, but I feel very feeble and am going to lie down. I love you always more, if this is possible [je vous aime toujours plus si c'est possible].

CHOPIN.

[FOOTNOTE: To the above, unfortunately undated, note, which was published for the first time in the Menestrel of February 15, 1885, and reprinted in "Un nid d'autographes," lettres incites recueillies et annotees par Oscar Comettant (Paris: E. Dentu), is appended the following P.S.:—"Do not forget, please, friend Herbeault. Till to-morrow, then; I expect you both."

La Mara's Musikerbriefe (Leipzig: Breitkopf and Hartel) contains likewise a friendly letter of Chopin to Camille Pleyel. It runs thus:

"Dearest friend,—I received the other day your piano, and give you my best thanks. It arrived in good tune, and is exactly at concert-pitch. As yet I have not played much on it, for the weather is at present so fine that I am almost always in the open air. I wish you as pleasant weather for your holidays. Write me a few words (if you find that you have not sufficiently exercised your pen in the course of the day). May you all remain well—and lay me at the feet of your mother and sister.—Your devoted, "F. CHOPIN."

The date given by La Mara is "Monday [May 20, 1842], Nohant, near La Chatre, Indre." This, however, cannot be right, for the 20th of May in 1842 was a Friday.]

And, again, how atrociously he reviles in the same letters the banker Leo, who lends him money, often takes charge of his manuscripts, procures payment for them, and in whose house he has been for years a frequent visitor. Mr. Ch. Halle informed me that Chopin was on particularly good terms with the Leos. From Moscheles' diary we learn that the writer made Chopin's acquaintance at the banker's house. Stephen Heller told me that he met Chopin several times at Leo's, and that the Polish composer visited there often, and continued to go there when he had given up going to many other houses. And from the same informant I learned also that Madame Leo as well as her husband took a kindly interest in Chopin, showing this, for instance, by providing him with linen. And yet Leo, this man who does him all sorts of services, and whose smiling guest he is before and after, is spoken of by Chopin as if he were the most "despicable wretch imaginable"; and this for no other reason than that everything has not been done exactly as he wished it to be done. Unless we assume these revilings to be no more than explosions of momentary ill-humour, we must find Chopin convicted of duplicity and ingratitude. In the letters to Fontana there are also certain remarks about Matuszynski which I do not like. Nor can they be wholly explained away by saying that they are in part fun and in part indirect flattery of his correspondent. It would rather seem that Chopin's undoubtedly real love for Matuszynski was not unmixed with a certain kind of contempt. And here I must tell the reader that while Poles have so high an opinion of their nation in comparison with other nations, and of their countrymen with other countrymen, they have generally a very mean opinion of each other. Indeed, I never met with a Pole who did not look down with a self-satisfied smile of pity on any of his fellow-countrymen, even on his best friend. It seems that their feeling of individual superiority is as great as that of their national superiority. Liszt's observations (see Vol. I., p. 259) and those of other writers (Polish as well as non-Polish) confirm mine, which else might rightly be supposed to be based on too limited an experience. To return to Matuszynski, he may have been too ready to advise and censure his friend, and not practical enough to be actively helpful. After reading the letters addressed to them one comes to the conclusion that Fontana's and Franchomme's serviceableness and readiness to serve went for something in his appreciation of them as friends. At any rate, he did not hesitate to exploiter them most unconscionably. Taking a general view of the letters written by him during the last twelve years of his life, one is struck by the absence of generous judgments and the extreme rareness of sympathetic sentiments concerning third persons. As this was not the case in his earlier letters, ill-health and disappointments suggest themselves naturally as causes of these faults of character and temper. To these principal causes have, however, to be added his nationality, his originally delicate constitution, and his cultivation of salon manners and tastes. His extreme sensitiveness, fastidiousness, and irritability may be easily understood to derive from one or the other of these conditions.

George Sand's Ma Vie throws a good deal of light on Chopin's character; let us collect a few rays from it:—

He [Chopin] was modest on principle and gentle [doux] by habit, but he was imperious by instinct, and full of a legitimate pride that did not know itself.

He was certainly not made to live long in this world, this extreme type of an artist. He was devoured by the dream of an ideal which no practical philosophic or compassionate tolerance combated. He would never compound with human nature.

He accepted nothing of reality. This was his vice and his virtue, his grandeur and his misery. Implacable to the least blemish, he had an immense enthusiasm for the least light, his excited imagination doing its utmost to see in it a sun.

He was the same in friendship [as in love], becoming enthusiastic at first sight, getting disgusted, and correcting himself [se reprenant] incessantly, living on infatuations full of charms for those who were the object of them, and on secret discontents which poisoned his dearest affections.

Chopin accorded to me, I may say honoured me with, a kind of friendship which was an exception in his life. He was always the same to me.

The friendship of Chopin was never a refuge for me in sadness. He had enough of his own ills to bear.

We never addressed a reproach to each other, except once, which, alas! was the first and the last time.

But if Chopin was with me devotion, kind attention, grace, obligingness, and deference in person, he had not for all that abjured the asperities of his character towards those who were about me. With them the inequality of his soul, in turn generous and fantastic, gave itself full course, passing always from infatuation to aversion, and vice versa.

Chopin when angry was alarming, and as, with me, he always restrained himself, he seemed almost to choke and die.

The following extracts from Liszt's book partly corroborate, partly supplement, the foregoing evidence:—

His imagination was ardent, his feelings rose to violence,— his physical organisation was feeble and sickly! Who can sound the sufferings proceeding from this contrast? They must have been poignant, but he never let them be seen.

The delicacy of his constitution and of his heart, in imposing upon him the feminine martyrdom of for ever unavowed tortures, gave to his destiny some of the traits of feminine destinies.

He did not exercise a decisive influence on any existence. His passion never encroached upon any of his desires; he neither pressed close nor bore down [n'a etreint ni masse] any mind by the domination of his own.

However rarely, there were nevertheless instances when we surprised him profoundly moved. We have seen him turn pale [palir et blemir] to such a degree as to assume green and cadaverous tints. But in his intensest emotions he remained concentrated. He was then, as usually, chary of words about what he felt; a minute's reflection [recueillement] always hid the secret of his first impression...This constant control over the violence of his character reminded one of the melancholy superiority of certain women who seek their strength in reticence and isolation, knowing the uselessness of the explosions of their anger, and having a too jealous care of the mystery of their passion to betray it gratuitously.

Chopin, however, did not always control his temper. Heller remembers seeing him more than once in a passion, and hearing him speak very harshly to Nowakowski. The following story, which Lenz relates in "Die grossen Pianoforte-Virtuosen unserer Zeit," is also to the point.

On one occasion Meyerbeer, whom I had not yet seen, entered Chopin's room when I was getting a lesson. Meyerbeer was not announced, he was king. I was playing the Mazurka in C (Op. 33), printed on one page which contains so many hundreds—I called it the epitaph of the idea [Grabschrift des Begriffs], so full of distress and sadness is the composition, the wearied flight of an eagle.

Meyerbeer had taken a seat, Chopin made me go on.

"This is two-four time," said Meyerbeer. Chopin denied this, made me repeat the piece, and beat time aloud with the pencil on the piano—his eyes were glowing.

"Two crotchets," repeated Meyerbeer, calmly.

Only once I saw Chopin angry, it was at this moment. It was beautiful to see how a light red coloured his pale cheeks.

"These are three crotchets," he said with a loud voice, he who spoke always so low

"Give it me," replied Meyerbeer, "for a ballet in my opera ("L'Africaine," at that time kept a secret), I shall show it you then."

"These are three crotchets," Chopin almost shouted, and played it himself. He played the mazurka several times, counted aloud, stamped time with his foot, was beside himself. But all was of no use, Meyerbeer insisted on TWO crotchets. They parted very angrily. I found it anything but agreeable to have been a witness of this angry scene. Chopin disappeared into his cabinet without taking leave of me. The whole thing lasted but a few minutes.

Exhibitions of temper like this were no doubt rare, indeed, hardly ever occurred except in his intercourse with familiars and, more especially, fellow-countrymen—sometimes also with pupils. In passing I may remark that Chopin's Polish vocabulary was much less choice than his French one. As a rule, Chopin's manners were very refined and aristocratic, Mr. Halle thinks they were too much so. For this refinement resulted in a uniform amiability which left you quite in the dark as to the real nature of the man. Many people who made advances to Chopin found like M. Marmontel—I have this from his own mouth—that he had a temperament sauvage and was difficult to get at. And all who came near him learned soon from experience that, as Liszt told Lenz, he was ombrageux. But while Chopin would treat outsiders with a chilly politeness, he charmed those who were admitted into his circle both by amiability and wit. "Usually," says Liszt, "he was lively, his caustic mind unearthed quickly the ridiculous far below the surface where it strikes all eyes." And again, "the playfulness of Chopin attacked only the superior keys of the mind, fond of witticism as he was, recoiling from vulgar joviality, gross laughter, common merriment, as from those animals more abject than venomous, the sight of which causes the most nauseous aversion to certain sensitive and delicate natures." Liszt calls Chopin "a fine connoisseur in raillery and an ingenious mocker." The testimony of other acquaintances of Chopin and that of his letters does not allow us to accept as holding good generally Mr. Halle's experience, who, mentioning also the Polish artist's wit, said to me that he never heard him utter a sarcasm or use a cutting expression.

Fondness of society is a characteristic trait in Chopin's mental constitution. Indeed, Hiller told me that his friend could not be without company. For reading, on the other hand, he did not much care. Alkan related to me that Chopin did not even read George Sand's works—which is difficult to believe—and that Pierre Leroux, who liked Chopin and always brought him his books, might have found them any time afterwards uncut on the pianist's table, which is not so difficult to believe, as philosophy and Chopin are contraries. According to what I learned from Hiller, Chopin took an interest in literature but read very little. To Heller it seemed that Chopin had no taste for literature, indeed, he made on him the impression of an uneducated man. Heller, I must tell the reader parenthetically, was both a great reader and an earnest thinker, over whom good books had even the power of making him neglect and forget mistress Musica without regret and with little compunction. But to return to Chopin. Franchomme excused his friend by saying that teaching and the claims of society left him no time for reading. But if Chopin neglected French literature—not to speak of other ancient and modern literatures—he paid some attention to that of his native country; at any rate, new publications of Polish books were generally to be found on his table. The reader will also remember that Chopin, in his letters to Fontana, alludes twice to books of poetry—one by Mickiewicz which was sent him to Majorca, the other by Witwicki which he had lost sight of.

Indeed, anything Polish had an especial charm and value for Chopin. Absence from his native country so far from diminishing increased his love for it. The words with which he is reported to have received the pianist Mortier de Fontaine, who came to Paris in 1833 and called on him with letters of introduction, are characteristic in this respect: "It is enough that you have breathed the air of Warsaw to find a friend and adviser in me." There is, no doubt, some exaggeration in Liszt's statement that whoever came to Chopin from Poland, whether with or without letters of introduction, was sure of a hearty welcome, of being received with open arms. On the other hand, we may fully believe the same authority when he says that Chopin often accorded to persons of his own country what he would not accord to anyone else—namely, the right of disturbing his habits; that he would sacrifice his time, money, and comfort to people who were perhaps unknown to him the day before, showing them the sights of the capital, having them to dine with him, and taking them in the evening to some theatre. We have already seen that his most intimate friends were Poles, and this was so in the aristocratic as well as in the conventionally less-elevated circles. However pleasant his relations with the Rothschilds may have been—indeed, Franchomme told me that his friend loved the house of Rothschild and that this house loved him, and that more especially Madame Nathaniel Rothschild preserved a touching remembrance of him [FOOTNOTE: Chopin dedicated to Madame la Baronne C. Rothschild the Waltz, Op. 64, No. 2 (Parisian Edition), and the Ballade, Op. 52.]—they can have been but of small significance in comparison with the almost passionate attachment he had to Prince Alexander Czartoryski and his wife the Princess Marcelline. And if we were to compare his friendship for any non-Polish gentleman or lady with that which he felt for the Countess Delphine Potocka, to whom he dedicated two of his happiest inspirations in two very different genres (the F minor Concerto, Op. 21, and the D flat major Waltz, Op. 64, No. I), the result would be again in favour of his compatriot. There were, indeed, some who thought that he felt more than friendship for this lady; this, however, he energetically denied.

[FOOTNOTE: Of this lady Kwiatkowski said that she took as much trouble and pride in giving choice musical entertainments as other people did in giving choice dinners. In Sowinski's Musiciens polonais we read that she had a beautiful soprano voice and occupied the first place among the amateur ladies of Paris. "A great friend of the illustrious Chopin, she gave formerly splendid concerts at her house with the old company of the Italians, which one shall see no more in Paris. To cite the names of Rubini, Lablache, Tamburini, Malibran, Grisi, Persiani, is to give the highest idea of Italian singing. The Countess Potocka sang herself according to the method of the Italian masters."]

But although Chopin was more devoted and more happy in his Polish friendships, he had beloved as well as loving friends of all nationalities— Germans, English, and even Russians. That as a good Pole he hated the Russians as a nation may be taken for granted. Of his feelings and opinions with regard to his English friends and the English in general, information will be forthcoming in a subsequent chapter. The Germans Chopin disliked thoroughly, partly, no doubt, from political reasons, partly perhaps on account of their inelegance and social awkwardness. Still, of this nation were some of his best friends, among them Hiller, Gutmann, Albrecht, and the Hanoverian ambassador Baron von Stockhausen.

[FOOTNOTE: Gutmann, in speaking to me of his master's dislike, positively ascribed it to the second of the above causes. In connection with this we must, however, not forget that the Germans of to-day differ from the Germans of fifty years ago as much socially as politically. Nor have the social characters of their neighbours, the French and the English, remained the same.]

Liszt has given a glowing description of an improvised soiree at Chopin's lodgings in the Rue de la Chaussee d'Antin—that is, in the years before the winter in Majorca. At this soiree, we are told, were present Liszt himself, Heine, Meyerbeer, Nourrit, Hiller, Delacroix, Niemcewicz, Mickiewicz, George Sand, and the Comtesse d'Agoult. Of course, this is a poetic licence: these men and women cannot have been at one and the same time in Chopin's salon. Indeed, Hiller informed me that he knew nothing of this party, and that, moreover, as long as he was in Paris (up to 1836) there were hardly ever more numerous gatherings at his friend's lodgings than of two or three. Liszt's group, however, brings vividly before us one section of Chopin's social surroundings: it shows us what a poetic atmosphere he was breathing, amidst what a galaxy of celebrities he was moving. A glimpse of the real life our artist lived in the early Paris years this extravagant effort of a luxuriant imagination does not afford. Such glimpses we got in his letters to Hiller and Franchomme, where we also met with many friends and acquaintances with less high-sounding names, some of whom Chopin subsequently lost by removal or death. In addition to the friends who were then mentioned, I may name here the Polish poet Stephen Witwicki, the friend of his youth as well as of his manhood, to whom in 1842 he dedicated his Op. 41, three mazurkas, and several of whose poems he set to music; and the Polish painter Kwiatkowski, an acquaintance of a later time, who drew and painted many portraits of the composer, and more than one of whose pictures was inspired by compositions of his friend. I have not been able to ascertain what Chopin's sentiments were with regard to Kwiatkowski, but the latter must have been a frequent visitor, for after relating to me that the composer was fond of playing in the dusk, he remarked that he heard him play thus almost all his works immediately after they were composed.

As we have seen in the chapters treating of Chopin's first years in Paris, there was then a goodly sprinkling of musicians among his associates—I use the word "associates" advisedly, for many of them could not truly be called friends. When he was once firmly settled, artistically and socially, not a few of these early acquaintances lapsed. How much this was due to the force of circumstances, how much to the choice of Chopin, is difficult to determine. But we may be sure that his distaste to the Bohemianism, the free and easy style that obtains among a considerable portion of the artistic tribe, had at least as much to do with the result as pressure of engagements. Of the musicians of whom we heard so much in the first years after his coming to Paris, he remained in close connection only with one-namely, with Franchomme. Osborne soon disappeared from his circle. Chopin's intercourse with Berlioz was in after years so rare that some of their common friends did not even know of its existence. The loosening of this connection was probably brought about by the departure of Hiller in 1836 and the quarrel with Liszt some time after, which broke two links between the sensitive Pole and the fiery Frenchman. The ageing Baillot and Cherubini died in 1842. Kalkbrenner died but a short time before Chopin, but the sympathy existing between them was not strong enough to prevent their drifting apart. Other artists to whom the new-comer had paid due homage may have been neglected, forgotten, or lost sight of when success was attained and the blandishments of the salons were lavished upon him. Strange to say, with all his love for what belonged to and came from Poland, he kept compatriot musicians at a distance. Fontana was an exception, but him he cherished, no doubt, as a friend of his youth in spite of his profession, or, if as a musician at all, chiefly because of his handiness as a copyist. For Sowinski, who was already settled in Paris when Chopin arrived there, and who assisted him at his first concert, he did not care. Consequently they had afterwards less and less intercourse, which, indeed, in the end may have ceased altogether. An undated letter given by Count Wodziriski in "Les trois Romans de Frederic Chopin," no doubt originally written in Polish, brings the master's feelings towards his compatriot, and also his irritability, most vividly before the reader.

Here he is! He has just come in to see me—a tall strong individual who wears moustaches; he sits down at the piano and improvises, without knowing exactly what. He knocks, strikes, and crosses his hands, without reason; he demolishes in five minutes a poor helpless key; he has enormous fingers, made rather to handle reins and whip somewhere on the confines of Ukraine. Here you have the portrait of S... who has no other merit than that of having small moustaches and a good heart. If I ever thought of imagining what stupidity and charlatanism in art are, I have now the clearest perception of them. I run through my room with my ears reddening; I have a mad desire to throw the door wide open; but one has to spare him, to show one's self almost affectionate. No, you cannot imagine what it is: here one sees only his neckties; one does him the honour of taking him seriously....There remains, therefore, nothing but to bear him. What exasperates me is his collection of little songs, compositions in the most vulgar style, without the least knowledge of the most elementary rules of harmony and poetry, concluding with quadrille ritornelli, and which he calls Recueil de Chants Polonais. You know how I wished to understand, and how I have in part succeeded in understanding, our national music. Therefore you will judge what pleasure I experience when, laying hold of a motive of mine here and there, without taking account of the fact that all the beauty of a melody depends on the accompaniment, he reproduces it with the taste of a frequenter of suburban taverns (guinguettes) and public-houses (cabarets). And one cannot say anything to him, for he comprehends nothing beyond what he has taken from you.

Edouard Wolff came to Paris in 1835, provided with a letter of introduction from Chopin's master Zywny; [FOOTNOTE: See Vol. I., p. 31.] but, notwithstanding this favourable opening of their acquaintanceship, he was only for some time on visiting terms with his more distinguished compatriot. Wolff himself told me that Chopin would never hear one of his compositions. From any other informant I would not have accepted this statement as probable, still less as true. [FOOTNOTE: Wolff dedicated in 1841 his Grand Allegro de Concert pour piano still, Op. 59, a son ami Chopin; but the latter never repaid him the compliment.] These remarks about Wolff remind me of another piece of information I got from this pianist-composer a few months before his death—namely, that Chopin hated all Jews, Meyerbeer and Halevy among the rest. What Pole does not hate the Jews? That Chopin was not enamoured of them we have seen in his letters. But that he hated Meyerbeer is a more than doubtful statement. Franchomme said to me that Meyerbeer was not a great friend of Chopin's; but that the latter, though he did not like his music, liked him as a man. If Lenz reports accurately, Meyerbeer's feelings towards Chopin were, no doubt, warmer than Chopin's towards Meyerbeer. When after the scene about the rhythm of a mazurka Chopin had left the room, Lenz introduced himself to Meyerbeer as a friend of the Counts Wielhorski, of St. Petersburg. On coming to the door, where a coupe was waiting, the composer offered to drive him home, and when they were seated said:—

I had not seen Chopin for a long time, I love him very much. I know no pianist like him, no composer for the piano like him. The piano lives on nuances and on cantilena; it is an instrument of intimacy [ein Intimitalsinstrument], I also was once a pianist, and there was a time when I trained myself to be a virtuoso. Visit me when you come to Berlin. Are we not now comrades? When one has met at the house of so great a man, it was for life.

Kwiatkowski told me a pretty story which se non vero is certainly ben trovato. When on one occasion Meyerbeer had fallen out with his wife, he sat down to the piano and played a nocturne or some other composition which Chopin had sent him. And such was the effect of the music on his helpmate that she came and kissed him. Thereupon Meyerbeer wrote Chopin a note telling him of what had taken place, and asking him to come and see their conjugal happiness. Among the few musicians with whom Chopin had in later years friendly relations stands out prominently, both by his genius and the preference shown him, the pianist and composer Alkan aine (Charles Henri Valentine), who, however, was not so intimate with the Polish composer as Franchomme, nor on such easy terms of companionship as Hiller and Liszt had been. The originality of the man and artist, his high aims and unselfish striving, may well have attracted Chopin; but as an important point in Alkan's favour must be reckoned the fact that he was also a friend of George Sand's. Indeed, some of the limitations of Chopin's intercourse were, no doubt, made on her account. Kwiatkowski told me that George Sand hated Chopin's Polish friends, and that some of them were consequently not admitted at all and others only reluctantly. Now suppose that she disliked also some of the non-Polish friends, musicians as well as others, would not her influence act in the same way as in the case of the Poles?

But now I must say a few words about Chopin and Liszt's friendship, and how it came to an end. This connection of the great pianists has been the subject of much of that sentimental talk of which writers on music and of musical biography are so fond. This, however, which so often has been represented as an ideal friendship, was really no friendship at all, but merely comradeship. Both admired each other sincerely as musicians. If Chopin did not care much for Liszt's compositions, he had the highest opinion of him as a pianist. We have seen in the letter of June 20, 1833, addressed to Hiller and conjointly written by Chopin and Liszt, how delighted Chopin was with Liszt's manner of playing his studies, and how he wished to be able to rob him of it. He said on one occasion to his pupil Mdlle. Kologrivof [FOOTNOTE: Afterwards Madame Rubio.]: "I like my music when Liszt plays it." No doubt, it was Liszt's book with its transcendentally-poetic treatment which induced the false notion now current. Yet whoever keeps his eyes open can read between the lines what the real state of matters was. The covert sneers at and the openly-expressed compassion for his comrade's whims, weaknesses, and deficiencies, tell a tale. Of Chopin's sentiments with regard to Liszt we have more than sufficient evidence. Mr. Halle, who arrived in Paris at the end of 1840, was strongly recommended to the banker Mallet. This gentleman, to give him an opportunity to make the acquaintance of the Polish pianist, invited both to dinner. On this occasion Mr. Halle asked Chopin about Liszt, but the reticent answer he got was indicative rather of dislike than of anything else. When in 1842 Lenz took lessons from Chopin, the latter defined his relations with Liszt thus: "We are friends, we were comrades." What he meant by the first half of the statement was, no doubt: "Now we meet only on terms of polite acquaintanceship." When the comradeship came to an end I do not know, but I think I do know how it came to an end. When I asked Liszt about the cause of the termination of their friendship, he said: "Our lady-loves had quarrelled, and as good cavaliers we were in duty bound to side with them." [FOOTNOTE: Liszt's words in describing to me his subsequent relation with Chopin were similar to those of Chopin to Lenz. He said: "There was a cessation of intimacy, but no enmity. I left Paris soon after, and never saw him again."] This, however, was merely a way to get rid of an inconvenient question. Franchomme explained the mystery to me, and his explanation was confirmed by what I learned from Madame Rubio. The circumstances are of too delicate a nature to be set forth in detail. But the long and short of the affair is that Liszt, accompanied by another person, invaded Chopin's lodgings during his absence, and made himself quite at home there. The discovery of traces of the use to which his rooms had been put justly enraged Chopin. One day, I do not know how long after the occurrence, Liszt asked Madame Rubio to tell her master that he hoped the past would be forgotten and the young man's trick (Junggesellenstuck) wiped out. Chopin then said that he could not forget, and was much better as he was; and further, that Liszt was not open enough, having always secrets and intrigues, and had written in some newspapers feuilleton notices unfavourable to him. This last accusation reminds one at once of the remark he made when he heard that Liszt intended to write an account of one of his concerts for the Gazette musicale. I have quoted the words already, but may repeat them here: "Il me donnera un petit royaume dans son empire" (He will give me a little kingdom in his empire). In this, as in most sayings of Chopin regarding Liszt, irritation against the latter is distinctly noticeable. The cause of this irritation may be manifold, but Liszt's great success as a concert-player and his own failure in this respect [FOOTNOTE: I speak here only of his inability to impress large audiences, to move great masses.] have certainly something to do with it. Liszt, who thought so likewise, says somewhere in his book that Chopin knew how to forgive nobly. Whether this was so or not, I do not venture to decide. But I am sure if he forgave, he never forgot. An offence remained for ever rankling in his heart and mind.

From Chopin's friends to his pupils is but one step, and not even that, for a great many of his pupils were also his friends; indeed, among them were some of those who were nearest to his heart, and not a few in whose society he took a particular delight. Before I speak, however, of his teaching, I must say a few words about a subject which equally relates to our artist's friends and pupils, and to them rather than to any other class of people with whom he had any dealings.

One of his [Chopin's] oddities [writes Liszt] consisted in abstaining from every exchange of letters, from every sending of notes; one could have believed that he had made a vow never to address letters to strangers. It was a curious thing to see him have recourse to all kinds of expedients to escape from the necessity of tracing a few lines. Many times he preferred traversing Paris from one end to the other in order to decline a dinner or give some slight information, to saving himself the trouble by means of a little sheet of paper. His handwriting remained almost unknown to most of his friends. It is said that he sometimes deviated from this habit in favour of his fair compatriots settled at Paris, of whom some are in possession of charming autographs of his, all written in

Polish. This breach of what one might have taken as a rule may be explained by the pleasure he took in speaking his language, which he employed in preference, and whose most expressive idioms he delighted in translating to others. Like the Slaves generally, he mastered the French language very well; moreover, owing to his French origin, it had been taught him with particular care. But he accommodated himself badly to it, reproaching it with having little sonority and being of a cold genius.

[FOOTNOTE: Notwithstanding his French origin, Chopin spoke French with a foreign accent, some say even with a strong foreign accent. Of his manner of writing French I spoke when quoting his letters to Franchomme (see Vol. I., p. 258).]

Liszt's account of Chopin's bizarrerie is in the main correct, although we have, of course, to make some deduction for exaggeration. In fact, Gutmann told me that his master sometimes began a letter twenty times, and finally flung down the pen and said: "I'll go and tell her [or "him," as the case might be] myself."

CHAPTER XXVIII

CHOPIN AS A TEACHER: HIS SUCCESS OR WANT OF SUCCESS AS SUCH; HIS PUPILS, AMATEUR AND PROFESSIONAL; METHOD OF TEACHING; AND TEACHING REPERTOIRE.

As Chopin rarely played in public and could not make a comfortable living by his compositions, there remained nothing for him but to teach, which, indeed, he did till his strength forsook him. But so far from regarding teaching as a burden, says his pupil Mikuli, he devoted himself to it with real pleasure. Of course, a teacher can only take pleasure in teaching when he has pupils of the right sort. This advantage, however, Chopin may have enjoyed to a greater extent than most masters, for according to all accounts it was difficult to be received as a pupil—he by no means gave lessons to anyone who asked for them. As long as he was in fair health, he taught during the season from four to five hours a day, in later years only, or almost only, at home. His fee for a lesson was twenty francs, which were deposited by the pupil on the mantelpiece.

Was Chopin a good teacher? His pupils without exception most positively affirm it. But outsiders ask: How is it, then, that so great a virtuoso has not trained players who have made the world ring with their fame? Mr. Halle, whilst pointing out the fact that Chopin's pupils have not distinguished themselves, did not wish to decide whether this was owing to a deficiency in the master or to some other cause. Liszt, in speaking to me on this subject, simply remarked: "Chopin was unfortunate in his pupils—none of them has become a player of any importance, although some of his noble pupils played very well." If we compare Liszt's pianistic offspring with Chopin's, the difference is indeed striking. But here we have to keep in mind several considerations—Chopin taught for a shorter period than Liszt; most of his pupils, unlike Liszt's, were amateurs; and he may not have met with the stuff out of which great virtuosos are made. That Chopin was unfortunate in his pupils may be proved by the early death of several very promising ones. Charles Filtsch, born at Hermannstadt, Transylvania (Hungary), about 1830, of whom Liszt and Lenz spoke so highly (see Chapter XXVI.), died on May 11, 1845, at Venice, after having in 1843 made a sensation in London and Vienna, both by the poetical and technical qualities of his playing. In London "little Filtsch" played at least twice in public (on June 14 at the St. James's Theatre between two plays, and on July 4 at a matinee of his own at the Hanover Square Rooms), repeatedly in private, and had also the honour to appear before the Queen at Buckingham Palace. J. W. Davison relates in his preface to Chopin's mazurkas and waltzes (Boosey & Co.) a circumstance which proves the young virtuoso's musicianship. "Engaged to perform Chopin's second concerto in public, the orchestral parts not being obtainable, Filtsch, nothing dismayed, wrote out the whole of them from memory." Another short-lived great talent was Paul Gunsberg. "This young man," Madame Dubois informed me, "was endowed with an extraordinary organisation. Chopin had made of him an admirable executant. He died of consumption, otherwise he would have become celebrated." I do not know in which year Gunsberg died. He was still alive on May 11, 1855. For on that day he played with his fellow-pupil Tellefsen, at a concert given by the latter in Paris, a duet of Schumann's. A third pupil of Chopin prematurely snatched away by death was Caroline Hartmann, the daughter of a manufacturer, born at Munster, near Colmar, in 1808. She came to Paris in 1833, and died the year after—of love for Chopin, as Edouard Wolff told me. Other authorities, however, ascribe the sad effect to a less romantic cause. They say that through persevering study under the direction of Chopin and Liszt she became an excellent pianist, but that the hard work brought on a chest complaint to which she succumbed on July 30, 1834. The GAZETTE MUSICALE of August 17, 1834, which notices her death, describes her as a pupil of Liszt, Chopin, and Pixis, without commenting on her abilities. Spohr admired her as a child. But if Chopin has not turned out virtuosos of the calibre of Tausig and Hans von Bulow, he has nevertheless formed many very clever pianists. It would serve no purpose except that of satisfying idle curiosity to draw up a list of all the master's ascertainable pupils. Those who wish, however, to satisfy this idle curiosity can do so to some extent by scanning the dedications of Chopin's works, as the names therein to be found—with a few and mostly obvious exceptions—are those of pupils. The array of princesses, countesses, &c., will, it is to be hoped, duly impress the investigator. Let us hear what the illustrious master Marmontel has to say on this subject:—

> Among the pianist-composers who have had the immense advantage
> of taking lessons from Chopin, to impregnate themselves with
> his style and manner, we must cite Gutmann, Lysberg, and our
> dear colleague G. Mathias. The Princesses de Chimay,
> Czartoryska, the Countesses Esterhazy, Branicka, Potocka, de
> Kalergis, d'Est; Mdlles. Muller and de Noailles were his
> cherished disciples [disciples affectionnees]. Madame Dubois,
> nee O'Meara, is also one of his favourite pupils [eleves de

predilection], and numbers among those whose talent has best preserved the characteristic traditions and procedures [procedes] of the master.

Two of Chopin's amateur and a few more of his professional pupils ought to be briefly noticed here—first and chiefly of the amateurs, the Princess Marcelline Czartoryska, who has sometimes played in public for charitable purposes, and of whom it has often been said that she is the most faithful transmitter of her master's style. Would the praise which is generally lavished upon her have been so enthusiastic if the lady had been a professional pianist instead of a princess? The question is ungracious in one who has not had the pleasure of hearing her, but not unnaturally suggests itself. Be this as it may, that she is, or was, a good player, who as an intimate friend and countrywoman thoroughly entered into the spirit of her master's music, seems beyond question.

[FOOTNOTE: "The Princess Marcelline Czartoryska," wrote Sowinski in 1857 in the article "Chopin" of his "Musicien polonais," "who has a fine execution, seems to have inherited Chopin's ways of procedure, especially in phrasing and accentuation. Lately the Princess performed at Paris with much success the magnificent F minor Concerto at a concert for the benefit of the poor." A critic, writing in the Gazette Musicale of March 11, 1855, of a concert given by the Princess—at which she played an andante with variations for piano and violoncello by Mozart, a rondo for piano and orchestra by Mendelssohn, and Chopin's F minor Concerto, being assisted by Alard as conductor, the violoncellist Franchomme, and the singers Madame Viardot and M. Fedor—praised especially her rendering of the ADAGIO in Chopin's Concerto. Lenz was the most enthusiastic admirer of the Princess I have met with. He calls her (in the Berliner Musikzeitung, Vol. XXVI) a highly-gifted nature, the best pupil [Schulerin] of Chopin, and the incarnation of her master's pianoforte style. At a musical party at the house of the Counts Wilhorski at St. Petersburg, where she performed a waltz and the Marche funebre by Chopin, her playing made such an impression that it was thought improper to have any more music on that evening, the trio of the march having, indeed, moved the auditors to tears. The Princess told Lenz that on one occasion when Chopin played to her this trio, she fell on her knees before him and felt unspeakably happy.]

G. Chouquet reminded me not to omit to mention among Chopin's pupils Madame Peruzzi, the wife of the ambassador of the Duke of Tuscany to the court of Louis Philippe:—

This virtuosa [wrote to me the late keeper of the Musee of the Paris Conservatoire] had no less talent than the Princess

Marcelline Czartoryska. I heard her at Florence in 1852, and I can assure you that she played Chopin's music in the true style and with all the unpublished traits of the master. She was of Russian origin.

But enough of amateurs. Mdlle. Friederike Muller, now for many years married to the Viennese pianoforte-maker J. B. Streicher, is regarded by many as the most, and is certainly one of the most gifted of Chopin's favourite pupils. [FOOTNOTE: She played already in public at Vienna in the fourth decade of this century, which must have been before her coming to Paris (see Eduard Hanslick, Geschichte des Concertwesens in Wien, p. 326). Marriage brought the lady's professional career to a close.] That the composer dedicated to her his Allegro de Concert, Op. 46, may be regarded as a mark of his love and esteem for her. Carl Mikuli found her assistance of great importance in the preparation of his edition of Chopin's works, as she had received lessons from the master for several years, and, moreover, had had many opportunities of hearing him on other occasions. The same authority refers to Madame Dubois (nee O'Meara) [FOOTNOTE: A relation of Edward Barry O'Meara, physician to the first Napoleon at St. Helena, and author of "Napoleon in Exile."] and to Madame Rubio (NEE Vera de Kologrivof) as to "two extremely excellent pianists [hochst ausgezeichnete Pianistinnen] whose talent enjoyed the advantage of the master's particular care." The latter lady was taught by Chopin from 1842 to 1849, and in the last years of his life assisted him, as we shall see, by taking partial charge of some of his pupils. Madame Dubois, who studied under Kalkbrenner from the age of nine to thirteen, became then a pupil of Chopin, with whom she remained five years. It was very difficult to obtain his consent to take another pupil, but the influence of M. Albrecht, a common friend of her father's and Chopin's, stood her in good stead. Although I heard her play only one or two of her master's minor pieces, and under very unfavourable circumstances too—namely, at the end of the teaching season and in a tropical heat—I may say that her suave touch, perfect legato, and delicate sentiment seemed to me to bear out the above-quoted remark of M. Marmontel. Madame Dubois, who is one of the most highly-esteemed teachers of the piano in Paris, used to play till recently in public, although less frequently in later than in earlier years. And here I must extract a passage from Madame Girardin's letter of March 7, 1847, in Vol. IV. of "Le Vicomte de Launay," where, after describing Mdlle. O'Meara's beauty, more especially her Irish look—"that mixture of sadness and serenity, of profound tenderness and shy dignity, which you never find in the proud and brilliant looks which you admire in the women of other nations "—she says:—

We heard her a few hours ago; she played in a really superior way the beautiful Concerto of Chopin in E flat minor [of course E minor]; she was applauded with enthusiasm. [FOOTNOTE: Chopin accompanied on a second piano. The occasion was a soiree at the house of Madame de Courbonne.] All we can say to give you an idea of Mdlle. O'Meara's playing is that there is in her playing all that is in her look, and in addition to it an admirable method, and excellent fingering. Her success has been complete; in hearing her, statesmen were moved... and the young ladies, those who are good musicians, forgave her her prettiness.

As regards Chopin's male pupils, we have to note George Mathias (born at Paris in 1826), the well-known professor of the piano at the Paris Conservatoire, [FOOTNOTE: He retired a year or two ago.] and still more widely-known composer of more than half-a-hundred important works (sonatas, trios, concertos, symphonic compositions, pianoforte pieces, songs, &c.), who enjoyed the master's teaching from 1839 to 1844; Lysberg (1821-1873), whose real name was Charles Samuel Bovy, for many years professor of the piano at the Conservatoire of his native town, Geneva, and a very fertile composer of salon pieces for the piano (composer also of a one-act comic opera, La Fills du Carillonneur), distinguished by "much poetic feeling, an extremely careful form, an original colouring, and in which one often seems to see pass a breath of Weber or Chopin"; [FOOTNOTE: Supplement et Complement to Fetis' Biographie universelle des Musiciens, published under the direction of Arthur Pougin.] the Norwegian Thomas Dyke Acland Tellefsen (1823-1874), a teacher of the piano in Paris and author of an edition of Chopin's works; Carl Mikuli (born at Czernowitz in 1821), since 1858 artistic director of the Galician Musical Society (conservatoire, concerts, &c.), and author of an edition of Chopin's works; and Adolph Gutmann, the master's favourite pupil par excellence, of whom we must speak somewhat more at length. Karasowski makes also mention of Casimir Wernik, who died at St. Petersburg in 1859, and of Gustav Schumann, a teacher of the piano at Berlin, who, however, was only during the winter of 1840-1841 with the Polish master. For Englishmen the fact of the late Brinley Richards and Lindsay Sloper having been pupils of Chopin—the one for a short, the other for a longer period—will be of special interest.

Adolph Gutmann was a boy of fifteen when in 1834 his father brought him to Paris to place him under Chopin. The latter, however, did not at first feel inclined to accept the proposed trust; but on hearing the boy play he conceived so high an idea of his capacities that he agreed to undertake his artistic education. Chopin seems to have always retained a thorough belief in his muscular pupil, although some of his great pianist friends thought this belief nothing but a strange delusion. There are also piquant anecdotes told by fellow-pupils with the purpose of showing that Chopin did not care very much for him. For instance, the following: Some one asked the master how his pupil was getting on, "Oh, he makes very good chocolate," was the answer. Unfortunately, I cannot speak of Gutmann's playing from experience, for although I spent eight days with him, it was on a mountain-top in the Tyrol, where there were no pianos. But Chopin's belief in Gutmann counts with me for something, and so does Moscheles' reference to him as Chopin's "excellent pupil"; more valuable, I think, than either is the evidence of Dr. A. C. Mackenzie, who at my request visited Gutmann several times in Florence and was favourably impressed by his playing, in which he noticed especially beauty of tone combined with power. As far as I can make out Gutmann planned only once, in 1846, a regular concert-tour, being furnished for it by Chopin with letters of introduction to the highest personages in Berlin, Warsaw, and St. Petersburg. Through the intervention of the Countess Rossi (Henriette Sontag), he was invited to play at a court-concert at Charlottenburg in celebration of the King's birthday. [FOOTNOTE: His part of the programme consisted of his master's E minor Concerto (2nd and 3rd movements) and No. 3 of the first book of studies, and his own tenth study.] But the day after the concert he was seized with such home-sickness that he returned forthwith to Paris, where he made his appearance to the great astonishment of Chopin. The reader may perhaps be interested in what a writer in the Gazette Musicale said about Chopin's favourite pupil on March 24, 1844:—

> M. Gutmann is a pianist with a neat but somewhat cold style of
> playing; he has what one calls fingers, and uses them with
> much dexterity. His manner of proceeding is rather that of
> Thalberg than of the clever professor who has given him
> lessons. He afforded pleasure to the lovers of the piano
> [amateurs de piano] at the musical SOIREE which he gave last
> Monday at M. Erard's. Especially his fantasia on the
> "Freischutz" was applauded.

Of course, the expression of any individual opinion is no conclusive proof. Gutmann was so successful as a teacher and in a way also as a composer (his compositions, I may say in passing, were not in his master's but in a light salon style) that at a comparatively early period of his life he was able to retire from his profession. After travelling for some time he settled at Florence, where he invented the art, or, at least, practised the art which he had previously invented, of painting with oil-colours on satin. He died at Spezzia on October 27, 1882.

[FOOTNOTE: The short notice of Gutmann in Fetis' Biographie Universelle des Musiciens, and those of the followers of this by no means infallible authority, are very incorrect. Adolfo Gutmann, Riccordi Biografici, by Giulio Piccini (Firenze: Guiseppe Polverini, 1881), reproduces to a great extent the information contained in Der Lieblingsschuler Chopin's in Bernhard Stavenow's Schone Geister (Bremen: Kuhlmann, 1879), both which publications, eulogistic rather than biographical, were inspired by Gutmann.]

Whatever interest the reader may have taken in this survey of Chopin's pupils, he is sure to be more deeply interested by the account of the master's manner and method of teaching. Such an account, which would be interesting in the case of any remarkable virtuoso who devoted himself to instruction, is so in a higher degree in that of Chopin: first, because it may help us to solve the question why so unique a virtuoso did not form a single eminent concert-player; secondly, because it throws still further light on his character as a man and artist; and thirdly, because, as Mikuli thinks may be asserted without exaggeration, "only Chopin's pupils knew the pianist in the fulness of his unrivalled height." The materials at my disposal are abundant and not less trustworthy than abundant. My account is based chiefly on the communications made to me by a number of the master's pupils—notably, Madame Dubois, Madame Rubio, M. Mathias, and Gutmann—and on Mikuli's excellent preface to his edition of Chopin's works. When I have drawn upon other sources, I have not done so without previous examination and verification. I may add that I shall use as far as possible the ipsissima verba of my informants:—

As to Chopin's method of teaching [wrote to me M. Mathias], it was absolutely of the old legato school, of the school of Clementi and Cramer. Of course, he had enriched it by a great variety of touch [d'une grande variete dans l'attaque de la touche]; he obtained a wonderful variety of tone and NUANCES of tone; in passing I may tell you that he had an extraordinary vigour, but only by flashes [ce ne pouvait etre que par eclairs].

The Polish master, who was so original in many ways, differed from his confreres even in the way of starting his pupils. With him the normal position of the hand was not that above the keys c, d, e, f, g (i.e., above five white keys), but that above the keys e, f sharp, g sharp, a sharp, b (I.E., above two white keys and three black keys, the latter lying between the former). The hand had to be thrown lightly on the keyboard so as to rest on these keys, the object of this being to secure for it not only an advantageous, but also a graceful position:—

[FOOTNOTE: Kleczynski, in Chopin: De l'interpretation de ses oeuvres—Trois conferences faites a Varsovie, says that he was told by several of the master's pupils that the latter sometimes held his hands absolutely flat. When I asked Madame Dubois about the correctness of this statement, she replied: "I never noticed Chopin holding his hands flat." In short, if Chopin put his hands at any time in so awkward a position, it was exceptional; physical exhaustion may have induced him to indulge in such negligence when the technical structure of the music he was playing permitted it.]

Chopin [Madame Dubois informed me] made his pupils begin with the B major scale, very slowly, without stiffness. Suppleness was his great object. He repeated, without ceasing, during the lesson: "Easily, easily" [facilement, facilement]. Stiffness exasperated him.

How much stiffness and jerkiness exasperated him may be judged from what Madame Zaleska related to M. Kleczynski. A pupil having played somewhat carelessly the arpeggio at the beginning of the first study (in A flat major) of the second book of Clementi's Preludes et Exercices, the master jumped from his chair and exclaimed: "What is that? Has a dog been barking?" [Qu'est-ce? Est-ce un chien qui vient d'aboyer?] The rudeness of this exclamation will, no doubt, surprise. But polite as Chopin generally was, irritation often got the better of him, more especially in later years when bad health troubled him. Whether he ever went the length of throwing the music from the desk and breaking chairs, as Karasowski says, I do not know and have not heard confirmed by any pupil. Madame Rubio, however, informed me that Chopin was very irritable, and when teaching amateurs used to have always a packet of pencils about him which, to vent his anger, he silently broke into bits. Gutmann told me that in the early stages of his discipleship Chopin sometimes got very angry, and stormed and raged dreadfully; but immediately was kind and tried to soothe his pupil when he saw him distressed and weeping.

To be sure [writes Mikuli], Chopin made great demands on the talent and diligence of the pupil. Consequently, there were often des lecons orageuses, as it was called in the school idiom, and many a beautiful eye left the high altar of the Cite d'Orleans, Rue St. Lazare, bedewed with tears, without, on that account, ever bearing the dearly-beloved master the least grudge. For was not the severity which was not easily satisfied with anything, the feverish vehemence with which the master wished to raise his disciples to his own stand-point, the ceaseless repetition of a passage till it was understood, a guarantee that he had at heart the progress of the pupil? A holy artistic zeal burnt in him then, every word from his lips was incentive and inspiring. Single lessons often lasted literally for hours at a stretch, till exhaustion overcame master and pupil.

Indeed, the pupils were so far from bearing their master the least grudge that, to use M. Marmontel's words, they had more for him than admiration: a veritable idolatry. But it is time that after this excursion—which hardly calls for an excuse—we return to the more important part of our subject, the master's method of teaching.

What concerned Chopin most at the commencement of his instruction [writes Mikuli] was to free the pupil from every stiffness and convulsive, cramped movement of the hand, and to give him thus the first condition of a beautiful style of playing, souplesse (suppleness), and with it independence of the fingers. He taught indefatigably that the exercises in question were no mere mechanical ones, but called for the intelligence and the whole will of the pupil, on which account twenty and even forty thoughtless repetitions (up to this time the arcanum of so many schools) do no good at all, still less the practising during which, according to Kalkbrenner's advice, one may occupy one's self simultaneously with some kind of reading(!).

He feared above all [remarked Madame Dubois to me] the abrutissement of the pupils. One day he heard me say that I practised six hours a day. He became quite angry, and forbade me to practise more than three hours. This was also the advice of Hummel in his pianoforte school.

To resume Mikuli's narrative:—

Chopin treated very thoroughly the different kinds of touch, especially the full-toned [tonvolle] legato.

[FOOTNOTE: Karasowski says that Chopin demanded absolutely from his pupils that they should practise the exercises, and especially the scales in major and minor, from piano to fortissimo, staccato as well as legato, and also with a change of accent, which was to be now on the second, now on the third, now on the fourth note. Madame Dubois, on the other hand, is sure she was never told by her master to play the scales staccato.]

"As gymnastic helps he recommended the bending inward and outward of the wrist, the repeated touch from the wrist, the extending of the fingers, but all this with the earnest warning against over-fatigue. He made his pupils play the scales with a full tone, as connectedly as possible, very slowly and only gradually advancing to a quicker TEMPO, and with metronomic evenness. The passing of the thumb under the other fingers and the passing of the latter over the former was to be facilitated by a corresponding turning inward of the hand. The scales with many black keys (B, F sharp, and D flat) were first studied, and last, as the most difficult, C major. In the same sequence he took up Clementi's Preludes et Exercices, a work which for its utility he esteemed very highly."

[FOOTNOTE: Kleczynski writes that whatever the degree of instruction was which Chopin's pupils brought with them, they had all to play carefully besides the scales the second book of Clementi's Preludes et Exercices, especially the first in A flat major.]

According to Chopin the evenness of the scales (also of the arpeggios) not merely depended on the utmost equal strengthening of all fingers by means of five-finger exercises and on a thumb entirely free at the passing under and over, but rather on a lateral movement (with the elbow hanging quite down and always easy) of the hand, not by jerks, but continuously and evenly flowing, which he tried to illustrate by the glissando over the keyboard. Of studies he gave after this a selection of Cramer's Etudes, Clementi's Gradus ad Parnassum, Moscheles' style-studies for the higher development (which were very sympathetic to him), and J. S. Bach's suites and some fugues from Das wohltemperirte Clavier. In a certain way Field's and his own nocturnes numbered likewise with the studies, for in them the pupil was—partly by the apprehension of his explanations, partly by observation and imitation (he played them to the pupil unweariedly)—to learn to know, love, and execute the beautiful smooth [gebundene] vocal tone and the legato.

[FOOTNOTE: This statement can only be accepted with much reserve. Whether Chopin played much or little to his pupil depended, no doubt, largely on the mood and state of health he was in at the time, perhaps also on his liking or disliking the pupil. The late Brinley Richards told me that when he had lessons from Chopin, the latter rarely played to him, making his corrections and suggestions mostly by word of mouth.]

With double notes and chords he demanded most strictly simultaneous striking, breaking was only allowed when it was indicated by the composer himself; shakes, which he generally began with the auxiliary note, had not so much to be played quick as with great evenness the conclusion of the shake quietly and without precipitation. For the turn (gruppetto) and the appoggiatura he recommended the great Italian singers as models. Although he made his pupils play octaves from the wrist, they must not thereby lose in fulness of tone.

All who have had the good fortune to hear Chopin play agree in declaring that one of the most distinctive features of his style of execution was smoothness, and smoothness, as we have seen in the foregoing notes, was also one of the qualities on which he most strenuously insisted in the playing of his pupils. The reader will remember Gutmann's statement to me, mentioned in a previous chapter, that all his master's fingering was calculated for the attainment of this object. Fingering is the mainspring, the determining principle, one might almost say the life and soul, of the pianoforte technique. We shall, therefore, do well to give a moment's consideration to Chopin's fingering, especially as he was one of the boldest and most influential revolutionisers of this important department of the pianistic art. His merits in this as in other respects, his various claims to priority of invention, are only too often overlooked. As at one time all ameliorations in the theory and practice of music were ascribed to Guido of Arezzo, so it is nowadays the fashion to ascribe all improvements and extensions of the pianoforte technique to Liszt, who more than any other pianist drew upon himself the admiration of the world, and who through his pupils continued to make his presence felt even after the close of his career as a virtuoso. But the cause of this false opinion is to be sought not so much in the fact that the brilliancy of his artistic personality threw all his contemporaries into the shade, as in that other fact, that he gathered up into one web the many threads new and old which he found floating about during the years of his development. The difference between Liszt and Chopin lies in this, that the basis of the former's art is universality, that of the latter's, individuality. Of the fingering of the one we may say that it is a system, of that of the other that it is a manner. Probably we have here also touched on the cause of Liszt's success and Chopin's want of success as a teacher. I called Chopin a revolutioniser of fingering, and, I think, his full enfranchisement of the thumb, his breaking-down of all distinctions of rank between the other fingers, in short, the introduction of a liberty sometimes degenerating into licence, justifies the expression. That this master's fingering is occasionally eccentric (presupposing peculiarly flexible hands and a peculiar course of study) cannot be denied; on the whole, however, it is not only well adapted for the proper rendering of his compositions, but also contains valuable contributions to a universal system of fingering. The following particulars by Mikuli will be read with interest, and cannot be misunderstood after what has just now been said on the subject:—

In the notation of fingering, especially of that peculiar to himself, Chopin was not sparing. Here pianoforte-playing owes him great innovations which, on account of their expedience, were soon adopted, notwithstanding the horror with which authorities like Kalkbrenner at first regarded them. Thus, for instance, Chopin used without hesitation the thumb on the black keys, passed it even under the little finger (it is true, with a distinct inward bend of the wrist), if this could facilitate the execution and give it more repose and evenness. With one and the same finger he took often two consecutive keys (and this not only in gliding down from a black to the next white key) without the least interruption of the sequence being noticeable. The passing over each other of the longer fingers without the aid of the thumb (see Etude, No. 2, Op. 10) he frequently made use of, and not only in passages where the thumb stationary on a key made this unavoidably necessary. The fingering of the chromatic thirds based on this (as he marked it in Etude, No. 5, Op. 25) affords in a much higher degree than that customary before him the possibility of the most beautiful legato in the quickest tempo and with a perfectly quiet hand.

But if with Chopin smoothness was one of the qualities upon which he insisted strenuously in the playing of his pupils, he was by no means satisfied with a mere mechanical perfection. He advised his pupils to undertake betimes thorough theoretical studies, recommending his friend, the composer and theorist Henri Reber as a teacher. He advised them also to cultivate ensemble playing—trios, quartets, &c., if first-class partners could be had, otherwise pianoforte duets. Most urgent, however, he was in his advice to them to hear good singing, and even to learn to sing. To Madame Rubio he said: "You must sing if you wish to play"; and made her take lessons in singing and hear much Italian opera—this last, the lady remarked, Chopin regarded as positively necessary for a pianoforte-player. In this advice we recognise Chopin's ideal of execution: beauty of tone, intelligent phrasing, truthfulness and warmth of expression. The sounds which he drew from the pianoforte were pure tone without the least admixture of anything that might be called noise. "He never thumped," was Gutmann's remark to me. Chopin, according to Mikuli, repeatedly said that when he heard bad phrasing it appeared to him as if some one recited, in a language he did not know, a speech laboriously memorised, not only neglecting to observe the right quantity of the syllables, but perhaps even making full stops in the middle of words. "The badly-phrasing pseudo-musician," he thought, "showed that music was not his mother-tongue, but something foreign, unintelligible to him," and that, consequently, "like that reciter, he must altogether give up the idea of producing any effect on the auditor by his rendering." Chopin hated exaggeration and affectation. His precept was: "Play as you feel." But he hated the want of feeling as much as false feeling. To a pupil whose playing gave evidence of nothing but the possession of fingers, he said emphatically, despairingly: "METTEZ-Y DONc TOUTE VOTRE AME!" (Do put all your soul into it!)

[FOOTNOTE: "In dynamical shading [im nuanciren]," says Mikuli, "he was exceedingly particular about a gradual increase and decrease of loudness." Karasowski writes: "Exaggeration in accentuation was hateful to him, for, in his opinion, it took away the poesy from playing, and gave it a certain didactic pedantry."]

On declamation, and rendering in general [writes Mikuli], he gave his pupils invaluable and significant instructions and hints, but, no doubt, effected more certain results by repeatedly playing not only single passages, but whole pieces, and this he did with a conscientiousness and enthusiasm that perhaps he hardly gave anyone an opportunity of hearing when he played in a concert-room. Frequently the whole hour passed without the pupil having played more than a few bars, whilst Chopin, interrupting and correcting him on a Pleyel cottage piano (the pupil played always on an excellent grand piano; and it was enjoined upon him as a duty to practise only on first-class instruments), presented to him for his admiration and imitation the life-warm ideal of the highest beauty.

With regard to Chopin's playing to his pupils we must keep in mind what was said in foot-note 12 on page 184. On another point in the above quotation one of Madame Dubois's communications to me throws some welcome light:—

Chopin [she said] had always a cottage piano [pianino] by the side of the grand piano on which he gave his lessons. It was marvellous to hear him accompany, no matter what compositions, from the concertos of Hummel to those of Beethoven. He performed the role of the orchestra most wonderfully [d'une facon prodigieuse]. When I played his own concertos, he accompanied me in this way.

Judging from various reports, Chopin seems to have regarded his Polish pupils as more apt than those of other nationalities to do full justice to his compositions. Karasowski relates that when one of Chopin's French pupils played his compositions and the auditors overwhelmed the performer with their praise, the master used often to remark that his pupil had done very well, but that the Polish element and the Polish enthusiasm had been wanting. Here it is impossible not to be reminded of the contention between Chopin on the one hand and Liszt and Hiller on the other hand about the possibility of foreigners comprehending Polish national music (See Vol. 1., p. 256). After revealing the mystery of Chopin's tempo rubato, Liszt writes in his book on this master:—

All his compositions have to be played with this sort of balancement accentue et prosodie, this morbidezza, of which it was difficult to seize the secret when one had not heard him often. He seemed desirous to teach this manner to his numerous pupils, especially to his compatriots, to whom he wished, more than to others, to communicate the breath of his inspiration. These [ceux-ci, ou plutot celles-la] seized it with that aptitude which they have for all matters of sentiment and poesy. An innate comprehension of his thought permitted them to follow all the fluctuations of his azure wave.

There is one thing which is worth inquiring into before we close this chapter, for it may help us to a deeper insight into Chopin's character as a teacher—I mean his teaching repertoire. Mikuli says that, carefully arranged according to their difficulty, Chopin placed before his pupils the following compositions: the concertos and sonatas of Clementi, Mozart, Bach, Handel, Scarlatti, Dussek, Field, Hummel, Ries, Beethoven; further, Weber, Moscheles, Mendelssohn, Hiller, Schumann, and his own works. This enumeration, however, does not agree with accounts from other equally authentic sources. The pupils of Chopin I have conversed and corresponded with never studied any Schumann under their master. As to the cultivation of Beethoven, it was, no doubt, limited. M. Mathias, it is true, told me that Chopin showed a preference for Clementi (Gradus ad Parnassum), Bach, Field (of him much was played, notably his concertos), and naturally for Beethoven, Weber, &c.—Clementi, Bach, and Field being always the composers most laid under contribution in the case of debutants. Madame Rubio, on the other hand, confined herself to stating that Chopin put her through Hummel, Moscheles, and Bach; and did not mention Beethoven at all. Gutmann's statements concerning his master's teaching contain some positive evidence with regard to the Beethoven question. What he said was this: Chopin held that dementi's Gradus ad Parnassum, Bach's pianoforte fugues, and Hummel's compositions were the key to pianoforte-playing, and he considered a training in these composers a fit preparation for his own works. He was particularly fond of Hummel and his style. Beethoven he seemed to like less. He appreciated such pieces as the first movement of the Moonlight Sonata (C sharp minor, Op. 27, No. 2). Schubert was a favourite with him. This, then, is what I learned from Gutmann. In parenthesis, as it were, I may ask: Is it not strange that no pupil, with the exception of Mikuli, mentions the name of Mozart, the composer whom Chopin is said to have so much admired? Thanks to Madame Dubois, who at my request had the kindness to make out a list of the works she remembers having studied under Chopin, we shall be able to form a pretty distinct idea of the master's course of instruction, which, to be sure, would be modified according to the capacities of his pupils and the objects they had in view. Well, Madame Dubois says that Chopin made her begin with the second book of Clementi's Preludes et Exercices, and that she also studied under him the same composer's Gradus ad Parnassum and Bach's forty-eight preludes and fugues. Of his high opinion of the teaching qualities of Bach's compositions we may form an idea from the recommendation to her at their last meeting—already mentioned in an earlier chapter—to practise them constantly, "ce sera votre meilleur moyen de progresser" (this will be your best means to make progress). The pieces she studied under him included the following ones: Of Hummel, the Rondo brillant sur un theme russe (Op. 98), La Bella capricciosa, the Sonata in F sharp minor (Op. 81), the Concertos in A minor and B minor, and the Septet; of Field, several concertos (the one in E flat among others) and several nocturnes ("Field" she says, "lui etait tres sympathique"); of Beethoven, the concertos and several sonatas (the Moonlight, Op. 27, No. 2; the one with the Funeral March, Op. 26; and the Appassionata, Op. 57); of Weber, the Sonatas in C and A flat major (Chopin made his pupils play these two works with extreme care); of Schubert, the

Landler and all the waltzes and some of the duets (the marches, polonaises, and the Divertissement hongrois, which last piece he admired sans reserve); of Mendelssohn, only the G minor Concerto and the Songs without Words; of Liszt, no more than La Tarantelle de Rossini and the Septet from Lucia ("mais ce genre de musique ne lui allait pas," says my informant); and of Schumann, NOTHING.

Madame Streicher's interesting reminiscences, given in Appendix III., form a supplement to this chapter.

CHAPTER XXIX

RUPTURE OF THE SAND-CHOPIN CONNECTION.—HER OWN, LISZT'S, AND KARASOWSKI'S ACCOUNTS.-THE LUCREZIA FLORIANI INCIDENT.—FURTHER INVESTIGATION OF THE CAUSES OF THE RUPTURE BY THE LIGHT OF LETTERS AND THE INFORMATION OF GUTMANN, FRANCHOMME, AND MADAME RUBIO.—SUMMING-UP OF THE EVIDENCE.—CHOPIN'S COMPOSITIONS IN 1847.—GIVES A CONCERT, HIS LAST IN PARIS (1848): WHAT AND HOW HE PLAYED; THE CHARACTER OF THE AUDIENCE.—GEORGE SAND AND CHOPIN MEET ONCE MORE.—THE FEBRUARY REVOLUTION; CHOPIN MAKES UP HIS MIND TO VISIT ENGLAND AND SCOTLAND.

WE now come to the catastrophe of Chopin's life, the rupture of his connection with George Sand. Although there is no lack of narratives in which the causes, circumstances, and time of this rupture are set forth with absolute positiveness, it is nevertheless an undeniable fact that we are not at the present moment, nor, all things well considered, shall be even in the most distant future, in a position to speak on this subject otherwise than conjecturally.

[FOOTNOTE: Except the letter of George Sand given on p. 75, and the note of Chopin to George Sand which will be given a little farther on, nothing, I think, of their correspondence has become public. But even if their letters were forth-coming, it is more likely than not that they would fail to clear up the mystery. Here I ought, perhaps, to reproduce the somewhat improbable story told in the World of December 14, 1887, by the Paris correspondent who signs himself "Theoc." He writes as follows: "I have heard that it was by saving her letters to Chopin that M. Alexandre Dumas won the friendship of George Sand. The anecdote runs thus: When Chopin died, his sister found amongst his papers some two hundred letters of Madame Sand, which she took with her to Poland. By chance this lady had some difficulties at the frontier with the Russian custom-house officials; her trunks were seized, and the box containing the letters was mislaid and lost. A few years afterwards, one of the custom-house officials found the letters and kept them, not knowing the name and the address of the Polish lady who had lost them. M. Dumas discovered this fact, and during a journey in Russia he explained to this official how painful it would be if by some indiscretion these letters of the illustrious novelist ever got into print. 'Let me restore them to Madame Sand,' said M. Dumas. 'And my duty?' asked the customs official. 'If anybody ever claims the letters,' replied M. Dumas, 'I authorise you to say that I stole them.' On this condition M. Dumas, then a young man, obtained the letters, brought them back to Paris, and restored them to Madame Sand, whose acquaintance he thus made. Madame Sand burnt all her letters to Chopin, but she never forgot the service that M. Dumas had rendered her."]

I have done my utmost to elucidate the tragic event which it is impossible not to regard as one of the most momentous crises in Chopin's life, and have succeeded in collecting besides the material already known much that is new; but of what avail is this for coming to a final decision if we find the depositions hopelessly contradictory, and the witnesses more or less untrustworthy—self-interest makes George Sand's evidence suspicious, the instability of memory that of others. Under the circumstances it seems to me safest to place before the reader the depositions of the various witnesses—not, however, without comment—and leave him to form his own conclusions. I shall begin with the account which George Sand gives in her Ma Vie:—

After the last relapses of the invalid, his mind had become extremely gloomy, and Maurice, who had hitherto tenderly loved him, was suddenly wounded by him in an unexpected manner about a trifling subject. They embraced each other the next moment, but the grain of sand had fallen into the tranquil lake, and little by little the pebbles fell there, one after another...All this was borne; but at last, one day, Maurice, tired of the pin-pricks, spoke of giving up the game. That could not be, and should not be. Chopin would not stand my legitimate and necessary intervention. He bowed his head and said that I no longer loved him.

What blasphemy after these eight years of maternal devotion! But the poor bruised heart was not conscious of its delirium. I thought that some months passed at a distance and in silence would heal the wound, and make his friendship again calm and his memory equitable. But the revolution of February came, and Paris became momentarily hateful to this mind incapable of yielding to any commotion in the social form. Free to return to Poland, or certain to be tolerated there, he had preferred languishing ten [and some more] years far from his family, whom he adored, to the pain of seeing his country transformed and deformed [denature]. He had fled from tyranny, as now he fled from liberty.

I saw him again for an instant in March, 1848. I pressed his trembling and icy hand. I wished to speak to him, he slipped away. Now it was my turn to say that he no longer loved me. I spared him this infliction, and entrusted all to the hands of Providence and the future.

I was not to see him again. There were bad hearts between us. There were good ones too who were at a loss what to do. There were frivolous ones who preferred not to meddle with such delicate matters; Gutmann was not there.

I have been told that he had asked for me, regretted me, and loved me filially up to the very end. It was thought fit to conceal this from me till then. It was also thought fit to conceal from him that I was ready to hasten to him.

Liszt's account is noteworthy because it gives us the opinion of a man who knew the two principal actors in the drama intimately, and had good opportunities to learn what contemporary society thought about it. Direct knowledge of the facts, however, Liszt had not, for he was no longer a friend either of the one or the other of the two parties:—

These commencements, of which Madame de Stael spoke, [FOOTNOTE: He alludes to her saying: En amour, il n'y a que des commencemens.] had already for a long time been exhausted between the Polish artist and the French poet. They had only survived with the one by a violent effort of respect for the ideal which he had gilded with its fatal brilliancy; with the other by a false shame which sophisticated on the pretension to preserve constancy in fidelity. The time came when this factitious existence, which succeeded no longer in galvanising fibres dried up under the eyes of the spiritualistic artist, seemed to him to surpass what honour permitted him not to perceive. No one knew what was the cause or the pretext of the sudden rupture; one saw only that after a violent opposition to the marriage of the daughter of the house, Chopin abruptly left Nohant never to return again.

However unreliable Liszt's facts may be, the PHILOSOPHY of his account shows real insight. Karasowski, on the other hand, has neither facts nor insight. He speaks with a novelist's confidence and freedom of characters whom he in no way knows, and about whom he has nothing to tell but the vaguest and most doubtful of second-hand hearsays:—

The depressed invalid became now to her a burden. At first her at times sombre mien and her shorter visits in the sick-room showed him that her sympathy for him was on the decrease; Chopin felt this painfully, but he said nothing...\The complaints of Madame Sand that the nursing of the invalid exhausted her strength, complaints which she often gave expression to in his presence, hurt him. He entreated her to leave him alone, to take walks in the fresh air; he implored her not to give up for his sake her amusements, but to frequent the theatre, to give parties, &c.; he would be contented in quietness and solitude if he only knew that she was happy. At last, when the invalid still failed to think of a separation from her, she chose a heroic means.

By this heroic means Karasowski understands the publication of George Sand's novel Lucrezia Floriani (in 1847), concerning which he says the story goes that "out of refined cruelty the proof-sheets were handed to him [Chopin] with the request to correct the misprints." Karasowski also reports as a "fact" that

the children of Madame Sand [who, by the way, were a man of twenty-three and a woman of eighteen] said to him [Chopin], pointing to the novel: "M. Chopin, do you know that you are meant by the Prince Karol?"...In spite of all this the invalid, and therefore less passionate, artist bore with the most painful feeling the mortification caused him by the novel...At the beginning of the year 1847 George Sand brought about by a violent scene, the innocent cause of which was her daughter, a complete rupture. To the unjust reproaches which she made to him, he merely replied: "I shall immediately leave your house, and wish henceforth no longer to be regarded by you as living." These words were very welcome to her; she made no objections, and the very same day the artist left for ever the house of Madame Sand. But the excitement and the mental distress connected with it threw him once more on the sick-bed, and for a long time people seriously feared that he would soon exchange it for a coffin.

George Sand's view of the Lucrezia Floriani incident must be given in full. In Ma Vie she writes as follows:—

It has been pretended that in one of my romances I have painted his [Chopin's] character with a great exactness of analysis. People were mistaken, because they thought they recognised some of his traits; and, proceeding by this system, too convenient to be sure, Liszt himself, in a Life of Chopin, a little exuberant as regards style, but nevertheless full of very good things and very beautiful pages, has gone astray in good faith. I have traced in Prince Karol the character of a man determined in his nature, exclusive in his sentiments, exclusive in his exigencies.

Chopin was not such. Nature does not design like art, however realistic it may be. She has caprices, inconsequences, probably not real, but very mysterious. Art only rectifies these inconsequences because it is too limited to reproduce them.

Chopin was a resume of these magnificent inconsequences which God alone can allow Himself to create, and which have their particular logic. He was modest on principle, gentle by habit, but he was imperious by instinct and full of a legitimate pride which was unconscious of itself. Hence sufferings which he did not reason and which did not fix themselves on a determined object.

Moreover, Prince Karol is not an artist. He is a dreamer, and nothing more; having no genius, he has not the rights of genius. He is, therefore, a personage more true than amiable, and the portrait is so little that of a great artist that Chopin, in reading the manuscript every day on my writing-desk, had not the slightest inclination to deceive himself, he who, nevertheless, was so suspicious.

And yet afterwards, by reaction, he imagined, I am told, that this was the case. Enemies, I had such about him who call themselves his friends; as if embittering a suffering heart was not murder, enemies made him believe that this romance was a revelation of his character. At that time his memory was, no doubt, enfeebled: he had forgotten the book, why did he not reread it!

This history is so little ours! It was the very reverse of it There were between us neither the same raptures [enivrements] nor the same sufferings. Our history had nothing of a romance; its foundation was too simple and too serious for us ever to have had occasion for a quarrel with each other, a propos of each other.

The arguments advanced by George Sand are anything but convincing; in fact, her defence is extremely weak. She does not even tell us that she did not make use of Chopin as a model. That she drew a caricature and not a portrait will hardly be accepted as an excuse, nay, is sure to be regarded as the very head and front of her offending. But George Sand had extraordinarily naive notions on this subject, notions which are not likely to be shared by many, at least not by many outside the fraternities of novelists and dramatists. Having mentioned, in speaking of her grand-uncle the Abbe de Beaumont, that she thought of him when sketching the portrait of a certain canon in Consuelo, and that she had very much exaggerated the resemblance to meet the requirements of the romance, she remarks that portraits traced in this way are no longer portraits, and that those who feel offended on recognising themselves do an injustice both to the author and themselves. "Caricature or idealisation," she writes, "it is no longer the original model, and this model has little judgment if it thinks it recognises itself, if it becomes angry or vain on seeing what art or imagination has been able to make of it." This is turning the tables with a vengeance; and if impudence can silence the voice of truth and humanity, George Sand has gained her case. In her account of the Lucrezia Floriani incident George Sand proceeds as usual when she is attacked and does not find it more convenient simply to declare that she will not condescend to defend herself—namely, she envelops the whole matter in a mist of beautiful words and sentiments out of which issues—and this is the only clearly-distinguishable thing—her own saintly self in celestial radiance. But notwithstanding all her arguments and explanations there remains the fact that Liszt and thousands of others, I one of them, read Lucrezia Floriani and were not a moment in doubt that Chopin was the prototype of Prince Karol. We will not charge George Sand with the atrocity of writing the novel for the purpose of getting rid of Chopin; but we cannot absolve her from the sin of being regardless of the pain she would inflict on one who once was dear to her, and who still loved her ardently. Even Miss Thomas, [FOOTNOTE: In George Sand, a volume of the "Eminent Women Series."] who generally takes George Sand at her own valuation, and in this case too tries to excuse her, admits that in Lucrezia Floriani there was enough of reality interwoven to make the world hasten to identify or confound Chopin with Prince Karol, that Chopin, the most sensitive of mortals, could not but be pained by the inferences which would be drawn, that "perhaps if only as a genius he had the right to be spared such an infliction," and that, therefore, "one must wish it could have appeared in this light to Madame Sand." This is a mild way of expressing disapproval of conduct that shows, to say the least, an inhuman callousness to the susceptibilities of a fellow-being. And to speak of the irresistible prompting of genius in connection with one who had her faculties so well under her control is downright mockery. It would, however, be foolish to expect considerateness for others in one who needlessly detailed and proclaimed to the world not only the little foibles but also the drunkenness and consequent idiocy and madness of a brother whose family was still living. Her practice was, indeed, so much at variance with her profession that it is preposterous rather to accept than to doubt her words. George Sand was certainly not the self-sacrificing woman she pretended to be; for her sacrifices never outlasted her inclinations, they were, indeed, nothing else than an abandonment to her desires. And these desires were the directors of her reason, which, aided by an exuberant imagination, was never at a loss to justify any act, be it ever so cruel and abject. In short, the chief characteristic of George Sand's moral constitution was her incapacity of regarding anything she did otherwise than as right. What I have said is fully borne out by her Ma Vie and the "Correspondance," which, of course, can be more easily and safely examined than her deeds and spoken words.

And now we will continue our investigations of the causes and circumstances of the rupture. First I shall quote some passages from letters written by George Sand, between which will be inserted a note from Chopin to her. If the reader does not see at once what several of these quotations have to do with the matter under discussion, he will do so before long.

Madame Sand to Madame Marliani; Nohant, September 1, 1846:—

It is exceedingly kind of you to offer me shelter [un gîte].
We have still our apartments in the Square Saint-Lazare
[Square d'Orleans], and nothing would prevent us from going
there.
Chopin to Madame Sand; Tuesday 2 1/2 [Paris, December 15,
1846]

[FOOTNOTE: The date is that of the postmark. A German
translation of the French original (in the Imperial Public
Library at St. Petersburg) will be found in La Mara's
"Musikerbriefe."]:—

Mademoiselle de Rozieres has found the piece of cloth in
question (it was in the camail-carton of Mdlle. Augustine),
and I sent it at once last night to Borie, [Victor Borie a
publicist and friend of George Sand] who, as Peter was told,
does not yet leave to-day. Here we have a little sun and
Russian snow. I am glad of this weather for your sake, and
imagine you walking about a great deal. Did Dib dance in last
night's pantomime? May you and yours enjoy good health!

Your most devoted,

C.

For your dear children.

I am well; but I have not the courage to leave my fireside for a moment.
Madame Sand to Madame Marliani; Nohant, May 6, 1847:—

Solange marries in a fortnight Clesinger, the sculptor, a man of great talent, who is making much money, and can give her the brilliant existence which, I believe, is to her taste. He is very violently in love with her, and he pleases her much. She was this time as prompt and firm in her determination as she was hitherto capricious and irresolute. Apparently she has met with what she dreamt of. May God grant it!

As regards myself, the young man pleases me also much and Maurice likewise. He is little civilised at first sight; but he is full of sacred fire and for some time past, since I noticed him making advances, I have been studying him without having the appearance of doing so...He has other qualities which compensate for all the defects he may have and ought to have.

...Somebody told me of him all the ill that can be said of a man [on making inquiries George Sand found that Clesinger was a man "irreproachable in the best sense of the word"].

M. Dudevant, whom he has been to see, consents. We do not know yet where the marriage will take place. Perhaps at Nerac, [FOOTNOTE: Where M. Dudevant, her whilom husband, resided.] in order to prevent M. Dudevant from falling asleep in the eternal to-morrow to the province.
Madame Sand to Mazzini; Nohant, May 22, 1847:—

I have just married and, I believe, well married my daughter to an artist of powerful inspiration and will. I had for her but one ambition—namely, that she should love and be loved; my wish is realised. The future is in the hand of God, but I believe in the duration of this love and this union.

Madame Sand to Charles Poncy; Nohant, August 9, 1847:—

My good Maurice is always calm, occupied, and lively. He sustains and consoles me. Solange is in Paris with her husband; they are going to travel. Chopin is in Paris also; his health has not yet permitted him to make the journey; but he is better.

The following letter, of an earlier date than those from which my last two excerpts are taken, is more directly concerned with Chopin.

Madame Sand to Gutmann; Nohant, May 12, 1847:—

Thanks, my good Gutmann, thanks from the bottom of my heart for the admirable care which you lavish on him [Chopin]. I know well that it is for him, for yourself, and not for me, that you act thus, but I do not the less feel the need of thanking you. It is a great misfortune for me that this happens at a moment like that in which I find myself. Truly, this is too much anxiety at one time! I would have gone mad, I believe, if I had learned the gravity of his illness before hearing that the danger was past. He does not know that I know of it, and on account, especially, of the embarras in which he knows I find myself, he wishes it to be concealed from me. He wrote to me yesterday as if nothing had taken place, and I have answered him as if I suspected as yet nothing. Therefore, do not tell him that I write to you, and that for twenty-four hours I have suffered terribly. Grzymala writes about you very kindly a propos of the tenderness with which you have taken my place by the side of him, and you especially, so that I will

tell you that I know it, and that my heart will keep account
of it seriously and for ever...

Au revoir, then, soon, my dear child, and receive my maternal
benediction. May it bring you luck as I wish!

George Sand.

[FOOTNOTE: This letter, which is not contained in the
"Correspondance," was, as far as I know, first published in
"Die Gegenwart" (Berlin, July 12, 1879)]

If all that George Sand here says is bona fide, the letter proves that the
rupture had not yet taken place. Indeed, Gutmann was of opinion that it did
not take place till 1848, shortly before Chopin's departure for England, that,
in-fact, she, her daughter, and son-in-law were present at the concert he gave
on February 16, 1848. That this, however, was not the case is shown both by
a letter written by George Sand from Nohant on February 18, 1848, and by
another statement of Gutmann's, according to which one of the causes of
the rupture was the marriage of Solange with Clesinger of which Chopin
(foreseeing unhappiness which did not fail to come, and led to separation)
did not approve. Another cause, he thought, was Chopin's disagreements
with Maurice Sand. There were hasty remarks and sharp retorts between
lover and son, and scenes in consequence. Gutmann is a very unsatisfactory
informant, everything he read and heard seemed to pass through the retort
of his imagination and reappear transformed as his own experience.

A more reliable witness is Franchomme, who in a letter to me summed
up the information which he had given me on this subject by word of mouth
as follows:—

Strange to say [chose bizarre], Chopin had a horror of the
figure 7; he would not have taken lodgings in a house which
bore the number 7; he would not have set out on a journey on
the 7th or 17th, &c. It was in 1837 that he formed the liaison
with George Sand; it was in 1847 that the rupture took place;
it was on the 17th October that my dear friend said farewell
to us. The rupture between Chopin and Madame Sand came about
in this way. In June, 1847, Chopin was making ready to start
for Nohant when he received a letter from Madame Sand to the

effect that she had just turned out her daughter and son-in-law, and that if he received them in his house all would be over between them [i.e., between George Sand and Chopin]. I was with Chopin at the time the letter arrived, and he said to me, "They have only me, and should I close my door upon them? No, I shall not do it!" and he did not do it, and yet he knew that this creature whom he adored would not forgive it him. Poor friend, how I have seen him suffer!

Of the quarrel at Nohant, Franchomme gave the following account:— There was staying at that time at Nohant a gentleman who treated Madame Clesinger invariably with rudeness. One day as Clesinger and his wife went downstairs the person in question passed without taking off his hat. The sculptor stopped him, and said, "Bid madam a good day"; and when the gentleman or churl, as the case may be, refused, he gave him a box on the ear. George Sand, who stood at the top of the stairs, saw it, came down, and gave in her turn Clesinger a box on the ear. After this she turned her son-in-law together with his wife out of her house, and wrote the above-mentioned letter to Chopin.

Madame Rubio had also heard of the box on the ear which George Sand gave Clesinger. According to this informant there were many quarrels between mother and daughter, the former objecting to the latter's frequent visits to Chopin, and using this as a pretext to break with him. Gutmann said to me that Chopin was fond of Solange, though not in love with her. But now we have again got into the current of gossip, and the sooner we get out of it the better.

Before I draw my conclusions from the evidence I have collected, I must find room for some extracts from two letters, respectively written on August 9, 1847, and December 14,1847, to Charles Poncy. The contents of these extracts will to a great extent be a mystery to the reader, a mystery to which I cannot furnish the key. Was Solange the chief subject of George Sand's lamentations? Had Chopin or her brother, or both, to do with this paroxysm of despair?

After saying how she has been overwhelmed by a chain of chagrins, how her purest intentions have had a fatal issue, how her best actions have been blamed by men and punished by heaven as crimes, she proceeds:—

And do you think I have reached the end? No, all I have told you hitherto is nothing, and since my last letter I have exhausted all the cup of life contains of tribulation. It is even so bitter and unprecedented that I cannot speak of it, at least I cannot write it. Even that would give me too much pain. I will tell you something about it when I see you...I hoped at least for the old age on which I was entering the recompense of great sacrifices, of much work, fatigue, and a whole life of devotion and abnegation. I asked for nothing but to render happy the objects of my affection. Well, I have been repaid with ingratitude, and evil has got the upper hand in a soul which I wished to make the sanctuary and the hearth of the beautiful and the good. At present I struggle against myself in order not to let myself die. I wish to accomplish my task unto the end. May God aid me! I believe in Him and hope!...Augustine has suffered much, but she has had great courage and a true feeling of her dignity; and her health, thank God, has not suffered.

[FOOTNOTE: Augustine Brault was according to the editor of the Correspondance a cousin of George Sand's; George Sand herself calls her in Ma Vie her parent, and tells us in a vague way how her connection with this young lady gave occasion to scandalous libels.]

The next quotation is from the letter dated Nohant, December 14, 1847. Desirez is the wife of Charles Poncy, to whom the letter is addressed.

You have understood, Desirez and you, you whose soul is delicate because it is ardent, that I passed through the gravest and most painful phase of my life. I nearly succumbed, although I had foreseen it for a long time. But you know one is not always under the pressure of a sinister foresight, however evident it may be. There are days, weeks, entire months even, when one lives on illusions, and when one flatters one's self one is turning aside the blow which threatens one. At last, the most probable misfortune always surprises us disarmed and unprepared. In addition to this development of the unhappy germ, which was going on unnoticed, there have arisen several very bitter and altogether unexpected accessory circumstances. The result is that I am broken in soul and body with chagrin. I believe that this chagrin is incurable; for the better I succeed in freeing myself from it for some hours, the more sombre and poignant does it re-enter into me in the following hours...I have undertaken a lengthy work [un ouvrage de longue haleine] entitled Histoire de ma Vie...However, I shall not reveal the whole of my life...It will be, moreover, a pretty good piece of business, which will put me on my feet again, and will relieve me of a part of my anxieties with regard to the future of Solange, which is rather compromised.

We have, then, the choice of two explanations of the rupture: George Sand's, that it was caused by the disagreement of Chopin and her son; and Franchomme's, that it was brought about by Chopin's disregard of George Sand's injunction not to receive her daughter and son-in-law. I prefer the latter version, which is reconcilable with George Sand's letters, confirmed by the testimony of several of Chopin's friends, and given by an honest, simple-minded man who may be trusted to have told a plain unvarnished tale.

[FOOTNOTE: The contradictions are merely apparent, and disappear if we consider that George Sand cannot have had any inclination to give to Gutmann and Poncy an explanation of the real state of matters. Moreover, when she wrote to the former the rupture had, according to Franchomme, not yet taken place.]

But whatever reason may have been alleged to justify, whatever circumstance may have been the ostensible cause of the rupture, in reality it was only a pretext. On this point all agree—Franchomme, Gutmann, Kwiatkowski, Madame Rubio, Liszt, &c. George Sand was tired of Chopin, and as he did not leave her voluntarily, the separation had to be forced upon him. Gutmann thought there was no rupture at all. George Sand went to Nohant without Chopin, ceased to write to him, and thus the connection came to an end. Of course, Chopin ought to have left her before she had recourse to the "heroic means" of kicking him, metaphorically speaking, out of doors. But the strength of his passion for this woman made him weak. If a tithe of what is rumoured about George Sand's amorous escapades is true, a lover who stayed with her for eight years must have found his capacity of overlooking and forgiving severely tested. We hear on all sides of the infidelities she permitted herself. A Polish friend of Chopin's informed me that one day when he was about to enter the composer's, room to pay him a visit, the married Berrichon female servant of George Sand came out of it; and Chopin, who was lying ill in bed, told him afterwards that she had been complaining of her mistress and husband. Gutmann, who said that Chopin knew of George Sand's occasional infidelities, pretended to have heard him say when she had left him behind in Paris: "I would overlook all if only she would allow me to stay with her at Nohant." I regard these and such like stories, especially the last one, with suspicion (is it probable that the reticent artist was communicative on so delicate a subject, and with Gutmann, his pupil and a much younger man?), but they cannot be ignored, as they are characteristic of how Chopin's friends viewed his position. And yet, tormented as he must have been in the days of possession, crushed as he was by the loss, tempted as he subsequently often felt to curse her and her deceitfulness, he loved and missed George Sand to the very end—even the day before his death he said to Franchomme that she had told him he would die in no other arms but hers (que je ne mourrais que dans ses bras).

If George Sand had represented her separation from Chopin as a matter of convenience, she would have got more sympathy and been able to make out a better case.

The friendship of Chopin [she writes in Ma Vie] has never been
for me a refuge in sadness. He had quite enough troubles of
his own to bear. Mine would have overwhelmed him; moreover, he
knew them only vaguely and did not understand them at all. He
would have appreciated them from a point of view very
different from mine.

Besides Chopin's illnesses became more frequent, his strength diminished from day to day, and care and attendance were consequently more than ever needful. That he was a "detestable patient" has already been said. The world takes it for granted that the wife or paramour of a man of genius is in duty bound to sacrifice herself for him. But how does the matter stand when there is genius on both sides, and self-sacrifice of either party entails loss to the world? By the way, is it not very selfish and hypocritical of this world which generally does so little for men of genius to demand that women shall entirely, self-denyingly devote themselves to their gifted lovers? Well, both George Sand and Chopin had to do work worth doing, and if one of them was hampered by the other in doing it, the dissolution of the union was justified. But perhaps this was not the reason of the separation. At any rate, George Sand does not advance such a plea. Still, it would have been unfair not to discuss this possible point of view.

The passage from the letter of George Sand dated September 1, 1846, which I quoted earlier in this chapter, justifies us, I think, in assuming that, although she was still keeping on her apartments in the Square d'Orleans, the phalanstery had ceased to exist. The apartments she gave up probably sometime in 1847; at any rate, she passed the winter of 1847-8, for the most part at least, at Nohant; and when after the outbreak of the revolution of 1848 she came to Paris (between the 9th and 14th of March), she put up at a hotel garni. Chopin continued to live in his old quarters in the Square d'Orldans, and, according to Gutmann, was after the cessation of his connection with George Sand in the habit of dining either with him (Gutmann) or Grzymala, that is to say, in their company.

It is much to be regretted that no letters are forthcoming to tell us of Chopin's feelings and doings at this time. I can place before the reader no more than one note, the satisfactory nature of which makes up to some extent for its brevity. It is addressed to Franchomme; dated Friday, October 1, 1847; and contains only these few words:—

Dear friend,—I thank you for your good heart, but I am very RICH this evening. Yours with all my heart.

In this year—i.e., 1847—appeared the three last works which Chopin published, although among his posthumous compositions there are two of a later date. The Trois Mazurkas, Op. 63 (dedicated to the Comtesse L. Czosnowska), and the Trois Valses, Op. 64 (dedicated respectively to Madame la Comtesse Potocka, Madame la Baronne de Rothschild, and Madame la Baronne Bronicka), appeared in September, and the Sonata for piano and violoncello, Op. 65 (dedicated to Franchomme), in October. Now I will say of these compositions only that the mazurkas and waltzes are not inferior to his previous works of this kind, and that the sonata is one of his most strenuous efforts in the larger forms. Mr. Charles Halle remembers going one evening in 1847 with Stephen Heller to Chopin, who had invited some friends to let them hear this sonata which he had lately finished. On arriving at his house they found him rather unwell; he went about the room bent like a half-opened penknife. The visitors proposed to leave him and to postpone the performance, but Chopin would not hear of it. He said he would try. Having once begun, he soon became straight again, warming as he proceeded. As will be seen from some remarks of Madame Dubois's, which I shall quote farther on, the sonata did not make an altogether favourable impression on the auditors.

The name of Madame Dubois reminds me of the soiree immortalised by a letter of Madame Girardin (see the one of March 7, 1847, in Vol. IV. of Le Vicomte de Launay), and already several times alluded to by me in preceding chapters. At this soiree Chopin not only performed several of his pieces, but also accompanied on a second piano his E minor Concerto which was played by his pupil, the youthful and beautiful Mdlle. Camille O'Meara. But the musical event par excellence of the period of Chopin's life with which we are concerned in this chapter is his concert, the last he gave in Paris, on February 16, 1848. Before I proceed with my account of it, I must quote a note, enclosing tickets for this concert, which Chopin wrote at this time to Franchomme. It runs thus: "The best places en evidence for Madame D., but not for her cook." Madame D. was Madame Paul Delaroche, the wife of the great painter, and a friend of Franchomme's.

But here is a copy of the original programme:—

FIRST PART.

Trio by Mozart, for piano, violin, and violoncello,
performed by MM. Chopin, Alard, and Franchomme.

Aria, sung by Mdlle. Antonia Molina di Mondi.

Nocturne, |
| —composed and performed by M. Chopin.
Barcarole, |

Air, sung by Mdlle. Antonia Molina di Mondi.

Etude, |
| —composed and performed by M. Chopin.
Berceuse, |

SECOND PART.

Scherzo, Adagio, and Finale of the Sonata in G minor, for
piano and violoncello, composed by M. Chopin, and performed
by the author and M. Franchomme.

Air nouveau from Robert le Diable, composed by M. Meyerbeer,
sung by M. Roger.

Preludes, |

|

Mazurkas, |—composed and performed by M. Chopin.

|

Valse, |

Accompanists:—MM. Aulary and de Garaude.

The report of "M. S." in the Gazette musicale of February 20, 1848, transports us at once into the midst of the exquisite, perfume-laden atmosphere of Pleyel's rooms on February 16:—

A concert by the Ariel of pianists is a thing too rare to be given, like other concerts, by opening both wings of the doors to whomsoever wishes to enter. For this one a list had been drawn up: everyone inscribed thereon his name: but everyone was not sure of obtaining the precious ticket: patronage was required to be admitted into the holy of holies, to obtain the favour of depositing one's offering, and yet this offering amounted to a louis; but who has not a louis to spare whep Chopin may be heard?

The outcome of all this naturally was that the fine flower of the aristocracy of the most distinguished women, the most elegant toilettes, filled on Wednesday Pleyel's rooms. There was also the aristocracy of artists and amateurs, happy to seize in his flight this musical sylph who had promised to let himself once more and for a few hours be approached, seen, and heard.

The sylph kept his word, and with what success, what enthusiasm! It is easier to tell you of the reception he got, the transport he excited, than to describe, analyse, divulge, the mysteries of an execution which was nothing analogous in our terrestrial regions. If we had in our power the pen which traced the delicate marvels of Queen Mab, not bigger than an agate that glitters on the finger of an alderman, of her liny chariot, of her diaphanous team, only then should we succeed in giving an idea of a purely ideal talent into which matter enters hardly at all. Only Chopin can make Chopin understood: all those who were present at the seance of Wednesday are convinced of this as well as we.

The programme announced first a trio of Mozart, which Chopin, Alard, and Franchomme executed in such a manner that one despairs of ever hearing it again so well performed. Then Chopin played studies, preludes, mazurkas, waltzes; he performed afterwards his beautiful sonata with Franchomme. Do not ask us how all these masterpieces small and great were rendered. We said at first we would not attempt to reproduce these thousands and thousands of nuances of an exceptional genius having in his service an organisation of the same kind. We shall only say that the charm did not cease to act a single instant on the audience, and that it still lasted after the concert was ended.

Let us add that Roger, our brilliant tenor, sang with his most expressive voice the beautiful prayer intercalated in Robert le Diable by the author himself at the debut of Mario at the Opera; that Mdlle. Antonia de Mendi [a niece of Pauline Viardot's; see the spelling of her name in the programme], the young and beautiful singer, carried off her share of bravos by her talent full of hope and promise.

There is a talk of a second concert which Chopin is to give on the 10th of March, and already more than 600 names are put down on the new list. In this there is nothing astonishing; Chopin owed us this recompense, and he well deserves this eagerness.

As this report, although it enables us to realise the atmosphere, is otherwise lacking in substance, we must try to get further information elsewhere. Happily, there is plenty at our disposal.

Before playing the violoncello sonata in public [wrote Madame Dubois to me], Chopin had tried it before some artists and intimate friends; the first movement, the masterpiece, was not understood. It appeared to the hearers obscure, involved by too many ideas, in short, it had no success. At the last moment Chopin dared not play the whole sonata before so worldly and elegant an audience, but confined himself to the Scherzo, Adagio, and Finale. I shall never forget the manner in which he executed the Barcarole, that adorable composition; the Waltz in D flat (la valse au petit chien) was encored amidst the acclamations of the public. A grande dame who was present at this concert wished to know Chopin's secret of making the scales so flowing on the piano [faire les gammes si coulees stir le piano]. The expression is good, and this limpidity has never been equalled.

Stephen Heller's remark to me, that Chopin became in his last years so weak that his playing was sometimes hardly audible, I have already related in a preceding chapter. There I have also mentioned what Mr. Charles Halle' told me—namely, that in the latter part of his life Chopin often played forte passages piano and even pianissimo, that, for instance, at the concert we are speaking of he played the two forte passages towards the end of the Barcarole pianissimo and with all sorts of dynamic finesses. Mr. Otto Goldschmidt, who was present at the concert on February 16, 1848, gave some interesting recollections of it, after the reading of a paper on the subject of Chopin, by Mr. G. A. Osborne, at one of the meetings of the Musical Association (see Proceedings, of the Musical Association for the year 1879-80):—

He [Chopin] was extremely weak, but still his playing—by reason of that remarkable quality which he possessed of gradation in touch—betrayed none of the impress of weakness which some attributed to piano playing or softness of touch; and he possessed in a greater degree than any pianoforte-player he [Mr. Goldschmidt] had ever heard, the faculty of passing upwards from piano through all gradations of tone...It was extremely difficult to obtain admission, for Chopin, who had been truly described as a most sensitive man—which seemed to be pre-eminently a quality of artistic organisations—not only had a list submitted to him of those who ought to be admitted, but he sifted that list, and made a selection from the selected list; he was, therefore, surrounded by none but friends and admirers. The room was beautifully decorated with flowers of all kinds, and he could truly say that even now, at the distance of thirty years, he had the most vivid recollection of the concert...The audience was so enraptured with his [Chopin's] playing that he was called forward again and again.

In connection with what Mr. Goldschmidt and the writer in the Gazette musicale say about the difficulty of admission and a sifted list, I have to record, and I shall do no more than record, Franchomme's denial. "I really believe," he said to me, "that this is a mere fiction. I saw Chopin every day; how, then, could I remain ignorant of it?"

To complete my account of Chopin's last concert in Paris, I have yet to add some scraps of information derived from Un nid d'autographes, by Oscar Comettant, who was present at it, and, moreover, reported on it in Le Siecle. The memory of the event was brought back to him when on looking over autographs in the possession of Auguste Wolff, the successor of Camille Pleyel, he found a ticket for the above described concert. As the concert so was also the ticket unlike that of any other artist. "Les lettres d'ecriture anglaise etaient gravees au burin et imprimees en taille-douce sur de beau papier mi-carton glace, d'un carre long elegant et distingue." It bore the following words and figures:—

SOIREE DE M. CHOPIN,

DANS L'UN DES SALONS DE MM. PLEYEL ET CIE.,

20, Rue Rochechouart,

Le mercredi 16 fevrier 1848 a 8 heures 1/2.

Rang....Prix 20 francs....Place reservee.

M. Comettant, in contradiction to what has been said by others about Chopin's physical condition, states that when the latter came on the platform, he walked upright and without feebleness; his face, though pale, did not seem greatly altered; and he played as he had always played. But M.

Comettant was told that Chopin, having spent at the concert all his moral and physical energy, afterwards nearly fainted in the artists' room.

In March Chopin and George Sand saw each other once more. We will rest satisfied with the latter's laconic account of the meeting already quoted: "Je serrai sa main tremblante et glacee. Je voulu lui parler, il s'echappa." Karasowski's account of this last meeting is in the feuilleton style and a worthy pendant to that of the first meeting:—

A month before his departure [he writes], in the last days of March, Chopin was invited by a lady to whose hospitable house he had in former times often gone. Some moments he hesitated whether he should accept this invitation, for he had of late years less frequented the salons; at last—as if impelled by an inner voice—he accepted. An hour before he entered the house of Madame H...

And then follow wonderful conversations, sighs, blushes, tears, a lady hiding behind an ivy screen, and afterwards advancing with a gliding step, and whispering with a look full of repentance: "Frederick!" Alas, this was not the way George Sand met her dismissed lovers. Moreover, let it be remembered she was at this time not a girl in her teens, but a woman of nearly forty-four.

The outbreak of the revolution on February 22, 1848, upset the arrangements for the second concert, which was to take place on the 10th of March, and, along with the desire to seek forgetfulness of the grievous loss he had sustained in a change of scene, decided him at last to accept the pressing and unwearied invitations of his Scotch and English friends to visit Great Britain. On April 2 the Gazette musicale announced that Chopin would shortly betake himself to London and pass the season there. And before many weeks had passed he set out upon his journey. But the history of his doings in the capital and in other parts of the United Kingdom shall be related in another chapter.

CHAPTER XXX

DIFFERENCE OF STYLE IN CHOPIN'S WORKS.——THEIR
CHARACTERISTICS DISCUSSED, AND POPULAR PREJUDICES
CONTROVERTED.——POLISH NATIONAL MUSIC AND ITS
INFLUENCE ON CHOPIN.——CHOPIN A PERSONAL AS WELL AS
NATIONAL TONE-POET.—A REVIEW OF SOME OF HIS LESS PERFECT
COMPOSITIONS AND OF HIS MASTERPIECES: BOLERO; RONDEAU;
VARIATIONS; TARANTELLE; ALLEGRO DE CONCERT; TWO
SONATAS FOR PIANOFORTE (OP. 38 AND 58); SONATA (OP. 65) AND
GRAND DUO CONCERTANT FOR PIANOFORTE AND VIOLONCELLO;
FANTAISIE; MAZURKAS; POLONAISES; VALSES; ETUDES; PRELUDES;
SCHERZI; IMPROMPTUS; NOCTURNES; BERCEUSE; BARCAROLE;
AND BALLADES——-THE SONGS.——VARIOUS EDITIONS.

Before we inquire into the doings and sufferings of Chopin in England
and Scotland, let us take a general survey of his life-work as a composer.
We may fitly do so now; as at the stage of his career we have reached, his
creative activity had come to a close. The last composition he published,
the G minor Sonata for piano and violoncello, Op. 65, appeared in October,
1847; and among his posthumous compositions published by Fontana there
are only two of later date—namely, the mazurkas, No. 2 of Op. 67 (G minor)
and No. 4 of Op. 68 (F minor), which came into existence in 1849. Neither
of these compositions can be numbered with the master's best works, but
the latter of them is interesting, because it seems in its tonal writhings and
wailings a picture of the bodily and mental torments Chopin was at the time
enduring.

A considerable number of the master's works I have already discussed
in Chapters III., VIII., and XIII. These, if we except the two Concertos,
Op. II and 21 (although they, too, do not rank with his chefs-d'oeuvre),
are, however, for us of greater importance biographically, perhaps also
historically, than otherwise. It is true, we hear now and then of some virtuoso
playing the Variations, Op. 2, or the Fantasia on Polish airs, Op. 13, nay, we
may hear even of the performance of the Trio, Op. 8; but such occurrences
are of the rarest rarity, and, considering how rich musical literature is in
unexceptionable concert-pieces and chamber compositions, one feels on the

whole pleased that these enterprising soloists and trio-players find neither much encouragement nor many imitators. While in examining the earlier works, the praise bestowed on them was often largely mixed with censure, and the admiration felt for them tempered by dissatisfaction; we shall have little else than pure praise and admiration for the works that remain to be considered, at least for the vast majority of them. One thing, however, seems to me needful before justice can be done to the composer Chopin: certain prejudices abroad concerning him have to be combated. I shall, therefore, preface my remarks on particular compositions and groups of compositions by some general observations.

It is sometimes said that there are hardly any traces of a development in the productions of Chopin, and that in this respect he is unlike all the other great masters. Such an opinion cannot be the result of a thorough and comprehensive study of the composer's works. So far from agreeing with those who hold it, I am tempted to assert that the difference of style between Chopin's early and latest works (even when juvenile compositions like the first two Rondos are left out of account) is as great as that between Beethoven's first and ninth Symphony. It would be easy to classify the Polish master's works according to three and even four (with the usual exceptions) successive styles, but I have no taste for this cheap kind of useless ingenuity. In fact, I shall confine myself to saying that in Chopin's works there are clearly distinguishable two styles—the early virtuosic and the later poetic style. The latter is in a certain sense also virtuosic, but with this difference, that its virtuosity is not virtuosity for virtuosity's sake. The poetic style which has thrown off the tinsel showiness of its predecessor does not, however, remain unchanged, for its texture becomes more and more close, and affords conclusive evidence of the increasing influence of Johann Sebastian Bach. Of course, the grand master of fugue does not appear here, as it were, full life-size, in peruke, knee-breeches, and shoe-buckles, but his presence in spite of transformation and attenuation is unmistakable. It is, however, not only in the closeness and complexity of texture that we notice Chopin's style changing: a striving after greater breadth and fulness of form are likewise apparent, and, alas! also an increase in sombreness, the result of deteriorating health. All this the reader will have to keep in mind when he passes in review the master's works, for I shall marshal them by groups, not chronologically.

Another prejudice, wide-spread, almost universal, is that Chopin's music is all languor and melancholy, and, consequently, wanting in variety. Now, there can be no greater error than this belief. As to variety, we should be obliged to wonder at its infiniteness if he had composed nothing but the pieces to which are really applicable the epithets dreamy, pensive, mournful, and despondent. But what vigour, what more than manly vigour, manifests itself in many of his creations! Think only of the Polonaises in A major (Op. 40, No. 1) and in A flat major (Op. 53), of many of his studies, the first three of his ballades, the scherzos, and much besides! To be sure, a great deal of this vigour is not natural, but the outcome of despair and maddening passion. Still, it is vigour, and such vigour as is not often to be met with. And, then, it is not the only kind to be found in his music. There is also a healthy vigour, which, for instance, in the A major Polonaise assumes a brilliantly-heroic form. Nor are serene and even joyous moods so rare that it would be permissible to ignore them. While thus controverting the so-called vox Dei (are not popular opinions generally popular prejudices?) and the pseudo-critics who create or follow it, I have no intention either to deny or conceal the Polish master's excess of languor and melancholy. I only wish to avoid vulgar exaggeration, to keep within the bounds of the factual. In art as in life, in biography as in history, there are not many questions that can be answered by a plain "yea" or "nay". It was, indeed, with Chopin as has been said of him, "his heart was sad, his mind was gay. "One day when Chopin, Liszt, and the Comtesse d'Agoult spent the after-dinner hours together, the lady, deeply moved by the Polish composer's playing, ventured to ask him "by what name he called the extraordinary feeling which he enclosed in his compositions, like unknown ashes in superb urns of most exquisitely-chiselled alabaster? "He answered her that—

her heart had not deceived her in its melancholy saddening,

for whatever his moments of cheerfulness might be, he never

for all that got rid of a feeling which formed, as it were,

the soil of his heart, and for which he found a name only in

his mother-tongue, no other possessing an equivalent to the

Polish word zal [sadness, pain, sorrow, grief, trouble,

repentance, &c.]. Indeed, he uttered the word repeatedly, as

if his ear had been eager for this sound, which for him

comprised the whole scale of the feelings which is produced by

an intense plaint, from repentance to hatred, blessed or

poisoned fruits of this acrid root.

After a long dissertation on the meaning of the word zal, Liszt, from whose book this quotation is taken, proceeds thus:—

Yes, truly, the zal colours with a reflection now argent, now

ardent, the whole of Chopin's works. It is not even absent

from his sweetest reveries. These impressions had so much the more importance in the life of Chopin that they manifested themselves distinctly in his last works. They little by little attained a kind of sickly irascibility, reaching the point of feverish tremulousness. This latter reveals itself in some of his last writings by a distortion of his thought which one is sometimes rather pained than surprised to meet. Suffocating almost under the oppression of his repressed transports of passion, making no longer use of the art except to rehearse to himself his own tragedy, he began, after having sung his feeling, to tear it to pieces.

Read together with my matter-of-fact statements, Liszt's hyperbolical and circumlocutional poetic prose will not be misunderstood by the reader. The case may be briefly summed up thus. Zal is not to be found in every one of Chopin's compositions, but in the greater part of them: sometimes it appears clearly on the surface, now as a smooth or lightly-rippled flow, now as a wildly-coursing, fiercely-gushing torrent; sometimes it is dimly felt only as an undercurrent whose presence not unfrequently becomes temporarily lost to ear and eye. We must, however, take care not to overlook that this zal is not exclusively individual, although its width and intensity are so.

The key-note [of Polish songs] [says the editor and translator into German of an interesting collection of Folk-songs of the Poles][FOOTNOTE: Volkslieder der Polen. Gesammelt und ubersetzt von W. P. (Leipzig,1833).] is melancholy—even in playful and naive songs something may be heard which reminds one of the pain of past sorrows; a plaintive sigh, a death-groan, which seems to accuse the Creator, curses His existence, and, as Tieck thinks, cries to heaven out of the dust of annihilation:

"What sin have I committed?"

These are the after-throes of whole races; these are the pains of whole centuries, which in these melodies entwine themselves in an infinite sigh. One is tempted to call them sentimental, because they seem to reflect sometimes on their own feeling;

but, on the other hand, they are not so, for the impulse to an annihilating outpouring of feeling expresses itself too powerfully for these musical poems to be products of conscious creativeness. One feels when one hears these songs that the implacable wheel of fate has only too often rolled over the terrene happiness of this people, and life has turned to them only its dark side. Therefore, the dark side is so conspicuous; therefore, much pain and poetry—unhappiness and greatness.

The remarks on Polish folk-music lead us naturally to the question of Chopin's indebtedness to it, which, while in one respect it cannot be too highly rated, is yet in another respect generally overrated. The opinion that every peculiarity which distinguishes his music from that of other masters is to be put to the account of his nationality, and may be traced in Polish folk-music, is erroneous. But, on the other hand, it is emphatically true that this same folk-music was to him a potent inspirer and trainer. Generally speaking, however, Chopin has more of the spirit than of the form of Polish folk-music. The only two classes of his compositions where we find also something of the form are his mazurkas and polonaises; and, what is noteworthy, more in the former, the dance of the people, than in the latter, the dance of the aristocracy. In Chopin's mazurkas we meet not only with many of the most characteristic rhythms, but also with many equally characteristic melodic and harmonic traits of this chief of all the Polish dances.

Polish national music conforms in part to the tonality prevailing in modern art-music, that is, to our major and minor modes; in part, however, it reminds one of other tonalities—for instance, of that of the mediaeval church modes, and of that or those prevalent in the music of the Hungarians, Wallachians, and other peoples of that quarter.

[FOOTNOTE: The strictly diatonic church modes (not to be confounded with the ancient Greek modes bearing the same names) differ from each other by the position of the two semitones: the Ionian is like our C major; the Dorian, Phrygian, Lydian, Mixolydian, Aeolian. &c., are like the series of natural notes starting respectively from d, c, f, g, a, &c. The characteristic interval of the Hungarian scale is the augmented second (a, b, c, d#, e, f, g#, a).]

The melodic progression, not always immediate, of an augmented fourth and major seventh occurs frequently, and that of an augmented second occasionally. Skips of a third after or before one or more steps of a second are very common. In connection with these skips of a third may be mentioned that one meets with melodies evidently based on a scale with a degree less than our major and minor scales, having in one place a step of a third instead of a second. [FOOTNOTE: Connoisseurs of Scotch music, on becoming acquainted with Polish music, will be incited by many traits of the latter to undertake a comparative study of the two.] The opening and the closing note stand often to each other in the relation of a second, sometimes also of a seventh. The numerous peculiarities to be met with in Polish folkmusic with regard to melodic progression are not likely to be reducible to one tonality or a simple system of tonalities. Time and district of origin have much to do with the formal character of the melodies. And besides political, social, and local influences direct musical ones—the mediaeval church music, eastern secular music, &c.—have to be taken into account. Of most Polish melodies it may be said that they are as capricious as they are piquant. Any attempt to harmonise them according to our tonal system must end in failure. Many of them would, indeed, be spoiled by any kind of harmony, being essentially melodic, not outgrowths of harmony.

[FOOTNOTE: To those who wish to study this subject may be recommended Oskar Kolberg's Piesni Ludu Polskiego (Warsaw, 1857), the best collection of Polish folk-songs. Charles Lipinski's collection, Piesni Polskie i Ruskie Luttu Galicyjskiego, although much less interesting, is yet noteworthy.]

To treat, however, this subject adequately, one requires volumes, not pages; to speak on it authoritatively, one must have studied it more thoroughly than I have done. The following melodies and snatches of melodies will to some extent illustrate what I have said, although they are chosen with a view rather to illustrate Chopin's indebtedness to Polish folk-music than Polish folk-music itself:—

[11 music score excerpts illustrated here]

Chopin, while piquantly and daringly varying the tonality prevailing in art-music, hardly ever departs from it altogether—he keeps at least in contact with it, however light that contact may be now and then in the mazurkas.

[FOOTNOTE: One of the most decided exceptions is the Mazurka, Op. 24, No. 2, of which only the A fiat major part adheres frankly to our tonality. The portion beginning with the twenty-first bar and extending over that and the next fifteen bars displays, on the other hand, the purest Lydian, while the other portions, although less definite as regards tonality, keep in closer touch with the mediaeval church smode [sic: mode] than with our major and minor.]

Further, he adopted only some of the striking peculiarities of the national music, and added to them others which were individual. These individual characteristics—those audacities of rhythm, melody, and harmony (in progressions and modulations, as well as in single chords)—may, however, be said to have been fathered by the national ones. As to the predominating chromaticism of his style, it is not to be found in Polish folk-music; although slight rudiments are discoverable (see Nos. 6-12 of the musical illustrations). Of course, no one would seek there his indescribably-exquisite and highly-elaborate workmanship, which alone enabled him to give expression to the finest shades and most sudden changes of gentle feelings and turbulent passions. Indeed, as I have already said, it is rather the national spirit than the form which manifests itself in Chopin's music. The writer of the article on Polish music in Mendel's Conversations-Lexikon remarks:—

What Chopin has written remains for all times the highest ideal of Polish music. Although it would be impossible to point out in a single bar a vulgar utilisation of a national theme, or a Slavonic aping of it, there yet hovers over the whole the spirit of Polish melody, with its chivalrous, proud, and dreamy accents; yea, even the spirit of the Polish language is so pregnantly reproduced in the musical diction as perhaps in no composition of any of his countrymen; unless it be that Prince Oginski with his polonaises and Dobrzynski in his happiest moments have approached him.

Liszt, as so often, has also in connection with this aspect of the composer Chopin some excellent remarks to offer.

He neither applied himself nor exerted himself to write Polish music; it is possible that he would have been astonished to hear himself called a Polish musician.

[FOOTNOTE: Liszt decidedly overshoots here the mark, and does so in a less degree in the rest of these observations. Did not Chopin himself say to Hiller that he wished to be to his countrymen what Uhland was to the Germans? And did he not write in one of his letters (see p. 168): "You know how I wish to understand, and how I have in part succeeded in understanding, our national music"?]

Nevertheless, he was a national musician par excellence...He summed up in his imagination, he represented in his talent, a poetic feeling inherent in his nation and diffused there among all his contemporaries. Like the true national poets, Chopin sang, without a fixed design, without a preconceived choice, what inspiration spontaneously dictated to him; it is thus that there arose in his music, without solicitation, without effort, the most idealised form of the emotions which had animated his childhood, chequered his adolescence, and embellished his youth...Without making any pretence to it, he collected into a luminous sheaf sentiments confusedly felt by all in his country, fragmentarily disseminated in their hearts, vaguely perceived by some.

George Sand tells us that Chopin's works were the mysterious and vague expression of his inner life. That they were the expression of his inner life is indeed a fact which no attentive hearer can fail to discover without the aid of external evidence. For the composer has hardly written a bar in which, so to speak, the beating of his heart may not be felt. Chopin revealed himself only in his music, but there he revealed himself fully. And was this expression of his inner life really "mysterious and vague"? I think not! At least, no effusion of words could have made clearer and more distinct what he expressed. For the communications of dreams and visions such as he dreamt and saw, of the fluctuating emotional actualities such as his sensitive heart experienced, musical forms are, no doubt, less clumsy than verbal and pictorial ones. And if we know something of his history and that of his nation, we cannot be at a loss to give names and local habitations to the impalpable, but emotionally and intellectually-perceptible contents of his music. We have to distinguish in Chopin the personal and the national tone-poet, the singer of his own joys and sorrows and that of his country's. But, while distinguishing these two aspects, we must take care not to regard them as two separate things. They were a duality the constitutive forces of which alternately assumed supremacy. The national poet at no time absorbed the personal, the personal poet at no time disowned the national. His imagination was always ready to conjure up his native atmosphere, nay, we may even say that, wherever he might be, he lived in it. The scene of his dreams and visions lay oftenest in the land of his birth. And what did the national poet dream and see in these dreams and visions? A past, present, and future which never existed and never will exist, a Poland and a Polish people glorified. Reality passed through the refining fires of his love and genius and reappeared in his music sublimated as beauty and poetry. No other poet has like Chopin embodied in art the romance of the land and people of Poland. And, also, no other poet has like him embodied in art the romance of his own existence. But whereas as a national poet he was a flattering idealist, he was as a personal poet an uncompromising realist.

The masterpieces of Chopin consist of mazurkas, polonaises, waltzes, etudes, preludes, nocturnes (with which we will class the berceuse and barcarole), scherzos and impromptus, and ballades. They do not, however, comprise all his notable compositions. And about these notable compositions which do not rank with his masterpieces, either because they are of less significance or otherwise fail to reach the standard of requisite perfectness, I shall first say a few words.

Chopin's Bolero, Op. 19, may be described as a Bolero a la polonaise. It is livelier in movement and more coquettish in character than the compositions which he entitles polonaises, but for all that its physiognomy does not on the whole strike one as particularly Spanish, certainly not beyond the first section of the Bolero proper and the seductive strains of the Pililento, the second tempo of the introduction. And in saying this I am not misled by the points of resemblance in the rhythmical accompaniment of these dances. Chopin published the Bolero in 1834, four years before he visited Spain, but one may doubt whether it would have turned out less Polish if he had composed it subsequently. Although an excellent imitator in the way of mimicry, he lacked the talent of imitating musical thought and character; at any rate, there are no traces of it in his works. The cause of this lack of talent lies, of course, in the strength of his subjectivism in the first place, and of his nationalism in the second. I said the Bolero was published four years before his visit to Spain. But how many years before this visit was it composed? I think a good many years earlier; for it has so much of his youthful style about it, and not only of his youthful style, but also of his youthful character—by which I mean that it is less intensely poetic. It is not impossible that Chopin was instigated to write it by hearing the Bolero in Auber's "La Muette de Portici" ("Masaniello"), which opera was first performed on February 28, 1828. These remarks are thrown out merely as hints. The second composition which we shall consider will show how dangerous it is to dogmatise on the strength of internal evidence.

Op. 16, a lightsome Rondeau with a dramatic Introduction, is, like the Bolero, not without its beauties; but in spite of greater individuality, ranks, like it, low among the master's works, being patchy, unequal, and little poetical.

If ever Chopin is not Chopin in his music, he is so in his Variations brillantes (in B flat major) sur le Rondeau favori: "Je vends des Scapulaires" de Ludovic, de Herold et Halevy, Op. 12. Did we not know that he must have composed the work about the middle of 1833, we should be tempted to class it with the works which came into existence when his individuality was as yet little developed. [FOOTNOTE: The opera Ludovic, on which Herold was engaged when he died on January 19, 1833, and which Halevy completed, was produced in Paris on May 16, 1833. From the German publishers of Chopin's Op. 12 I learned that it appeared in November, 1833. In the Gazette musicale of January 26, 1834, may be read a review of it.] But knowing what we do, we can only wonder at the strange phenomenon. It is as if Chopin had here thrown overboard the Polish part of his natal inheritance and given himself up unrestrainedly and voluptuously to the French part. Besides various diatonic runs of an inessential and purely ornamental character, there is in the finale actually a plain and full-toned C flat major scale. What other work of the composer could be pointed out exhibiting the like feature? Of course, Chopin is as little successful in entirely hiding his serpentining and chromaticising tendency as Mephistopheles in hiding the limp arising from his cloven foot. Still, these fallings out of the role are rare and transient, and, on the whole, Chopin presents himself as a perfect homme du monde who knows how to say the most insignificant trifles with the most exquisite grace imaginable. There can. be nothing more amusing than the contemporary critical opinions regarding this work, nothing more amusing than to see the at other times censorious Philistines unwrinkle their brows, relax generally the sternness of their features, and welcome, as it were, the return of the prodigal son. We wiser critics of to-day, who, of course, think very differently about this matter, can, nevertheless, enjoy and heartily applaud the prettiness and elegance of the simple first variation, the playful tripping second, the schwarmerische melodious third, the merry swinging fourth, and the brilliant finale.

From Chopin's letters we see that the publication of the Tarantelle, Op. 43, which took place in the latter part of 1841, was attended with difficulties and annoyances. [FOOTNOTE: Herr Schuberth, of Leipzig, informed me that a honorarium of 500 francs was paid to Chopin for this work on July 1, 1841. The French publisher deposited the work at the library of the Conservatoire in October, 1841.] What these difficulties and annoyances were, is, however, only in part ascertainable. To turn from the publication to the composition itself, I may say that it is full of life, indeed, spirited in every respect, in movement and in boldness of harmonic and melodic conception. The Tarantelle is a translation from Italian into Polish, a transmutation of Rossini into Chopin, a Neapolitan scene painted with opaque colours, the south without its transparent sky, balmy air, and general brightness. That this composition was inspired by impressions received from Rossini's Tarantella, and not from impressions received in Italy (of which, as has already been related, he had a short glimpse in 1839), is evident. A comparison of Chopin's Op. 43 with Liszt's glowing and intoxicating transcription of Rossini's composition may be recommended as a study equally pleasant and instructive. Although not an enthusiastic admirer of Chopin's Tarantelle, I protest in the interest of the composer and for justice's sake against Schumann's dictum: "Nobody can call that beautiful music; but we pardon the master his wild fantasies, for once he may let us see also the dark sides of his inner life."

The Allegro de Concert, Op. 46, which was published in November, 1841, although written for the pianoforte alone, contains, nevertheless, passages which are more distinctly orchestral than anything Chopin ever wrote for the orchestra. The form resembles somewhat that of the concerto. In the first section, which occupies the place of the opening tutti, we cannot fail to distinguish the entrances of single instruments, groups of instruments, and the full orchestra. The soloist starts in the eighty-seventh bar, and in the following commences a cadenza. With the a tempo comes the first subject (A major), and the passage-work which brings up the rear leads to the second subject (E major), which had already appeared in the first section in A major. The first subject, if I may dignify the matter in question with that designation, does not recur again, nor was it introduced by the tutti. The central and principal thought is what I called the second subject. The second section concludes with brilliant passage-work in E major, the time— honoured shake rousing the drowsy orchestra from its sweet repose. The hint is not lost, and the orchestra, in the disguise of the pianoforte, attends to its duty right vigorously. With the poco rit. the soloist sets to work again, and in the next bar takes up the principal subject in A minor. After that we have once more brilliant passage-work, closing this time in A major, and then a final tutti. The Allegro de Concert gives rise to all sorts of surmises. Was it written first for the pianoforte and orchestra, as Schumann suspects? Or may we make even a bolder guess, and suppose that the composer, at a more advanced age, worked up into this Allegro de Concert a sketch for the first movement of a concerto conceived in his younger days? Have we, perhaps, here a fragment or fragments of the Concerto for two pianos which Chopin, in a letter written at Vienna on December 21, 1830, said he would play in public with his friend Nidecki, if he succeeded in writing it to his satisfaction? And is there any significance in the fact that Chopin, when (probably in the summer of 1841) sending the manuscript of this work to Fontana, calls it a Concerto? Be this as it may, the principal subject and some of the passage-work remind one of the time of the concertos; other things, again, belong undoubtedly to a later period. The tutti and solo parts are unmistakable, so different is the treatment of the pianoforte: in the former the style has the heaviness of an arrangement, in the latter it has Chopin's usual airiness. The work, as a whole, is unsatisfactory, nay, almost indigestible. The subjects are neither striking nor important. Of the passage-work, that which follows the second subject contains the most interesting matter. Piquant traits and all sorts of fragmentary beauties are scattered here and there over the movement. But after we have considered all, we must confess that this opus adds little or nothing to the value of our Chopin inheritance.

[FOOTNOTE: In justice to the composer I must here quote a criticism which since I wrote the above appeared in the Athenaum (January 21, 1888):—"The last-named work [the Allegro de Concert, Op. 46] is not often heard, and is generally regarded as one of Chopin's least interesting and least characteristic pieces. Let us hasten to say that these impressions are distinctly wrong; the executive difficulties of the work are extremely great, and a mere mastery of them is far from all that is needed. When M. de Pachmann commenced to play it was quickly evident that his reading would be most remarkable, and in the end it amounted to an astounding revelation. That which seemed dry and involved became under his fingers instinct with beauty and feeling; the musicians and amateurs present listened as if spellbound, and opinion was unanimous that the performance was nothing short of an artistic creation. For the sake of the composer, if not for his own reputation, the pianist should repeat it, not once, but many times." Notwithstanding this decided judgment of a weighty authority—for such everyone will, without hesitation, acknowledge the critic in question to be—I am unable, after once more examining the work, to alter my previously formed opinion.]

As a further confirmation of the supposed origin of the Allegro de Concert, I may mention the arrangement of it for piano and orchestra (also for two pianos) by Jean Louis Nicode.

[FOOTNOTE: Nicode has done his work well so far as he kept close to the text of Chopin; but his insertion of a working-out section of more than seventy bars is not justifiable, and, moreover, though making the work more like an orthodox first movement of a concerto, does not enhance its beauty and artistic value.]

To the Sonata in B flat minor, Op. 35 (published in May, 1840), this most powerful of Chopin's works in the larger forms, Liszt's remark, "Plus de volonte que d'inspiration," is hardly applicable, although he used the expression in speaking of Chopin's concertos and sonatas in general;

for there is no lack of inspiration here, nor are there traces of painful, unrewarded effort. Each of the four pieces of which the sonata consists is full of vigour, originality, and interest. But whether they can be called a sonata is another question. Schumann, in his playful manner, speaks of caprice and wantonness, and insinuates that Chopin bound together four of his maddest children, and entitled them sonata, in order that he might perhaps under this name smuggle them in where otherwise they would not penetrate. Of course, this is a fancy of Schumann's. Still, one cannot help wondering whether the composer from the first intended to write a sonata and obtained this result—amphora coepit institui; currente rota cur urceus exit?—or whether these four movements got into existence without any predestination, and were afterwards put under one cover. [FOOTNOTE: At any rate, the march was finished before the rest of the work. See the quotation from one of Chopin's letters farther on.] With all Schumann's admiration for Chopin and praise of this sonata, it appears to me that he does not give Chopin his due. There is something gigantic in the work which, although it does not elevate and ennoble, being for the most part a purposeless fuming, impresses one powerfully. The first movement begins with four bars grave, a groan full of pain; then the composer, in restless, breathless haste, is driven by his feelings onward, ever onward, till he comes to the lovely, peaceful second subject (in D flat major, a real contrast this time), which grows by-and-by more passionate, and in the concluding portion of the first part transcends the limits of propriety—VIDE those ugly dissonances. The connection of the close of the first part with the repetition of this and the beginning of the second part by means of the chord of the dominant seventh in A flat and that in D flat with the suspended sixth, is noteworthy. The strange second section, in which the first subject is worked out, has the appearance rather of an improvisation than of a composition. After this a few bars in 6/4 time, fiercely wild (stretto) at first, but gradually subsiding, lead to the repeat in B flat major of the second subject—the first subject does not appear again in its original form. To the close, which is like that of the corresponding section in the first part (6/4), is added a coda (2/2) introducing the characteristic motive of the first subject. In the scherzo, the grandest movement and the climax of the sonata, the gloom and the threatening power which rise to a higher and higher pitch become quite weird and fear-inspiring; it affects one like lowering clouds, rolling of thunder, and howling and whistling of the wind—to the latter, for instance, the chromatic successions of chords of the sixth may not inappropriately be likened. The piu lento is certainly one of the most scherzo-like thoughts in Chopin's scherzos—so light and joyful, yet a volcano is murmuring under this serenity. The return of this piu lento, after the repeat of the first section, is very fine and beneficently refreshing, like nature after a storm. The Marche funebre ranks among Chopin's best-known and most highly-appreciated pieces. Liszt mentions it with particular distinction, and grows justly eloquent over it. I do not altogether understand Schumann's objection: "It is still more gloomy than the scherzo," he says, "and contains even much that is repulsive; in its place an adagio, perhaps in D flat, would have had an incomparably finer effect." Out of the dull, stupefied brooding, which is the fundamental mood of the first section, there rises once and again (bars 7 and 8, and 11 and 12) a pitiable wailing, and then an outburst of passionate appealing (the forte passage in D flat major), followed by a sinking helplessness (the two bars with the shakes in the bass), accompanied by moans and deep breathings. The two parts of the second section are a rapturous gaze into the beatific regions of a beyond, a vision of reunion of what for the time is severed. The last movement may be counted among the curiosities of composition—a presto in B flat minor of seventy-five bars, an endless series of triplets from beginning to end in octaves. It calls up in one's mind the solitude and dreariness of a desert. "The last movement is more like mockery than music," says Schumann, but adds, truly and wisely—

and yet one confesses to one's self that also out of this unmelodious and joyless movement a peculiar dismal spirit breathes upon us, who keeps down with a strong hand that which would revolt, so that we obey, as if we were charmed, without murmuring, but also without praising, for that is no music. Thus the sonata concludes, as it began, enigmatically, like a sphinx with a mocking smile.

J. W. Davison, in the preface to an edition of Chopin's mazurkas, relates that Mendelssohn, on being questioned about the finale of one of Chopin's sonatas (I think it must have been the one before us), said briefly and bitterly, "Oh, I abhor it!" H. Barbedette remarks in his "Chopin," a criticism without insight and originality, of this finale, "C'est Lazare grattant de ses ongles la pierre de son tombeau et tombant epuise de fatigue, de faim et de desespoir." And now let the reader recall the words which Chopin wrote from Nohant to Fontana in the summer of 1839:—

I am composing here a Sonata in B flat minor, in which will be the funeral march which you have already. There is an Allegro, then a Scherzo, in E flat minor, the March, and a short Finale of about three pages. The left hand unisono with the right hand are gossiping after the March [ogaduja po Marszu].

The meaning of which somewhat obscure interpretation seems to be, that after the burial the good neighbours took to discussing the merits of the departed, not without a spice of backbiting.

The Sonata in B minor, Op. 58, the second of Chopin's notable pianoforte sonatas (the third if we take into account the unpalatable Op. 4), made its appearance five years later, in June, 1845. Unity is as little discernible in this sonata as in its predecessor. The four movements of which the work consists are rather affiliated than cognate; nay, this may be said even of many parts of the movements. The first movement by far surpasses the other three in importance: indeed, the wealth of beautiful and interesting matter which is here heaped up—for it is rather an unsifted accumulation than an artistic presentation and evolution—would have sufficed many a composer for several movements. The ideas are very unequal and their course very jerky till we come to the second subject (D major), which swells out into a broad stream of impassioned melody. Farther on the matter becomes again jerky and mosaic-like. While the close of the first part is very fine, the beginning of the second is a comfortless waste. Things mend with the re-entrance of the subsidiary part of the second subject (now in D flat major), which, after being dwelt upon for some time and varied, disappears, and is followed by a repetition of portions of the first subject, the whole second subject (in B major), and the closing period, which is prolonged by a coda to make the close more emphatic and satisfying. A light and graceful quaver figure winds with now rippling, now waving motion through the first and third sections of the scherzo; in the contrasting second section, with the sustained accompaniment and the melody in one of the middle parts, the entrance of the bright A major, after the gloom of the preceding bars, is very effective. The third movement has the character of a nocturne, and as such cannot fail to be admired. In the visionary dreaming of the long middle section we imagine the composer with dilated eyes and rapture in his look—it is rather a reverie than a composition. The finale surrounds us with an emotional atmosphere somewhat akin to that of the first movement, but more agitated. After eight bold introductory bars with piercing dissonances begins the first subject, which, with its rhythmically differently-accompanied repetition, is the most important constituent of the movement. The rest, although finely polished, is somewhat insignificant. In short, this is the old story, plus de volonte que d'inspiration, that is to say, inspiration of the right sort. And also, plus de volonte que de savoir-faire.

There is one work of Chopin's to which Liszt's dictum, plus de volnte que d'inspiratio, applies in all, and even more than all its force. I allude to the Sonata (in G minor) for piano and violoncello, Op. 65 (published in September, 1847), in which hardly anything else but effort, painful effort, manifests itself. The first and last movements are immense wildernesses with only here and there a small flower. The middle movements, a Scherzo and an Andante, do not rise to the dignity of a sonata, and, moreover, lack distinction, especially the slow movement, a nocturne-like dialogue between the two instruments. As to the beauties—such as the first subject of the first movement (at the entrance of the violoncello), the opening bars of the Scherzo, part of the ANDANTE, &c.—they are merely beginnings, springs that lose themselves soon in a sandy waste. Hence I have not the heart to controvert Moscheles who, in his diary, says some cutting things about this work: "In composition Chopin proves that he has only isolated happy thoughts which he does not know how to work up into a rounded whole. In the just published sonata with violoncello I find often passages which sound as if someone were preluding on the piano and knocked at all the keys to learn whether euphony was at home." [FOOTNOTE: Aus Moscheles' Leben; Vol. II., p. 171.] An entry of the year 1850 runs as follows: "But a trial of patience of another kind is imposed on me by Chopin's Violoncello Sonata, which I am arranging for four hands. To me it is a tangled forest, through which now and then penetrates a gleam of the sun." [FOOTNOTE: Ibid., Vol. II., p. 216.] To take up after the last-discussed work a composition like the Grand Duo Concertant for piano and violoncello, on themes from "Robert le Diable," by Chopin and A. Franchomme, is quite a relief, although it is really of no artistic importance. Schumann is right when he says of this DUO, which saw the light of publicity (without OPUS number) in 1833:14 [FOOTNOTE: The first performance of Meyerbeer's "Robert le Diable" took place at the Paris Opera on November 21, 1831.] "A piece for a SALON where behind the shoulders of counts and countesses now and then rises the head of a celebrated artist." And he may also be right when he says:—

> It seems to me that Chopin sketched the whole of it, and that
> Franchomme said "yes" to everything; for what Chopin touches
> takes his form and spirit, and in this minor salon-style he
> expresses himself with grace and distinction, compared with
> which all the gentility of other brilliant composers together
> with all their elegance vanish into thin air.

The mention of the DUO is somewhat out of place here, but the Sonata, Op. 65, in which the violoncello is employed, naturally suggested it.

We have only one more work to consider before we come to the groups of masterpieces in the smaller forms above enumerated. But this last work is one of Chopin's best compositions, and in its way no less a masterpiece than these. Unfettered by the scheme of a definite form such as the sonata or concerto, the composer develops in the Fantaisie, Op. 49 (published in November, 1841), his thought with masterly freedom. There is an enthralling weirdness about this work, a weirdness made up of force of passion and an indescribable fantastic waywardness. Nothing more common than the name of Fantasia, here we have the thing! The music falls on our ears like the insuppressible outpouring of a being stirred to its heart's core, and full of immeasurable love and longing. Who would suspect the composer's fragility and sickliness in this work? Does it not rather suggest a Titan in commotion? There was a time when I spoke of the Fantasia in a less complimentary tone, now I bow down my head regretfully and exclaim peccavi. The disposition of the composition may be thus briefly indicated. A tempo di marcia opens the Fantasia—it forms the porch of the edifice. The dreamy triplet passages of the poco a poco piu mosso are comparable to galleries that connect the various blocks of buildings. The principal subject, or accumulation of themes, recurs again and again in different keys, whilst other subjects appear only once or twice between the repetitions of the principal subject.

The mazurkas of Chopin are a literature in themselves, said Lenz, and there is some truth in his saying. They may, indeed, be called a literature in themselves for two reasons—first, because of their originality, which makes them things sui generis; and secondly, because of the poetical and musical wealth of their contents. Chopin, as I have already said, is most national in the mazurkas and polonaises, for the former of which he draws not only inspiration, but even rhythmic, melodic, and harmonic motives from his country's folk-music. Liszt told me, in a conversation I had with him, that he did not care much for Chopin's mazurkas. "One often meets in them with bars which might just as well be in another place." But he added, "And yet as Chopin puts them, perhaps nobody else could have put them." And mark, those are the words of one who also told me that when he sometimes played half-an-hour for his amusement, he liked to resort to Chopin. Moscheles, I suspect, had especially the mazurkas in his mind when, in 1833, [FOOTNOTE: At this time the published compositions of Chopin were, of course, not numerous, but they included the first two books of Mazurkas, Op. 6 and 7.] he said of the Polish master's compositions that he found "much charm in their originality and national colouring," and that "his thoughts and through them the fingers stumbled over certain hard, inartistic modulations." Startling progressions, unreconciled contrasts, and abrupt changes of mood are characteristic of Slavonic music and expressive of the Slavonic character. Whether they ought to be called inartistic or not, we will leave time to decide, if it has not done so already; the Russian and other Slavonic composers, who are now coming more and more to the front, seem to be little in doubt as to their legitimacy. I neither regard Chopin's mazurkas as his most artistic achievements nor recommend their capriciousness and fragmentariness for general imitation. But if we view them from the right stand-point, which is not that of classicism, we cannot help admiring them. The musical idiom which the composer uses in these, notwithstanding their capriciousness and fragmentariness, exquisitely-finished miniatures, has a truly delightful piquancy. Yet delightful as their language is, the mazurkas have a far higher claim to our admiration. They are poems—social poems, poems of private life, in distinction from the polonaises, which are political poems. Although Chopin's mazurkas and polonaises are no less individual than the other compositions of this most subjective of subjective poets, they incorporate, nevertheless, a good deal of the poetry of which the national dances of those names are the expression or vehicle. And let it be noted, in Poland so-called civilisation did not do its work so fast and effectually as in Western Europe; there dancing had not yet become in Chopin's days a merely formal and conventional affair, a matter of sinew and muscle.

It is, therefore, advisable that we should make ourselves acquainted with the principal Polish dances; such an acquaintance, moreover, will not only help us to interpret aright Chopin's mazurkas and polonaises, but also to gain a deeper insight into his ways of feeling and seeing generally. Now the reader will become aware that the long disquisitions on Poland and the Poles at the commencement of this biography were not superfluous accessories. For completeness' sake I shall preface the description of the mazurka by a short one of the krakowiak, the third of the triad of principal Polish dances. The informants on whom I shall chiefly rely when I am not guided by my own observations are the musician Sowinski and the poet Brodzinski, both Poles:

The krakowiak [says Albert Sowinski in chant polonais] bubbles

over with esprit and gaiety; its name indicates its origin. It

is the delight of the salons, and especially of the huts. The

Cracovians dance it in a very agitated and expressive manner,

singing at the same time words made for the occasion of which

they multiply the stanzas and which they often improvise.

These words are of an easy gaiety which remind one strangely

of the rather loose [semi-grivoises] songs so popular in

France; others again are connected with the glorious epochs of

history, with the sweet or sad memories which it calls up, and

are a faithful expression of the character and manners of the nation.

Casimir Brodzinski describes the dance as follows:—
The krakowiak resembles in its figures a simplified polonaise;
it represents, compared with the latter, a less advanced
social state. The boldest and strongest takes the position of
leader and conducts the dance; he sings, the others join in
chorus; he dances, they imitate him. Often also the krakowiak
represents, in a kind of little ballet, the simple course of a
love-affair: one sees a couple of young people place
themselves before the orchestra; the young man looks proud,
presumptuous, preoccupied with his costume and beauty. Before
long he becomes meditative, and seeks inspiration to improvise
verses which the cries of his companions ask for, and which
the time beaten by them provoke, as well as the manoeuvre of
the young girl, who is impatient to dance. Arriving before the
orchestra after making a round, the dancer generally takes the
liberty of singing a refrain which makes the young girl blush;
she runs away, and it is in pursuing her that the young man
displays all his agility. At the last round it is the young
man who pretends to run away from his partner; she tries to
seize his arm, after which they dance together until the
ritornello puts an end to their pleasure.

As a technical supplement to the above, I may say that this lively dance
is in 2/4 time, and like other Polish dances has the rhythmical peculiarity
of having frequently the accent on a usually unaccented part of the bar,
especially at the end of a section or a phrase, for instance, on the second
quaver of the second and the fourth bar, thus:—

[Here, the author illustrates with a rhythm diagram consisting of a line
of notes divided in measures: 1/8 1/16 1/16 1/8 1/8 | 1/8 1/4 1/8 | 1/8 1/16 1/16
1/8 1/8 | 1/8 1/4 dot]

Chopin has only once been inspired by the krakowiak—namely, in
his Op. 14, entitled Krakowiak, Grand Rondeau de Concert, a composition
which was discussed in Chapter VIII. Thus much of the krakowiak; now to
the more interesting second of the triad.

The mazurek [or mazurka], whose name comes from Mazovia, one
of our finest provinces, is the most characteristic dance-tune

—it is the model of all our new tunes. One distinguishes, however, these latter easily from the ancient ones on account of their less original and less cantabile form. There are two kinds of mazureks: one, of which the first portion is always in minor and the second in major, has a romance-like colouring, it is made to be sung, in Polish one says "to be heard" (do sludninin); the other serves as an accompaniment to a dance, of which the figures are multiplied passes and coiuluiles. Its movement is in time, and yet less quick than the waltz. The motive is in dotted notes, which must be executed with energy and warmth, but not without a certain dignity.

Now the mazurka is generally written in 3/4-time; Chopin's are all written thus. The dotted rhythmical motive alluded to by Sowinski is this, or similar to this—

[Another rhythm diagram: 1/8 dot 1/16 1/4 1/4 | 1/8 dot 1/16 1/2]

But the dotted notes are by no means de rigueur. As motives like the following—

[Another rhythm diagram: 1/4 1/2 | 1/8 1/8 1/4 1/4 | triplet 1/4 1/4 | triple 1/8 1/8 1/8 1/8]

are of frequent occurrence, I would propose a more comprehensive definition—namely, that the first part of the bar consists mostly of quicker notes than the latter part. But even this more comprehensive definition does not comprehend all; it is a rule which has many exceptions. [FOOTNOTE: See the musical illustrations on pp. 217-218.] Le Sowinski mentions only one classification of mazurkas. Several others, however, exist. First, according to the district from which they derive—mazurkas of Kujavia, of Podlachia, of Lublin, &c.; or, secondly, according to their character, or to the purpose or occasion for which they were composed: wedding, village, historical, martial, and political mazurkas. And now let us hear what the poet Brodzinski has to say about the nature of this dance:— The mazurek in its primitive form and as the common people dance is only a kind of krakowiak, only less lively and less sautillant. The agile Cracovians and the mountaineers of the Carpathians call the mazurek danced by the inhabitants of the plain but a dwarfed krakowiak. The proximity of the Germans, or rather the sojourn of the German troops, has caused the true character of the mazurek among the people to be lost; this dance hap become a kind of awkward waltz.

With the people of the capital the real dances of the country
are disfigured not only by the influx of foreigners, but
especially also by the unfortunate employment of barrel-
organs....It is this instrument which crushes among the people
the practice of music, and takes the means of subsistence from
the village fiddler, who becomes more and more rare since
every tavern-keeper, in buying a barrel-organ, easily puts an
end to all competition. We see already more and more disappear
from our country sides these sweet songs and improvised
refrains which the rustic minstrels remembered and repeated,
and the truly national music gives way, alas! to the themes
borrowed from the operas most in vogue.

The mazurek, thus degenerated among the people, has been
adopted by the upper classes who, in preserving the national
allures, perfected it to the extent of rendering it, beyond
doubt, one of the most graceful dances in Europe. This dance
has much resemblance with the French quadrille, according to
what is analogous in the characters of the two nations; in
seeing these two dances one might say that a French woman
dances only to please, and that a Polish woman pleases by
abandoning herself to a kind of maiden gaiety—the graces
which she displays come rather from nature than from art. A
French female dancer recalls the ideal of Greek statues; a
Polish female dancer has something which recalls the
shepherdesses created by the imagination of the poets; if the
former charms us, the latter attaches us.

As modern dances lend themselves especially to the triumph of
the women, because the costume of the men is so little
favourable, it is noteworthy that the mazurek forms here an
exception; for a young man, and especially a young Pole,
remarkable by a certain amiable boldness, becomes soon the
soul and hero of this dance. A light and in some sort pastoral

dress for the women, and the Polish military costume so advantageous for the men, add to the charm of the picture which the mazurek presents to the eye of the painter. This dance permits to the whole body the most lively and varied movements, leaves the shoulders full liberty to bend with that ABANDON which, accompanied by a joyous laisser-aller and a certain movement of the foot striking the floor, is exceedingly graceful.

One finds often a magic effect in the animated enthusiasm which characterises the different movements of the head—now proudly erect, now tenderly sunk on the bosom, now lightly inclined towards the shoulder, and always depicting in large traits the abundance of life and joy, shaded with simple, graceful, and delicate sentiments. Seeing in the mazurek the female dancer almost carried away in the arms and on the shoulders of her cavalier, abandoning herself entirely to his guidance, one thinks one sees two beings intoxicated with happiness and flying towards the celestial regions. The female dancer, lightly dressed, scarcely skimming the earth with her dainty foot, holding on by the hand of her partner, in the twinkling of an eye carried away by several others, and then, like lightning, precipitating herself again into the arms of the first, offers the image of the most happy and delightful creature. The music of the mazurek is altogether national and original; through its gaiety breathes usually something of melancholy—one might say that it is destined to direct the steps of lovers, whose passing sorrows are not without charm.

Chopin himself published forty-one mazurkas of his composition in eleven sets of four, five, or three numbers—Op. 6, Quatre Mazurkas, and Op. 7, Cinq Mazurkas, in December, 1832; Op. 17, Quatre Mazurkas, in May, 1834; Op. 24, Quatre Mazurkas, in November, 1835; Op. 30, Quatre Maazurkas, in December, 1837; Op. 33, Quatre Mazurkas, in October, 1838; Op. 41, Quatre Mazurkas, in December, 1840; Op. 50, Trois Mazurkas, in November, 1841; Op, 56, Trois Mazurkas, in August, 1844; Op. 59, Trois

Mazurkas, in April, 1846; and Op. 63, Trois Mazurkas, in September, 1847. In the posthumous works published by Fontana there are two more sets, each of four numbers, and respectively marked as Op. 67 and 68. Lastly, several other mazurkas composed by or attributed to Chopin have been published without any opus number. Two mazurkas, both in A minor, although very feeble compositions, are included in the editions by Klindworth and Mikuli. The Breitkopf and Hartel edition, which includes only one of these two mazurkas, comprises further a mazurka in G major and one in B flat major of 1825, one in D major of 1829-30, a remodelling of the same of 1832—these have already been discussed—and a somewhat more interesting one in C major of 1833. Of one of the two mazurkas in A minor, a poor thing and for the most part little Chopinesque, only the dedication (a son ami Rmile Gaillard) is known, but not the date of composition. The other (the one not included in Breitkopf and Hartel's, No. 50 of Mikuli's and Klindworth's edition) appeared first as No. 2 of Noire Temps, a publication by Schott's Sohne. On inquiry I learned that Notre Temps was the general title of a series of 12 pieces by Czerny, Chopin, Kalliwoda, Rosenhain, Thalberg, Kalkbrenner, Mendelssohn, Bertini, Wolff, Kontski, Osborne, and Herz, which appeared in 1842 or 1843 as a Christmas Album. [FOONOTE: I find, however, that Chopin's Mazurka was already separately announced as "Notre Temps, No. 2," in the Monatsberichte of February, 1842.] Whether a Mazurka elegante by Fr, Chopin, advertised in La France Musicale of April 6, 1845, as en vente au Bureau de musique, 29, Place de la Bourse, is identical with one of the above-enumerated mazurkas I have not been able to discover. In the Klindworth edition [FOOTNOTE: That is to say, in the original Russian, not in the English (Augener and Co.'s) edition; and there only by the desire of the publishers and against the better judgment of the editor.] is also to be found a very un-Chopinesque Mazurka in F sharp major, previously published by J. P. Gotthard, in Vienna, the authorship of which Mr. E. Pauer has shown to belong to Charles Mayer.

[FOOTNOTE: In an article, entitled Musical Plagiarism in the Monthly Musical Record of July 1, 1882 (where also the mazurka in question is reprinted), we read as follows:—"In 1877 Mr. E. Pauer, whilst preparing a comprehensive guide through the entire literature of the piano, looked through many thousand pieces for that instrument published by German firms, and came across a mazurka by Charles Mayer, published by Pietro Mechetti (afterwards C. A. Spinal, and entitled Souvenirs de la Pologne. A few weeks later a mazurka, a posthumous work of F. Chopin, published by J. Gotthard, came into his hands. At first, although the piece 'struck him as being an old acquaintance,' he could not fix the time when and the place where he had heard it; but at last the Mayer mazurka mentioned above returned to his remembrance, and on comparing the two, he found that they were one and the same piece. From the appearance of the title-page and the size of the notes, Mr. Pauer, who has had considerable experience in these matters, concluded that the Mayer copy must have been published between the years 1840 and 1845, and wrote to Mr. Gotthard pointing out the similarity of Chopin's posthumous work, and asking how he came into possession of the Chopin manuscript. Mr. Gotthard replied,'that he had bought the mazurka as Chopin's autograph from a Polish countess, who, being in sad distress, parted, though with the greatest sorrow, with the composition of her illustrious compatriot.' Mr. Pauer naturally concludes that Mr. Gotthard had been deceived, that the manuscript was not a genuine autograph, and 'that the honour of having composed the mazurka in question belongs to Charles Mayer.' Mr. Pauer further adds: 'It is not likely that C. Mayer, even if Chopin had made him a present of this mazurka, would have published it during Chopin's lifetime as a work of his own, or have sold or given it to the Polish countess. It is much more likely that Mayer's mazurka was copied in the style of Chopin's handwriting, and after Mayer's death in 1862 sold as Chopin's autograph to Mr. Gotthard.'"]

Surveying the mazurkas in their totality, we cannot but notice that there is a marked difference between those up to and those above Op. 41. In the later ones we look in vain for the beautes sauvages which charm us in the earlier ones—they strike us rather by their propriety of manner and scholarly elaboration; in short, they have more of reflective composition and less of spontaneous effusion about them. This, however, must not be taken too literally. There are exceptions, partial and total. The "native wood-notes wild" make themselves often heard, only they are almost as often stifled in the close air of the study. Strange to say, the last opus (63) of mazurkas published by Chopin has again something of the early freshness and poetry. Schumann spoke truly when he said that some poetical trait, something new, was to be found in every one of Chopin's mazurkas. They are indeed teeming with interesting matter. Looked at from the musician's point of view, how much do we not see that is novel and strange, and beautiful and fascinating withal? Sharp dissonances, chromatic passing notes, suspensions and anticipations, displacements of accent, progressions of perfect fifths (the horror of schoolmen), [FOOTNOTE: See especially the passage near the close of Op. 30, No. 4, where there are four bars of simultaneous consecutive fifths and sevenths.] sudden turns and unexpected digressions that are so unaccountable, so out of the line of logical sequence, that one's following the composer is beset with difficulties, marked rhythm picture to us the graceful motions of the dancers, and suggest the clashing of the spurs and the striking of heels against the ground. The second mazurka might be called "the request." All the arts of persuasion are tried, from the pathetic to the playful, and a vein of longing, not unmixed with sadness, runs through the whole, or rather forms the basis of it. The tender commencement of the second part is followed, as it were, by the several times repeated questions— Yes? No? (Bright sunshine? Dark clouds?) But there comes no answer, and the poor wretch has to begin anew. A helpless, questioning uncertainty and indecision characterise the third mazurka. For a while the composer gives way (at the beginning of the second part) to anger, and speaks in a defiant tone; but, as if perceiving the unprofitableness of it, returns soon to his first strain. Syncopations, suspensions, and chromatic passing notes form here the composer's chief stock in trade, displacement of everything in melody, harmony, and rhythm is the rule. Nobody did anything like this before Chopin, and, as far as I know, nobody has given to the world an equally minute and distinct representation of the same intimate emotional experiences. My last remarks hold good with the fourth mazurka, which is bleak and joyless till, with the entrance of A major, a fairer prospect opens. But those jarring tones that strike in wake the dreamer pitilessly. The commencement of the mazurka, as well as the close on the chord of the sixth, the chromatic glidings of the harmonies, the strange twirls and skips, give a weird character to this piece.

The origin of the polonaise (Taniec Polski, Polish dance), like that of the, no doubt, older mazurka, is lost in the dim past. For much credit can hardly be given to the popular belief that it developed out of the measured procession, to the sound of music, of the nobles and their ladies, which is said to have first taken place in 1574, the year after his election to the Polish throne, when Henry of Anjou received the grandees of his realm. The ancient polonaises were without words, and thus they were still in the time of King Sobieski (1674-96). Under the subsequent kings of the house of Saxony, however, they were often adapted to words or words were adapted to them. Celebrated polonaises of political significance are: the Polonaise of the 3rd of May, adapted to words relative to the promulgation of the famous constitution of the 3rd of May, 1791; the Kosciuszko Polonaise, with words adapted to already existing music, dedicated to the great patriot and general when, in 1792, the nation rose in defence of the constitution; the Oginski Polonaise, also called the Swan's song and the Partition of Poland, a composition without words, of the year 1793 (at the time of the second partition), by Prince Michael Cleophas Oginski. Among the Polish composers of the second half of the last century and the beginning of the present whose polonaises enjoyed in their day, and partly enjoy still, a high reputation, are especially notable Kozlowski, Kamienski, Elsner, Deszczynski, Bracicki, Wanski, Prince Oginski, Kurpinski, and Dobrzynski. Outside Poland the polaise, both as an instrumental and vocal composition, both as an independent piece and part of larger works, had during the same period quite an extraordinary popularity. Whether we examine the productions of the classics or those of the inferior virtuosic and drawing-room composers, [FOOTNOTE: I should have added "operatic composers."] everywhere we find specimens of the polonaise. Pre-eminence among the most successful foreign cultivators of this Polish dance has, however, been accorded to Spohr and Weber. I said just now "this dance," but, strictly speaking, the polonaise, which has been called a marche dansante, is not so much a dance as a figured walk, or procession, full of gravity and a certain courtly etiquette. As to the music of the polonaise, it is in 3/4 time, and of a moderate movement (rather slow than quick). The flowing and more or less florid melody has rhythmically a tendency to lean on the second crotchet and even on the second quaver of the bar (see illustration No. 1, a and b), and generally concludes each of its parts with one of certain stereotyped formulas of a similar rhythmical cast (see illustration No. 2, a, b, c, and d). The usual accompaniment consists of a bass note at the beginning of the bar followed, except at the cadences, by five quavers, of which the first may be divided into semiquavers. Chopin, however, emancipated himself more and more from these conventionalities in his later poetic polonaises.

[Two music score excerpts here, labeled No. 1 and No. 2]

The polonaise [writes Brodzinski] is the only dance which

suits mature age, and is not unbecoming to persons of elevated

rank; it is the dance of kings, heroes, and even old men; it

alone suits the martial dress. It does not breathe any

passion, but seems to be only a triumphal march, an expression

of chivalrous and polite manners. A solemn gravity presides

always at the polonaise, which, perhaps, alone recalls neither

the fire of primitive manners nor the gallantry of more

civilised but more enervated ages. Besides these principal

characteristics, the polonaise bears a singularly national and

historical impress; for its laws recall an aristocratic

republic with a disposition to anarchy, flowing less from the

character of the people than from its particular legislation.

In the olden times the polonaise was a kind of solemn

ceremony. The king, holding by the hand the most distinguished

personage of the assembly, marched at the head of a numerous train of couples composed of men alone: this dance, made more effective by the splendour of the chivalrous costumes, was only, strictly speaking, a triumphal march.

If a lady was the object of the festival, it was her privilege to open the march, holding by the hand another lady. All the others followed until the queen of the ball, having offered her hand to one of the men standing round the room, induced the other ladies to follow her example.

The ordinary polonaise is opened by the most distinguished person of the gathering, whose privilege it is to conduct the whole file of the dancers or to break it up. This is called in Polish rey wodzic, figuratively, to be the leader, in some sort the king (from the Latin rex). To dance at the head was also called to be the marshal, on account of the privileges of a marshal at the Diets. The whole of this form is connected with the memories and customs of raising the militia (pospolite), or rather of the gathering of the national assemblies in Poland. Hence, notwithstanding the deference paid to the leaders, who have the privilege of conducting at will the chain of dancers, it is allowable, by a singular practice made into a law, to dethrone a leader every time any bold person calls out odbiianego, which means retaken by force or reconquered; he who pronounces this word is supposed to wish to reconquer the hand of the first lady and the direction of the dance; it is a kind of act of liberum veto, to which everyone is obliged to give way. The leader then abandons the hand of his lady to the new pretender; every cavalier dances with the lady of the following couple, and it is only the cavalier of the last couple who finds himself definitively ousted if he has not the boldness to insist likewise upon his privilege of equality by demanding odbiianego, and placing himself at the head.

But as a privilege of this nature too often employed would throw the whole ball into complete anarchy, two means are established to obviate this abuse—namely, the leader makes use of his right to terminate the polonaise, in imitation of a king or marshal dissolving a Diet, or else, according to the predominating wish, all the cavaliers leave the ladies alone in the middle, who then choose new partners and continue the dance, excluding the disturbers and discontented, which recalls the confederations employed for the purpose of making the will of the majority prevail.

The polonaise breathes and paints the whole national character; the music of this dance, while admitting much art, combines something martial with a sweetness marked by the simplicity of manners of an agricultural people. Foreigners have distorted this character of the polonaises; the natives themselves preserve it less in our day in consequence of the frequent employment of motives drawn from modern operas. As to the dance itself, the polonaise has become in our day a kind of promenade which has little charm for the young, and is but a scene of etiquette for those of a riper age. Our fathers danced it with a marvellous ability and a gravity full of nobleness; the dancer, making gliding steps with energy, but without skips, and caressing his moustache, varied his movements by the position of his sabre, of his cap, and of his tucked-up coat-sleeves, distinctive signs of a free man and warlike citizen. Whoever has seen a Pole of the old school dance the polonaise in the national costume will confess without hesitation that this dance is the triumph of a well-made man, with a noble and proud tournure, and with an air at once manly and gay.

After this Brodzinski goes on to describe the way in which the polonaise used to be danced. But instead of his description I shall quote a not less true and more picturesque one from the last canto of Mickiewicz's "Pan Tadeusz":—

It is time to dance the polonaise. The President comes forward; he lightly throws back the fausses manches of his overcoat, caresses his moustache, presents his hand to Sophia: and, by a respectful salute, invites her for the first couple. Behind them range themselves the other dancers, two and two; the signal is given, the dance is begun, the President directs it.

His red boots move over the green sward, his belt sends forth flashes of light; he proceeds slowly, as if at random: but in every one of his steps, in every one of his movements, one can read the feelings and the thoughts of the dancer. He stops as if to question his partner; he leans towards her, wishes to speak to her in an undertone. The lady turns away, does not listen, blushes. He takes off his cap, and salutes her respectfully. The lady is not disinclined to look at him, but persists in being silent. He slackens his pace, seeks to read in her eyes, and smiles. Happy in her mute answer, he walks more quickly, looking proudly at his rivals; now he draws his cap with the heron-feathers forward, now he pushes it back. At last he puts it on one side and turns up his moustaches. He withdraws; all envy him, all follow his footsteps. He would like to disappear with his lady. Sometimes he stops, raises politely his hand, and begs the dancers to pass by him. Sometimes he tries to slip dexterously away, changing the direction. He would like to deceive his companions; but the troublesome individuals follow him with a nimble step, entwine him with more and more tightened loops. He becomes angry; lays his right hand on his sword as if he wished to say: "Woe to the jealous!" He turns, pride on his countenance, a challenge in his air, and marches straight on the company, who give way at his approach, open to him a passage, and soon, by a rapid evolution, are off again in pursuit of him.

On all sides one hears the exclamation: "Ah! this is perhaps the last. Look, young people, perhaps this is the last who will know how to conduct thus the polonaise!"

Among those of Chopin's compositions which he himself published are, exclusive of the "Introduction et Polonaise brillante" for piano and violoncello, Op. 3, eight polonaises—namely: "Grande Polonaise brillante" (in E flat major), "precedee d'un Andante spianato" (in G major), "pour le piano avec orchestre," Op. 22; "Deux Polonaises" (in C sharp minor and E flat minor), Op. 26; "Deux Polonaises" (in A major and C minor), Op. 40; "Polonaise" (F sharp minor), Op. 44; "Polonaise" (in A flat major), Op. 53; [FOOTNOTE: This polonaise is called the "eighth" on the title-page, which, of course, it is only by including the "Polonaise," Op. 3, for piano and violoncello.] and "Polonaise-Fantaisie" (in A flat major), Op. 61. The three early polonaises posthumously-published by Fontana as Op. 71 have already been discussed in Chapter VIII. Other posthumously-published polonaises—such as the Polonaise in G sharp minor, to be found in Mikuli's edition, and one in B flat minor of the year 1826, first published in the supplement of the journal "Echo Muzyczne"—need not be considered by us. [FOOTNOTE: Both polonaises are included in the Breitkopf and Hartel edition, where the one in G sharp minor bears the unlikely date 1822. The internal evidence speaks against this statement.]

Chopin's Polonaises Op. 26, 40, 53, and 61 are pre-eminently political, they are the composer's expression of his patriotic feelings. It is not difficult to recognise in them proud memories of past splendours, sad broodings over present humiliations, bright visions of a future resurrection. They are full of martial chivalry, of wailing dejection, of conspiracy and sedition, of glorious victories. The poetically-inferior Polonaise, Op. 22, on the other hand, while unquestionably Polish in spirit, is not political. Chopin played this work, which was probably composed, or at least sketched, in 1830, [FOOTNOTE: See Vol. I., Chapter xiii., pp. 201, 202.] and certainly published in July, 1836, for the first time in public at a Paris Conservatoire concert for the benefit of Habeneck on April 26, 1835; and this was the only occasion on which he played it with orchestral accompaniments. The introductory Andante (in G major, and 6/8 time), as the accompanying adjective indicates, is smooth and even. It makes one think of a lake on a calm, bright summer day. A boat glides over the pellucid, unruffled surface of the water, by-and-by halts at a shady spot by the shore, or by the side of some island (3/4 time), then continues its course (f time), and finally returns to its moorings (3/4). I can perceive no connection between the Andante and the following Polonaise (in E flat major) except the factitious one of a formal and forced transition, with which the orchestra enters on the scene of action (Allegro molto, 3/4). After sixteen bars of tutti, the pianoforte commences, unaccompanied, the polonaise. Barring the short and in no way attractive and remarkable test's, the orchestra plays a very subordinate and often silent role, being, indeed, hardly missed when the pianoforte part is played alone. The pronounced bravura character of the piece would warrant the supposition that it was written expressly for the concert-room, even if the orchestral accompaniments were not there to prove the fact. A proud bearing, healthful vigour, and sprightly vivacity distinguish Chopin on this occasion. But notwithstanding the brave appearance, one misses his best qualities. This polonaise illustrates not only the most brilliant, but also the least lovable features of the Polish character—ostentatiousness and exaggerated rhetoric. In it Chopin is discovered posturing, dealing in phrases, and coquetting with sentimental affectations. In short, the composer comes before us as a man of the world, intent on pleasing, and sure of himself and success. The general airiness of the style is a particularly-noticeable feature of this piece of Chopin's virtuosic period.

The first bars of the first (in C sharp minor) of the two Polonaises, Op. 26 (published in July, 1836), fall upon one's ear like a decision of irresistible, inexorable fate. Indignation flares up for a moment, and then dies away, leaving behind sufficient strength only for a dull stupor (beginning of the second part), deprecation, melting tenderness (the E major in the second part, and the closing bars of the first and second parts), and declarations of devotion (meno mosso). While the first polonaise expresses weak timidity, sweet plaintiveness, and a looking for help from above, the second one (in E flat minor) speaks of physical force and self-reliance—it is full of conspiracy and sedition. The ill-suppressed murmurs of discontent, which may be compared to the ominous growls of a volcano, grow in loudness and intensity, till at last, with a rush and a wild shriek, there follows an explosion. The thoughts flutter hither and thither, in anxious, helpless agitation. Then martial sounds are heard—a secret gathering of a few, which soon grows in number and in boldness. Now they draw nearer; you distinguish the clatter of spurs and weapons, the clang of trumpets (D flat major). Revenge and death are their watchwords, and with sullen determination they stare desolation in the face (the pedal F with the trebled part above). After an interesting transition the first section returns. In the meno mosso (B major) again a martial rhythm is heard; this time, however, the gathering is not one for revenge and death, but for battle and victory. From the far-off distance the winds carry the message that tells of freedom and glory. But what is this (the four bars before the tempo I.)? Alas! the awakening from a dream. Once more we hear those sombre sounds, the shriek and explosion, and so on. Of the two Polonaises, Op. 26, the second is the grander, and the definiteness which distinguishes it from the vague first shows itself also in the form.

A greater contrast than the two Polonaises, Op. 40 (published in November, 1840), can hardly be imagined. In the first (in A major) the mind of the composer is fixed on one elating thought—he sees the gallantly-advancing chivalry of Poland, determination in every look and gesture; he hears rising above the noise of stamping horses and the clash of arms their bold challenge scornfully hurled at the enemy. In the second (in C minor), on the other hand, the mind of the composer turns from one depressing or exasperating thought to another—he seems to review the different aspects of his country's unhappy state, its sullen discontent, fretful agitation, and uncertain hopes. The manly Polonaise in A major, one of the simplest (not easiest) compositions of Chopin, is the most popular of his polonaises. The second polonaise, however, although not so often heard, is the more interesting one, the emotional contents being more varied, and engaging more our sympathy. Further, the pianoforte, however fully and effectively employed, cannot do justice to the martial music of the one, while its capacities are well suited for the rendering of the less material effect of the other. In conclusion, let me point out in the C minor Polonaise the chafing agitation of the second part, the fitful play between light and shade of the trio-like part in A flat major, and the added wailing voice in the recurring first portion at the end of the piece. [FOOTNOTE: In connection with the A major Polonaise, see last paragraph on next page.]

If Schiller is right in saying "Ernst ist das Leben, heiter ist die Kunst," then what we find in the Polonaise (in F sharp minor), Op. 44 (published in November, 1841), cannot be art. We look in vain for beauty of melody and harmony; dreary unisons, querulous melodic phrases, hollow-eyed chords, hard progressions and modulations throughout every part of the polonaise proper. We receive a pathological rather than aesthetical impression. Nevertheless, no one can deny the grandeur and originality that shine through this gloom. The intervening Doppio movimento, tempo di Mazurka, sends forth soft beneficent rays—reminiscences of long ago, vague and vanishing, sweet and melancholy. But there is an end to this as to all such dreams. Those harassing, exasperating gloomy thoughts (Tempo di Polacca) return. The sharp corners which we round so pleasantly and beautifully in our reconstructions of the past make themselves only too soon felt in the things of the present, and cruelly waken us to reality and its miseries.

The Polonaise, Op. 53 (in A flat major; published in December, 1843), is one of the most stirring compositions of Chopin, manifesting an overmastering power and consuming fire. But is it really the same Chopin, is it the composer of the dreamy nocturnes, the elegant waltzes, who here fumes and frets, struggling with a fierce, suffocating rage (mark the rushing succession of chords of the sixth, the growling semiquaver figures, and the crashing dissonances of the sixteen introductory bars), and then shouts forth, sure of victory, his bold and scornful challenge? And farther on, in the part of the polonaise where the ostinato semiquaver figure in octaves for the left hand begins, do we not hear the trampling of horses, the clatter of arms and spurs, and the sound of trumpets? Do we not hear—yea, and see too—a high-spirited chivalry approaching and passing? Only pianoforte giants can do justice to this martial tone-picture, the physical strength of the composer certainly did not suffice.

The story goes that when Chopin played one of his polonaises in the night-time, just after finishing its composition, he saw the door open, and a long train of Polish knights and ladies, dressed in antique costumes, enter through it and defile past him. This vision filled the composer with such terror that he fled through the opposite door, and dared not return to the room the whole night. Karasowski says that the polonaise in question is the last-mentioned one, in A flat major; but from M. Kwiatkowski, who depicted the scene three times, [FOOTNOTE: "Le Reve de Chopin," a water-colour, and two sketches in oils representing, according to Chopin's indication (d'apres l'avis de Chopin), the polonaise.] learned that it is the one in A major, No. 1 of Op. 40, dedicated to Fontana.

I know of no more affecting composition among all the productions of Chopin than the "Polonaise-Fantaisie" (in A flat major), Op. 61 (published in September, 1846). What an unspeakable, unfathomable wretchedness reveals itself in these sounds! We gaze on a boundless desolation. These lamentations and cries of despair rend our heart, these strange, troubled wanderings from thought to thought fill us with intensest pity. There are thoughts of sweet resignation, but the absence of hope makes them perhaps the saddest of all. The martial strains, the bold challenges, the shouts of triumph, which we heard so often in the composer's polonaises, are silenced.

> An elegiac sadness [says Liszt] predominates, intersected by
> wild movements, melancholy smiles, unexpected starts, and
> intervals of rest full of dread such as those experience who
> have been surprised by an ambuscade, who are surrounded on all
> sides, for whom there dawns no hope upon the vast horizon, and
> to whose brain despair has gone like a deep draught of Cyprian

wine, which gives a more instinctive rapidity to every gesture, a sharper point to every emotion, causing the mind to arrive at a pitch of irritability bordering on madness.

Thus, although comprising thoughts that in beauty and grandeur equal—I would almost say surpass-anything Chopin has written, the work stands, on account of its pathological contents, outside the sphere of art.

Chopin's waltzes, the most popular of his compositions, are not poesie intime like the greater number of his works. [FOOTNOTE: Op. 34, No. 2, and Op. 64, No. 2, however, have to be excepted, to some extent at least.] In them the composer mixes with the world-looks without him rather than within—and as a man of the world conceals his sorrows and discontents under smiles and graceful manners. The bright brilliancy and light pleasantness of the earlier years of his artistic career, which are almost entirely lost in the later years, rise to the surface in the waltzes. These waltzes are salon music of the most aristocratic kind. Schumann makes Florestan say of one of them, and he might have said it of all, that he would not play it unless one half of the female dancers were countesses. But the aristocraticalness of Chopin's waltzes is real, not conventional; their exquisite gracefulness and distinction are natural, not affected. They are, indeed, dance-poems whose content is the poetry of waltz-rhythm and movement, and the feelings these indicate and call forth. In one of his most extravagantly-romantic critical productions Schumann speaks, in connection with Chopin's Op. 18, "Grande Valse brillante," the first-published (in June, 1834) of his waltzes, of "Chopin's body and mind elevating waltz," and its "enveloping the dancer deeper and deeper in its floods." This language is altogether out of proportion with the thing spoken of; for Op. 18 differs from the master's best waltzes in being, not a dance-poem, but simply a dance, although it must be admitted that it is an exceedingly spirited one, both as regards piquancy and dash. When, however, we come to Op. 34, "Trois Valses brillantes" (published in December, 1838), Op. 42, "Valse" (published in July, 1840), and Op. 64, "Trois Valses" (published in September, 1847), the only other waltzes published by him, we find ourselves face to face with true dance-poems. Let us tarry for a moment over Op. 34. How brisk the introductory bars of the first (in A flat major) of these three waltzes! And what a striking manifestation of the spirit of that dance all that follows! We feel the wheeling motions; and where, at the seventeenth bar of the second part, the quaver figure enters, we think we see the flowing dresses sweeping round. Again what vigour in the third part, and how coaxingly tender the fourth! And, lastly, the brilliant conclusion—the quavers intertwined with triplets! The second waltz (in A minor; Lento) is of quite another, of a more retired and private, nature, an exception to the rule. The composer evidently found pleasure in giving way to this delicious languor, in indulging in these melancholy thoughts full of sweetest, tenderest loving and longing. But here words will not avail. One day when Stephen Heller—my informant—was at Schlesinger's music-shop in Paris, Chopin entered. The latter, hearing Heller ask for one of his waltzes, inquired of him which of them he liked best. "It is difficult to say which I like best," replied Heller, "for I like them all; but if I were pressed for an answer I would probably say the one in A minor." This gave Chopin much pleasure. "I am glad you do," he said; "it is also my favourite." And in an exuberance of amiability he invited Heller to lunch with him, an invitation which was accepted, the two artists taking the meal together at the Cafe Riche. The third waltz (in F major; Vivace) shows a character very different from the preceding one. What a stretching of muscles! What a whirling! Mark the giddy motions of the melody beginning at bar seventeen! Of this waltz of Chopin's and the first it is more especially true what Schumann said of all three: "Such flooding life moves within these waltzes that they seem to have been improvised in the ball-room." And the words which the same critic applies to Op. 34 may be applied to all the waltzes Chopin published himself—"They must please; they are of another stamp than the usual waltzes, and in the style in which they can only be conceived by Chopin when he looks in a grandly-artistic way into the dancing crowd, which he elevates by his playing, thinking of other things than of what is being danced." In the A flat major waltz which bears the opus number 42, the duple rhythm of the melody along with the triple one of the accompaniment seems to me indicative of the loving nestling and tender embracing of the dancing couples. Then, after the smooth gyrations of the first period, come those sweeping motions, free and graceful like those of birds, that intervene again and again between the different portions of the waltz. The D flat major part bubbles over with joyousness. In the sostenuto, on the other hand, the composer becomes sentimental, protests, and heaves sighs. But at the very height of his rising ardour he suddenly plunges back into that wild, self-surrendering, heaven and earth-forgetting joyousness—a stroke of genius as delightful as it is clever. If we do not understand by the name of scherzo a fixed form, but rather a state of mind, we may say that Chopin's waltzes are his scherzos and not the pieces to which he has given that name. None of Chopin's waltzes is more popular than the first of Op. 64 (in D flat major). And no wonder! The life, flow, and oneness are unique; the charm of the multiform motions is indescribable. That it has been and why it has been called valse au petit chien need here only be recalled to the reader's recollection (see Chapter XXVI., p. 142). No. 2 (in C sharp minor); different as it is, is in its own way nearly as perfect as No. 1. Tender, love-sick longing cannot be depicted more truthfully, sweetly, and entrancingly. The excellent

No. 3 (in A flat major), with the exquisite serpentining melodic lines, which play so important a part in Chopin's waltzes, and other beautiful details, is in a somewhat trying position beside the other two waltzes. The non-publication by the composer of the waltzes which have got into print, thanks to the zeal of his admirers and the avidity of publishers, proves to me that he was a good judge of his own works. Fontana included in his collection of posthumous compositions five waltzes—"Deux Valses," Op. 69 (in F minor, of 1836; in B minor, of 1829);. and "Trois Valses," Op. 70 (in G flat major, of 1835; in F minor, of 1843; in D flat major, of 1830). There are further a waltz in E minor and one in E major (of 1829). [FOOTNOTE: The "Deux Valses melancoliques" (in F minor and B minor), ecrits sur l'album de Madame la Comtesse P., 1844 (Cracow: J. Wildt), the English edition of which (London: Edwin Ashdown) is entitled "Une soiree en 1844," "Deux Valses melancoliques," are Op. 70. No. 2, and Op. 69, No. 2, of the works of Chopin posthumously published by Fontana.] Some of these waltzes I discussed already when speaking of the master's early compositions, to which they belong. The last-mentioned waltz, which the reader will find in Mikuli's edition (No. 15 of the waltzes), and also in Breitkopf and Hartel's (No. 22 of the Posthumous works), is a very weak composition; and of all the waltzes not published by the composer himself it may be said that what is good in them has been expressed better in others.

We have of Chopin 27 studies: Op. 10, "Douze Etudes," published in July, 1833; Op. 25, "Douze Etudes," published in October, 1837; and "Trois nouvelles Etudes," which, before being separately published, appeared in 1840 in the "Methode des Methodes pour le piano" by F. J. Fetis and I. Moscheles. The dates of their publication, as in the case of many other works, do not indicate the approximate dates of their composition. Sowinski tells us, for instance, that Chopin brought the first book of his studies with him to Paris in 1831. A Polish musician who visited the French capital in 1834 heard Chopin play the studies contained in Op. 25. And about the last-mentioned opus we read in a critical notice by Schumann, who had, no doubt, his information directly from Chopin: "The studies which have now appeared [that is, those of Op. 25] were almost all composed at the same time as the others [that is, those of Op. 10] and only some of them, the greater masterliness of which is noticeable, such as the first, in A flat major, and the splendid one in C minor [that is, the twelfth] but lately." Regarding the Trois nouvelles Etudes without OPUS number we have no similar testimony. But internal evidence seems to show that these weakest of the master's studies—which, however, are by no means uninteresting, and certainly very characteristic—may be regarded more than Op. 25 as the outcome of a gleaning. In two of Chopin's letters of the year 1829, we meet with announcements of his having composed studies. On the 20th of October he writes: "I have composed a study in my own manner"; and on the 14th of November: "I have written some studies." From Karasowski learn that the master composed the twelfth study of Op. 10 during his stay in Stuttgart, being inspired by the capture of Warsaw by the Russians, which took place on September 8, 1831. Whether looked at from the aesthetical or technical point of view, Chopin's studies will be seen to be second to those of no composer. Were it not wrong to speak of anything as absolutely best, their excellences would induce one to call them unequalled. A striking feature in them compared with Chopin's other works is their healthy freshness and vigour. Even the slow, dreamy, and elegiac ones have none of the faintness and sickliness to be found in not a few of the composer's pieces, especially in several of the nocturnes. The diversity of character exhibited by these studies is very great. In some of them the aesthetical, in others the technical purpose predominates; in a few the two are evenly balanced: in none is either of them absent. They give a summary of Chopin's ways and means, of his pianoforte language: chords in extended positions, wide-spread arpeggios, chromatic progressions (simple, in thirds, and in octaves), simultaneous combinations of contrasting rhythms, &c—nothing is wanting. In playing them or hearing them played Chopin's words cannot fail to recur to one's mind: "I have composed a study in my own manner." Indeed, the composer's demands on the technique of the executant were so novel at the time when the studies made their first public appearance that one does not wonder at poor blind Rellstab being staggered, and venting his feelings in the following uncouthly-jocular manner: "Those who have distorted fingers may put them right by practising these studies; but those who have not, should not play them, at least not without having a surgeon at hand." In Op. 10 there are three studies especially noteworthy for their musical beauty. The third (Lento ma non troppo, in E major) and the sixth (Andante, in E flat minor) may be reckoned among Chopin's loveliest compositions. They combine classical chasteness of contour with the fragrance of romanticism. And the twelfth study (Allegro con fuoco, in C minor), the one composed at Stuttgart after the fall of Warsaw, how superbly grand! The composer seems to be fuming with rage: the left hand rushes impetuously along and the right hand strikes in with passionate ejaculations. With regard to the above-named Lento ma non troppo (Op. 10, No. 3), Chopin said to Gutmann that he had never in his life written another such beautiful melody (CHANT); and on one occasion when Gutmann was studying it the master lifted up his arms with his hands clasped and exclaimed: "O, my fatherland!" ("O, me patrie!") I share with Schumann the opinion that the total weight of Op. 10 amounts to more than that of Op. 25. Like him I regard also Nos. 1 and 12 as the most important items of the latter collection of studies: No. 1

(Allegro sostenuto, in A flat major)—a tremulous mist below, a beautiful breezy melody floating above, and once or twice a more opaque body becoming discernible within the vaporous element—of which Schumann says that "after listening to the study one feels as one does after a blissful vision, seen in a dream, which, already half-awake, one would fain bring back": [FOOTNOTE: See the whole quotation, Vol. I., p. 310.] and No. 12 (in C minor, Allegro molto con fuoco), in which the emotions rise not less than the waves of arpeggios (in both hands) which symbolise them. Stephen Heller's likings differ from Schumann's. Discussing Chopin's Op. 25 in the Gazette musicale of February 24, 1839, he says:—

What more do we require to pass one or several evenings in as perfect a happiness as possible? As for me, I seek in this collection of poesy (this is the only name appropriate to the works of Chopin) some favourite pieces which I might fix in my memory rather than others. Who could retain everything? For this reason I have in my note book quite particularly marked the numbers 4, 5, and 7 of the present poems. Of these twelve much-loved studies (every one of which has a charm of its own) these three numbers are those I prefer to all the rest.

In connection with the fourth, Heller points out that it reminds him of the first bar of the Kyrie (rather the Requiem aeternam) of Mozart's Requiem. And of the seventh study he remarks:—

It engenders the sweetest sadness, the most enviable torments; and if in playing it one feels one's self insensibly drawn towards mournful and melancholy ideas, it is a disposition of the soul which I prefer to all others. Alas! how I love these sombre and mysterious dreams, and Chopin is the god who creates them.

This No. 7 (in C sharp minor, lento), a duet between a HE and a SHE, of whom the former shows himself more talkative and emphatic than the latter, is, indeed, very sweet, but perhaps, also somewhat tiresomely monotonous, as such tete-a-tete naturally are to third parties. As a contrast to No. 7, and in conclusion—leaving several aerial flights and other charming conceptions undiscussed—I will yet mention the octave study, No. 10, which is a real pandemonium; for a while holier sounds intervene, but finally hell prevails.

The genesis of the Vingt-quatre Preludes, Op. 28, published in September, 1839, I have tried to elucidate in the twenty-first chapter. I need, therefore, not discuss the question here. The indefinite character and form of the prelude, no doubt, determined the choice of the title which, however, does not describe the contents of this OPUS. Indeed, no ONE name could do so. This heterogeneous collection of pieces reminds me of nothing so much as of an artist's portfolio filled with drawings in all stages of advancement—finished and unfinished, complete and incomplete compositions, sketches and mere memoranda, all mixed indiscriminately together. The finished works were either too small or too slight to be sent into the world separately, and the right mood for developing, completing, and giving the last touch to the rest was gone, and could not be found again. Schumann, after expressing his admiration for these preludes, as well he might, adds: "This book contains morbid, feverish, and repellent matter." I do not think that there is much that could justly be called repellent; but the morbidity and feverishness of a considerable portion must be admitted.

I described the preludes [writes Schumann] as remarkable. To confess the truth, I expected they would be executed like the studies, in the grandest style. Almost the reverse is the case; they are sketches, commencements of studies, or, if you will, ruins, single eagle-wings, all strangely mixed together. But in his fine nonpareil there stands in every piece:— "Frederick Chopin wrote it." One recognises him by the violent breathing during the rests. He is, and remains, the proudest poet-mind of the time.

The almost infinite and infinitely-varied beauties collected in this treasure-trove denominated Vingt-quatre Preludes could only be done justice to by a minute analysis, for which, however, there is no room here. I must content myself with a word or two about a few of them, picked out at random. No. 4 is a little poem the exquisitely-sweet languid pensiveness of which defies description. The composer seems to be absorbed in the narrow sphere of his ego, from which the wide, noisy world is for the time being shut out. In No. 6 we have, no doubt, the one of which George Sand said that it occurred to Chopin one evening while rain was falling, and that it "precipitates the soul into a frightful depression." [FOOTNOTE: See George Sand's account and description in Chapter XXI., p. 43.] How wonderfully the contending rhythms of the accompaniment, and the fitful, jerky course of the melody, depict in No. 8 a state of anxiety and agitation! The premature conclusion of that bright vivacious thing No. 11 fills one with regret. Of the beautifully-melodious No. 13, the piu lento and the peculiar closing bars are especially noteworthy. No. 14 invites a comparison with the finale of the B flat minor Sonata. In the middle section (in C sharp minor) of the following number (in D flat major), one of the larger pieces, rises before one's mind the cloistered court of the monastery of Valdemosa, and a procession of monks chanting lugubrious prayers, and carrying in the dark hours of night their departed brother to his last resting-place. It reminds one of the words of George Sand, that the monastery was to Chopin full of terrors and phantoms. This C sharp minor portion of No. 15 affects one like an oppressive dream; the re-entrance of the opening D flat major, which dispels the dreadful nightmare, comes upon one with the smiling freshness of dear, familiar nature—only after these horrors of the imagination can its serene beauty be fully appreciated. No. 17, another developed piece, strikes one as akin to Mendelssohn's Songs without Words. I must not omit to mention No. 21, one of the finest of the collection, with its calming cantilena and palpitating quaver figure. Besides the set of twenty-four preludes, Op. 28, Chopin published a single one, Op. 45, which appeared in December, 1841. This composition deserves its name better than almost anyone of the twenty-four; still, I would rather call it an improvisata. It seems unpremeditated, a heedless outpouring when sitting at the piano in a lonely, dreary hour, perhaps in the twilight. The quaver figure rises aspiringly, and the sustained parts swell out proudly. The piquant cadenza forestalls in the progression of diminished chords favourite effects of some of our more modern composers. The modulation from C sharp minor to D major and back again (after the cadenza) is very striking and equally beautiful.

It can hardly be said, although Liszt seemed to be of a different opinion, that Chopin created a new type by his preludes—they are too unlike each other in form and character. On the other hand, he has done so by his four scherzos—Op. 20 (in B minor), published in February, 1835; Op. 31 (B flat minor), published in December, 1837; Op. 39 (C sharp minor), published in October, 1840; and Op. 54 (in E major), published in December, 1843. "How is 'gravity' to clothe itself, if 'jest' goes about in dark veils?" exclaims Schumann. No doubt, scherzo, if we consider the original meaning of the word, is a misnomer. But are not Beethoven's scherzos, too, misnamed? To a certain extent they are. But if Beethoven's scherzos often lack frolicsomeness, they are endowed with humour, whereas Chopin's have neither the one nor the other. Were it not that we attach, especially since Mendelssohn's time, the idea of lightness and light-heartedness to the word capriccio, this would certainly be the more descriptive name for the things Chopin entitled SCHERZO. But what is the use of carping at a name? Let us rather look at the things, and thus employ our time better. Did ever composer begin like Chopin in his Premier Scherzo, Op. 20? Is this not like a shriek of despair? and what follows, bewildered efforts of a soul shut in by a wall of circumstances through which it strives in vain to break? at last sinking down with fatigue, dreaming· a dream of idyllic beauty? but beginning the struggle again as soon as its strength is recruited? Schumann compared the second SCHERZO, Op. 31, to a poem of Byron's, "so tender, so bold, as full of love as of scorn." Indeed, scorn—an element which does not belong to what is generally understood by either frolicsomeness or humour—plays an important part in Chopin's scherzos. The very beginning of Op. 31 offers an example.

[FOOTNOTE: "It must be a question [the doubled triplet figure A, B flat, d flat, in the first bar], taught Chopin, and for him it was never question enough, never piano enough, never vaulted (tombe) enough, as he said, never important enough. It must be a charnel-house, he said on one occasion." (W. von Lenz, in Vol. XXVI. of the Berliner Musikzeitung.)]

And then, we do not meet·with a phrase of a more cheerful nature which is not clouded by sadness. Weber—I mention his name intentionally—would, for instance, in the D flat major portion have concluded the melodic phrase in diatonic progression and left the harmony pure. Now see what Chopin does. The con anima has this mark of melancholy still more distinctly impressed upon it. After the repetition of the capricious, impulsively-passionate first section (in B flat minor and D flat major) follows the delicious second, the expression of which is as indescribable as that of Leonardo da Vinci's "La Gioconda." It is a pondering and wondering full of longing. In the deep, tender yearning, with the urging undercurrent of feeling, of the C sharp minor portion, the vague dreaming of the preceding portion of the section grows into wakefulness, and the fitful imagination is concentrated on one object. Without continuing the emotional or entering on a formal analysis of this scherzo, I venture to say that it is a very important composition, richer and more varied in emotional incidents than the other works of Chopin which bear the same name. More than to any one of the master's scherzos, the name capriccio would be suitable to his third "Scherzo," Op. 39, with its capricious starts and changes, its rudderless drifting. Peevishness, a fierce scornfulness, and a fretful agitation, may be heard in these sounds, of jest and humour there is nothing perceptible. At any rate, the curled lip, as it were, contradicts the jesting words, and the careless exterior does not altogether conceal the seething rage within. But with the meno mosso (D flat major) come pleasanter thoughts. The hymn-like snatches of sustained melody with the intervening airy interludes are very lovely. These are the principal features, to describe all the whims is of course impossible. You may call this work an extravaganza, and point out its grotesqueness; but you must admit that only by this erratic character of the form and these spasmodic movements, could be expressed the peculiar restiveness, fitfulness, and waywardness of thought and feeling that characterise Chopin's individuality. To these unclassical qualities—for classical art is above all plastic and self-possessed—combined as they are with a high degree of refinement and delicacy, his compositions owe much of their peculiar charm. The absence of scorn distinguishes the fourth "Scherzo," Op. 54, from the other three; but, like them, although less closely wrapped, it wears dark veils. The tripping fairy steps which we find in bars 17-20 and in other places are a new feature in Chopin. As to the comparative value of the work, it seems to me inferior to its brothers. The first section is too fragmentary to give altogether satisfaction. One is hustled from one phrase to another, and they are as unlike each other as can well be imagined. The beauty of many of the details, however, must be acknowledged; indeed, the harmonic finesses, the melodic cunning, and rhythmical piquancy, are too potent to be ignored. The resting-place and redeeming part of this scherzo is the sweetly-melodious second section, with its long, smooth, gently and beautifully-curved lines. Also the return to the repetition of the first section is very interesting. This scherzo has the appearance of being laboured, painfully hammered and welded together. But as the poet is born, not made—which "being born" is not brought about without travail, nor makes the less desirable a careful bringing-up—so also does a work of art owe what is best in it to a propitious concurrence of circumstances in the natal hour.

The contents of Chopin's impromptus are of a more pleasing nature than those of the scherzos. Like the latter they are wayward, but theirs is a charming, lovable waywardness. The composer's three first impromptus were published during his lifetime: Op. 29 in December, 1837; Op. 36 in May, 1840; and Op. 51 in February, 1843. The fourth impromptu ("Fantaisie-Impromptu"), Op. 66, is a posthumous publication. What name has been more misapplied than that of impromptu? Again and again we meet with works thus christened which bear upon them the distinct marks of painful effort and anxious filing, which maybe said to smell of the midnight lamp, and to be dripping with the hard-working artificer's sweat. How Chopin produced the "Impromptu," Op. 29 (in A flat major), I do not know. Although an admired improviser, the process of composition was to him neither easy nor quick. But be this as it may, this impromptu has quite the air of a spontaneous, unconstrained outpouring. The first section with its triplets bubbles forth and sparkles like a fountain on which the sunbeams that steal through the interstices of the overhanging foliage are playing. The F minor section is sung out clearly and heartily, with graces beautiful as nature's. The song over, our attention is again attracted by the harmonious murmuring and the changing lights of the water. The

"Deuxieme Impromptu," Op. 36 (in F sharp major), is, like the first, a true impromptu, but while the first is a fresh and lusty welling forth of joy amidst the pleasures of a present reality, this is a dreamy lingering over thoughts and scenes of the imagination that appear and vanish like dissolving views. One would wish to have a programme of this piece. Without such assistance the D major section of the impromptu is insignificant. We want to see, or at least to know, who the persons that walk in the procession which the music accompanies are. Some bars in the second half of this section remind one of Schumann's "Fantasia" in C. After this section a curious transition leads in again the theme, which first appeared in F sharp major, in F major, and with a triplet accompaniment. When F sharp major is once more reached, the theme is still further varied (melodically), till at last the wondrous, fairy-like phrase from the first section brings the piece to a conclusion. This impromptu is inferior to the first, having less pith in it; but its tender sweetness and euphony cannot be denied. The idle forgetfulness of the more serious duties and the deep miseries of life in the enjoyment of a dolce far niente recalls Schubert and the "Fantasia," Op. 78, and other works of his. In the "Troisieme Impromptu" (in G flat major), Op. 51, the rhythmical motion and the melodical form of the two parts that serpentine their lines in opposite directions remind one of the first impromptu (in A flat), but the characters of these pieces are otherwise very unlike. The earlier work is distinguished by a brisk freshness; the later one by a feverish restlessness and faint plaintiveness. After the irresolute flutter of the relaxing and enervating chromatic progressions and successions of thirds and sixths, the greater steadiness of the middle section, more especially the subdued strength and passionate eloquence at the D flat major, has a good effect. But here, too, the languid, lamenting chromatic passing and auxiliary notes are not wanting, and the anxious, breathless accompaniment does not make things more cheerful. In short, the piece is very fine in its way, but the unrelieved, or at least very insufficiently relieved, morbidezza is anything but healthy. We may take note of the plain chord progressions which intervene in the first and last sections of the impromptu; such progressions are of frequent occurrence in Chopin's works. Is there not something pleonastic in the title "Fantaisie-Impromptu?" Whether the reader may think so or not, he will agree with me that the fourth impromptu (in C sharp minor), Op. 66, is the most valuable of the compositions published by Fontana; indeed, it has become one of the favourites of the pianoforte-playing world. Spontaneity of emotional expression and effective treatment of the pianoforte distinguish the Fantaisie-Impromptu. In the first section we have the restless, surging, gushing semiquavers, carrying along with them a passionate, urging melody, and the simultaneous waving triplet accompaniment; in the second section, where the motion of the accompaniment is on the whole preserved, the sonorous, expressive cantilena in D flat major; the third section repeats the first, which it supplements with a coda containing a reminiscence of the cantilena of the second section, which calms the agitation of the semiquavers. According to Fontana, Chopin composed this piece about 1834. Why did he keep it in his portfolio? I suspect he missed in it, more especially in the middle section, that degree of distinction and perfection of detail which alone satisfied his fastidious taste.

Among Chopin's nocturnes some of his most popular works are to be found. Nay, the most widely-prevailing idea of his character as a man and musician seems to have been derived from them. But the idea thus formed is an erroneous one; these dulcet, effeminate compositions illustrate only one side of the master's character, and by no means the best or most interesting. Notwithstanding such precious pearls as the two Nocturnes, Op. 37, and a few others, Chopin shows himself greater both as a man and a musician in every other class of pieces he has originated and cultivated, more especially in his polonaises, ballades, and studies. That, however, there is much to be admired in the class now under consideration will be seen from the following brief comments on the eighteen nocturnes (leaving out of account the one of the year 1828 published by Fontana as Op. 72, No. 1, and already discussed in an earlier chapter) which Chopin gave to the world—Op. 9, Trois Nocturnes, in January, 1833; Op. 15, Trois Nocturnes, in January, 1834; Op. 27, Deux Nocturnes, in May, 1836; Op. 32, Deux Nocturnes, December, 1837; Op. 37, Deux Nocturnes, in May, 1840; Op. 48, Deux Nocturnes, in November, 1841; Op. 55, Deux Nocturnes, in August, 1844; and Op. 62, Deux Nocturnes, in September, 1846. Rellstab remarked in 1833 of the Trois Nocturnes, Op. 9, that Chopin, without borrowing directly from Field, copied the latter's melody and manner of accompaniment. There is some truth in this; only the word "copy" is not the correct one. The younger received from the elder artist the first impulse to write in this form, and naturally adopted also something of his manner. On the whole, the similitude is rather generic than specific. Even the contents of Op. 9 give Chopin a just claim to originality; and the Field reminiscences which are noticeable in Nos. 1 and 2 (most strikingly in the commencement of No. 2) of the first set of nocturnes will be looked for in vain in the subsequent ones.

Where Field smiles [said the above-mentioned critic], Chopin

makes a grinning grimace; where Field sighs, Chopin groans;

where Field shrugs his shoulders, Chopin twists his whole

body; where Field puts some seasoning into the food, Chopin

empties a handful of Cayenne pepper...In short, if one holds

Field's charming romances before a distorting concave mirror, so that every delicate expression becomes a coarse one, one gets Chopin's work...We implore Mr. Chopin to return to nature.

Now, what remains of this statement after subtracting prejudices and narrow-mindedness? Nothing but that Chopin is more varied and passionate than Field, and has developed to the utmost some of the means of expression used by the latter. No. 1 (in B flat minor) of Op. 9 is pervaded by a voluptuous dreaminess and cloying sweetness: it suggests twilight, the stillness of night, and thoughts engendered thereby. The tone of sentiment and the phraseology of No. 2 (in E fiat major) have been made so common by fashionable salon composers that one cannot help suspecting that it is not quite a natural tone—not a tone of true feeling, but of sentimentality. The vulgar do not imitate the true and noble, but the false and ostentatious. In this piece one breathes drawing-room air, and ostentation of sentiment and affectation of speech are native to that place. What, however, the imitations often lack is present in every tone and motion of the original: eloquence, grace, and genuine refinement.

[FOOTNOTE: Gutmann played the return of the principal subject in a way very different from that in which it is printed, with a great deal of ornamentation, and said that Chopin played it always in that way. Also the cadence at the end of the nocturne (Op. 9, No. 2) had a different form. But the composer very frequently altered the ornamentions of his pieces or excogitated alternative readings.]

The third is, like the preceding nocturne, exquisite salon music. Little is said, but that little very prettily. Although the atmosphere is close, impregnated with musk and other perfumes, there is here no affectation. The concluding cadenza, that twirling line, reads plainly "Frederic Chopin." Op. 15 shows a higher degree of independence and poetic power than Op. 9. The third (in G minor) of these nocturnes is the finest of the three. The words languido e rubato describe well the wavering pensiveness of the first portion of the nocturne, which finds its expression in the indecision of the melodic progressions, harmonies, and modulations. The second section is marked religiose, and may be characterised as a trustful prayer, conducive to calm and comfort. The Nocturnes in F major and F sharp major, Op. 15, are more passionate than the one we just now considered, at least in the middle sections. The serene, tender Andante in F major, always sweet, and here and there with touches of delicate playfulness, is interrupted by thoughts of impetuous defiance, which give way to sobs and sighs, start up again with equal violence, and at last die away into the first sweet, tender serenity. The contrast between the languid dreaming and the fiery upstarting is striking and effective, and the practical musician, as well as the student of aesthetics, will do well to examine by what means these various effects are produced. In the second nocturne, F sharp major, the brightness and warmth of the world without have penetrated into the world within. The fioriture flit about as lightly as gossamer threads. The sweetly-sad longing of the first section becomes more disquieting in the doppio movimento, but the beneficial influence of the sun never quite loses its power, and after a little there is a relapse into the calmer mood, with a close like a hazy distance on a summer day. The second (in D flat major) of Op. 27 was, no doubt, conceived in a more auspicious moment than the first (in C sharp minor), of which the extravagantly wide-meshed netting of the accompaniment is the most noteworthy feature. [FOOTNOTE: In most of the pieces where, as in this one, the left-hand accompaniment consists of an undulating figure, Chopin wished it to be played very soft and subdued. This is what Gutmann said.] As to the one in D flat, nothing can equal the finish and delicacy of execution, the flow of gentle feeling, lightly rippled by melancholy, and spreading out here and there in smooth expansiveness. But all this sweetness enervates; there is poison in it. We should not drink in these thirds, sixths, &c., without taking an antidote of Bach or Beethoven. Both the nocturnes of Op. 32 are pretty specimens of Chopin's style of writing in the tender, calm, and dreamy moods. Of the two (in B major and A flat major) I prefer the quiet, pellucid first one. It is very simple, ornaments being very sparingly introduced. The quietness and simplicity are, however, at last disturbed by an interrupted cadence, sombre sounds as of a kettle-drum, and a passionate recitative with intervening abrupt chords. The second nocturne has less originality and pith. Deux Nocturnes (in G minor and G major), Op. 37, are two of the finest, I am inclined to say, the two finest, of this class of Chopin's pieces; but they are of contrasting natures. The first and last sections of the one in G minor are plaintive and longing, and have a wailing accompaniment; the chord progressions of the middle section glide along hymn-like. [FOOTNOTE: Gutmann played this section quicker than the rest, and said that Chopin forgot to mark the change of movement.] Were it possible to praise one part more emphatically than another without committing an injustice, I would speak of the melodic exquisiteness of the first motive. But already I see other parts rise reproachfully before my repentant conscience. A beautiful sensuousness distinguishes the nocturne in G major: it is luscious, soft, rounded, and not without a certain degree of languor. The successions of thirds and, sixths, the semitone progressions, the rocking motion, the modulations (note especially those of the first section and the transition from that to the second), all tend to express the essential character. The second section in C major reappears in E major, after a repetition of part of the first section; a few bars of the latter and a reminiscence of the former conclude the nocturne. But let us not tarry too long in the treacherous atmosphere of this Capua—it bewitches and unmans. The two nocturnes (in C minor and F sharp minor) which form Op. 48 are not of the number of those that occupy foremost places among their companions. Still, they need not be despised. The melody of the C minor portion of the first is very expressive, and the second has in the C sharp minor portion the peculiar Chopinesque flebile dolcezza. In playing these nocturnes there occurred to me a remark of Schumann's, made when he reviewed some nocturnes by Count Wielhorski. He said, on that occasion, that the quicker middle movements which Chopin frequently introduces into his nocturnes are often weaker than his first conceptions, meaning the first portions of the nocturnes. Now, although the middle parts in the present instances are, on the contrary, slower movements, yet the judgment holds good; at least, with respect to the first nocturne, the middle part of which has nothing to recommend it but the effective use of a full and sonorous instrumentation, if I may use this word in speaking of one instrument. The middle part of the second (f, D flat, Molto piu lento), however, is much finer; in it we meet again, as we did in some other nocturnes, with soothing, simple chord progressions. When Gutmann studied the C sharp minor nocturne with Chopin, the master told him that the middle section (the Molto piu lento, in D flat major) should be played as a recitative: "A tyrant commands" (the first two chords), he said, "and the other asks for mercy." Regarding the first nocturne (in F minor) of Op. 55, we will note only the flebile dolcezza of the first and the last section, and the inferiority of the more impassioned middle section. The second nocturne (in E flat major) differs in form from the other nocturnes in this, that it has no contrasting second section, the melody flowing onward from begining to end in a uniform manner. The monotony of the unrelieved sentimentality does not fail to make itself felt. One is seized by an ever-increasing longing to get out of this oppressive atmosphere, to feel the fresh breezes and warm sunshine, to see smiling faces and the many-coloured dress of Nature, to hear the rustling of leaves, the murmuring of streams, and voices which have not yet lost the clear, sonorous ring that joy in the present and hope in the future impart. The two nocturnes, Op. 62, seem to owe their existence rather to the sweet habit of activity than to inspiration. At any rate, the tender flutings, trills, roulades, syncopations, &c., of the first nocturne (in B major), and the sentimental declarations and confused, monotonous agitation of the second (in E major), do not interest me sufficiently to induce me to discuss their merits and demerits.

One day Tausig, the great pianoforte-virtuoso, promised W. von Lenz to play him Chopin's "Barcarolle," Op. 60 (published in September, 1846), adding, "That is a performance which must not be undertaken before more than two persons. I shall play you my own self (meinen Menschen). I love the piece, but take it up only rarely." Lenz, who did not know the barcarolle, thereupon went to a music-shop and read it through attentively. The piece, however, did not please him at all; it seemed to him a long movement in the nocturne-style, a Babel of figuration on a lightly-laid foundation. But he found that he had made a mistake, and, after hearing it played by Tausig, confessed that the virtuoso had infused into the "nine pages of enervating music, of one and the same long-breathed rhythm (12/8), so much interest, so much motion, and so much action," that he regretted the long piece was not longer. And now let us hear what remarks Tausig made with regard to the barcarolle:—

> There are two persons concerned in the affair; it is a love-scene in a discrete gondola; let us say this mise en scene is the symbol of a lovers' meeting generally. This is expressed in the thirds and sixths; the dualism of two notes (persons) is maintained throughout; all is two-voiced, two-souled. In this modulation here in C sharp major (superscribed dolce sfogato), there are kiss and embrace! This is evident! When, after three bars of introduction, the theme, lightly rocking in the bass solo, enters in the fourth, this theme is nevertheless made use of throughout the whole fabric only as an accompaniment, and on this the cantilena in two parts is laid; we have thus a continuous, tender dialogue.

Both Lenz's first and last impressions were correct. The form of the barcarolle is that of most of Chopin's nocturnes—consisting of three sections, of which the third is a modified repetition of the first—only everything is on a larger scale, and more worked out. Unfortunately, the contrast of the middle section is not great enough to prevent the length, in spite of the excellence of the contents, from being felt. Thus we must also subscribe to the "nine pages of enervating music." Still, the barcarolle is one of the most important of Chopin's compositions in the nocturne-style. It has distinctive features which decidedly justify and make valuable its existence. Local colouring is not wanting. The first section reminded me of Schumann's saying that Chopin in his melodies leans sometimes over Germany towards Italy. If properly told, this love-laden romance cannot fail to produce effect.

Of the pieces that bear the name "Berceuse," Chopin's Op. 57 (published in June, 1845) is the finest, or at least one of the finest and happiest conceptions. It rests on the harmonic basis of tonic and dominant. The triad of the tonic and the chord of the dominant seventh divide every bar between them in a brotherly manner. Only in the twelfth and thirteenth bars from the end (the whole piece contains seventy) the triad of the subdominant comes forward, and gives a little breathing time to the triad of the tonic, the chord of the dominant having already dropped off. Well, on this basis Chopin builds, or let us rather say, on this rocking harmonic fluid he sets afloat a charming melody, which is soon joined by a self-willed second part. Afterwards, this melody is dissolved into all kinds of fioriture, colorature, and other trickeries, and they are of such fineness, subtlety, loveliness, and gracefulness, that one is reminded of Queen Mab, who comes—

In shape no bigger than an agate-stone

On the fore-finger of an alderman.

Drawn with a team of little atomies

Athwart men's noses as they lie asleep;

Her waggon-spokes made of long spinners' legs,

The cover of the wings of grasshoppers;

The traces of the smallest spider's web;

The collars of the moonshine's watery beams;

Her whip of cricket's bone; the lash of film;

Her waggoner a small grey-coated gnat.

[FOOTNOTE: Shakespeare, Romeo and Juliet, I., iv., 59-68]

But who does not know the delightful description of the fairy in her hazel-nut coach, and the amusing story of her frolics and pranks? By-and-by the nimble motions of the colorature become slower, and finally glide into the original form of the melody, which, however, already after the third bar comes to a stand-still, is resumed for a short phrase, then expires, after a long-drawn chord of the dominant seventh, on the chord of the tonic, and all is rest and silence. Alexandre Dumas fils speaks in the "Affaire Clemenceau" of the "Berceuse" as—

this muted music [musique en sourdine] which penetrated little
by little the atmosphere and enveloped us in one and the same
sensation, comparable perhaps to that which follows a Turkish
bath, when all the senses are confounded in a general
apaisement, when the body, harmoniously broken, has no longer
any other wish than rest, and when, the soul, seeing all the
doors of its prison open, goes wherever it lists, but always
towards the Blue, into the dream-land.

None of Chopin's compositions surpass in masterliness of form and beauty and poetry of contents his ballades. In them he attains, I think, the acme of his power as an artist. It is much to be regretted that they are only four in number—Op. 23, published in June, 1836; Op. 38, in September, 1840; Op. 47, in November, 1841; and Op 52, in December, 1843. When Schumann reviewed the second ballade he wrote: "Chopin has already written a piece under the same title, one of his wildest and most individual compositions." Schumann relates also that the poems of Mickiewicz incited Chopin to write his ballades, which information he got from the Polish composer himself. He adds significantly: "A poet, again, might easily write words to them [Chopin's ballades]. They move the innermost depth of the soul." Indeed, the "Ballade" (in G minor), Op. 23, is all over quivering with intensest feeling, full of sighs, sobs, groans, and passionate ebullitions. The seven introductory bars (Lento) begin firm, ponderous, and loud, but gradually become looser, lighter, and softer, terminating with a dissonant chord, which some editors have thought fit to correct. [FOOTNOTE: For the correctness of the suspected note we have the testimony of pupils—Gutmann, Mikuli, &c.] Yet this dissonant E flat may be said to be the emotional key-note of the whole poem. It is a questioning thought that, like a sudden pain, shoots through mind and body. And now the story-teller begins his simple but pathetic tale, heaving every now and then a sigh. After the ritenuto the matter becomes more affecting; the sighs and groans, yet for a while kept under restraint, grow louder with the increasing agitation, till at last the whole being is moved to its very depths. On the uproar of the passions follows a delicious calm that descends like a heavenly vision (meno mosso, E flat major). But this does not last, and before long there comes, in the train of the first theme, an outburst of passion with mighty upheavings and fearful lulls that presage new eruptions. Thus the ballade rises and falls on the sea of passion till a mad, reckless rush (presto con fuoco) brings it to a conclusion. Schumann tells us a rather interesting fact in his notice of the "Deuxieme Ballade" (in F major), Op. 38. He heard Chopin play it in Leipzig before its publication, and at that time the passionate middle parts did not exist, and the piece closed in F major, now it closes in A minor. Schumann's opinion of this ballade is, that as a work of art it stands below the first, yet is not less fantastic and geistreich. If two such wholly dissimilar things can be compared and weighed in this fashion, Schumann is very likely right; but I rather think they cannot. The second ballade possesses beauties in no way inferior to those of the first. What can be finer than the simple strains of the opening section! They sound as if they had been drawn from the people's storehouse of song. The entrance of the presto surprises, and seems out of keeping with what precedes; but what we hear after the return of the tempo primo—the development of those simple strains, or rather the cogitations on them—justifies the presence of the presto. The second appearance of the latter leads to an urging, restless coda in A minor, which closes in the same key and pianissimo with a few bars of the simple, serene, now veiled, first strain. The "Troisieme Ballade" (in A flat major), Op. 47, does not equal its sisters in emotional intensity, at any rate, not in emotional tumultuousness. On this occasion the composer shows himself in a fundamentally caressing mood. But the fine gradations, the iridescence of feeling, mocks at verbal definition. Insinuation and persuasion cannot be more irresistible, grace and affection more seductive. Over everything in melody, harmony, and rhythm, there is suffused a most exquisite elegance. A quiver of excitement runs through the whole piece. The syncopations, reversions of accent, silences on accented parts of the bar (sighs and suspended respiration, felicitously expressed), which occur very frequently in this ballade, give much charm and piquancy to it. As an example, I may mention the bewitching subject in F major of the second section. The appearances of this subject in different keys and in a new guise are also very effective. Indeed, one cannot but be struck with wonder at the ease, refinement, and success with which Chopin handles here the form, while in almost every work in the larger forms we find him floundering lamentably. It would be foolish and presumptuous to pronounce this or that one of the ballades the finest; but one may safely say that the fourth (in F minor), Op. 52, is fully worthy of her sisters. The emotional key-note of the piece is longing sadness, and this key-note is well preserved throughout; there are no long or distant excursions from it. The variations of the principal subject are more emphatic restatements of it: the first is more impressive than the original, the second more eloquently beseeching than either of them. I resist, though with difficulty, the temptation to point out in detail the interesting course of the composer's thoughts, and proceed at once to the coda which, palpitating and swelling with passion, concludes the fourth and, alas! last ballade.

We have now passed in review not only all the compositions published by Chopin himself, but also a number of those published without his authorisation. The publications not brought about by the master himself were without exception indiscretions; most of them, no doubt, well meant, but nevertheless regrettable. Whatever Fontana says to the contrary in the preface to his collection of Chopin's posthumous works, [FOOTNOTE: The Chopin compositions published by Fontana (in 1855) comprise the Op. 66-74; the reader will see them enumerated in detail in the list of cur composer's works at the end of this volume.] the composer unequivocally expressed the wish that his manuscripts should not be published. Indeed, no one acquainted with the artistic character of the master, and the nature of the works published by himself, could for a moment imagine that the latter would at any time or in any circumstances have given his consent to the publication of insignificant and imperfect compositions such as most of those presented to the world by his ill-advised friend are. Still, besides the "Fantaisie-Impromptu," which one would not like to have lost, and one or two mazurkas, which cannot but be prized, though perhaps less for their artistic than their human interest, Fontana's collection contains an item which, if it adds little value to Chopin's musical legacy, attracts at least the attention of the lover and student of his music-namely, Op. 74, Seventeen Polish Songs, composed in the years 1824-1844, the only vocal compositions of this pianist-composer that have got into print. The words of most of these songs are by his friend Stephen Witwicki; others are by Adam Mickiewicz, Bogdan Zaleski, and Sigismond Krasinski, poets with all of whom he was personally acquainted. As to the musical settings, they are very unequal: a considerable number of them decidedly commonplace— Nos. 1, 5, 8, and also 4 and 12 may be instanced; several, and these belong to the better ones, exceedingly simple and in the style of folk-songs—No. 2 consists of a phrase of four bars (accompanied by a pedal bass and the tonic and dominant harmonies) repeated alternately in G minor and B flat major; and a few more developed in form and of a more artistic character. In the symphonies (the preludes, interludes, &c.) of the songs, we meet now and then with reminiscences from his instrumental pieces. In one or two cases one notices also pretty tone-painting—for instance, No. 10, "Horseman before the Battle," and No. 15, "The return Home" (storm). Among the most noteworthy are: the already-described No. 2; the sweetly-melancholy No. 3; the artistically more dignified No. 9; the popular No. 13; the weird No. 15; and the impressive, but, by its terrible monotony, also oppressive No. 17 ("Poland's Dirge"). The mazurka movement and the augmented fourth degree of the scale (Nos. 2 and 4) present themselves, apart from the emotional contents, as the most strikingly-national features of these songs. Karasowski states that many songs sung by the people in Poland are attributed to Chopin, chief among them one entitled "The third of May."

I must not conclude this chapter without saying something about the editions of Chopin's works. The original French, German, and English editions all leave much to be desired in the way of correctness. To begin with, the composer's manuscripts were very negligently prepared, and of the German and the English, and even of the French edition, he did not always see the proofs; and, whether he did or not, he was not likely to be a good proof-reader, which presupposes a special talent, or rather disposition. Indeed, that much in the preparation of the manuscripts for the press and the correction of the proofs was left to his friends and pupils may be gathered both from his letters and from other sources. "The first comprehension of the piece," says Schumann, in speaking of the German edition of the Tarantella, "is, unfortunately, rendered very difficult by the misprints with which it is really swarming." Those who assisted Chopin in the work incident to publication—more especially by copying his autographs—were Fontana, Wolff, Gutmann, and in later years Mikuli and Tellefsen.

Here I may fitly insert a letter written by Chopin to Maurice Schlesinger on July 22, 1843 (not 1836, as La Mara supposes), which has some bearing on the subject under discussion. The Impromptu spoken of is the third, Op. 51, in G flat major:—

Dear friend,—In the Impromptu which you have issued with the paper [Gazette musicals] of July 9, there is a confusion in the paging, which makes my composition unintelligible. Though I cannot at all pretend to taking the pains which our friend Moscheles bestows on his works, I consider myself, however, with regard to your subscribers, in duty bound to ask you on this occasion to insert in your next number an erratum:—

If you are too busy or too lazy to write to me, answer me through the erratum in the paper, and that shall signify to me that you, Madame Schlesinger, and your children are all well. —Yours very truly, July 22, 1843. F. CHOPIN.

The first complete edition of Chopin's works was, according to Karasowski, [FOOTNOTE: More recently the same firm brought out the works of Chopin edited by Jean Kleczynski.] that published in 1864, with the authorisation of the composer's family, by Gebethner and Wolff, of Warsaw. But the most important editions—namely, critical editions—are Tellefsen's (I mention them in chronological order), Klindworth's, Scholtz's, and Breitkopf and Hartel's. Simon Richault, of Paris, the publisher of the first-named edition, which appeared in 1860, says in the preface to it that Telléfsen had in his possession a collection of the works of Chopin corrected by the composer's own hand. As to the violoncello part of the Polonaise, it was printed as Franchomme always played it with the composer. The edition was also to be free from all marks of expression that were not Chopin's own. Notwithstanding all this, Tellefsen's edition left much to be desired.

My friend and fellow-pupil, Thomas Tellefsen [writes Mikuli], who, till Chopin's last breath, had the happiness to be in uninterrupted intercourse with him, was quite in a position to bring out correctly his master's works in the complete edition undertaken by him for Richault. Unfortunately, a serious illness and his death interrupted this labour, so that numerous misprints remained uncorrected.

[FOOTNOTE: Mikuli's spelling of the name is Telefsen, whereas it is Tellefsen on the Norwegian's edition of Chopin's works, in all the dictionaries that mention him, and in the contemporary newspaper notices and advertisements I have come across.]

[FOOTNOTE: I do not know how to reconcile this last remark with the publisher's statement that the edition appeared in 1860 (it was entered at Stationers' Hall on September 20, 1860), and Tellefsen's death at Paris in October, 1874.]

Klindworth's edition, the first volume of which appeared in October, 1873, and the last in March, 1876, at Moscow (P. Jurgenson), in six volumes, is described on the title-page as "Complete works of Fr. Chopin critically revised after the original French, German, and Polish editions, carefully corrected and minutely fingered for pupils." [FOOTNOTE: This edition has been reprinted by Augener & Co., of London.] The work done by Klindworth is one of the greatest merit, and has received the highest commendations of such men as Liszt and Hans von Bulow. Objections that can be made to it are, that the fingering, although excellent, is not always Chopinesque; and that the alteration of the rhythmically-indefinite small notes of the original into rhythmically-definite ones, although facilitating the execution for learners, counteracts the composer's intention. Mikuli holds that an appeal to Chopin's manuscripts is of no use as they are full of slips of the pen—wrong notes and values, wrong accidentals and clefs, wrong slurs and 8va markings, and omissions of dots and chord-intervals. The original French, German, and English editions he regards likewise as unreliable. But of them he gives the preference to the French editions, as the composer oftener saw proofs of them. On the other hand, the German editions, which, he thinks, came out later than the Paris ones, contain subsequently-made changes and improvements. [FOOTNOTE: Take note, however, in connection with this remark, of Chopin's letter of August 30, 1845, on pp. 119-120 of this volume.] Sometimes, no doubt, the Paris edition preceded the German one, but not as a rule. The reader will remember from the letters that Chopin was always anxious that his works should appear simultaneously in all countries, which, of course, was not always practicable. Mikuli based his edition (Leipzig: Fr. Kistner), the preface to which is dated "Lemberg, September, 1879," on his own copies, mostly of Parisian editions, copies which Chopin corrected in the course of his lessons; and on other copies, with numerous corrections from the hand of the master, which were given him by the Countess Delphine Potocka. He had also the assistance of Chopin's pupils the Princess Marcelline Czartoryska and Madame Friederike Streicher (nee Muller), and also of Madame Dubois and Madame Rubio, and of the composer's friend Ferdinand Hiller. Mikuli's edition, like Klindworth's, is fingered, and, as the title-page informs us, "for the most part according to the author's markings." Hermann Scholtz, who edited Chopin's works for Peters, of Leipzig, says in the preface (dated "Dresden, December, 1879") that his critical apparatus consisted of the original French, German, and English editions, various autographs (the Preludes, Op. 28; the Scherzo, Op. 54; the Impromptu, Op. 51; the Nocturnes, Op. 48; the Mazurka, Op. 7, No. 3, and a sketch of the Mazurka, Op. 30, No. 4), and three volumes of Chopin's compositions with corrections, additions, and marks of expression by his own hand, belonging to the master's pupil Madame von Heygendorf (nee von Konneritz). In addition to these advantages he enjoyed the advice of M. Mathias, another pupil of Chopin. The critically-revised edition published (March, 1878— January, 1880) by Breitkopf and Hartel was edited by Woldemar Bargiel, Johannes Brahms, Auguste Franchomme, Franz Liszt (the Preludes), Carl Reinecke, and Ernst Rudorff. The prospectus sets forth that the revision was based on manuscript material (autographs and proofs with the composer's corrections and additions) and the original French and German editions; and that Madame Schumann, M. Franchomme, and friends and pupils of the composer had been helpful with their counsel. Breitkopf and Hartel's edition is the most complete, containing besides all the pianoforte solo and ensemble works published by the composer himself, a greater number of posthumous works (including the songs) than is to be found in any other edition. Klindworth's is a purely pianoforte edition, and excludes the trio, the pieces with violoncello, and the songs. The above enumeration, however, does not exhaust the existing Chopin editions, which, indeed, are almost innumerable, as in the last decade almost every publisher, at least, almost every German publisher, has issued one—among others there are

Schuberth's, edited by Alfred Richter, Kahnt's, edited by S. Jadassohn, and Steingraber's, edited by Ed. Mertke. [FOOTNOTE: Among earlier editions I may mention the incomplete OEuvres completes, forming Vols. 21-24 of the Bibliotheque des Pianistes, published by Schonenberger (Paris, 1860).] Voluminous as the material for a critical edition of Chopin's works is, its inconclusiveness, which constantly necessitates appeals to the individual taste and judgment of the editor, precludes the possibility of an edition that will satisfy all in all cases. Chopin's pupils, who reject the editing of their master's works by outsiders, do not accept even the labours of those from among their midst. These reasons have determined me not to criticise, but simply to describe, the most notable editions. In speaking of the disputes about the correctness of the various editions, I cannot help remembering a remark of Mendelssohn's, of which Wenzel told me. "Mendelssohn said on one occasion in his naive manner: 'In Chopin's music one really does not know sometimes whether a thing is right or wrong.'"

CHAPTER XXXI

CHOPIN'S ARRIVAL IN LONDON.—MUSICAL ASPECT OF THE BRITISH METROPOLIS IN 1848.—CULTIVATION OF CHOPIN'S MUSIC IN ENGLAND.—CHOPIN AT EVENING PARTIES, &C.—LETTERS GIVING AN ACCOUNT OF HIS DOINGS AND FEELINGS.—TWO MATINEES MUSICALES GIVEN BY CHOPIN; CRITICISMS ON THEM.—ANOTHER LETTER.—KINDNESS SHOWN HIM.—CHOPIN STARTS FOR SCOTLAND.—A LETTER WRITTEN AT EDINBURGH AND CALDER HOUSE.—HIS SCOTCH FRIENDS AND ACQUAINTANCES.—HIS STAY AT DR. LYSCHINSKI'S.—PLAYS AT A CONCERT IN MANCHESTER.—RETURNS TO SCOTLAND, AND GIVES A MATINEE MUSICALE IN GLASGOW AND IN EDINBURGH.—MORE LETTERS FROM SCOTLAND.—BACK TO LONDON.—OTHER LETTERS.—PLAYS AT A "GRAND POLISH BALL AND CONCERT" IN THE GUILDHALL.—LAST LETTER FROM LONDON, AND JOURNEY AND RETURN TO PARIS.

CHOPIN arrived in London, according to Mr. A. J. Hipkins, on April 21, 1848.

[FOOTNOTE: The indebtedness of two writers on Chopin to Mr. Hipkins has already been adverted to in the Preface. But his vivid recollection of Chopin's visit to London in this year, and of the qualities of his playing, has been found of great value also in other published notices dealing with this period. The present writer has to thank Mr. Hipkins, apart from second-hand obligations, for various suggestions, answers to inquiries, and reading the proof-sheets of this chapter.]

He took up his quarters first at 10, Bentinck Street, but soon removed to the house indicated in the following letter, written by him to Franchomme on May 1, 1848:—

Dearest friend,—Here I am, just settled. I have at last a room—fine and large—where I shall be able to breathe and play, and the sun visits me to-day for the first time. I feel less suffocated this morning, but all last week I was good for nothing. How are you and your wife and the dear children? You begin at last to become more tranquil, [FOOTNOTE: This, I think, refers to some loss Franchomme had sustained in his family] do you not? I have some tiresome visits; my letters of introduction are not yet delivered. I trifle away my time, and VOILA. I love you, and once more VOILA.

Yours with all my heart.

My kindest regards to Madame Franchomme.

48, Dover Street.

Write to me, I will write to you also.

Were Chopin now to make his appearance in London, what a stir there would be in musical society! In 1848 Billet, Osborne, Kalkbrenner, Halle, and especially Thalberg, who came about the same time across the channel, caused more curiosity. By the way, England was just then heroically enduring an artistic invasion such as had never been seen before; not only from France, but also from Germany and other musical countries arrived day after day musicians who had found that their occupation was gone on the Continent, where people could think of nothing but politics and revolutions. To enumerate all the celebrities then congregated in the British Metropolis would be beyond my power and the scope of this publication, but I must at least mention that among them was no less eminent a creative genius than Berlioz, no less brilliant a vocal star than Pauline Viardot-Garcia. Of other high-priests and high-priestesses of the art we shall hear in the sequel. But although Chopin did not set the Thames on fire, his visit was not altogether ignored by the press. Especially the Athenaeum (H. F. Chorley) and the Musical World (J. W. Davison) honoured themselves by the notice they took of the artist. The former journal not only announced (on April 29) his arrival, but also some weeks previously (on April 8) his prospective advent, saying: "M. Chopin's visit is an event for which we most heartily thank the French Republic."

In those days, and for a long time after, the appreciation and cultivation of Chopin's music was in England confined to a select few. Mr. Hipkins told me that he "had to struggle for years to gain adherents to Chopin's music, while enduring the good-humoured banter of Sterndale Bennett and J. W. Davison." The latter—the author of An Essay on the Works of Frederic Chopin (London, 1843), the first publication of some length on the subject, and a Preface to, or, to be more precise, a Memoir prefixed to Boosey & Co.'s The Mazurkas and Valses of F. Chopin—seems to have in later years changed his early good opinion of the Polish master.

[FOOTNOTE: Two suggestions have been made to me in explanation of this change of opinion: it may have been due to the fear that the rising glory of Chopin might dim that of Mendelssohn; or Davison may have taken umbrage at Chopin's conduct in an affair relative to Mendelssohn. I shall not discuss the probability of these suggestions, but will say a few words with regard to the last-mentioned matter. My source of information is a Paris letter in the Musical World of December 4, 1847. After the death of Mendelssohn some foreign musicians living in Paris proposed to send a letter of condolence to Mrs. Mendelssohn. One part of the letter ran thus: "May it be permitted to us, German artists, far from our country, to offer," &c. The signatures to it were: Rosenhain, Kalkbrenner, Panofka, Heller, Halle, Pixis, and Wolff. Chopin when applied to for his signature wrote: "La lettre venant des Allemands, comment voulez-vous que je m'arroge le droit de la signer?" One would think that no reasonable being could take exception to Chopin's conduct in this affair, and yet the writer in the Musical World comments most venomously on it.]

The battle fought in the pages of the Musical World in 1841 illustrates the then state of matters in England. Hostilities commenced on October 28 with a criticism of the Mazurkas, Op. 41. Of its unparalleled nature the reader shall judge himself:—

Monsieur Frederic Chopin has, by some means or other which we cannot divine, obtained an enormous reputation, a reputation but too often refused to composers of ten times his genius. M. Chopin is by no means a putter down of commonplaces; but he is, what by many would be esteemed worse, a dealer in the most absurd and hyperbolical extravagances. It is a striking satire on the capability for thought possessed by the musical profession, that so very crude and limited a writer should be esteemed, as he is very generally, a profound classical musician. M. Chopin does not want ideas, but they never extend beyond eight or sixteen bars at the utmost, and then he is invariably in nubibus... the works of the composer give us invariably the idea of an enthusiastic school-boy, whose parts are by no means on a par with his enthusiasm, who WILL be original whether he CAN or not. There is a clumsiness about his harmonies in the midst of their affected strangeness, a sickliness about his melodies despite their evidently FORCED unlikeness to familiar phrases, an utter ignorance of design everywhere apparent in his lengthened works...The entire works of Chopin present a motley surface of ranting hyperbole and excruciating cacophony. When he is not THUS singular, he is no better than Strauss or any other waltz compounder... such as admire Chopin, and they are legion, will admire these Mazurkas, which are supereminently Chopin-ical; that do NOT we.

Wessel and Stapleton, the publishers, protested against this shameful criticism, defending Chopin and adducing the opinions of numerous musicians in support of their own. But the valorous editor "ventures to assure the distinguished critics and the publishers that there will be no difficulty in pointing out a hundred palpable faults, and an infinitude of meretricious uglinesses, such as, to real taste and judgment, are intolerable." Three more letters appeared in the following numbers—two for (Amateur and Professor) and one against (Inquirer) Chopin; the editor continuing to insist with as much violence as stupidity that he was right. It is pleasant to turn from this senseless opposition to the friends and admirers of the master. Of them we learn something in Davison's Essay on the Works of F. Chopin, from which I must quote a few passages:—

This Concerto [the E minor] has been made known to the amateurs of music in England by the artist-like performance of Messrs. W. H. Holmes, F. B. Jewson, H. B. Richards, R. Barnett, and other distinguished members of the Royal Academy, where it is a stock piece...The Concerto [in F minor] has been made widely known of late by the clever performance of that true little prodigy Demoiselle Sophie Bohrer....These charming bagatelles [the Mazurkas] have been made widely known in England through the instrumentality of Mr. Moscheles, Mr. Cipriani Potter, Mr. Kiallmark, Madame de Belleville-Oury, Mr. Henry Field (of Bath), Mr. Werner, and other eminent pianists, who enthusiastically admire and universally recommend them to their pupils...To hear one of those eloquent streams of pure loveliness [the nocturnes] delivered by such pianists as Edouard Pirkhert, William Holmes, or Henry Field, a pleasure we frequently enjoyed, is the very transcendency of delight.

[FOOTNOTE: Information about the above-named pianists may be found in the musical biographical dictionaries, with three exceptions-namely, Kiallmark, Werner, and Pirkhert. George Frederick Kiallmark (b. November 7, 1804; d. December 13, 1887), a son of the violinist and composer George Kiallmark, was for many years a leading professor in London. He is said to have had a thorough appreciation and understanding of Chopin's genius, and even in his last years played much of that master's music. He took especial delight in playing Chopin's Nocturnes, no Sunday ever passed without his family hearing him play two or three of them.—Louis Werner (whose real name was Levi) was the son of a wealthy and esteemed Jewish family living at Clapham. He studied music in London under Moscheles, and, though not an eminent pianist, was a good teacher. His amiability assured him a warm welcome in society.—Eduard Pirkhert died at Vienna, aged 63, on February 28, 1881. To Mr. Ernst Pauer, who is never appealed to in vain, I am indebted for the following data as well as for the subject—matter of my notice on Werner: "Eduard Pirkhert, born at Graz in 1817, was a pupil of Anton Halm and Carl Czerny. He was a shy and enormously diligent artist, who, however, on account of his nervousness, played, like Henselt, rarely in public. His execution was extraordinary and his tone beautiful. In 1855 he became professor at the Vienna Conservatorium." Mr. Pauer never heard him play Chopin.]

After this historical excursus let us take up again the record of our hero's doings and sufferings in London.

Chopin seems to have gone to a great many parties of various kinds, but he could not always be prevailed upon to give the company a taste of his artistic quality. Brinley Richards saw him at an evening party at the house of the politician Milner Gibson, where he did not play, although he was asked to do so. According to Mr. Hueffer, [FOOTNOTE: Chopin in Fortnightly Review of September, 1877, reprinted in Musical Studies (Edinburgh: A. & C. Black, 1880).] he attended, likewise without playing, an evening party

(May 6) at the house of the historian Grote. Sometimes ill-health prevented him from fulfilling his engagements; this, for instance, was the case on the occasion of a dinner which Macready is said to have given in his honour, and to which Thackeray, Mrs. Procter, Berlioz, and Julius Benedict were invited. On the other hand, Chopin was heard at the Countess of Blessington's (Gore House, Kensington) and the Duchess of Sutherland's (Stafford House). On the latter occasion Benedict played with him a duet of Mozart's. More than thirty years after, Sir Julius had still a clear recollection of "the great pains Chopin insisted should be taken in rehearsing it, to make the rendering of it at the concert as perfect as possible." John Ella heard Chopin play at Benedict's. Of another of Chopin's private performances in the spring of 1848 we read in the Supplement du Dictionnaire de la Conversation, where Fiorentino writes:

> We were at most ten or twelve in a homely, comfortable little salon, equally propitious to conversation and contemplation. Chopin took the place of Madame Viardot at the piano, and plunged us into ineffable raptures. I do not know what he played to us; I do not know how long our ecstasy lasted: we were no longer on earth; he had transported us into unknown regions, into a sphere of flame and azure, where the soul, freed from all corporeal bonds, floats towards the infinite.
> This was, alas! the song of the swan.

The sequel will show that the concluding sentence is no more than a flourish of the pen. Whether Chopin played at Court, as he says in a letter to Gutmann he expected to do, I have not ascertained. Nor have I been able to get any information about a dinner which, Karasowski relates, some forty countrymen of Chopin's got up in his honour when they heard of his arrival in London. According to this authority the pianist-composer rose when the proceedings were drawing to an end, and many speeches extolling him as a musician and patriot had been made, and spoke, if not these words, to this effect: "My dear countrymen! The proofs of your attachment and love which you have just given me have truly moved me. I wish to thank you, but lack the talent of expressing my feelings in words; I invite you therefore to accompany me to my lodgings and to receive there my thanks at the piano." The proposal was received with enthusiasm, and Chopin played to his delighted and insatiable auditors till two o'clock in the morning. What a crush, these forty or more people in Chopin's lodgings! However, that is no business of mine.

[FOOTNOTE: After reading the above, Mr. Hipkins remarked: "I fancy this dinner resembled the dinner which will go down to posterity as given by the Hungarians of London to Liszt in 1886, which was really a private dinner given by Mrs. Bretherton to fifteen people, of whom her children and mine were four. NO Hungarians."]

The documents—letters and newspaper advertisements and notices—bearing on this period of Chopin's life are so plentiful that they tell the story without the help of many additions and explanatory notes. This is satisfactory, for one grain of fact is more precious than a bushel of guesses and hearsays.

Chopin to Gutmann; London, 48, Dover Street, Piccadilly, Saturday, May 6, 1848:—

Dear friend,—Here I am at last, settled in this whirlpool of London. It is only a few days since I began to breathe; for it is only a few days since the sun showed itself. I have seen M. D'Orsay, and notwithstanding all the delay of my letter he received me very well. Be so good as to thank the duchess for me and him. I have not yet made all my calls, for many persons to whom I have letters of introduction are not yet here. Erard was charming; he sent me a piano. I have a Broadwood and a Pleyel, which makes three, and yet I do not find time to play them. I have many visitors, and my days pass like lightning—I have not even had a moment to write to Pleyel. Let me know how you are getting on. In what state of mind are you? How are your people? With my people things are not going well. I am much vexed about this. In spite of that I must think of making a public appearance; a proposal has been made to me to play at the Philharmonic, [FOOTNOTE: "Chopin, we are told," says the Musical World of May 27, 1848, "was invited to play at the Philharmonic, but declined."] but I would rather not. I shall apparently finish off, after playing at Court before the Queen [chez la reine], by giving a matinee, limited to a number of persons, at a private residence [hotel particulier]. I wish that this would terminate thus. But these projects are only projects in the air. Write to me a great deal about yourself. —Yours ever, my old Gut.,

CHOPIN.

P.S.—I heard the other evening Mdlle. Lind in La Sonnambula. [FOOTNOTE: Jenny Lind made her first appearance at Her Majesty's Theatre in the season 1848, on May 4, as Amina, in La Sonnambula. The Queen was present on that occasion. Pauline Garcia made her first appearance, likewise as Amina, at Covent Garden Theatre, on May 9.] It was very fine; I have made her acquaintance. Madame Viardot also came to see me. She will make her debuts at the rival theatre [Covent Garden], likewise in La Sonnambula. All the pianists of Paris are here. Prudent played his Concerto at the Philharmonic with little success, for it is necessary to play classical music there. Thalberg is engaged for twelve concerts at the theatre where Lind is [Her Majesty's, Haymarket]. Halle is going to play Mendelssohn at the rival theatre.

Chopin to his friend Grzymala; Thursday, May 11, 1848:—

I have just come from the Italian Opera, where Jenny Lind appeared to-day, for the first time, as Sonnambula, and the Queen showed herself for the first time to the people after a long retirement. [FOOTNOTE: Chopin must have begun this letter on the 4th of May, and dated it later on; for on the 11th of May Jenny Lind sang in La Figlia del Reggimento, and the presence of the Queen at the performance is not mentioned in the newspaper accounts of it. See preceding foot-note.] Both were, of course, of much interest to me; more especially, however, Wellington, who, like an old, faithful dog in a cottage, sat in the box below his crowned mistress. I have also made Jenny Lind's personal acquaintance: when, a few days afterwards, I paid her a visit, she received me in the most amiable manner, and sent me an excellent "stall" for the opera performance. I was capitally seated and heard excellently. This Swede is indeed an original from top to toe! She does not show herself in the ordinary light, but in the magic rays of an aurora borealis. Her singing is infallibly pure and sure; but what I admired most was her piano, which has an indescribable charm. "Your

FREDERICK.

Of Chopin's visit Jenny Lind-Goldschmidt had to the last years of her life a most pleasing and vivid recollection. She sang to him Polskas, [FOOTNOTE: Polskas are dances of Polish origin, popular in Sweden, whose introduction dates from the time of the union of the crowns of Sweden and Poland in 1587.] which delighted him greatly. The way Madame Goldschmidt spoke of Chopin showed unmistakably that he made the best possible impression upon her, not only as an artist, but also as a man—she was sure of his goodness, and that he could not but have been right in the Sand affair, I mean as regards the rupture. She visited him when she went in the following year (1849) to Paris.

In his letter to Gutmann, Chopin speaks of his intention to give a matinee at a private house. And he more than realised it; for he not only gave one, but two—the first at the house of Mrs. Sartoris (nee Adelaide Kemble) and the second at the house of Lord Falmouth. Here are two advertisements which appeared in the Times.

June 15, 1848:—

Monsieur Chopin will give a Matinee musicale, at No. 99, Eaton Place, on Friday, June 23, to commence at 3 o'clock. A limited number of tickets, one guinea each, with full particulars, at Cramer, Beale & Co.'s, 201, Regent Street.

July 3 and 4, 1848:—

Monsieur Chopin begs to announce that his second Matinee musicale will take place on Friday next, July 7, at the residence of the Earl of Falmouth, No. 2, St. James's Square. To commence at half-past 3. Tickets, limited in number, and full particulars at Cramer, Beale & Co.'s, 201, Regent Street.

The Musical World (July 8, 1848) says about these
performances:—

M. Chopin has lately given two performances of his own
pianoforte music at the residence of Mrs. Sartoris (late Miss
Adelaide Kemble), which seem to have given much pleasure to
his audiences, among whom Mdlle. Lind, who was present at the
first, seems to be the most enthusiastic. We were not present
at either, and, therefore, have nothing to say on the subject.

[FOOTNOTE: Of course, the above-quoted advertisements prove
the reporter to be wrong in this particular; there was only
one at the house of Mrs. Sartoris.]

From an account of the first matinee in the Athenaeum we learn that
Chopin played nocturnes, etudes, mazurkas, two waltzes, and the Berceuse,
but none of his more developed works, such as sonatas, concertos, scherzos,
and ballades. The critic tries to analyse the master's style of execution—a
"mode" in which "delicacy, picturesqueness, elegance, and humour are
blended so as to produce that rare thing, a new delight"—pointing out his
peculiar fingering, treatment of scale and shake, tempo rubato, &c. But
although the critic speaks no less appreciatively of the playing than of the
compositions, the tenor of the notice of the second matinee (July 15, 1848)
shows that the former left nevertheless something to be desired. "Monsieur
Chopin played better at his second than at his first matinee—not with more
delicacy (that could hardly be), but with more force and brio." Along with
other compositions of his, Chopin played on this occasion his Scherzo in
B flat and his Etude in C sharp minor. Another attraction of the matinee
was the singing of Madame Viardot-Garcia, "who, besides her inimitable
airs with Mdlle. de Mendi, and her queerly-piquant Mazurkas, gave the
Cenerentola rondo, graced with great brilliancy; and a song by Beethoven,
'Ich denke dein.'"

[FOOTNOTE: No doubt, those Mazurkas by Chopin which, adapting
to them Spanish words, she had arranged for voice and piano. Hiller wrote
mostenthusiastically of these arrangements and her performance of them.]

Mr. Salaman said, at a meeting of the London Musical Association (April
5, 1880), in the course of a discussion on the subject of Chopin, that he was
present at the matinee at the house of Mrs. Sartoris, and would never forget
the concert-giver's playing, especially of the waltz in D flat. "I remember

every bar, how he played it, and the appearance of his long, attenuated fingers during the time he was playing. [FOOTNOTE: Their thinness may have made them appear long, but they were not really so. See Appendix III.] He seemed quite exhausted." Mr. Salaman was particularly struck by the delicacy and refinement of Chopin's touch, and the utmost exquisiteness of expression.

To Chopin, as the reader will see in the letter addressed to Franchomme, and dated August 6th and 11th, these semi-public performances had only the one redeeming point—that they procured him much-needed money, otherwise he regarded them as a great annoyance. And this is not to be wondered at, if we consider the physical weakness under which he was then labouring. When Chopin went before these matinees to Broadwood's to try the pianoforte on which he was to play, he had each time to be carried up the flight of stairs which led to the piano-room. Chopin had also to be carried upstairs when he came to a concert which his pupil Lindsay Sloper gave in this year in the Hanover Square Rooms. But nothing brings his miserable condition so vividly before us as his own letters.

Chopin to Grzymala, London, July 18, 1848:—

My best thanks for your kind lines and the accompanying letter from my people. Heaven be thanked, they are all well; but why are they concerned about me? I cannot become sadder than I am, a real joy I have not felt for a long time. Indeed, I feel nothing at all, I only vegetate, waiting patiently for my end. Next week I go to Scotland to Lord Torphichen, the brother-in-law of my Scottish friends, the Misses Stirling, who are already with him (in the neighbourhood of Edinburgh). He wrote to me and invited me heartily, as did also Lady Murray, an influential lady of high rank there, who takes an extraordinary interest in music, not to mention the many invitations I have received from various parts of England. But I cannot wander about from one place to another like a strolling musician; such a vagabond' life is hateful to me, and not conducive to my health. I intend to remain in Scotland till the 29th of August, on which day I go as far as Manchester, where I am engaged to play in public. I shall play there twice without orchestra, and receive for this 60 [pounds]. The Alboni comes also, but all this does not interest me—I just seat myself at the piano, and begin to play. I shall stay during this time with rich manufacturers, with whom also Neukomm [FOOTNOTE: Karasowski has Narkomm, which is, of course, either a misreading or a misprint, probably the former, as it is to be found in all editions of his book.] has stayed. What I shall do next I don't know yet. If only someone could foretell whether I shall not fall sick here during the winter..."Your

FREDERICK.

Had Chopin, when he left Paris, really in view the possibility of settling in London? There was at the time a rumour of this being the case. The Athenaeum (April 8, 1848), in the note already adverted to, said:—"M. Chopin is expected, if not already here—it is even added to remain in England." But if he embraced the idea at first, he soon began to loosen his grasp of it, and, before long, abandoned it altogether. In his then state of health existence would have been a burden anywhere, but it was a greater one away from his accustomed surroundings. Moreover, English life to be enjoyable requires a robustness of constitution, sentimental and intellectual as well as physical, which the delicately-organised artist, even in his best time, could not boast of. If London and the rest of Britain was not to the mind of Chopin, it was not for want of good-will among the people. Chopin's letters show distinctly that kindness was showered upon him from all sides. And these letters do not by any means contain a complete roll of those who were serviceable to him. The name of Frederick Beale, the publisher, for instance, is not to be found there, and yet he is said, with what truth I do not know, to have attached himself to the tone-poet.

[FOOTNOTE: Mr. Hipkins heard Chopin play at Broadwood's to Beale the Waltzes in D flat major and C sharp minor (Nos. 1 and 2 of Op. 64), subsequently published by Cramer, Beale and Co. But why did the publisher not bring out the whole opus (three waltzes, not two), which had already been in print in France and Germany for nine or ten months? Was his attachment to the composer weaker than his attachment to his cash-box?]

The attentions of the piano-makers, on the other hand, are duly remembered. In connection with them I must not forget to record the fact that Mr. Henry Fowler Broadwood had a concert grand, the first in a complete iron frame, expressly made for Chopin, who, unfortunately, did not live to play upon it.

[FOOTNOTE: For particulars about the Broadwood pianos used by Chopin in England and Scotland (and he used there no others at his public concerts and principal private entertainments), see the List of John Broadwood & Sons' Exhibits at the International Inventions Exhibition (1885), a pamphlet full of interesting information concerning the history and construction of the pianoforte. It is from the pen of A. J. Hipkins.]

A name one misses with surprise in Chopin's letters is that of his Norwegian pupil Tellefsen, who came over from Paris to London, and seems to have devoted himself to his master. [FOOTNOTE: Tellefsen, says Mr. Hipkins, was nearly always with Chopin.] Of his ever-watchful ministering friend Miss Stirling and her relations we shall hear more in the following letters.

Chopin started for Scotland early in August, 1848, for on the 6th August he writes to Franchomme that he had left London a few days before.

Chopin to Franchomme; Edinburgh, August 6 1848. Calder House, August 11:—

Very dear friend,—I do not know what to say. The best, it seems to me, is not even to attempt to console you for the loss of your father. I know your grief—time itself assuages little such sorrows. I left London a few days ago. I made the journey to Edinburgh (407 miles) in twelve hours. After having taken a day's rest in Edinburgh, I went to Calder House, twelve miles from Edinburgh, the mansion of Lord Torphichen, brother-in-law of Madame Erskine, where I expect to remain till the end of the month and to rest after my great doings in London. I gave two matinees, which it appears have given pleasure, but which, for all that, did not the less bore me. Without them, however, I do not know how I could have passed three months in this dear London, with large apartments (absolutely necessary), carriage, and valet. My health is not altogether bad, but I become more feeble, and the air here does not yet agree with me. Miss Stirling was going to write to you from London, and asks me to beg you to excuse her. The fact is that these ladies had many preparations to make before their journey to Scotland, where they intend to remain some months. There is in Edinburgh a pupil of yours, Mr. Drechsler, I believe.

[FOOTNOTE: Louis Drechsler (son of the Dessau violoncellist Carl Drechsler and uncle of the Edinburgh violoncellist and conductor Carl Drechsler Hamilton), who came to Edinburgh in August, 1841, and died there on June 25,1860. From an obituary notice in a local paper I gather that he studied under Franchomme in 1845.]

He came to see me in London; he appeared to me a fine young fellow, and he loves you much. He plays duets [fait de la musique] with a great lady of this country, Lady Murray, one of my sexagenarian pupils in London, to whom I have also promised a visit in her beautiful mansion. [FOOTNOTE: The wife of Lord (Sir John Archibald) Murray, I think. At any rate, this lady was very musical and in the habit of playing with Louis Drechsler.] But I do not know how I shall do it, for I have promised to be in Manchester on the 28th of August to play at a concert for 60 pounds. Neukomm is there, and, provided that he does not improvise on the same day [et pourvu qu'il ne m'improvise pas le meme jour], I reckon on earning my 60 francs [he means, of course, "60 pounds"].

[FOOTNOTE: Thinking that this remark had some hidden meaning, I applied to Franchomme for an explanation; but he wrote to me as follows: "Chopin trouvait que Neukomm etait un musicien ennuyeux, et il lui etait desagreable de penser que Neukomm pourrait improviser dans le concert dans lequel il devrait jouer."]

After that I don't know what will become of me. I should like

very much if they were to give me a pension for life for
having composed nothing, not even an air a la Osborne or
Sowinski (both of them excellent friends), the one an
Irishman, the other a compatriot of mine (I am prouder of them
than of the rejected representative Antoine de Kontski—
Frenchman of the north and animal of the south). [FOOTNOTE:
"Frenchmen of the north" used to be a common appellation of
the Poles.]

After these parentheses, I will tell you truly that I know
[FOOTNOTE: Here probably "not" ought to be added.] what will
become of me in autumn. At any rate, if you get no news from
me do not complain of me, for I think very often of writing to
you. If you see Mdlle. de Rozieres or Grzymala, one or the
other of them will have heard something—if not from me, from
some friends. The park here is very beautiful, the lord of the
manor very excellent, and I am as well as I am permitted to
be. Not one proper musical idea. I am out of my groove; I am
like, for instance, an ass at a masked ball, a chanterelle
[first, i.e., highest string] of a violin on a double bass—
astonished, amazed, lulled to sleep as if I were hearing a
trait [a run or a phrase] of Bodiot [FOOTNOTE: That is,
Charles Nicolas Baudiot (1773-1849), the violoncellist, at one
time professor at the Conservatoire. He published a school and
many compositions for his instrument.] (before the 24th of
February), [FOOTNOTE: The revolution of February 24, 1848.] or
a stroke of the bow of M. Cap [FOOTNOTE: This gentleman was an
amateur player of the violoncello and other stringed
instruments.] (after the June days). [FOOTNOTE: The
insurrection of the Red Republicans on June 23-26, 1848.] I
hope they are still flourishing, for I cannot do without them
in writing. But another real question is, that I hope you have
no friends to deplore in all these terrible affairs. And the

health of Madame Franchomme and of the little children? Write me a line, and address it to London, care of Mr. Broadwood, 33, Great Pulteney Street, Golden Square. I have here a perfect (material) tranquillity, and pretty Scotch airs. I wish I were able to compose a little, were it only to please these good ladies—Madame Erskine and Mdlle. Stirling. I have a Broadwood piano in my room, the Pleyel of Miss Stirling in my salon. I lack neither paper nor pens. I hope that you also will compose something, and may God grant that I hear it soon newly born. I have friends in London who advise me to pass there the winter.—But I shall listen only to my I do not know what [mon je ne sais quoi]; or, rather, I shall listen to the last comer—this comes often to the same thing as weighing well. Adieu dear, dear friend! My most sincere wishes to Madame Franchomme for her children. I hope that Rene amuses himself with his bass, that Cecile works well, and that their little sister always reads her books. Remember me to Madame Lasserve, I pray you, and correct my orthography as well as my French.

The following words are written along the margin:—

The people here are ugly, but, it would seem, good. As a compensation there are charming, apparently mischievous, cattle, perfect milk, butter, eggs, and tout ce qui s'en suit, cheese and chickens.

To save the reader from becoming confused by allusions in Chopin's letters to names of unknown persons and places, I will now say a few words about the composer's Scotch friends. The Stirlings of Keir, generally regarded as the principal family of the name, are said to be descended from Walter de Striveline, Strivelyn, or Strivelyng, Lucas of Strivelyng (1370-1449) being the first possessor of Keyr. The family was for about two centuries engaged in the East India and West India trade. Archibald Stirling, the father of the late baronet, went, as William Fraser relates in The Stirlings of Keir, like former younger sons, to Jamaica, where he was a planter for nearly twenty-five years. He succeeded his brother James in 1831, greatly improved the mansion, and died in 1847. When Chopin visited Keir it was in the possession of William Stirling, who, in 1865, became Sir William Stirling-Maxwell (his mother was a daughter of Sir John Maxwell), and is well-known by his literary works—Annals of the Artists of Spain (1848), The Cloister Life of the Emperor Charles V. (1852), Velasquez (1855), &c. He was the uncle of Jane Stirling and Mrs. Erskine, daughters (the former the youngest daughter) of John Stirling, of Kippendavie and Kippenross, and friends of Chopin. W. Hanna, the editor of the Letters of Thomas Erskine of Linlathen, says that Jane Stirling was a cousin and particular friend of Thomas Erskine. The latter used in later life to regard her and the Duchess de Broglie as the most remarkable women he had ever met:—

In her later years she lived much in Paris, and counted among her friends there Ary Scheffer. In his "Christus Consolator," this eminent artist has presented in one of the figures his ideal of female beauty, and was struck on being first introduced to Miss Stirling to find in her the almost exact embodiment of that ideal. She was introduced afterwards in many of his pictures.

In a letter addressed to Mrs. Schwabe, and dated February 14, 1859, we read about her:—

She was ill for eight weeks, and suffered a great deal...I know you will feel this deeply, for you could appreciate the purity and beauty of that stream of love which flowed through her whole life. I don't think that I ever knew anyone who seemed more entirely to have given up self, and devoted her whole being to the good of others. I remember her birth like yesterday, and I never saw anything in her but what was lovable from the beginning to the end of her course.

Lindsay Sloper, who lived in Paris from 1841 to 1846, told me that Miss Stirling, who was likewise staying there, took for some time lessons from him. As she wished to become a pupil of Chopin, he spoke to his master about her. Chopin, Lindsay Sloper said, was pleased with her playing, and soon began to like her.

[FOOTNOTE: To the above I must append a cautionary foot-note. In his account to me Lindsay Sloper made two mistakes which prove that his memory was not one of the most trustworthy, and suggest even the possibility that his Miss Stirling was a different person from Chopin's friend. His mistakes were these: he called Mrs. Erskine, who was with Miss Stirling in Paris, her aunt instead of her sister; and thought that Miss Stirling was about eighteen years old when he taught her. The information I shall give farther on seems to show that she was older rather than younger than Chopin; indeed, Mr Hipkins is of opinion that she was in 1848 nearer fifty than forty.]

To her the composer dedicated his Deux Nocturnes, Op. 55, which he published in August, 1844. It was thought that she was in love with Chopin, and there were rumours of their going to be married. Gutmann informed me that Chopin said to him one day when he was ill: "They have married me to Miss Stirling; she might as well marry death." Of Miss Jane Stirling's elder sister Katherine, who, in 1811, married her cousin James Erskine, and lost her husband already in 1816, Thomas Erskine says: "She was an admirable woman, faithful and diligent in all duties, and unwearied in her efforts to help those who needed her help." Lord Torphichen, at whose residence (Calder House, twelve miles from Edinburgh) Chopin passed much of his time in Scotland, was, as we learn from the composer's letters, a brother-in-law of Miss Stirling and Mrs. Erskine. Johnstone Castle (twelve miles from Glasgow), where Chopin was also received as a guest, belonged to the Houston family, friends of the Erskines and Stirlings, but, I think, no relations. The death of Ludovic Houston, Esq., in 1862, is alluded to in one of Thomas Erskine's letters.

But Chopin, while in Scotland, was not always staying in manors and castles, now and then he was housed less aristocratically, though perhaps not less, nay, probably more, comfortably. Such humbler quarters he found at the house (10, Warriston Crescent) of Dr. Lyschinski, a Pole by birth, and a refugee, who after studying medicine in Edinburgh practised it there until a few years ago when he removed to London. For the information which I am now going to give I am indebted to Mrs. Lyschinski. Among those who received Chopin at the Edinburgh railway station was Dr. Lyschinski who addressed him in Polish. The composer put up at an hotel (perhaps the London Hotel, in St. Andrew's Square). Next day—Miss Paterson, a neighbour, having placed her carriage at Chopin's disposal—Mrs. Lyschinski took him out for a drive. He soon got tired of the hotel, in fact, felt it quite unbearable, and told the doctor, to whom he had at once taken a fancy, that he could not do without him. Whereupon the latter said: "Well, then you must come to my house; and as it is rather small, you must be satisfied with the nursery." So the children were sent to a friend's house, and the nursery was made into a bedroom for the illustrious guest, an adjoining bedroom being prepared for his servant Daniel, an Irish-Frenchman. Unless the above refers to Chopin's return to Scotland in September, after his visit to Manchester, Mrs. Lyschinski confuses her reminiscences a little, for, as the last-quoted letter proves, he tarried, on his first arrival, only one day in Edinburgh. But the facts, even if not exactly grouped, are, no doubt, otherwise correctly remembered. Chopin rose very late in the day, and in the morning had soup in his room. His hair was curled daily by the servant, and his shirts, boots, and other things were of the neatest—in fact, he was a petit-maitre, more vain in dress than any woman. The maid-servants found themselves strictly excluded from his room, however indispensable their presence might seem to them in the interests of neatness and cleanliness. Chopin was so weak that Dr. Lyschinski had always to carry him upstairs. After dinner he sat before the fire, often shivering with cold. Then all on a sudden he would cross the room, seat himself at the piano, and play himself warm. He could bear neither dictation nor contradiction: if you told him to go to the fire, he would go to the other end of the room where the piano stood. Indeed, he was imperious. He once asked Mrs. Lyschinski to sing. She declined. At this he was astonished and quite angry. "Doctor, would you take it amiss if I were to force your wife to do it?" The idea of a woman refusing him anything seemed to him preposterous. Mrs. Lyschinski says that Chopin was gallant to all ladies alike, but thinks that he had no heart. She used to tease him about women, saying, for instance, that Miss Stirling was a particular friend of his. He replied that he had no particular friends among the ladies, that he gave to all an equal share of his attention. "Not even George Sand then," she asked, "is a particular friend?" "Not even George Sand," was the reply. Had Mrs. Lyschinski known the real state of matters between Chopin and George Sand, she certainly would not have asked that question. He, however, by no means always avoided the mention of his faithless love. Speaking one day of his thinness he remarked that she used to call him mon cher cadavre. Miss Stirling was much about Chopin. I may mention by the way that Mrs. Lyschinski told me that Miss Stirling was much older than Chopin, and her love for him, although passionate, purely Platonic. Princess Czartoryska arrived some time after Chopin, and accompanied him, my informant says, wherever he went. But, as we see from one of his letters, her stay in Scotland was short. The composer was always on the move. Indeed, Dr. Lyschinski's was hardly more than a pied-a-terre for him: he never stayed long, and generally came unexpectedly. A number of places where Chopin was a guest are mentioned in his letters. Mrs. Lyschinski thinks that he also visited the Duke of Hamilton.

At the end of August and at the end of September and beginning of October, this idling was interrupted by serious work, and a kind of work which, at no time to his liking, was particularly irksome in the then state of his health.

The Manchester Guardian of August 19, 1848, contained the following advertisement:—

Concert Hall.—The Directors beg to announce to the Subscribers that a Dress Concert has been fixed for Monday, the 28th of August next, for which the following performers have already been engaged: Signora Alboni, Signora Corbari, Signer Salvi, and Mons. Chopin.

From an account of the concert in the same paper (August 30), the writer of which declares the concert to have been the most brilliant of the season, we learn that the orchestra, led by Mr. Seymour, played three overtures—Weber's Ruler of the Spirits, Beethoven's Prometheus, and Rossini's Barbiere di Siviglia; and that Chopin performed an Andante and Scherzo, and a Nocturne, Etudes, and the Berceuse of his own composition. With regard to Chopin we read in this critique:—

With the more instrumental portion of the audience, Mons. Chopin was perhaps an equal feature of interest with Alboni, as he was preceded by a high musical reputation. Chopin appears to be about thirty years of age. [FOOTNOTE: Chopin, says Mr. Hipkins, had a young look, although much wasted.] He is very spare in frame, and there is an almost painful air of feebleness in his appearance and gait. This vanishes when he seats himself at the instrument, in which he seems for the time perfectly absorbed. Chopin's music and style of performance partake of the same leading characteristics— refinement rather than vigour—subtle elaboration rather than simple comprehensiveness in composition—an elegant rapid touch, rather than a firm, nervous grasp of the instrument. Both his compositions and playing appear to be the perfection of chamber music—fit to be associated with the most refined instrumental quartet and quartet playing—but wanting breadth and obviousness of design, and executive power, to be effective in a large hall. These are our impressions from hearing Mons. Chopin for the first time on Monday evening. He was warmly applauded by many of the most accomplished amateurs in the town, and he received an encore in his last piece, a compliment thus accorded to each of the four London artists who appeared at the concert.

From the criticism of the Manchester Courier and Lancashire General Advertiser (August 30, 1848), I cull the following remarks:—

We can, with great sincerity, say that he delighted us. Though we did not discover in him the vigour of Thalberg, yet there was a chasteness and purity of style, a correctness of manipulation combined with a brilliance of touch, and delicate sensibility of expression which we never heard excelled. He played in the second act [part]... and elicited a rapturous encore. He did not, however, repeat any part, but treated the audience with what appeared to be a fragment of great beauty.

Mr. Osborne, in a paper on Chopin read before the London Musical Association, says:—

On a tour which I made with Alboni, I met Chopin at Manchester, where he was announced to play at a grand concert without orchestra. He begged I should not be present. "You, my dear Osborne," said he, "who have heard me so often in Paris, remain with those impressions. My playing will be lost in such a large room, and my compositions will be ineffective. Your presence at the concert will be painful both to you and me."

Mr. Osborne told his audience further that notwithstanding this appeal he was present in a remote corner of the room. I may add that although he could absent himself from the hall for the time Chopin was playing, he could not absent himself from the concert, for, as the papers tell us, he acted as accompanist. The impression which Chopin's performance on this occasion left upon his friend's mind is described in the following few sad words: "His playing was too delicate to create enthusiasm, and I felt truly sorry for him."

Soon after the concert Chopin returned to Scotland. How many days (between August 23 and September 7?) he remained in Manchester, I do not know, but it is well known that while staying there he was the guest of Mr. and Mrs. Salis Schwabe. To Mrs. Salis Schwabe, a lady noted for her benevolence, Thomas Erskine addressed the letter concerning Miss Jane Stirling a part of which I quoted on one of the foregoing pages of this chapter. The reader remembers, of course, Chopin's prospective allusions to the Manchester concert in his letters to Franchomme (August 6, 1848) and Grzymala (July 18, 1848).

About a month after the concert at which he played in Manchester, Chopin gave one of his own in Glasgow. Here is what may be read in the Courier of September 28 and previous days:—

Monsieur Chopin has the honour to announce that his Matinee musicals will take place on Wednesday, the 27th September, in the Merchant Hall, Glasgow. To commence at half-past two o'clock. Tickets, limited in number, half-a-guinea each, and full particulars to be had from Mr. Muir Wood, 42, Buchanan Street.

The net profits of this concert are said to have been 60 pounds. Mr. Muir Wood relates:—

I was then a comparative stranger in Glasgow, but I was told that so many private carriages had never been seen at any concert in the town. In fact, it was the county people who turned out, with a few of the elite of Glasgow society. Being a morning concert, the citizens were busy otherwise, and half-a-guinea was considered too high a sum for their wives and daughters.

No doubt Chopin's playing and compositions must have been to the good Glasgow citizens of that day what caviare is to the general. In fact, Scotland, as regards music, had at that period not yet emerged from its state of primitive savagery. But if we may believe the learned critic in the Glasgow Courier, Chopin's matinee was numerously attended, and the audience, which consisted of "the beauty and fashion, indeed of the very elite of the West-end," thoroughly enjoyed the playing of the concert-giver and the singing of Madame Adelasio de Margueritte who assisted him. I think the reader will be interested by the following specimen of criticism for more than one reason:—

The performance was certainly of the highest order in point of musical attainment and artistic skill, and was completely successful in interesting and delighting everyone present for an hour and a half. Visited as we now are by the highest musical talent, by this great player and the other eminent composer, it must be difficult for each successive candidate for our patronage and applause to produce in sufficient quantity that essential element to success—novelty; but M. Chopin has proved satisfactorily that it is not easy to estimate the capabilities of the instrument he handles with so much grace and ingenuity, or limit the skill and power whose magic touch makes it pour forth its sublime strains to electrify and delight anew the astonished listener. M. Chopin's treatment of the pianoforte is peculiar to himself, and his style blends in beautiful harmony and perfection the elegant, the picturesque, and the humorous. We cannot at present descend to practical illustrations in proof of these observations, but feel persuaded we only express the feelings of all who attended yesterday when we say that the pianist produces, without extraordinary effort, not only pleasing, but new musical delights. Madame Adelasio has a beautiful voice, which she manages with great ease and occasional brilliancy. She sang several airs with much taste and great acceptance. We may mention that all the pieces were rapturously applauded, and the audience separated with expressions of the highest gratification.

Clearly this critic was not without judgment, although his literary taste and skill leave much to be desired. That there were real Chopin enthusiasts in Glasgow is proved by an effusion, full of praise and admiration, which the editor received from a correspondent and inserted on September 30, two days after the above criticism. But, without indulging our curiosity further, we will now take our leave of Glasgow and Glasgow critics.

On October 4, Chopin gave an evening concert in Edinburgh. Here is the programme:—

HOPETOUN ROOMS, QUEEN STREET.
MONSIEUR CHOPIN'S SOIREE MUSICALE.

Programme.

1. Andante et Impromptu.

2. Etudes.

3. Nocturne et Berceuse.

4. Grande Valse Brillante.

5. Andante precede d'un Largo.

6. Preludes, Ballade, Mazurkas et Valses.

To commence at half-past eight o'clock. Tickets,
limited to number, half-a-guinea each. To be had, &c.

Mrs. Lyschinski told me that this concert was chiefly attended by the nobility. Half-a-guinea had never been charged for admission to a concert (which is probably overstating the case), and Chopin was little known. Miss Stirling, who was afraid the hall might not be filled, bought fifty pounds' worth of tickets. The piano on which Chopin played (one sent by Broadwood, and used in Glasgow as well as in Edinburgh) was afterwards sold for 30 pounds above the price. Thus, at any rate, runs the legend.

In the Edinburgh Courant, which contained on September 30 and on other days an advertisement similar to the Glasgow one (with the addition of a programme, consisting, however, only of the 1st, 2nd, 3rd, and 6th items of the one above given), there appeared on October 7, 1848, a notice of the concert, a part of which may find a place here:—

This talented pianist gratified his admirers by a performance
on Wednesday evening in the Hopetoun Rooms, where a select and
highly fashionable audience assembled to welcome him on his
first appearance in Edinburgh...Chopin's compositions have
been too long before the musical portion of Europe, and have
been too highly appreciated to require any comment, further
than that they are among the best specimens of classical
excellence in pianoforte music. Of his execution we need say
nothing further than that it is the most finished we have ever
heard. He has neither the ponderosity nor the digital power of
a Mendelssohn, a Thalberg, or Liszt; consequently his
execution would appear less effective in a large room; but as
a chamber pianist he stands unrivalled. Notwithstanding the
amount of musical entertainment already afforded the Edinburgh
public this season, the rooms were filled with an audience
who, by their judicious and well-timed applause, testified

their appreciation of the high talent of Monsieur Chopin.

An Edinburgh correspondent of the Musical World, who signs himself "M.," confirms (October 14, 1848) the statements of the critic of the Courant. From this communication we learn that one of the etudes played was in F minor (probably No. 2 of Op. 25, although there are two others in the same key—No. 9 of Op. 10 and No. 1 of Trois Etudes without opus number). The problematical Andante precede d'un Largo was, no doubt, a juxtaposition of two of his shorter compositions, this title being chosen to vary the programme. From Mr. Hipkins I learned that at this Chopin played frequently the slow movement from his Op. 22, Grande Polonaise preceded d'un Andante Spianato.

And now we will let Chopin again speak for himself.

Chopin to Grzymala; Keir, Perthshire, Sunday, October 1, 1848:—

No post, no railway, also no carriage (not even for taking the air), no boat, not a dog to be seen—all desolate, desolate!

My dearest friend,—Just at the moment when I had already begun to write to you on another sheet, your and my sister's letters were brought to me. Heaven be thanked that cholera has hitherto spared them. But why do you not write a word about yourself? and yet to you corresponding is much easier than to me; for I have been writing to you daily for a whole week already—namely, since my return from northern Scotland (Strachur [FOOTNOTE: A small town, eight miles south of Inveraray, in Argyleshire.])—without getting done. I know, indeed, that you have an invalid in Versailles; for Rozaria [FOOTNOTE: Mdlle. de Rozieres.] wrote to me that you had paid her a visit, and then in great haste had gone to an invalid in Versailles. I hope it is not your grandfather or grandchild, or one of your dear neighbours, the Rochanskis. Here one hears as yet nothing of cholera, but in London it appears already here and there.

With your letter, which I received at Johnstone Castle, and in which you informed me that you had been with Soli [FOOTNOTE: I suppose Solange, Madame Clesinger, George Sand's daughter.] at the Gymnase Theatre, there came at the same time one from

Edinburgh, from Prince Alexander Czartoryski, with the news that he and his wife had arrived, and that he would be very glad to see me. Although tired, I at once took the train and found them still in Edinburgh. Princess Marcelline was as kind as she always is to me. The intercourse with them reanimated me, and gave me strength to play in Glasgow, where the whole haute volee had gathered for my concert. The weather was magnificent, and the princely family had even come from Edinburgh with little Marcel, who is growing nicely, and sings already my compositions, yes, and even corrects when he hears someone making mistakes. It was on Wednesday afternoon, at 3 o'clock, and the princely couple did me the kindness to accept along with me an invitation to a dinner at Johnstone Castle (by the way, twelve English miles from Glasgow) after the concert; in this way, then, I passed the whole day with them. Lord and Lady Murray and the old Lord Torphichen (who had come a distance of a hundred miles) drove also thither with us, and the next day all were quite charmed with the amiability of Princess Marcelline. The princely pair returned to Glasgow, whence, after a visit to Loch Tamen, [FOOTNOTE: There is no such loch. Could it possibly be Loch Lomond? Loch Leven seems to me less likely.] they wished to go back at once to London, and thence to the Continent. The Prince spoke of you with sincere kindness. I can very well imagine what your noble soul must suffer when you see what is now going on in Paris. You cannot think how I revived, how lively I became that day in the society of such dear countrymen; but to-day I am again very depressed. O, this mist! Although, from the window at which I write, I have before me the most beautiful view of Stirling Castle—it is the same, as you will remember, which delighted Robert Bruce—and mountains, lochs, a charming park, in one word, the view most celebrated for its beauty in Scotland; I see nothing, except now and then, when the mist gives way to the sun. The owner of this mansion, whose name is

Stirling, is the uncle of our Scotch ladies, and the head of the family. I made his acquaintance in London; he is a rich bachelor, and has a very beautiful picture-gallery, which is especially distinguished by works of Murillo and other Spanish masters. He has lately even published a very interesting book on the Spanish school; he has travelled much (visited also the East), and is a very intelligent man. All Englishmen of note who come to Scotland go to him; he has always an open house, so that there are daily on an average about thirty people at dinner with him. In this way one has opportunities of seeing the most different English beauties; lately there was, for instance, for some days a Mrs. Boston here, but she is already gone. As to dukes, earls, and lords, one now sees here more of them than ever, because the Queen has sojourned in Scotland. Yesterday she passed close by us by rail, as she had to be at a certain time in London, and there was such a fog on the sea that she preferred to return from Aberdeen to London by land, and not (as she had come) by boat—to the great regret of the navy, which had prepared various festivities for her. It is said that her consort, Prince Albert, was very much pleased at this, as he becomes always sea-sick on board, while the Queen, like a true ruler of the sea, is not inconvenienced by a voyage. I shall soon have forgotten Polish, speak French like an Englishman, and English like a Scotchman—in short, like Jawurek, jumble together five languages. If I do not write to you a Jeremiad, it is not because you cannot comfort me, but because you are the only one who knows everything; and if I once begin to complain, there will be no end to it, and it will always be in the same key. But it is incorrect when I say: "always in the same key," for things are getting worse with me every day. I feel weaker; I cannot compose, not for want of inclination, but for physical reasons, and because I am every week in a different place. But what shall I do? At least, I shall save something for the winter. Invitations I have in plenty, and cannot even go where I should like, for instance, to the Duchess of Argyll and Lady Belhaven, as the season is already too far advanced and too dangerous for my enfeebled health. I am all the morning unable to do anything, and when I have dressed myself I feel again so fatigued that I must rest. After dinner I must sit two hours with the gentlemen, hear what they say, and see how much they drink. Meanwhile I feel bored to death. I think of something totally different, and then go to the drawing-room, where I require all my strength to revive, for all are anxious to hear me. Afterwards my good Daniel carries me upstairs to my bedroom, undresses me, puts me to bed, leaves the candle burning, and then I am again at liberty to sigh and to dream until morning, to pass the next day just like the preceding one. When I have settled down in some measure, I must continue my travels, for my Scotch ladies do not allow me—to be sure with the best intentions in the world—any rest. They fetch me to introduce me to all their relations; they will at last kill me with their kindness, and I must bear it all out of pure amiability.—

Your

FREDERICK.

Chopin to Gutmann; Calder House, October 16, 1848 (twelve miles from Edinburgh):—

Very dear friend,—What are you doing? How are your people, your country, your art? you are unjustly severe upon me, for you know my infirmity in the matter of letter-writing. I have thought of you much, and on reading the other day that there was a disturbance at Heidelberg, I tried some thirty rough draughts [brouillons] in order to send you a line, the end of them all being to be thrown into the fire. This page will perhaps reach you and find you happy with your good mother. Since I had news from you, I have been in Scotland, in this beautiful country of Walter Scott, with so many memories of

Mary Stuart, the two Charleses, &c. I drag myself from one lord to another, from one duke to another. I find everywhere, besides extreme kindness and hospitality without limit, excellent pianos, beautiful pictures, choice libraries; there are also hunts, horses, dogs, interminable dinners, and cellars of which I avail myself less. It is impossible to form an idea of all the elaborate comfort which reigns in the English mansions. The Queen having passed this year some weeks in Scotland, all England followed her, partly out of courtesy, partly because of the impossibility of going to the disturbed Continent. Everything here has become doubly splendid, except the sun, which has done nothing more than usual; moreover, the winter advances, and I do not know yet what will become of me. I am writing to you from Lord Torphichen's. In this mansion, above my apartment, John Knox, the Scotch reformer, dispensed for the first time the Sacrament. Everything here furnishes matter for the imagination—a park with hundred-year-old trees, precipices, walls of the castle in ruins, endless passages with numberless old ancestors—there is even a certain Red-cowl which walks there at midnight. I walk there my incertitude. [Il y a meme un certain bonnet rouge, qui s'y promene a minuit. J'y promene mon incertitude.]

Cholera is coming; there is fog and spleen in London, and no president in Paris. It does not matter where I go to cough and suffocate, I shall always love you. Present my respects to your mother, and all my wishes for the happiness of you all. Write me a line to the address: Dr. Lishinsky, [FOOTNOTE: The letter I shall next place before the reader is addressed by Chopin to "Dr. Lishinski." In an Edinburgh medical directory the name appeared as Lyszynski.] 10, Warriston Crescent, Edinburgh, Scotland.—Yours, with all my heart,
CHOPIN.

P.S.—I have played in Edinburgh; the nobility of the neighbourhood came to hear me; people say the thing went off well—a little success and money. There were this year in Scotland Lind, Grisi, Alboni, Mario, Salvi—everybody.

From Chopin's letters may be gathered that he arrived once more in London at the end of October or beginning of November.

Chopin to Dr. Lyschinski; London, November 3, 1848:—

I received yesterday your kind words with the letter from Heidelberg. I am as perplexed here as when I was with you, and have the same love in my heart for you as when I was with you. My respects to your wife and your neighbours. May God bless you!

I embrace you cordially. I have seen the Princess [Czartoryska]; they were inquiring about you most kindly.

My present abode is 4, St. James's Place. If anything should come for me, please send it to that address.

3rd November, 1848.

Pray send the enclosed note to Miss Stirling, who, no doubt, is still at Barnton.

[FOOTNOTE: In this case, as when writing to Woyciechowski, Matuszynski, Fontana, Franchomme and Gutmann, Chopin uses in addressing his correspondent, the pronoun of the second person singular. Here I may also mention the curious monogram on his seal: three C's in the form of horns (with mouthpieces and bells) intertwined.]

The following letter shows in what state of mind and body Chopin was at the time.

Chopin to Grzymala; London, October [should be November] 17-18, 1848:—

My dearest friend,—For the last eighteen days, that is, since my arrival in London, I have been ill, and had such a severe cold in my head (with headache, difficult breathing, and all my bad symptoms) that I did not get out of doors at all. The physician visits me daily (a homoeopathist of the name of Mallan, the same whom my Scotch ladies have and who has here a great reputation, and is married to a niece of Lady Gainsborough). He has succeeded in restoring me so far that yesterday I was able to take part in the Polish Concert and Ball; I went, however, at once home, after I had gone through my task. The whole night I could not sleep, as I suffered, besides cough and asthma, from very violent headache. As yet the mist has not been very bad, so that, in order to breathe a little fresh air, I can open the windows of my apartments notwithstanding the keen cold. I live at No. 4, St. James's Street, see almost every day the excellent Szulczewski, Broadwood, Mrs. Erskine, who followed me hither with Mr. Stirling, and especially Prince Alexander [Czartoryski] and his wife.

[FOOTNOTE: Charles Francis Szulczewski, son of Charles Szulczewski, Receiver General for the District of Orlow, born on January 18, 1814, was educated at the Military School at Kalisz, served during the War of 1831 in the Corps of Artillery under General Bem, obtained the Cross of Honour (virtuti militari) for distinguishing himself at Ostrolenka, passed the first years of his refugee life in France, and in 1842 took up his residence in London, where, in 1845, he became Secretary of the Literary Association of the Friends of Poland. He was promoted for his services to the rank of Major in the Polish Legion, which was formed in Turkey under the command of Ladislas Zamoyski, and after the treaty of Paris (1856) the English Government appointed him to a post in the War Office. Major Szulczewski, who died on October 18, 1884, was an ardent patriot, highly esteemed not only by his countrymen, but also by all others who came in contact with him, numbering among his friends the late Lord Dudley Stuart and the late Earl of Harrowby.]

Address your letters, please, to Szulczewski. I cannot yet come to Paris, but I am always considering what is to be done to return there. Here in these apartments, which for any healthy man would be good, I cannot remain, although they are beautifully situated and not dear (four and a half guineas a week, inclusive of bed, coals, &c.); they are near Lord Stuart's, [FOOTNOTE: Lord Dudley Cuotts Stuart, a staunch and generous friend of the Poles.] who has just left me. This worthy gentleman came to inquire how I felt after last night's concert. Probably I shall take up my quarters with him, because he has much larger rooms, in which I can breathe more freely. En tout cas—inquire, please, whether there are not somewhere on the Boulevard, in the neighbourhood of the Rue de la Paix or Rue Royale, apartments to be had on the first etage with windows towards the south; or, for aught I care, in the Rue des Mathurin, but not in the Rue Godot or other gloomy, narrow streets; at any rate, there must be included a room for the servant. Perhaps Franck's old quarters, which were above mine, at the excellent Madame Etienne's, in the Square No. 9 (Cite d'Orleans), are unoccupied; for I know from experience that I cannot keep on my old ones during the winter. If there were only on the same story a room for the servant, I should go again and live with Madame Etienne, but I should not like to let my Daniel go away, as, should I at any time wish or be able to return to England, he will be acquainted with everything.

Why I bother you with all this I don't know myself; but I must think of myself, and, therefore, I beg of you, assist me in this. I have never cursed anyone, but now I am so weary of life that I am near cursing Lucrezia! [FOOTNOTE: George Sand. This allusion after what has been said in a previous chapter about her novel Lucrezia Floriani needs no further explanation.] But she suffers too, and suffers more because she grows daily older in wickedness. What a pity about Soli! [FOOTNOTE: I suppose Solange, Madame Clesinger, George Sand's daughter.] Alas! everything is going wrong in this world. Think only that Arago with the eagle on his breast now represents France!!! Louis Blanc attracts here nobody's attention. The deputation of the national guard drove Caussidier out of the Hotel de la Sablonniere (Leicester Square) from the table d'hote with the exclamation: "Vous n'etes pas francais!"

Should you find apartments, let me know at once; but do not give up the old ones till then.—Your

FREDERICK.

The Polish Ball and Concert alluded to in the above letter deserves our attention, for on that occasion Chopin was heard for the last time in public, indeed, his performance there may be truly called the swan's song.

The following is an advertisement which appeared in the DAILY NEWS of November 1, 1848:—

Grand Polish Ball and Concert at Guildhall, under Royal and distinguished patronage, and on a scale of more than usual magnificence, will take place on Thursday, the 16th of November, by permission of the Lord Mayor and Corporation of the City of London; particulars of which will be shortly announced to the public.

JAMES R. CARR, HONORARY SECRETARY.

The information given in this advertisement is supplemented in one of November 15:—

The magnificent decorations used on the Lord Mayor's day are, by permission, preserved. The concert will comprise the most eminent vocalists. Tickets (refreshments included), for a lady and gentleman, 21/-; for a gentleman, 15/-; for a lady, 10/6; to be had of, &c.

On the 17th of November the TIMES had, of course, an account of the festivity of the preceding night:—

The patrons and patronesses of this annual or rather perennial demonstration in favour of foreign claims on domestic charity assembled last night at Guildhall much in the same way as they assembled last year and on previous occasions, though certainly not in such numbers, nor in such quality as some years ago. The great hall was illuminated and decorated as at the Lord Mayor's banquet. The appearance was brilliant without being particularly lively.

Then the dancing, Mr. Adams' excellent band, the refreshment rooms, a few noble Lords, the Lord Mayor, and some of the civic authorities (who "diversified the plain misters and mistresses who formed the majority"), the gay costumes of some Highlanders and Spaniards, and Lord Dudley (the great lion of the evening)—all these are mentioned, but there is not a word about Chopin. Of the concert we read only that it "was much the same as on former anniversaries, and at its conclusion many of the company departed." We learn, moreover, that the net profit was estimated at less than on former occasions.

The concert for which Chopin, prompted by his patriotism and persuaded by his friends, lent his assistance, was evidently a subordinate part of the proceedings in which few took any interest. The newspapers either do not notice it at all or but very briefly; in any case the great pianist-composer is ignored. Consequently, very little information is now to be obtained about this matter. Mr. Lindsay Sloper remembered that Chopin played among other things the "Etudes" in A flat and F minor (Op. 25, Nos. 1 & 2). But the best account we have of the concert are some remarks of one present at it which Mr. Hueffer quotes in his essay on Chopin in "Musical Studies":—

The people, hot from dancing, who went into the room where he played, were but little in the humour to pay attention, and anxious to return to their amusement. He was in the last stage of exhaustion, and the affair resulted in disappointment. His playing at such a place was a well-intentioned mistake.

What a sad conclusion to a noble artistic career!

Although Chopin was longing for Paris in November, he was still in London in the following January.

Chopin to Grzymaia; London, Tuesday, January, 1849:—

My dearest friend,—To-day I am again lying almost the whole day, but Thursday I shall leave the to me unbearable London. The night from Thursday to Friday I shall remain at Boulogne, and, I hope, go to bed on Friday night in the Place d'Orleans. To other ailments is now added neuralgia. Please see that the sheets and pillows are quite dry and cause fir-nuts to be bought; Madame Etienne is not to spare anything, so that I may warm myself when I arrive. I have written to Drozewski that he is to provide carpets and curtains. I shall pay the paper-hanger Perrichon at once after my arrival. Tell Pleyel to send me a piano on Thursday; let it be closed and a nosegay of violets be bought, so that there may be a nice fragrance in the salon. I should like to find a little poesy in my rooms and in my bedroom, where I in all probability shall lie down for a long time.

Friday evening, then, I expect to be in Paris; a day longer here, and I shall go mad or die! My Scotch ladies are good, but so tedious that—God have mercy on us! They have so attached themselves to me that I cannot easily get rid of them; only Princess Marcelline [Czartoryska] and her family, and the excellent Szulczewski keep me alive. Have fires lighted in all rooms and the dust removed—perhaps I may yet recover.—Yours ever,

FREDERICK.

Mr. Niedzwiecki told me that he travelled with Chopin, who was accompanied by his servant, from London to Paris.

[FOOTNOTE: Leonard Niedzwiecki, born in the Kingdom of Poland in 1807, joined the National Army in 1830, distinguished himself on several battlefields, came in 1832 as a refugee to England, made there a livelihood by literary work and acted as honorary librarian of the Literary Association of the friends of Poland, left about 1845 London for Paris and became Private Secretary, first to General Count Ladislas Zamoyski, and after the Count's death to the widowed Countess. M. Niedzwiecki, who is also librarian of the Polish Library at Paris, now devotes all his time to historical and philological research.]

The three had a compartment to themselves. During the journey the invalid suffered greatly from frequent attacks of breathlessness. Chopin was delighted when he saw Boulogne. How hateful England and the English were to him is shown by the following anecdote. When they had left Boulogne and Chopin had been for some time looking at the landscape through which they were passing, he said to Mr. Niedzwiecki: "Do you see the cattle in this meadow? Ca a plus d'intelligence que les Anglais." Let us not be wroth at poor Chopin: he was then irritated by his troubles, and always anything but a cosmopolitan.

CHAPTER XXXII

DETERIORATION OF CHOPIN'S STATE OF HEALTH.—TWO
LETTERS.—REMOVES FROM THE SQUARE D'ORLEANS TO THE RUE
CHAILLOT.—PECUNIARY CIRCUMSTANCES.—A CURIOUS STORY.—
REMINISCENCES AND LETTERS CONNECTED WITH CHOPIN'S STAY
IN THE RUE CHAILLOT.—REMOVES TO NO. 12, PLACE VENDOME.—
LAST DAYS, AND DEATH.—FUNERAL.—LAST RESTING-PLACE.—
MONUMENT AND COMMEMORATION IN 1850.

The physical condition in which we saw Chopin in the preceding
chapter was not the outcome of a newly-contracted disease, but only an
acuter phase of that old disease from which he had been suffering more
or less for at least twelve years, and which in all probability he inherited
from his father, who like himself died of a chest and heart complaint.
[FOOTNOTE: My authority for this statement is Dr. Lyschinski, who must
have got his information either from Chopin himself or his mother. That
Chopin's youngest sister, Emilia, died of consumption in early life cannot
but be regarded as a significant fact.] Long before Chopin went in search of
health to Majorca, ominous symptoms showed themselves; and when he
returned from the south, he was only partly restored, not cured.

My attachment [writes George Sand in "Ma Vie"] could work this
miracle of making him a little calm and happy, only because
God had approved of it by preserving a little of his health.
He declined, however, visibly, and I knew no longer what
remedies to employ in order to combat the growing irritation
of his nerves. The death of his friend Dr. Matuszynski, then
that of his own father, [FOOTNOTE: Nicholas Chopin died on May
3, 1844. About Matuszynski's death see page 158.] were to him
two terrible blows. The Catholic dogma throws on death
horrible terrors. Chopin, instead of dreaming for these pure
souls a better world, had only dreadful visions, and I was
obliged to pass very many nights in a room adjoining his,
always ready to rise a hundred times from my work in order to
drive away the spectres of his sleep and wakefulness. The idea

of his own death appeared to him accompanied with all the
superstitious imaginings of Slavonic poetry. As a Pole he
lived under the nightmare of legends. The phantoms called him,
clasped him, and, instead of seeing his father and his friend
smile at him in the ray of faith, he repelled their fleshless
faces from his own and struggled under the grasp of their icy
hands.

But a far more terrible blow than the deaths of his friend and his father
was his desertion by George Sand, and we may be sure that it aggravated his
disease a hundredfold. To be convinced of this we have only to remember
his curse on Lucrezia (see the letter to Grzymala of November 17-18, 1848).

Jules Janin, in an obituary notice, says of Chopin that "he lived ten
years, ten miraculous years, with a breath ready to fly away" (il a vecu
dix ans, dix ans de miracle, d'un souffle pret a s'envoler). Another writer
remarks: "In seeing him [Chopin] so puny, thin, and pale, one thought for a.
long time that he was dying, and then one got accustomed to the idea that
he could live always so." Stephen Heller in chatting to me about Chopin
expressed the same idea in different words: "Chopin was often reported to
have died, so often, indeed, that people would not believe the news when
he was really dead." There was in Chopin for many years, especially since
1837, a constant flux and reflux of life. To repeat another remark of Heller's:
"Now he was ill, and then again one saw him walking on the boulevards
in a thin coat." A married sister of Gutmann's remembers that Chopin had
already, in 1843-4, to be carried upstairs, when he visited her mother, who
in that year was staying with her children in Paris; to walk upstairs, even
with assistance, would have been impossible to him.

For a long time [writes M. Charles Gavard] Chopin had been,
moving about with difficulty, and only went out to have
himself carried to a few faithful friends. He visited them by
no means in order that they might share his misery, on the
contrary, he seemed even to forget his troubles, and at sight
of the family life, and in the midst of the demonstrations of
love which he called forth from everyone, he found new impulse
and new strength to live.

[FOOTNOTE: In a manuscript now before me, containing
reminiscences of the last months of Chopin's life. Karasowski,

at whose disposal the author placed his manuscript, copies LITERALY, in the twelfth chapter of his Chopin biography, page after page, without the customary quotation marks.]

Edouard Wolff told me that, in the latter part of Chopin's life, he did not leave the carriage when he had any business at Schlesinger's music-shop; a shopman came out to the composer, who kept himself closely wrapped in his blue mantle. The following reminiscence is, like some of the preceding ones, somewhat vague with regard to time. Stephen Heller met Chopin shortly before the latter fell ill. On being asked where he was going, Chopin replied that he was on his way to buy a new carpet, his old one having got worn, and then he complained of his legs beginning to swell. And Stephen Heller saw indeed that there were lumps of swelling. M. Mathias, describing to me his master as he saw him in 1847, wrote: "It was a painful spectacle to see Chopin at that time; he was the picture of exhaustion—the back bent, the head bowed forward—but always amiable and full of distinction." That Chopin was no longer in a condition to compose (he published nothing after October, 1847), and that playing in public was torture to him and an effort beyond his strength, we have already seen. But this was not all the misery; he was also unable to teach. Thus all his sources of income were cut off. From Chopin's pupil Madame Rubio (nee Vera de Kologrivof) I learned that latterly when her master was ill and could not give many lessons, he sent to her several of his pupils, among whom was also Miss Stirling, who then came to him only once a week instead of oftener. But after his return from England Chopin was no longer able to teach at all. [FOOTNOTE: "When languor [son mal de langueur] took hold of him," relates Henri Blaze de Bury in "Etudes et Souvenirs," "Chopin gave his lessons, stretched on a sofa, having within reach a piano of which he made use for demonstration."] This is what Franchomme told me, and he, in the last years especially, was intimately acquainted with Chopin, and knew all about his financial affairs, of which we shall hear more presently.

As we saw from the letter quoted at the end of the last chapter, Chopin took up his quarters in the Square d'Orleans, No. 9. He, however, did not find there the recovery of his health, of which he spoke in the concluding sentences. Indeed, Chopin knew perfectly by that time that the game was lost. Hope showed herself to him now and then, but very dimly and doubtfully. Nothing proves the gravity of his illness and his utter prostration so much as the following letters in which he informs his Titus, the dearest friend of his youth, that he cannot go and meet him in Belgium.

Chopin to Titus Woyciechowski; Paris, August 20, 1849:—

Square d'Orleans, Rue St. Lazare, No 9.

My dearest friend,—Nothing but my being so ill as I really am could prevent me from leaving Paris and hastening to meet you at Ostend; but I hope that God will permit you to come to me. The doctors do not permit me to travel. I drink Pyrenean waters in my own room. But your presence would do me more good than any kind of medicine.—Yours unto death,

FREDERICK.
Paris, September 12, 1849.

My dear Titus,—I had too little time to see about the permit for your coming here; [FOOTNOTE: As a Russian subject, Woyciechowski required a special permission from the Rusian authorities to visit Paris, which was not readily granted to Poles.] I cannot go after it myself, for the half of my time I lie in bed. But I have asked one of my friends, who has very great influence, to undertake this for me; I shall not hear anything certain, about it till Saturday. I should have liked to go by rail to the frontier, as far as Valenciennes, to see you again; but the doctors do not permit me to leave Paris, because a few days ago I could not get as far as Ville d'Avraye, near Versailles, where I have a goddaughter. For the same reason they do not send me this winter to a warmer climate. It is, then, illness that retains me; were I only tolerably well I should certainly have visited you in Belgium.

Perhaps you may manage to come here. I am not egotistic enough to ask you to come only on my account; for, as I am ill, you would have with me weary hours and disappointments, but, perhaps, also hours of comfort, and of beautiful reminiscences of our youth, and I wish only that our time together may be a time of happiness.—Yours ever,

FREDERICK.

When Chopin wrote the second of the above letters he was staying in a part of Paris more suitable for summer quarters than the Square d'Orleans — namely, in the Rue Chaillot, whither he had removed in the end of August.

The Rue Chaillot [writes M. Charles Gavard] was then a very quiet street, where one thought one's self rather in the province than in the capital. A large court-yard led to Chopin's apartments on the second story and with a view of Paris, which can be seen from the height of Chaillot.

The friends who found these apartments for the invalid composer made him believe that the rent was only 200 francs. But in reality it was 400 francs, and a Russian lady, Countess Obreskoff, [FOOTNOTE: Madame Rubio, differing in this one particular from Franchomme, said that Chopin paid 100 francs and Countess Obreskoff 200.] paid one half of it. When Chopin expressed surprise at the lowness of the rent, he was told that lodgings were cheap in summer.

This last story prompts me to say a few words about Chopin's pecuniary circumstances, and naturally leads me to another story, one more like romance than reality. Chopin was a bad manager, or rather he was no manager at all. He spent inconsiderately, and neglecting to adapt his expenditure to his income, he was again and again under the necessity of adapting his income to his expenditure. Hence those borrowings of money from friends, those higglings with and dunnings of publishers, in short, all those meannesses which were unworthy of so distinguished an artist, and irreconcilable with his character of grand seigneur. Chopin's income was more than sufficient to provide him with all reasonable comforts; but he spent money like a giddy-headed, capricious woman, and unfortunately for him had not a fond father or husband to pay the debts thus incurred. Knowing in what an unsatisfactory state his financial affairs were when he was earning money by teaching and publishing, we can have no difficulty in imagining into what straits he must have been driven by the absolute cessation of work and the consequent cessation of income. The little he had saved in England and Scotland was soon gone, gone unawares; indeed, the discovery of the fact came to him as a surprise. What was to be done? Franchomme, his right hand, and his head too, in business and money matters — and now, of course, more than ever — was at his wits' end. He discussed the disquieting, threatening problem with some friends of Chopin, and through one of them the composer's destitution came to the knowledge of Miss Stirling. She cut the Gordian knot by sending her master 25,000 francs. [FOOTNOTE: M. Charles Gavard says 20,000 francs.] This noble gift, however; did not at once reach the hands of Chopin. When Franchomme, who knew what had been done, visited Chopin a few days afterwards, the invalid lamented as on previous occasions his impecuniosity, and in answer to the questions of his astonished friend stated that he had received nothing. The enquiries which were forthwith set on foot led to the envelope with the precious enclosure being found untouched in the clock of the portiere, who intentionally or unintentionally had omitted to deliver it. The story is told in various ways, the above is the skeleton of apparently solid facts. I will now make the reader acquainted with the hitherto unpublished account of Madame Rubio, who declared solemnly that her version was correct in every detail. Franchomme's version, as given in Madame Audley's book on Chopin, differs in several points from that of Madame Rubio; I shall, therefore, reproduce it for comparison in a foot-note.

One day in 1849 Franchomme came to Madame Rubio, and said that something must be done to get money for Chopin. Madame Rubio thereupon went to Miss Stirling to acquaint her with the state of matters. When Miss Stirling heard of Chopin's want of money, she was amazed, and told her visitor that some time before she had, without the knowledge of anyone, sent Chopin 25,000 francs in a packet which, in order to conceal the sender, she got addressed and sealed in a shop. The ladies made enquiries as to the whereabouts of the money, but without result. A Scotch gentleman, a novelist (Madame Rubio had forgotten the name at the time she told the story, but was sure she would recall it, and no doubt would have done so, had not her sudden death soon after [FOOTNOTE: In the summer of 1880] intervened), proposed to consult the clairvoyant Alexandre. [FOOTNOTE: Madame Rubio always called the clairvoyant thus. See another name farther on.] The latter on being applied to told them that the packet along with a letter had been delivered to the portiere who had it then in her possession, but that he could not say more until he got some of her hair. One evening when the portiere was bathing Chopin's feet, he—who had in the meantime been communicated with—talked to her about her hair and asked her to let him cut off one lock. She allowed him to do so, and thus Alexandre was enabled to say that the money was in the clock in the portiere's room. Having got this information, they went to the woman and asked her for the packet. She turned pale, and, drawing it out of the clock, said that at the time she forgot to give it to Chopin, and when she remembered it afterwards was afraid to do so. The packet of notes was unopened. Madame Rubio supposed that the portiere thought Chopin would soon die and that then she might keep the contents of the parcel.

[FOOTNOTE: After relating that an intimate friend of Chopin's told Miss Stirling of the latter's straitened circumstances, received from her bank-notes to the amount of 25,000 francs, and handed them enclosed in an envelope to the master's portiere with the request to deliver the packet immediately to its address, Madame Audley proceeds with her story (which Franchomme's death prevented me from verifying) thus: "Here, then, was a gleam of light in this darkened sky, and the reassured friends breathed more freely." "But what was my surprise," said M. Franchomme, from whom I have the story, "when some time after I heard Chopin renew his complaints and speak of his distress in the most poignant terms. Becoming impatient, and being quite at a loss as to what was going on," I said at last to him: "But, my dear friend, you have no cause to torment yourself, you can wait for the return of your health, you have money now!"—"I, money!" exclaimed Chopin; "I have nothing."—"How! and these 25,000 francs which were sent you lately?"—"25,000 francs? Where are they? Who sent them to me? I have not received a sou!"—"Ah! really, that is too bad!" Great commotion among the friends. It was evident that the money given to the portiere had not arrived at its destination; but how to be assured of this? and what had become of it? Here was a curious enough fact, as if a little of the marvellous must always be mingled with Chopin's affairs. Paris at that time possessed a much run-after clairvoyant, the celebrated Alexis; they thought of going to consult him. But to get some information it was necessary to put him en rapport, directly or indirectly, with the person suspected. Now this person was, naturally, the portiere. By ruse or by address they got hold of a little scarf that she wore round her neck and placed it in the hands of the clairvoyant. The latter unhesitatingly declared that the 25,000 francs were behind the looking-glass in the loge. The friend who had brought them immediately presented himself to claim them; and our careful portiere, fearing, no doubt, the consequences of a too prolonged sequestration, drew the packet from behind the clock and held it out to him, saying: 'Eh bien, la v'la, vot' lettre!'"]

Chopin, however, refused to accept the whole of the 25,000 francs. According to Madame Rubio, he kept only 1,000 francs, returning the rest to Miss Stirling, whilst Franchomme, on the other hand, said that his friend kept 12,000 francs.

During Chopin's short stay in the Rue Chaillot, M. Charles Gavard, then a very young man, in fact, a youth, spent much of his time with the suffering composer:—

The invalid [he writes] avoided everything that could make me
sad, and, to shorten the hours which we passed together,
generally begged me to take a book out of his library and to
read to him. For the most part he chose some pages out of

Voltaire's Dictionnaire Philosophique. He valued very highly the finished form of that clear and concise language, and that so sure judgment on questions of taste. Thus, for instance, I remember that the article on taste was one of the last I read to him.

What M. Gavard says of how slowly, in pain, and often in loneliness, the hours passed for Chopin in the spacious, rooms of his lodgings in the Rue Chaillot, reminds me of a passage in Hector Berlioz's admirable article on his friend in the Journal des Debats (October 27, 1849):—

> His weakness and his sufferings had become so great that he could no longer either play the piano or compose; even the slightest conversation fatigued him in an alarming manner. He endeavoured generally to make himself understood as far as possible by signs. Hence the kind of isolation in which he wished to pass the last months of his life, an isolation which many people wrongly interpreted—some attributing it to a scornful pride, others to a melancholic temper, the one as well as the other equally foreign to the character of this, charming artist.

During his stay in the Rue Chaillot Chopin wrote the following note and letter to Franchomme:—

> Dear friend,—Send me a little of your Bordeaux. I must take a little wine to-day, and have none. How distrustful I am! Wrap up the bottle, and put your seal on it. For these porters! And I do not know who will take charge of this commission.
>
> Yours, with all my heart.
> Sunday after your departure, September 17, 1849.

> Dear friend,—I am very sorry that you were not well at Le Mans. Now, however, you are in Touraine, whose sky will have been more favourable to you. I am less well rather than better. MM. Cruveille, Louis, and Blache have had a consultation, and have come to the conclusion that I ought not to travel, but only to take lodgings in the south and remain

at Paris. After much seeking, very dear apartments, combining all the desired conditions, have been found in the Place Vendome, No. 12. Albrecht has now his offices there. Meara [FOOTNOTE: This is a very common French equivalent for O'Meara.] has been of great help to me in the search for the apartments. In short, I shall see you all next winter—well housed; my sister remains with me, unless she is urgently required in her own country. I love you, and that is all I can tell you, for I am overcome with sleep and weakness. My sister rejoices at the idea of seeing Madame Franchomme again, and I also do so most sincerely. This shall be as God wills. Kindest regards to M. and Madame Forest. How much I should like to be some days with you! Is Madame de Lauvergeat also at the sea-side? Do not forget to remember me to her, as well as to M. de Lauvergeat. Embrace your little ones. Write me a line. Yours ever. My sister embraces Madame Franchomme.

After a stay of less than six weeks Chopin removed from the Rue Chaillot to the apartments in No. 12, Place Vendome, which M. Albrecht and Dr. O'Meara had succeeded in finding for him. About this time Moscheles came to Paris. Of course he did not fail to inquire after his brother-artist and call at his house. What Moscheles heard and thought may be gathered from the following entry in his diary:-"Unfortunately, we heard of Chopin's critical condition, made ourselves inquiries, and found all the sad news confirmed. Since he has been laid up thus, his sister has been with him. Now the days of the poor fellow are numbered, his sufferings great. Sad lot!" Yes, Chopin's condition had become so hopeless that his relations had been communicated with, and his sister, Louisa Jedrzejewicz, [FOOTNOTE: The same sister who visited him in 1844, passed on that occasion also some time at Nohant, and subsequently is mentioned in a letter of Chopin's to Franchomme.] accompanied by her husband and daughter, had lost no time in coming from Poland to Paris. For the comfort of her presence he was, no doubt, thankful. But he missed and deplored very much during his last illness the absence of his old, trusted physician, Dr. Molin, who had died shortly after the composer's return from England.

The accounts of Chopin's last days—even if we confine ourselves to those given by eye-witnesses—are a mesh of contradictions which it is impossible to wholly disentangle. I shall do my best, but perhaps the most I can hope for is to avoid making confusion worse confounded.

In the first days of October Chopin was already in such a condition that unsupported he could not sit upright. His sister and Gutmann did not leave him for a minute, Chopin holding a hand of the latter almost constantly in one of his. By the 15th of October the voice of the patient had lost its sonority. It was on this day that took place the episode which has so often and variously been described. The Countess Delphine Potocka, between whom and Chopin existed a warm friendship, and who then happened to be at Nice, was no sooner informed of her friend's fatal illness than she hastened to Paris.

When the coming of this dear friend was announced to Chopin [relates M. Gavard], he exclaimed: "Therefore, then, has God delayed so long to call me to Him; He wished to vouchsafe me yet the pleasure of seeing you." Scarcely had she stepped up to him when he expressed the wish that she should let him hear once more the voice which he loved so much. When the priest who prayed beside the bed had granted the request of the dying man, the piano was moved from the adjoining room, and the unhappy Countess, mastering her sorrow and suppressing tier sobs, had to force herself to sing beside the bed where her friend was exhaling his life. I, for my part, heard nothing; I do not know what she sang. This scene, this contrast, this excess of grief had over-powered my-sensibility; I remember only the moment when the death-rattle of the departing one interrupted the Countess in the middle of the second piece. The instrument was quickly removed, and beside the bed remained only the priest who said the prayers for the dying, and the kneeling friends around him.

However, the end was not yet come, indeed, was not to come till two days after. M. Gavard, in saying that he did not hear what the Countess Potocka sang, acts wisely, for those who pretended to have heard it contradict each other outright. Liszt and Karasowski, who follows him, say that the Countess sang the Hymn to the Virgin by Stradella, and a Psalm by Marcello; on the other hand, Gutmann most positively asserted that she sang a Psalm by Marcello and an air by Pergolesi; whereas Franchomme insisted on her having sung an air from Bellini's Beatrice di Tenda, and that only once, and nothing else. As Liszt was not himself present, and does not give the authority for his statement, we may set it, and with it Karasowski's, aside; but the two other statements, made as they were by two musicians who were ear witnesses, leave us in distressing perplexity with regard to what really took place, for between them we cannot choose. Chopin, says M. Gavard, looked forward to his death with serenity.

Some days after his removal to the Place Vendome, Chopin, sitting upright and leaning on the arm of a friend, remained silent for a long time and seemed lost in deep meditation. Suddenly he broke the silence with the words: "Now my death-struggle begins" [Maintenant j'entre en agonie]. The physician, who was feeling his pulse, wished to comfort him with some commonplace words of hope. But Chopin rejoined with a superiority which admitted of no reply: "God shows man a rare favour when He reveals to him the moment of the approach of death; this grace He shows me. Do not disturb me."

M. Gavard relates also that on the 16th October Chopin twice called his friends that were gathered in his apartments around him. "For everyone he had a touching word; I, for my part, shall never forget the tender words he spoke to me." Calling to his side the Princess Czartoryska and Mdlle. Gavard, [FOOTNOTE: A sister of M. Charles Gavard, the pupil to whom Chopin dedicated his Berceuse.] he said to them: "You will play together, you will think of me, and I shall listen to you." And calling to his side Franchomme, he said to the Princess: "I recommend Franchomme to you, you will play Mozart together, and I shall listen to you." [FOOTNOTE: The words are usually reported to have been "Vous jouerez du Mozart en memoire de moi."] "And," added Franchomme when he told me this, "the Princess has always been a good friend to me."

And George Sand? Chopin, as I have already mentioned, said two days before his death to Franchomme: "She had said to me that I would die in no arms but hers" [Elle n'avait dit que je ne mourrais que dans ses bras]. Well, did she not come and fulfil her promise, or, at least, take leave of her friend of many years? Here, again, all is contradiction. M. Gavard writes:—

Among the persons who called and were not admitted was a certain Madame M., who came in the name of George Sand—who was then much occupied with the impending representation of one of her dramas—to inquire after Chopin's state of health. None of us thought it proper to disturb the last moments of the master by the announcement of this somewhat late remembrance.

Gutmann, on the other hand, related that George Sand came to the landing of the staircase and asked him if she might see Chopin; but that he advised her strongly against it, as it was likely to excite the patient too much. Gutmann, however, seems to have been by no means sure about this part of his recollections, for on two occasions he told me that it was Madame Clesinger (George Sand's daughter, Solange) who asked if it was advisable for her mother to come. Madame Clesinger, I may say in passing, was one of those in loving attendance on Chopin, and, as Franchomme told me, present, like himself, when the pianist-composer breathed his last. From the above we gather, at least, that it is very uncertain whether Chopin's desire to see George Sand was frustrated by her heartlessness or the well-meaning interference of his friends.

During this illness of Chopin a great many of his friends and acquaintances, in fact, too many, pressed forward, ready to be of use, anxious to learn what was passing. Happily for the dying man's comfort, most of them were not allowed to enter the room in which he lay.

In the back room [writes M. Gavard] lay the poor sufferer, tormented by fits of breathlessness, and only sitting in bed resting in the arms of a friend could he procure air for his oppressed lungs. It was Gutmann, the strongest among us, who knew best how to manage the patient, and who mostly thus supported him. At the head of his bed sat the Princess Marcelline Czartoryska: she never left him, guessing his most secret wishes, nursing him like a sister of mercy with a serene countenance, which did not betray her deep sorrow. Other friends gave a helping hand or relieved her, everyone according to his power; but most of them stayed in the two adjoining rooms. Everyone had assumed a part; everyone helped as much as he could: one ran to the doctors, to the apothecary; another introduced the persons asked for; a third shut the door on the intruders. To be sure, many who had anything but free entrance came, and called to take leave of him just as if he were about to start on a journey. This anteroom of the dying man, where every one of us hopelessly waited and watched, was like a guard-house or a camp.

M. Gavard probably exaggerates the services of the Princess Czartoryska, but certainly forgets those of the composer's sister. Liszt, no doubt, comes nearer the truth when he says that among those who assembled in the salon adjoining Chopin's bedroom, and in turn came to him and watched his gestures and looks when he had lost his speech, the Princess Marcelline Czartoryska was the most assiduous.

> She passed every day a couple of hours with the dying man. She
> left him at the last only after having prayed for a long time
> beside him who had just then fled from this world of illusions
> and sorrows....

After a bad night Chopin felt somewhat better on the morning of the 16th. By several authorities we are informed that on this day, the day after the Potocka episode, the artist received the sacrament which a Polish priest gave him in the presence of many friends. Chopin got worse again in the evening. While the priest was reading the prayers for the dying, he rested silently and with his eyes closed upon Gutmann's shoulder; but at the end of the prayers he opened his eyes wide and said with a loud voice: "Amen."

The Polish priest above mentioned was the Abbe Alexander Jelowicki. Liszt relates that in the absence of the Polish priest who was formerly Chopin's confessor, the Abbe called on his countryman when he heard of his condition, although they had not been on good terms for years. Three times he was sent away by those about Chopin without seeing him. But when he had succeeded in informing Chopin of his wish to see him, the artist received him without delay. After that the Abbe became a daily visitor. One day Chopin told him that he had not confessed for many years, he would do so now. When the confession was over and the last word of the absolution spoken, Chopin embraced his confessor with both arms a la polonaise, and exclaimed: "Thanks! Thanks! Thanks to you I shall not die like a pig." That is what Liszt tells us he had from Abbe Jelowicki's own lips. In the account which the latter has himself given of how Chopin was induced by him to receive the sacrament, induced only after much hesitation, he writes:—

> Then I experienced an inexpressible joy mixed with an
> indescribable anguish. How should I receive this precious soul
> so as to give it to God? I fell on my knees, and cried to God
> with all the energy of my faith: "You alone receive it, O my
> God!" And I held out to Chopin the image of the crucified
> Saviour, pressing it firmly in his two hands without saying a
> word. Then fell from his eyes big tears. "Do you believe?" I

asked him. — "I believe." — "Do you believe as your mother taught you?" — "As my mother taught me." And, his eyes fixed on the image of his Saviour, he confessed while shedding torrents of tears. Then he received the viaticum and the extreme unction which he asked for himself. After a moment he desired that the sacristan should be given twenty times more than was usually given to him. When I told him that this would be far too much, he replied: "No, no, this is not too much, for what I have received is priceless." From this moment, by God's grace, or rather under the hand of God Himself, he became quite another, and one might almost say he became a saint. On the same day began the death-struggle, which lasted four days and four nights. His patience and resignation to the will of God did not abandon him up to the last minute....

When Chopin's last moments approached he took "nervous cramps" (this was Gutmann's expression in speaking of the matter), and the only thing which seemed to soothe him was Gutmann's clasping his wrists and ankles firmly. Quite near the end Chopin was induced to drink some wine or water by Gutmann, who supported him in his arms while holding the glass to his lips. Chopin drank, and, sinking back, said "Cher ami!" and died. Gutmann preserved the glass with the marks of Chopin's lips on it till the end of his life.

[FOOTNOTE: In B. Stavenow's sketch already more than once alluded to by me, we read that Chopin, after having wetted his lips with the water brought him by Gutmann, raised the latter's hand, kissed it, and with the words "Cher ami!" breathed his last in the arms of his pupil, whose sorrow was so great that Count Gryzmala was obliged to lead him out of the room. Liszt's account is slightly different. "Who is near me?" asked Chopin, with a scarcely audible voice. He bent his head to kiss the hand of Gutmann who supported him, giving up his soul in this last proof of friendship and gratitude. He died as he had lived, loving.]

M. Gavard describes the closing hours of Chopin's life as follows: —
The whole evening of the 16th passed in litanies; we gave the responses, but Chopin remained silent. Only from his difficult breathing could one perceive that he was still alive. That evening two doctors examined him. One of them, Dr. Cruveille, took a candle, and, holding it before Chopin's face, which had

become quite black from suffocation, remarked to us that the senses had already ceased to act. But when he asked Chopin whether he suffered, we heard, still quite distinctly, the answer "No longer" [Plus]. This was the last word I heard from his lips. He died painlessly between three and four in the morning [of October 17, 1849]. When I saw him some hours afterwards, the calm of death had given again to his countenance the grand character which we find in the mould taken the same day [by Clesinger], and still more in the simple pencil sketch which was drawn by the hand of a friend, M. Kwiatkowski. This picture of Chopin is the one I like best.

Liszt, too, reports that Chopin's face resumed an unwonted youth, purity, and calm; that his youthful beauty so long eclipsed by suffering reappeared. Common as the phenomenon is, there can be nothing more significant, more impressive, more awful, than this throwing-off in death of the marks of care, hardship, vice, and disease—the corruption of earthly life; than this return to the innocence, serenity, and loveliness of a first and better nature; than this foreshadowing of a higher and more perfect existence. Chopin's love of flowers was not forgotten by those who had cherished and admired him now when his soul and body were parted. "The bed on which he lay," relates Liszt, "the whole room, disappeared under their varied colours; he seemed to repose in a garden." It was a Polish custom, which is not quite obsolete even now, for the dying to choose for themselves the garments in which they wished to be dressed before being laid in the coffin (indeed, some people had their last habiliments prepared long before the approach of their end); and the pious, more especially of the female sex, affected conventual vestments, men generally preferring their official attire. That Chopin chose for his grave-clothes his dress-suit, his official attire, in which he presented himself to his audiences in concert-hall and salon, cannot but be regarded as characteristic of the man, and is perhaps more significant than appears at first sight. But I ought to have said, it would be if it were true that Chopin really expressed the wish. M. Kwiatkowski informed me that this was not so.

For some weeks after, from the 18th October onwards, the French press occupied itself a good deal with the deceased musician. There was not, I think, a single Paris paper of note which did not bring one or more long articles or short notes regretting the loss, describing the end, and estimating the man and artist. But the phenomenal ignorance, exuberance of imagination, and audacity of statement, manifested by almost every one of the writers of these articles and notes are sufficient to destroy one's faith in journalism completely and for ever. Among the offenders were men of great celebrity, chief among them Theophile Gautier (Feuilleton de la Presse, November 5, 1849) and Jules Janin (Feuilleton du Journal des Debuts, October 22, 1849), the latter's performance being absolutely appalling. Indeed, if we must adjudge to French journalists the palm for gracefulness and sprightliness, we cannot withhold it from them for unconscientiousness. Some of the inventions of journalism, I suspect, were subsequently accepted as facts, in some cases perhaps even assimilated as items of their experience, by the friends of the deceased, and finally found their way into AUTHENTIC biography. One of these myths is that Chopin expressed the wish that Mozart's Requiem should be performed at his funeral. Berlioz, one of the many journalists who wrote at the time to this effect, adds (Feuilleton du Journal des Debuts, October 27, 1849) that "His [Chopin's] worthy pupil received this wish with his last sigh." Unfortunately for Berlioz and this pretty story, Gutmann told me that Chopin did not express such a wish; and Franchomme made to me the same statement. I must, [I must, however, not omit to mention here that M. Charles Gavard says that Chopin drew up the programme of his funeral, and asked that on that occasion Mozart's Requiem should be performed.] Also the story about Chopin's wish to be buried beside Bellini is, according to the latter authority, a baseless invention. This is also the place to dispose of the question: What was done with Chopin's MSS.? The reader may know that the composer is said to have caused all his MSS. to be burnt. Now, this is not true. From Franchomme I learned that what actually took place was this. Pleyel asked Chopin what was to be done with the MSS. Chopin replied that they were to be distributed among his friends, that none were to be published, and that fragments were to be destroyed. Of the pianoforte school which Chopin is said to have had the intention to write, nothing but scraps, if anything, can have been found.

M. Gavard pere made the arrangements for the funeral, which, owing to the extensiveness of the preparations, did not take place till the 30th of October. Ready assistance was given by M. Daguerry, the curate of the Madeleine, where the funeral service was to be held; and thanks to him permission was received for the introduction of female singers into the church, without whom the performance of Mozart's Requiem would have been an impossibility.

Numerous equipages [says Eugene Guinot in the Feuilleton du Siecle of November 4] encumbered last Tuesday the large avenues of the Madeleine church, and the crowd besieged the doors of the Temple where one was admitted only on presenting a letter of invitation. Mourning draperies announced a funeral ceremony, and in seeing this external pomp, this concourse of carriages and liveried servants, and this privilege which permitted only the elect to enter the church, the curious congregated on the square asked: "Who is the great lord [grand seigneur] whom they are burying?" As if there were still grands seigneurs! Within, the gathering was brilliant; the elite of Parisian society, all the strangers of distinction which Paris possesses at this moment, were to be found there...

Many writers complain of the exclusiveness which seems to have presided at the sending out of invitations. M. Guinot remarks in reference to this point:

His testamentary executors [executrices] organised this solemnity magnificently. But, be it from premeditation or from forgetfulness, they completely neglected to invite to the ceremony most of the representatives of the musical world. Members of the Institute, celebrated artists, notable writers, tried in vain to elude the watch-word [consigne] and penetrate into the church, where the women were in a very great majority. Some had come from London, Vienna, and Berlin.

In continuation of my account of the funeral service I shall quote from a report in the Daily News of November 2, 1849:—

The coffin was under a catafalque which stood in the middle of the area. The semicircular space behind the steps of the altar was screened by a drapery of black cloth, which being festooned towards the middle, gave a partial view of the vocal and instrumental orchestra, disposed not in the usual form of a gradual ascent from the front to the back, but only on the level of the floor....

The doors of the church were opened at eleven o'clock, and at noon (the time fixed for the commencement of the funeral service) the vast area was filled by an assembly of nearly three thousand persons, all of whom had received special invitations, as being entitled from rank, from station in the world of art and literature, or from friendship for the lamented deceased, to be present on so solemn and melancholy an occasion.

A trustworthy account of the whole ceremony, and especially a clear and full report of the musical part of the service, we find in a letter from the Paris correspondent of The Musical World (November 10, 1849). I shall quote some portions of this letter, accompanying them with elucidatory and supplementary notes:—

The ceremony, which took place on Tuesday (the 30th ult.), at noon, in the church of the Madeleine, was one of the most imposing we ever remember to have witnessed. The great door of the church was hung with black curtains, with the initials of the deceased, "F. C.," emblazoned in silver. On our entry we found the vast area of the modern Parthenon entirely crowded. Nave, aisles, galleries, &c., were alive with human beings who had come to see the last of Frederick Chopin. Many, perhaps, had never heard of him before....In the space that separates the nave from the choir, a lofty mausoleum had been erected, hung with black and silver drapery, with the initials "F.C." emblazoned on the pall. At noon the service began. The orchestra and chorus (both from the Conservatoire, with M. Girard as conductor and the principal singers (Madame Viardot-Garcia, Madame Castellan, Signor Lablache, and M. Alexis Dupont)) were placed at the extreme end of the church, a black drapery concealing them from view.

[FOOTNOTE: This statement is confirmed by one in the Gazette musicals, where we read that the members of the Societe des Concerts "have made themselves the testamentary executors of this wish" —namely, to have Mozart's Requiem performed. Madame Audley, misled, I think, by a dubious phrase of Karasowski's, that has its origin in a by no means dubious phrase of

Liszt's, says that Meyerbeer conducted (dirigeait l'ensemble).
Liszt speaks of the conducting of the funeral procession.]

When the service commenced the drapery was partially withdrawn
and exposed the male executants to view, concealing the women,
whose presence, being uncanonical, was being felt, not seen. A
solemn march was then struck up by the band, during the
performance of which the coffin containing the body of the
deceased was slowly carried up the middle of the nave...As
soon as the coffin was placed in the mausoleum, Mozart's
Requiem was begun...The march that accompanied the body to the
mausoleum was Chopin's own composition from his first
pianoforte sonata, instrumented for the orchestra by M. Henri
Reber.

[FOOTNOTE: Op. 35, the first of those then published, but in
reality his second, Op. 4 being the first. Meyerbeer
afterwards expressed to M. Charles Gavard his surprise that he
had not been asked to do the deceased the homage of scoring
the march.]

During the ceremony M. Lefebure-Wely, organist of the
Madeleine, performed two of Chopin's preludes [FOOTNOTE: Nos.
4 and 6, in E and B minor] upon the organ...After the service
M. Wely played a voluntary, introducing themes from Chopin's
compositions, while the crowd dispersed with decorous gravity.
The coffin was then carried from the church, all along the
Boulevards, to the cemetery of Pere-Lachaise-a distance of
three miles at least—Meyerbeer and the other chief mourners,
who held the cords, walking on foot, bareheaded.

[FOOTNOTE: Liszt writes that Meyerbeer and Prince Adam
Czartoryski conducted the funeral procession, and that Prince
Alexander Czartoryski, Delacroix, Franchomme, and Gutmann were

the pall-bearers. Karasowski mentions the same gentlemen as pall-bearers; Madame Audley, on the other hand, names Meyerbeer instead of Gutmann. Lastly, Theophile Gautier reported in the Feuilleton de la Presse of November 5, 1849, that MM. Meyerbeer, Eugene Delacroix, Franchomme, and Pleyel held the cords of the pall. The Gazette musicale mentions Franchomme, Delacroix, Meyerbeer, and Czartoryski.]

A vast number of carriages followed...

[FOOTNOTE: "Un grand nombre de voitures de deuil et de voitures particulieres," we read in the Gazette musicals, "ont suivi jusqu'au cimetiere de l'Est, dit du Pere-Lachaise, le pompeux corbillard qui portait le corps du defunt. L'elite des artistes de Paris lui a servi de cortege. Plusieurs dames, ses eleves, en grand deuil, ont suivi le convoi, a pied, jusqu'au champ de repos, ou l'artiste eminent, convaincu, a eu pour oraisons funebres des regrets muets, profondement sentis, qui valent mieux que des discours dans lesquels perce toujours une vanite d'auteur ou d'orateur"]

At Pere-Lachaise, in one of the most secluded spots, near the tombs of Habeneck and Marie Milanollo, the coffin was deposited in a newly-made grave. The friends and admirers took a last look, ladies in deep mourning threw garlands and flowers upon the coffin, and then the gravedigger resumed his work...The ceremony was performed in silence.

One affecting circumstance escaped the attention of our otherwise so acute observer—namely, the sprinkling on the coffin, when the latter had been lowered into the grave, of the Polish earth which, enclosed in a finely-wrought silver cup, loving friends had nearly nineteen years before, in the village of Wola, near Warsaw, given to the departing young and hopeful musician who was never to see his country again.

Chopin's surroundings at Pere-Lachaise are most congenial. Indeed, the neighbourhood forms quite a galaxy of musical talent—close by lie

Cherubini, Bellini, Gretry, Boieldieu, Bocquillon-Wilhem, Louis Duport, and several of the Erard family; farther away, Ignace Pleyel, Rodolphe Kreutzer, Pierre Galin, Auguste Panseron, Mehul, and Paer. Some of these, however, had not yet at that time taken possession of their resting-places there, and Bellini has since then (September 15, 1876) been removed by his compatriots, to his birthplace, Catania, in Sicily.

Not the whole of Chopin's body, however, was buried at Pere-Lachaise; his heart was conveyed to his native country and is preserved in the Holy Cross Church at Warsaw, where at the end of 1879 or beginning of 1880 a monument was erected, consisting of a marble bust of the composer in a marble niche. Soon after Chopin's death voluntary contributions were collected, and a committee under Delacroix's presidence was formed, for the erection of a monument, the execution of which was entrusted to Clesinger, the husband of Madame Sand's daughter, Solange. Although the sculptor's general idea is good—a pedestal bearing on its front a medallion, and surmounted by a mourning muse with a neglected lyre in her hand— the realisation leaves much to be desired. This monument was unveiled in October, 1850, on the anniversary of Chopin's death.

[FOOTNOTE: On the pedestal of the monument are to be read besides the words "A. Frederic Chopin" above the medallion, "Ses amis" under the medallion, and the name of the sculptor and the year of its production (J. Clesinger, 1850), the following incorrect biographical data: "Frederic Chopin, ne en Pologne a Zelazowa Wola pres de Varsovie: Fils d'un emigre francais, marie a Mile. Krzyzanowska, fille d'un gentilhomme Polonais."]

The friends of the composer, as we learn from an account in John Bull (October 26, 1850), assembled in the little chapel of Pere-Lachaise, and after a religious service proceeded with the officiating priest at their head to Chopin's grave. The monument was then unveiled, flowers and garlands were scattered over and around it, prayers were said, and M. Wolowski, the deputy, [FOOTNOTE: Louis Francois Michel Raymond Wolowski, political economist, member of the Academie des Sciences Morales, and member of the Constituante. A Pole by birth, he became a naturalised French subject in 1834.] endeavoured to make a speech, but was so much moved that he could only say a few words.

[FOOTNOTE: In the Gazette muticale of October 20, 1850, we read: "Une messe commemorative a ete dite jeudi dernier [i.e., on the 17th] dans la chapelle du cimetiere du Pere-Lachaise a la memoire de Frederic Chopin et pour l'inauguration de son monument funebre."]

The Menestrel of November 3, 1850, informed its readers that in the course of the week (it was on the 30th October at eleven o'clock) an anniversary mass had been celebrated at the Madeleine in honour of Chopin, at which from two to three hundred of his friends were present, and that Franchomme on the violoncello and Lefebure-Wely on the organ had played some of the departed master's preludes, or, to quote our authority literally, "ont redit aux assistants emus les preludes si pleins de melancolie de l'illustre defunt."

EPILOGUE

We have followed Chopin from his birthplace, Zelazowa Wola, to Warsaw, where he passed his childhood and youth, and received his musical as well as his general education; we have followed him in his holiday sojourns in the country, and on his more distant journeys to Reinerz, Berlin, and Vienna; we have followed him when he left his native country and, for further improvement, settled for a time in the Austrian capital; we have followed him subsequently to Paris, which thenceforth became his home; and we have followed him to his various lodgings there and on the journeys and in the sojourns elsewhere—to 27, Boulevard Poissonniere, to 5 and 38, Chaussee d'Antin, to Aix-la-Chapelle, Carlsbad, Leipzig, Heidelberg, Marienbad, and London, to Majorca, to Nohant, to 5, Rue Tronchet, 16, Rue Pigalle, and 9, Square d'Orleans, to England and Scotland, to 9, Square d'Orleans once more, Rue Chaillot, and 12, Place Vendome; and, lastly, to the Pere-Lachaise cemetery. We have considered him as a pupil at the Warsaw Lyceum and as a student of music under the tuition of Zywny and Elsner; we have considered him as a son and as a brother, as a lover and as a friend, as a man of the world and as a man of business; and we have considered him as a virtuoso, as a teacher, and as a composer. Having done all this, there remains only one thing for me to do—namely, to summarise the thousands of details of the foregoing account, and to point out what this artist was to his and is to our time. But before doing this I ought perhaps to answer a question which the reader may have asked himself. Why have I not expressed an opinion on the moral aspect of Chopin's connection with George Sand? My explanation shall be brief. I abstained from pronouncing judgment because the incomplete evidence did not seem to me to warrant my doing so. A full knowledge of all the conditions and circumstances. I hold to be indispensable if justice is to be done; the rash and ruthless application of precepts drawn from the social conventions of the day are not likely to attain that end. Having done my duty in placing before the reader the ascertainable evidence, I leave him at liberty to decide on it according to his wisdom and charity.

Henri Blaze de Bury describes (in Etudes et Souvenirs) the portrait which Ary Scheffer painted of Chopin in these words:—

It represents him about this epoch [when "neither physical nor moral consumption of any kind prevented him from attending freely to his labours as well as to his pleasures"], slender, and in a nonchalant attitude, gentlemanlike in the highest degree: the forehead superb, the hands of a rare distinction, the eyes small, the nose prominent, but the mouth of an exquisite fineness and gently closed, as if to keep back a melody that wishes to escape.

M. Marmontel, with, "his [Chopin's] admirable portrait" by Delacroix before him, penned the following description:—

This is the Chopin of the last years, ailing, broken by suffering; the physiognomy already marked by the last seal [le sceau supreme], the look dreamy, melancholy, floating between heaven and earth, in the limbos of dream and agony. The attenuated and lengthened features are strongly accentuated: the relief stands out boldly, but the lines of the countenance remain beautiful; the oval of the face, the aquiline nose and its harmonious curve, give to this sickly physiognomy the stamp of poetic distinction peculiar to Chopin.

Poetic distinction, exquisite refinement, and a noble bearing are the characteristics which strike one in all portraits of Chopin, [FOOTNOTE: See Appendix IV.] and which struck the beholder still more strongly in the real Chopin, where they were reinforced by the gracefulness of his movements, and by manners that made people involuntarily treat him as a prince...[FOOTNOTE: See my description of Chopin, based on the most reliable information, in Chapter XX.] And pervading and tincturing every part of the harmonious whole of Chopin's presence there was delicacy, which was indeed the cardinal factor in the shaping not only of his outward conformation, but also of his character, life, and art-practice. Physical delicacy brought with it psychical delicacy, inducing a delicacy of tastes, habits, and manners, which early and continued intercourse with the highest aristocracy confirmed and developed. Many of the charming qualities of the man and artist derive from this delicacy. But it is likewise the source of some of the deficiencies and weaknesses in the man and artist. His exclusiveness, for instance, is, no doubt, chargeable to the superlative sensitiveness which shrank from everything that failed to satisfy his fastidious, exacting nature, and became more and more morbid as delicacy, of which it was a concomitant, degenerated into disease. Yet, notwithstanding the lack of robustness and all it entails, Chopin might have been moderately happy, perhaps even have continued to enjoy moderately good health, if body and soul had been well matched. This, however, was not the case. His thoughts were too big, his passions too violent, for the frail frame that held them; and the former grew bigger and more violent as the latter grew frailer and frailer. He could not realise his aspirations, could not compass his desires, in short, could not fully assert himself. Here, indeed, we have lit upon the tragic motive of Chopin's life-drama, and the key to much that otherwise would be enigmatical, certainly not explicable by delicacy and disease alone. His salon acquaintances, who saw only the polished outside of the man, knew nothing of this disparity and discrepancy; and even the select few of his most intimate friends, from whom he was not always able to conceal the irritation that gnawed at his heart, hardly more than guessed the true state of matters. In fact, had not Chopin been an artist, the tale of his life would have for ever remained a tale untold. But in his art, as an executant and a composer, he revealed all his strength and weakness, all his excellences and insufficiencies, all his aspirations and failures, all his successes and disappointments, all his dreams and realities.

Chopin [wrote Anton Schindler in 1841] [FOOTNOTE: Beethoven in Paris, p. 71] is the prince of all pianists, poesy itself at the piano... His playing does not impress by powerfulness of touch, by fiery brilliancy, for Chopin's physical condition forbids him every bodily exertion, and spirit and body are constantly at variance and in reciprocal excitement. The cardinal virtue of this great master in pianoforte-playing lies in the perfect truth of the expression of every feeling within his reach [dessen er sich bemeistern darf], which is altogether inimitable and might lead to caricature were imitatior attempted.

Chopin was not a virtuoso in the ordinary sense of the word. His sphere was the reunion intime, not the mixed crowd of concert audiences. If, however, human testimony is worth anything, we may take it as proven that there never was a pianist whose playing exercised a charm equal to that of Chopin. But, as Liszt has said, it is impossible to make those who have not heard him understand this subtle, penetrating charm of an ineffable poesy. If words could give an idea of Chopin's playing, it would be given by such expressions as "legerete impalpable," "palais aeriens de la Fata Morgana," "wundersam und marchenhaft," and other similar ones used with regard to it by men who may safely be accepted as authorities.

As a pianist Chopin was sorely restricted by lack of physical vigour, which obliged him often to merely suggest, and even to leave not a little wholly unexpressed. His range as a composer was much wider, as its limits were those of his spirit. Still, Chopin does not number among those masterminds who gather up and grasp with a strong hand all the acquisitions of the past and present, and mould them into a new and glorious synthesis-the highest achievement possible in art, and not to be accomplished without a liberal share of originality in addition to the comprehensive power. Chopin, then, is not a compeer of Bach, Handel, Mozart, and Beethoven. But if he does not stand on their level, he stands on a level not far below them. And if the inferiority of his intellectual stamina prevented him from achieving what they achieved, his delicate sensibility and romantic imagination enabled him to achieve what they were disqualified from achieving. Of universality there was not a trace in him, but his individuality is one of the most interesting. The artistico-historical importance of Chopin lies in his having added new elements to music, originated means of expression for the communication and discrimination of moods and emotions, and shades of moods and emotions, that up to his time had belonged to the realm of the unuttered and unutterable. Notwithstanding the high estimation in which Chopin is held, it seems to me that his importance for the development of the art is not rated at its full value. His influence on composers for the pianoforte, both as regards style and subject-matter, is generally understood; but the same cannot be said of his less obvious wider influence. Indeed, nothing is more common than to overlook his connection with the main current of musical history altogether, to regard him as a mere hors d'oeuvre in the musical MENU of the universe. My opinion, on the contrary, is that among the notable composers who have lived since the days of Chopin there is not to be found one who has not profited more or less, consciously or unconsciously, directly or indirectly, by this truly creative genius. To trace his influence we must transport ourselves back fifty or sixty years, and see what the state of music then was, what composers expressed and what means of expression they had at their disposal. Much that is now familiar, nay, even commonplace, was then a startling novelty. The appearance of Chopin was so wonderful a phenomenon that it produced quite an electrical effect upon Schumann. "Come," said Berlioz to Legouve in the first years of the fourth decade of this century, "I am going to let you see something which you have never seen, and someone whom you will never forget." This something and someone was Chopin. Mendelssohn being questioned about his enthusiasm for one of this master's preludes replied: "I love it,

I cannot tell you how much, or why; except, perhaps, that it is something which I could never have written at all." Of course, Chopin's originality was not universally welcomed and appreciated. Mendelssohn, for instance, was rather repelled than attracted by it; at any rate, in his letters there are to be found frequent expressions of antipathy to Chopin's music, which seemed to him" mannered "(see letter to Moscheles of February 7, 1835). But even the heartless and brainless critic of the Musical World whose nonsense I quoted in Chapter XXXI. admits that Chopin was generally esteemed by the "professed classical musicians," and that the name of the admirers of the master's compositions was legion. To the early popularity of Chopin's music testify also the many arrangements for other instruments (the guitar not excepted) and even for voices (for instance, OEuvres celebres de Chopin, transcrites a une ou deux voix egales par Luigi Bordese) to which his compositions were subjected. This popularity was, however, necessarily limited, limited in extent or intensity. Indeed, popular, in the comprehensive sense of the word, Chopin's compositions can never become. To understand them fully we must have something of the author's nature, something of his delicate sensibility and romantic imagination. To understand him we must, moreover, know something of his life and country. For, as Balzac truly remarked, Chopin was less a musician than une ame qui se rend sensible. In short, his compositions are the "celestial echo of what he had felt, loved, and suffered"; they are his memoirs, his autobiography, which, like that of every poet, assumes the form of "Truth and Poetry."

APPENDICES

APPENDIX I
THE GOLDEN AGE OP POLISH MUSIC

(VOL. I., p. 66.)

As yet it is difficult to speak with any degree of certainty of the early musical history of Poland. Our general histories of music have little or nothing to say on the matter, and a special history exists neither in the Polish nor in any other language. The Abbe Joseph Surzynski, who by his labours is endeavouring to remove the reproach of indifference and ignorance now lying on his countrymen in this respect, says: [FOOTNOTE: In the preface to the Monumenta Musices sacra, selected works of the best composers of classical religious music in Poland, published by him. The first two parts of this publication, respectively issued in 1885 and 1887, contain compositions by Thomas Szadek, Nicolas Zielenski, G. G. Gorczycki, Venceslas, Szamotulski, and Sebastian of Felsztyn.] "The compositions of our old masters are buried in the archives and libraries—no one cares to make them known to the public; many Polish musicians, not even supposing that these compositions exist, are very far from believing that the authors of these pieces deserve to be ranked with the best composers of the Roman Catholic Church. Now, in studying these works, we find in the century of Palestrina and Vittoria among our artists: Marcin ze Lwowa (Martin Leopolita), Christopher Borek, Thomas Szadek, Venceslas Szamotulski, and especially Zielenski and Gomolka—distinguished masters who deserve to be known by the friends of the musical art, either on account of their altogether national genius, or on account of their inspiration and the perfection of the forms which manifest themselves in their compositions." One of the first illustrious names in the history of music in Poland is the German Henry Finck, the chapel-master of the Polish Kings, John Albert (1492-1501) and Alexander (1501-1506). From the fact that this excellent master got his musical education in Poland we may safely conclude—and it is not the only fact which justifies our doing so—that in that country already in the fifteenth century good contrapuntists were to be found. The

Abbe Surzynski regards Zielenski as the best of the early composers, having been impressed both by the profound religious inspiration and the classical form of his works. Of Gomolka, who has been called the Polish Palestrina as Sebastian of Felsztyn the Polish Goudimel, the Abbe remarks: "Among the magnificent musical works of Martin Leopolita, Szadek, and Zielenski, the compositions of Gomolka present themselves like miniature water-colours, in which, nevertheless, every line, every colour, betrays the painter of genius. His was a talent thoroughly indigenous—his compositions are of great simplicity; no too complicated combinations of parts, one might even say that they are homophonous; nevertheless what wealth of thought, what beauty of harmony, what profoundness of sentiment do we find there! These simple melodies clothed in pure and truly holy harmonies, written, as Gomolka said himself, not for the Italians, but for the Poles, who are happy in their own country, are the best specimens of the national style. "In speaking of the early Polish church music I must not forget to mention the famous College of the Roratists, [FOOTNOTE: The duties of these singers were to sing Rorate masses and Requiem masses for the royal family. Their name was derived from the opening word of the Introit, "Rorate coeli."] the Polish Sistine Chapel, attached to the Cracow Cathedral. It was founded in 1543 and subsisted till 1760. With the fifteenth of seventeen conductors of the college, Gregor Gorczycki, who died in 1734, passed away the last of the classical school of Polish church music. Music was diligently cultivated in the seventeenth century, especially under the reigns of Sigismund III. (1587-1632), and Wladislaw IV. (1632-1648); but no purpose would be served by crowding these pages with unknown names of musicians about whom only scanty information is available; I may, however, mention the familiar names of three of many Italian composers who, in the seventeenth century, like many more of their countrymen, passed a great part of their lives in Poland—namely, Luca Marenzio, Asprilio Pacelii, and Marco Scacchi.

APPENDIX II
EARLY PERFORMANCES OF CHOPIN'S WORKS IN GERMANY

(VOL. I., p. 268.)

The first performance of a composition by Chopin at the Leipzig Gewandhaus took place on October 27, 1831. It was his Op. 1, the variations on La ci darem la mano, which Julius Knorr played at a concert for the benefit of the Pension-fund of the orchestra, but not so as to give the audience pleasure—at least, this was the opinion of Schumann, as may be seen from his letter to Frederick Wieck of January 4, 1832. Chopin relates already on June 5, 1830, that Emilie Belleville knew his variations by heart and had played them in Vienna. Clara Wieck was one of the first who performed Chopin's compositions in public. On September 29, 1833, she played at a Leipzig Gewandhaus concert the last movement of the E minor Concerto, and on May 5, 1834, in the same hall at an extra concert, the whole work and two Etudes. Further information about the introduction and repetitions of Chopin's compositions at the Leipzig Gewandhaus, is to be found in the statistical part (p. 13) of Alfred Dorffel's Die Gewandhausconcerte.

APPENDIX III
MADAME SCHUMANN ON
CHOPIN'S VISIT TO LEIPZIG

(VOL. I., p. 290.)

Through a kind communication from Madame Schumann I have learned that Wenzel's account does not quite agree with her diary. There she finds written that her father, Friedrich Wieck, felt offended because Chopin, for whose recognition in Germany he had done so much, had not called upon him immediately after his arrival. Chopin made his appearance only two hours before his departure, but then did not find Wieck at home, for he, to avoid Chopin, had gone out and had also taken his daughter Clara with him. When Wieck returned an hour later, he found unexpectedly Chopin still there. Clara had now to play to the visitor. She let him hear Schumann's F sharp minor Sonata, two Etudes by Chopin, and a movement of a Concerto by herself. After this Chopin played his E flat major Nocturne. By degrees Wieck's wrath subsided, and finally he accompanied Chopin to the post-house, and parted from him in the most friendly mood.

APPENDIX IV
REBECCA DIRICHLET ON
CHOPIN AT MARIENBAD

(VOL. I., p. 309.)

When Rebecca Dirichlet came with her husband to Marienbad, she learnt that Chopin did not show himself, and that his physician and a Polish countess, who completely monopolised him, did not allow him to play. Having, however, heard so much of his playing from her brothers, she was, in order to satisfy her curiosity, even ready to commit the bassesse of presenting herself as the soeur de Messieurs Paul et Felix Mendelssohn Bartholdy. As she humorously wrote a few days later: "The bassesse towards Chopin has been committed and has completely failed. Dirichlet went to him, and said that a soeur, &c.—only a mazurka—impossible, mal aux nerfs, mauvais piano—et comment se porte cette chere Madame Hensel, el Paul est marie? heureux couple, &c.—allez vous promener—the first and the last time that we do such a thing."

APPENDIX V
PALMA AND VALDEMOSA

(VOL. II., pp. 22-48.)

The Argosy of 1888 contains a series of Letters from Majorca by Charles W. Wood, illustrated by views of Palma, Valdemosa, and other parts of the island. The illustrations in the April number comprise a general view of the monastery of Valdemosa, and views of one of its courts and of the cloister in which is situated the cell occupied by George Sand and Chopin in the winter of 1838-1839. The cloister has a groined vault, on one side the cell doors, and on the other side, opening on the court, doors and rectangular windows with separate circular windows above them. The letters have been republished in book form (London: Bentley and Sons).

APPENDIX VI
ON TEMPO RUBATO

(VOL. II., p. 101.)

An earlier practiser of the tempo rubato than the lady mentioned by Quanz (see Vol. II., p. 101 of this work) was Girolamo Frescobaldi, who speaks of this manner of musical rendering in the preface to Il primo libra di Capricci fatti sopra diversi sogetti et Arie in partitura (1624). An extract from this preface is to be found in A. G. Ritter's Zur Geschichte des Orgelspiels, Vol. I., p. 34. F. X. Haberl remarks in the preface to his collection of pieces by Frescobaldi (Leipzig: Breitkopf and Hartel): "A chief trait of Frescobaldi's genius is the so-called tempo rubato, an absolute freedom in the employment of a quicker and slower tempo."

APPENDIX VII
CAROLINE HARTMANN

(VOL. II., p. 171.)

On page 175 of this volume I made an allusion to Spohr in connection with Chopin's pupil Caroline Hartmann. To save the curious reader trouble, I had better point out that the information is to be found in Spohr's autobiography under date Munster, near Colmar, March 26, 1816 (German edition, pp. 245-250; English edition, pp. 229-232). Jacques Hartmann, the father of Caroline, was a cotton manufacturer and an enthusiastic lover of music. He had an orchestra consisting of his family and employes. Spohr calls the father a bassoon-virtuoso; what he says of the daughter will be seen in the following sentences: "His sister and his daughter play the pianoforte. The latter, a child eight years old, is the star of the amateur orchestra. She plays with a dexterity and exactness that are worthy of admiration. I was still more astonished at her fine ear, with which (away from the piano) she recognises the intervals of the most intricate and full dissonant chords which one strikes, and names the notes of which they consist in their sequence. If the child is well guided, she is sure to become one day an excellent artist."

APPENDIX VIII
MADAME PERUZZI

(VOL. II., p. 177.)

The reader will be as grateful as I am for the following interesting communications of Madame Peruzzi (nee Elise Eustaphieve, whose father was Russian Consul-General to the United States of America) about her intercourse with Chopin.

"I first met Chopin at the house of the American banker, Samuel Welles, in Paris, where I, like every one present, was enchanted listening to his mazurkas, waltzes, nocturnes, &c., which he played on a wretched square piano. I lived as dame en chambre (a very convenient custom for ladies alone), at a pension, or rather a regular boarding-school, with rooms to let for ladies. The lady of the house was acquainted with many of the musical people, and I had a splendid American grand piano which was placed in the large drawing-room of the establishment, so that I felt quite at home, and there received Chopin, Liszt, and Herz (Miss Herz, his sister, gave lessons in the school), and often played four-hand pieces with them.

"My intimacy with Chopin began after my marriage. He often dined with us, was very fond of my husband, and after dinner we were not at home if any one else came, but remained at our two pianos (Erard had sent me one), playing together, and I used to amuse him by picking out of his music little bits that seemed like questions for him to answer on the other piano. He lived very near us, so we very often passed mornings at his house, where he asked me to play with him all Weber's duets. This was delightful to me, the more so, as he complimented me on my reading and entering at first sight into the spirit of the music. He made me acquainted with the beautiful duet of Moscheles, and was the first with whom I played Hummel's splendid duet. He was a great admirer of Weber. We frequently had morning concerts with double quartet, and Chopin would very kindly turn the leaves for me. He was particularly fond of doing so when I played Hummel's Septet, and was so encouraging. Even when playing to him his own music, he would approve some little thing not indicated and say, 'What a good idea of yours that is!' My husband begged him to give me lessons; but he always refused, and did give them; for I studied so many things with him, among others his two concertos. The one in E minor I once played accompanied by himself on a second piano. We passed many pleasant evenings at Mr. and Madame Leo's house, a very musical one. Madame Moscheles was a niece of theirs. Chopin was fond of going there, where he was quite a pet. He always appeared to best advantage among his most intimate friends. I was one who helped to christen the Berceuse. You ask me in what years I knew Chopin, 1838 is the date of the manuscript in my collection which he gave me after I was married, and the last notes of that little jewel he wrote on the desk of the piano in our presence. He said it would not be published because they would play it....Then he would show how they would play it, which was very funny. It came out after his death, it is a kind of waltz-mazurka [the Valse, Op. 69, No. I], Chopin's intimate friend, Camille Pleyel, called it the story of a D flat, because that note comes in constantly. One morning we took Paganini to hear Chopin, and he was enchanted; they seemed to understand each other so well. When I knew him he was a sufferer and would only occasionally play in public, and then place his piano in the middle of Pleyel's room whilst his admirers were around the piano. His speciality was extreme delicacy, and his pianissimo extraordinary. Every little note was like a bell, so clear. His fingers seemed to be without any bones; but he would bring out certain effects by great elasticity. He got very angry at being accused of not keeping time; calling his left hand his maitre de chapelle and allowing his right to wander about ad libitum."

APPENDIX IX

MADAME STREICHER'S (nee FRIEDERIKE MULLER) RECOLLECTIONS OF CHOPIN, BASED ON EXTRACTS FROM HER CAREFULLY-KEPT DIARY OF THE YEARS 1839, 1840, AND 1841. (VOL. II., p. 177.)

In March, 1839, I went to Paris, accompanied by a kind aunt, who was a highly-cultured musical connoisseur, animated by the wish to get if possible lessons from Chopin, whose compositions inspired me with enthusiasm. But he was from home and very ill; indeed, it was feared he would not return to Paris even in the winter. However, at last, at last, in October, 1839, he came. I had employed this long time in making myself acquainted with the musical world in Paris, but the more I heard, nay, even admired, the more was my intention to wait till Chopin's return confirmed. And I was quite right.

On the 30th of October, 1839, we, my kind aunt and I, went to him. At that time he lived in Rue Tronchet, No. 5. Anxiously I handed him my letters of introduction from Vienna, and begged him to take me as a pupil. He said very politely, but very formally: "You have played with applause at a matinee at the house of Countess Appony, the wife of the Austrian ambassador, and will hardly require my instruction." I became afraid, for I was wise enough to understand he had not the least inclination to accept me as a pupil. I quickly protested that I knew very well I had still very, very much to learn. And, I added timidly, I should like to be able to play his wondrously-beautiful compositions well. "Oh!" he exclaimed, "it would be sad if people were not in a position to play them well without my instruction." "I certainly am not able to do so," I replied anxiously. "Well, play me something," he said. And in a moment his reserve had vanished. Kindly and indulgently he helped me to overcome my timidity, moved the piano, inquired whether I were comfortably seated, let me play till I had become calm, then gently found fault with my stiff wrist, praised my correct comprehension, and accepted me as a pupil. He arranged for two lessons a week, then turned in the most amiable way to my aunt, excusing himself beforehand if he should often be obliged to change the day and hour of the lesson on account of his delicate health. His servant would always inform us of this.

Alas! he suffered greatly. Feeble, pale, coughing much, he often took opium drops on sugar and gum-water, rubbed his forehead with eau de Cologne, and nevertheless he taught with a patience, perseverance, and zeal which were admirable. His lessons always lasted a full hour, generally he was so kind as to make them longer. Mikuli says: "A holy artistic zeal burnt in him then, every word from his lips was incentive and inspiring. Single lessons often lasted literally for hours at a stretch, till exhaustion overcame master and pupil." There were for me also such blessed lessons. Many a Sunday I began at one o'clock to play at Chopin's, and only at four or five o'clock in the afternoon did he dismiss us. Then he also played, and how splendidly but not only his own compositions, also those of other masters, in order to teach the pupil how they should be performed. One morning he played from memory fourteen Preludes and Fugues of Bach's, and when I expressed my joyful admiration at this unparalleled performance, he replied: "Cela ne s'oublie jamais," and smiling sadly he continued: "Depuis un an je n'ai pas etudie un quart d'heure de sante, je n'ai pas de force, pas d'energie, j'attends toujours un peu de sante pour reprendre tout cela, mais... j'attends encore." We always spoke French together, in spite of his great fondness for the German language and poetry. It is for this reason that I give his sayings in the French language, as I heard them from him. In Paris people had made me afraid, and told me how Chopin caused Clementi, Hummel, Cramer, Moscheles, Beethoven, and Bach to be studied, but not his own compositions. This was not the case. To be sure, I had to study with him the works of the above-mentioned masters, but he also required me to play to him the new and newest compositions of Hiller, Thalberg, and Liszt, &c. And already in the first lesson he placed before me his wondrously—beautiful Preludes and Studies. Indeed, he made me acquainted with many a composition before it had appeared in print.

I heard him often preluding in a wonderfully-beautiful manner. On one occasion when he was entirely absorbed in his playing, completely detached from the world, his servant entered softly and laid a letter on the music-desk. With a cry Chopin left off playing, his hair stood on end—what I had hitherto regarded as impossible I now saw with my own eyes. But this lasted only for a moment.

His playing was always noble and beautiful, his tones always sang, whether in full forte, or in the softest piano. He took infinite pains to teach the pupil this legato, cantabile way of playing. "Il [ou elle] ne sait pas lier deux notes" was his severest censure. He also required adherence to the strictest rhythm, hated all lingering and dragging, misplaced rubatos, as well as exaggerated ritardandos. "Je vous prie de vous asseoir," he said on such an occasion with gentle mockery. And it is just in this respect that people make such terrible mistakes in the execution of his works. In the use of the pedal he had likewise attained the greatest mastery, was uncommonly strict regarding the misuse of it, and said repeatedly to the pupil: "The correct employment of it remains a study for life."

When I played with him the study in C major, the first of those he dedicated to Liszt, he bade me practise it in the mornings very slowly. "Cette etude vous fera du bien," he said. "Si vous l'etudiez comme je l'entends, cela elargit la main, et cela vous donne des gammes d'accords, comme les coups d'archet. Mais souvent malheureusement au lieu d'apprendre tout cela, elle fait desapprendre." I am quite aware that it is a generally-prevalent error, even in our day, that one can only play this study well when one possesses a very large hand. But this is not the case, only a supple hand is required.

Chopin related that in May, 1834, he had taken a trip to Aix-la-Chapelle with Hiller and Mendelssohn. "Welcomed there in a very friendly manner, people asked me when I was introduced: 'You are, I suppose, a brother of the pianist?' I answered in the affirmative, for it amused me, and described my brother the pianist. 'He is tall, strong, has black hair, a black moustache, and a very large hand.'" To those who have seen the slightly-built Chopin and his delicate hand, the joke must have been exceedingly amusing.

On the 20th of April, 1840, Liszt, who had come back to Paris after extended artistic tours, gave a matinee to an invited audience in Erard's saloon. He played, as he did always, very brilliantly, and the next morning I had to give a minute account to Chopin of what and how he had played. He himself was too unwell to be present. When I spoke of Liszt's artistic self-control and calmness in overcoming the greatest technical difficulties, he exclaimed: "Ainsi il parait que mon avis est juste. La derniere chose c'est la simplicite. Apres avoir epuise toutes les difficultes, apres avoir joue une immense quantite de notes, et de notes, c'est la simplicite qui sort avec tout son charme, comme le dernier sceau de l'art. Quiconque veut arriver de suite a cela n'y parviendra jamais, on ne peut commencer par la fin. Il faut avoir etudie beaucoup, meme immensement pour atteindre ce but, ce n'est pas une chose facile. II m'etait impossible," he continued, "d'assister a sa matinee. Avec ma sante ou ne peut rien faire. Je suis toujours embrouille avec mes affaires, de maniere que je n'ai pas un moment libre. Que j'envie les gens forts qui sont d'une sante robuste et qui n'ont rien a faire! Je suis bien fache, je n'ai pas le temps d'etre malade."

When I studied his Trio he drew my attention to some passages which now displeased him, he would now write them differently. At the end of the Trio he said: "How vividly do the days when I composed it rise up in my memory! It was at Posen, in the castle surrounded by vast forests of Prince Radziwill. A small but very select company was gathered together there. In the mornings there was hunting, in the evenings music. Ah! and now," he added sadly, "the Prince, his wife, his son, all, all are dead."

At a soiree (Dec. 20, 1840) he made me play the Sonata with the Funeral March before a large assemblage. On the morning of the same day I had once more to play over to him the Sonata, but was very nervous. "Why do you play less well to-day?" he asked. I replied that I was afraid. "Why? I consider you play it well," he rejoined very gravely, indeed, severely. "But if you wish to play this evening as nobody played before you, and nobody will play after you, well then!"...These words restored my composure. The thought that I played to his satisfaction possessed me also in the evening; I had the happiness of gaining Chopin's approval and the applause of the audience. Then he played with me the Andante of his F minor Concerto, which he accompanied magnificently on the second piano. The entire assemblage assailed him with the request to perform some more of his compositions, which he then did to the delight of all.

For eighteen months (he did not leave Paris this summer) I was allowed to enjoy his instruction. How willingly would I have continued my studies with him longer! But he himself was of opinion that I should now return to my fatherland, pursue my studies unaided, and play much in public. On parting he presented me with the two manuscripts of his C sharp major and E major studies (dedicated to Liszt), and promised to write during his stay in the country a concert-piece and dedicate it to me.

In the end of the year 1844 I went again to Paris, and found Chopin looking somewhat stronger. At that time his friends hoped for the restoration of, or at least for a considerable improvement in, his health.

The promised concert-piece, Op. 46, had to my inexpressible delight been published. I played it to him, and he was satisfied with my playing of it; rejoiced at my successes in Vienna, of which he had been told, exerted himself with the amiability peculiar to him to make me still better known to the musical world of Paris. Thus I learned to know Auber, Halevy, Franchomme, Alkan, and others. But in February, 1845,1 was obliged to return to Vienna; I had pupils there who were waiting for me. On parting he spoke of the possibility of coming there for a short time, and I had quite made up my mind to return for another visit to Paris in eighteen months, in order again to enjoy his valuable instruction and advice. But this, to my deepest regret, was not to be.

I saw Madame Sand in the year 1841 and again in the year 1845 in a box in a theatre, and had an opportunity of admiring her beauty. I never spoke to her.

APPENDIX X
PORTRAITS OF CHOPIN

A biography is incomplete without some account of the portraits of the hero or heroine who is the subject of it. M. Mathias regards as the best portrait of Chopin a lithograph by Engelmann after a drawing by Vigneron, of 1833, published by Maurice Schlesinger, of Paris. In a letter to me he writes: "This portrait is marvellous for the absolutely exact idea it gives of Chopin: the graceful fall of the shoulders, the Polish look, the charm of the mouth." Continuing, he says: "Another good likeness of Chopin, but of a later date, between the youthful period and that of his decay, is Bovy's medallion, which gives a very exact idea of the outlines of his hair and nose. Beyond these there exists nothing, all is frightful; for instance, the portrait in Karasowski's book, which has a stupid look." The portrait here alluded to is a lithographic reproduction of a drawing by A. Duval. As a rule, the portraits of Chopin most highly prized by his pupils and acquaintances are those by A. Bovy and T. Kwiatkowski. Madame Dubois, who likes Bovy's medallion best, and next to it the portraits by Kwiatkowski, does not care much for Ary Scheffer's portrait of her master, in whose apartments she had of course frequent opportunities to examine it. "It had the appearance of a ghost [d'un ombre], and was more pale and worn than Chopin himself." Of a bust by Clesinger Madame Dubois remarks that it does not satisfy those who knew Chopin. M. Marmontel writes in a letter to me that the portrait of Chopin by Delacroix in his possession is a powerful sketch painted in oil, "reproducing the great artist in the last period of his life, when he was about to succumb to his chest disease. My dear friend Felix Barrias has been inspired, or, to be more exact, has reproduced this beautiful and poetic face in his picture of the dying Chopin asking the Countess Potocka to sing to him." Gutmann had in his possession two portraits of his master, both pencil drawings; the one by Franz Winterhalter, dated May 2, 1847, the other by Albert Graefle, dated October 19, 1849. The former of these valuable portraits shows Chopin in his decline, the latter on his death-bed. Both seem good likenesses, Graefle's drawing having a strong resemblance with Bovy's medallion.

[FOOTNOTE: The authorship alone is sufficient to make a drawing by George Sand interesting. Madame Dubois says (in a letter written to me) that the portrait, after a drawing of George Sand, contained in the French edition of Chopin's posthumous works, published by Fontana, is not at all a good likeness. Herr Herrmann Scholtz in Dresden has in his possession a faithful copy of a drawing by George Sand made by a nephew of the composer, a painter living at Warsaw. Madame Barcinska, the sister of Chopin, in whose possession the original is, spoke of it as a very good likeness. This picture, however, is not identical with that mentioned by Madame Dubois.]

The portrait by A. Regulski in Szulc's book can only be regarded as a libel on Chopin, and ought perhaps also to be regarded as a libel on the artist. Various portraits in circulation are curiosities rather than helps to a realisation of the outward appearance of Chopin. Schlesinger, of Berlin, published a lithograph after a drawing by Maurir; and Schuberth, of Hamburg, an engraving on steel, and Hofmeister, of Leipzig, a lithograph, after I don't know what original. Several other portraits need not be mentioned, as they are not from life, but more or less fancy portraits based on one or more of the authentic delineations. Bovy's medallion graces Breitkopf and Hartel's Gesammtausgabe and Thematic Catalogue of the master's published works. The portrait by Ary Scheffer may be seen lithographically reproduced by Waldow in the German edition of Chopin's posthumous works, published by Fontana. A wood-cut after the drawing by Graefle appeared in 1879 in the German journal Die Gartenlaube. Prefixed to the first volume of the present biography the reader will find one of the portraits by Kwiatkowski, an etching after a charming pencil drawing in my possession, the reproduction of which the artist has kindly permitted. M. Kwiatkowski has portrayed Chopin frequently, and in many ways and under various circumstances, alive and dead. Messrs. Novello, Ewer & Co. have in their possession a clever water-colour drawing by Kwiatkowski of Chopin on his death-bed. A more elaborate picture by the same artist represents Chopin on his death-bed surrounded by his sister, the Princess Marcellince Czartoryska, Grzymala, the Abbe Jelowicki, and the portrayer. On page 321 of this volume will be found M. Charles Gavard's opinion of two portrayals of Chopin, respectively by Clesinger and Kwiatkowski. In conclusion, I recall to the reader's attention what has been said of the master's appearance and its pictorial and literary reproductions on pp. 65 and 246 of Vol. I. and pp. 100, 135, and 329 of Vol. II.

REMARKS PRELIMINARY TO THE LIST OF CHOPIN'S WORKS.

The original editions were three in number: the German, the French, and the English (see p. 272). To avoid overcrowding, only the names of the original German and French publishers will be given in the following list, with two exceptions, however,—Op. 1 and 5, which were published in Poland (by Brzezina & Co., of Warsaw) long before they made their appearance elsewhere. [FOOTNOTE: What is here said, however, does not apply to Section IV.] Some notes on the publication of the works in England are included in these preliminary remarks.

In the list the publishers will be always placed in the same order—the German first, and the French second (in the two exceptional cases, Op. 1 and 5, they will be second and third). The dates with an asterisk and in parentheses (*) are those at which a copy of the respective works was deposited at the Paris Bibliotheque du Conservatoire de Musique, the dates without an asterisk in parentheses are derived from advertisements in French musical journals; the square brackets [ ] enclose conjectural and approximate dates and additional information; and lastly, the dates without parentheses and without brackets were obtained by me direct from the successors of the original German publishers, and consequently are more exact and trustworthy than the others. In a few cases where the copyright changed hands during the composer's lifetime, and where unacquaintance with this change might give rise to doubts and difficulties, I have indicated the fact.

The publishing firms mentioned in the list are the following:—Maurice Schlesinger, Brandus &Cie. (the successors of M. Schlesinger), Eugene Troupenas & Cie., Joseph Meissonnier, Joseph Meissonnier fils H. Lemoine, Ad. Catelin & Cie. (Editeurs des Compositeurs reunis, Rue Grange Bateliere, No. 26), Pacini (Antonio Francesco Gaetano), Prilipp & Cie. (Aquereurs d'une partie du Fond d'lgn. Pleyel & Cie.), S. Richault (i.e., Charles Simon Richault, to whom succeeded his son Guillaume Simon, who in his turn was succeeded by his son Leon.—Present style: Richault et Cie., Successeurs), and Schonenberger, all of Pans;-Breitkopf & Hartel, Probst-Kistner (since 1836 Friedrich Kistner), Friedrich Hofmeister, and C. F. Peters, of Leipzig;— Ad. M. Schlesinger, Stern & Co.(from 1852 J. Friedlander; later on annexed to Peters, of Leipzig), and Bote and Bock, of Berlin;—Tobias Haslinger, Carl Haslinger quondam Tobias, and Pietro Mechetti (whose widow was succeeded by C. A. Spina), of Vienna;—Schuberth & Co., of Hamburg (now Julius Schuberth, of Leipzig);—B. Schott's Sohne, of Mainz;—Andr. Brzezina & Co. and Gebethner & Wolff, of Warsaw;—J. Wildt and W. Chaberski, of Cracow;—and J. Leitgeber, of Posen.

From 1836 onward the course of the publication of Chopin's works in England can be followed in the advertisement columns of the Musical World. Almost all the master's works were published in England by Wessel. On March 8, 1838, Messrs. Wessel advertised Op. 1-32 with the exception of Op. 4, 11, and 29. This last figure has, no doubt, to be read as 28, as the Preludes could hardly be in print at that time, and the Impromptu, Op. 29, was advertised on October 20, 1837, as OP. 28. With regard to Op.

12 it has to be noted that it represents not the Variations brillantes sur le Rondo favori "Je vends des Scapulaires," but the Grand Duo concertant for piano and violoncello, everywhere else published without opus number. The Studies, Op. 10, were offered to the public "revised with additional fingering by his pupil I. [sic] Fontana." On November 18, 1841, Wessel and Stapleton (the latter having come in as a partner in 1839) advertised Op. 33-43, and subsequently Op. 44-48. On February 22, 1844, they announced that they had "the sole copyright of the COMPLETE and entire works" of Chopin. On May 15, 1845, were advertised Op. 57 and 58; on January 17, 1846, Op. 59; on September 26, 1846, Op. 60, 61, and 62. The partnership with Stapleton having in 1845 been dissolved, the style of the firm was now Wessel & Co. Thenceforth other English publishers came forward with Chopin compositions. On June 3, 1848, Cramer, Beale & Co. advertised Chopin's "New Valses and Mazurkas for the pianoforte"; and on the title-pages of the French edition of Op. 63, 64, and 65 I found the words: "London, Jullien et Cie." But also before this time Wessel seems to have had competitors; for on the title-page of the French edition of Op. 22 may be read: "London, Mori et Lavenu," and on September 20, 1838, Robert Cocks advertised "Five Mazurkas and Three Nocturnes." On September 23, 1848, however, Wessel & Co. call themselves sole proprietors of Chopin's works; and on November 24, 1849, they call themselves Publishers of the Complete Works of Chopin. Information received from Mr. Ashdown, the present proprietor of the business, one of the two successors (Mr. Parry retired in 1882) of Christian Rudolph Wessel, who retired in 1860 and died in 1885, throws some further light on the publication of Chopin's works in England. We have already seen in a former part of this book (p. 117) that Wessel discontinued to deal with Chopin after Op. 62. "Cramer, Beale & Co.," writes Mr. Ashdown, "published the Mazurkas, Op. 63, and two only of the Waltzes, Op. 64; these, being non-copyright in England, Mr. Wessel added to his edition, together with the third waltz of Op. 64. The name of Jullien on the French edition was probably put on in consequence of negotiations for the sale of English copyright having been entered upon, but without result." With the exception of Op. 12 and 65, Wessel published all the works with opus numbers of Chopin that were printed during the composer's lifetime. Cramer, Addison & Beale published the Variations, Op. 12; Chappell, the Trois Nouvelles Etudes; R. Cocks, the posthumous Sonata, Op. 4, and the Variations stir un air allemand without opus number; and Stanley Lucas, Weber & Co., the Seventeen Polish Songs, Op. 74. The present editions issued by the successor of Wessel are either printed from the original plates or re-engraved (which is the case in about half of the number) from the old Wessel copies, with here and there a correction.

Simultaneous publication was aimed at, as we see from Chopin's letters, but the dates of the list show that it was rarely attained. The appearance of the works in France seems to have in most cases preceded that in Germany; in the case of the Tarantelle, Op. 43, I found the English edition first advertised (October 28, 1841). Generally there was approximation if not simultaneity.

I—WORKS PUBLISHED WITH OPUS NUMBERS DURING THE COMPOSER'S LIFETIME

DATES ORIGINAL

OF GERMAN & FRENCH

PUBLICATION TITLES WITH REFERENCES PUBLISHERS.

1825. OP.1. Premier Rondeau [C minor] Brzezina.

pour le piano. Dedie a Mme. de A. M. Schlesinger.

Linde.—Vol. I, pp. 52, 53-54, M. Schlesinger

55, 112;—Vol. II, p.87

[1830, OP.2. La ci darem la mano [B flat T. Haslinger

about March] major] varie pour le piano, avec M. Schlesinger

(September accompagnement d'orchestre. Dedie

21, 1834.) a Mr. Woyciechowski.—Vol. I., pp.

53, 62, 95, 96, 97, 99, 100, 101,

105, 112, 116-118, 120, 163, 241;

Vol. II., p.87, 212

[1833 in OP.3. Introduction et Polonaise Mechetti

print.] brillante [C major], pour piano S. Richault

June, 1835) et violincelle Dediee d Mr. Joseph

Merk.—Vol.I., pp. 129, 200-201;

—Vol. II., p. 87.

Op.4. As this work was published

posthumously, it had to be placed

in Section III. Nevertheless, it

differs from the works with which

it is classed in one important

respect—it was intended for

publication by the composer himself,

who sent it to Vienna in 1828.

[1827?] Op.5. Rondeau a la Mazur [F major] Brzezina.
May, 1836 pour le piano. Dediee a Mlle. la Hofmeister.
Comtesse Alexandrine de Moriolles. Schonenberger.
—Vol. I., pp. 54-55, 56, 112, 168;
—Vol. II., p.87
Dec., 1832 Op.6. Quatre Mazurkas [F sharp minor Probst-Kistner.
(Nov. 23, C Sharp minor, E major, and E flat M. Schlesinger.
1834.) minor] pour le piano. Dediees a
Mlle. la Comtesse Pauline Plater.
—Vol. I., p. 268;—Vol. II, pp.231-
232.234-239.
Dec.1832 Op.7. Cinq Mazurkas [B flat major, Probst-Kistner
(Nov. 23, A minor, F minor, A flat major, and M. Schlesinger.
1834.) C major] pour le piano. Dediees a
Mr. Johns.—Vol. I., pp.250,268,
276 (No. 1);—Vol. II, pp. 231-232
234-239.
March, 1833.) Op.8. Premier Trio [G minor] pour Probst-Kistner
(Nov. 23, piano, violon, et violoncelle. M. Schlesinger
1834.) Dedie a Mr. le Prince Antonine
Radziwill—Vol. I., pp. 62, 88,
112, 113-115, 268;—Vol. II., p.
212,342
Jan. 1833. Op.9. Trois Nocturnes (B flat Probst-Kistner
(Nov. 23, minor, E flamajor, and B major] M. Schlesinger
1834.) pour le piano Dedies a Mme.
Camille Pleyel—Vol.l.,268;
—Vol. II., pp.87. 261-63
August, 1833. Op.10.Douze Grandes Etudes [C major Probst-Kistner
(July 6,1833.) A minor, E major, C sharp minor M. Schlesinger
G flat major, E flat minor, C [who sold them
major, F major, F minor, A flat afterwards to
major, E flat major, and C minor] Lemoine].
pour le piano. Dediees a Mr. Fr.

Liszt.—Vol. I., p.201,268; Vol.
II., p. 55 (No. 5), 251-254.

Sept., 1833 Op.11.Grand Concerto [E minor] pour Probst-Kistner
(July 6, le piano avec orchestre. Dedie a M. Schlesinger
1833.) Mr. Fr. Kalkbrenner.—Vol. I., pp
127, 146, 147, 150, 151, 152, 156,
189, 195, 203-208, 210-212, 233, 240,
241, 268, 281; Vol. II., pp. 16, 211

Nov., 1833 Op.12.Variations brillantes [B flat Breitkopf & Hartel
(Jan.26, major] pour le piano sur le Rondeau M. Schlesinger
1834) favori de Ludovic de Herold: "Je
vends des Scapulaires." Dediees a
Mlle. Emma Horsford.—Vol.I.,p.268;
Vol. II., p.221.

May, 1834 Op.13.Grande Fantaisie [A major] sur Probst-Kistner
(April, des airs polonais, pour le piano M. Schlesinger
1834) avec orchestre. Dediee a Mr. J.
P. Pixis—Vol.I., pp. 112,116.
118-120,132,152,197,268; Vol.
II., p.212.

July, 1834. Op.14 Krakowiak, Grand Rondeau de Probst-Kistner
(June, Concert [F major] pour le piano M. Schlesinger
1834.) avec orchestre. Deidie a Mme. la
Princesse Adam Czartoryska.
Vol.I.,pp.88,96,97,98,99,101,
102.112,116,118-120,134,268;
Vol. II., 233.

Jan., 1834 OP. 15. Trois Nocturnes [F major, F Breitkopf &
[Copies sharp major, and G minor] pour le Hartel.
sent to piano. Dedies a Mr. Ferd. Hiller.—
M. Schlesinger.
composer Vol. II., pp. 87, 261, 263
already in
Dec.,

1833].

(Jan.

12,1834.)

March, OP. 16. Rondeau [E flat major] pour Breitkopf &
1834. le piano. Dedie a Mlle. Caroline Hartel.
Hartmann.—Vol. I., p. 269; Vol. M. Schlesinger.
II., p. 221.

May, 1834. OP. 17. Quatre Mazurkas [B flat Breitkopf &
major, E minor, A flat major, and A Hartel.
minor] pour le piano, Dediees a Mme. M. Schlesinger.
Lina Freppa.—Vol. I., p. 268; Vol.
II., 231-232, 234-239.

July, 1834. OP. 18. Grande Valse [E fiat major] Breitkopf &
(June, pour le piano. Dediee a Mlle. Laura Hartel.
1834.*) Harsford [thus in all the editions, M. Schlesinger
but should probably be Horsford. See [who sold it
Op. 12.]—Vol. I., pp. 268, 273; afterwards to
Vol. II., 249. Lemoine].

March, OP. 20. Premier Scherzo [B minor] Breitkopf &
1835. pour le piano. Dedie a Mr. Hartel.
(Feb., T.Albrecht.—Vol. I., p. 294; Vol. M. Schlesinger.
1835.*) II., pp. 27,87, 256-257.

April, OP. 21. Second Concerto [F minor] Breitkopf and
1836. pour le piano avec orchestre. Dedie Hartel.
(Aug., a Mme. la Comtesse Delphine Potocka. M. Schlesinger.
1836.) —Vol. I., pp. 128, 131-132, 134,
156, 163, 200, 203-210, 212, 241,
294; II., p. 211.

Aug., 1836. OP. 22. Grande Polonaise brillante Breitkopf &
(July, [E flat major], precedee d'un Hartel.
1836.*) Andante spianato, pour le piano avec M. Schlesinger.
orchestre. Dediee a Mme. la Baronne
d'Est.—Vol. I., pp. 201-202, 295;
Vol. II., pp. 239-243, 244.

June, 1836. OP. 23. Ballade [G minor] pour le Breitkopf &
(July, piano. Dediee a Mr. le Baron de Hartel.
1836.*) Stockhausen.—Vol. I., pp. 294, 295 M. Schlesinger.
Vol. II., pp. 87, 268-9.
Nov., 1835. Op. 24 Quatre Mazurkas [G minor, C Breitkopf &
(Jan., major, A flat major, and B flat Hartel.
1836.) minor]. Dediees a Mr. le Comte de M. Schlesinger.
Perthuis.-Vol. I., pp. 294,
295; Vol. II., pp. 218 (No. 2), 231-
2, 234 9.
Oct., 1837. Op. 25 Douze Etudes [A flat major, F Breitkopf &
(Oct.22, minor, F major, A minor, E minor, G Hartel.
1837.) sharp minor, C sharp minor, D flat M. Schlesinger
major G flat major, B minor, A minor, [who sold the
& C minor] pour le piano. Dediees & copyright
Mme. la Comtesse d'Agoult.—Vol. I., afterwards to
pp. 276, 295, 310; Vol. II., pp. 15, Lemoine].
251-4.

July, 1836. Op. 26. Deux Polonaises [C sharp Breitkopf &
(July, minor and E flat minor] pour le Hartel.
1836.*) piano. Dediees a Mr. J. Dessauer.—
M. Schlesinger.
Vol. I., p. 295; Vol. II., pp. 239-
244; 245-6.
May, 1836. Op. 27. Deux Nocturnes [C sharp Breitkopf &
(July, minor and D flat major] pour le Hartel.
1836.*) piano. Dediees a Mme. la Comtesse M. Schlesinger.
d'Appony.-Vol. I., pp. 294, 295;
Vol. II., pp. 87, 261, 263-4.
Sept., Op. 28. Vingt-quatre Preludes pour Breitkopf &
1839. le piano. Dediees a son ami Pleyel Hartel.
(Sept., [in the French and in the English Ad. Catelin et
1839.*) edition; a Mr. J. C. Kessler in the Cie.

German edition. The French edition appeared in two books and without opus number].—Vol. II., pp. 20, 24, 27, 28, 29-30, 30-31, 42-45, 50, 51, 71, 72, 76, 77, 254-6.

Jan., 1838. Op. 29. Impromptu [A flat major] Breitkopf & (Dec., pour le piano. Dedie a Mile, la Hartel. 1837.*) Comtesse de Lobau.—Vol. II., pp. M. Schlesinger. 15, 259.

Jan., 1838. Op. 30. Quatre Mazurkas [C minor, B Breitkopf & (Dec., minor, D flat major, and C sharp Hartel. 1837.*) minor] pour le piano. Dediees a Mme. M. Schlesinger. la Princesse de Wurtemberg, nee Princesse Czartoryska.—Vol. II., pp. 15, 231-2, 234-9.

Feb., 1838. Op. 31. Deuxieme Scherzo [B flat Breitkopf & (Dec., minor] pour le piano. Dedie a Mile, Hartel. 1837.*) la Comtesse Adele de Fursienslein. M. Schlesinger. —Vol. II., pp. 15, 87, 256, 257.

(Dec., OP. 32. Deux Nocturnes [B major and A. M. 1837.*) A flat major] pour le Piano. Dedies Schlesinger. a Mme. la Baronne de Billing.—Vol. M. Schlesinger. II., pp. 15, 87, 264.

Nov., 1838. OP. 33. Quatre Mazurkas [G sharp Breitkopf & (Nov., minor, D major, C major, and B Hartel. 1838.) minor] pour le piano. Dediees a M. Schlesinger. Mlle. la Comtesse Mostowska.—Vol. II., pp. 15, 231-2, 234-9.

Dec., 1838. OP. 34. Trois Valses brillantes [A Breitkopf & (Jan., flat major, A minor, and F major] Hartel. 1839.*) pour le piano. Dediees [No. 1] a M. Schlesinger. Mlle. deThun-Hohenstein; [No. 2] a Mme. G. d'Ivri; [No. 3] d Mile. A.

d'Eichthal.—Vol. I., p. 200 (No.
I); Vol. II., pp. 15, 30; 248, 249.

May, 1840. OP. 35. Sonate [B flat minor] pour Breitkopf &
(May, le piano.—Vol. II., pp. 45, 62, 72, Hartel.
1840.*) 77, 94, 225-8. Troupenas et
Cie.

May, 1840. OP. 36. Deuxieme Impromptu [F sharp Breitkopf &
(May, minor] pour le piano.—Vol. II., pp. Hartel.
1840.*) 259-60. Troupenas et
Cie.

May, 1840. OP. 37. Deux Nocturnes [G minor and Breitkopf &
(June, G major] pour le piano.—Vol. II., Hartel.
1840.*) p. 45, 62, 87, 261, 264. Troupenas et
Cie.

Sept., OP. 38. Deuxieme Ballade [F major] Breitkopf &
1840. pour le piano. Dediee a Mr. R. Hartel.
(Sept., Schumann.—Vol. II., pp. 45, 50, 51, Troupenas et
1840.*) 52,54,77,268,269. Cie.

Oct., 1840. Op. 39. Troisieme Scherzo [C sharp Breitkopf &
(Dec., minor] pour le piano. Dedie a Mr. A. Hartel.
1840.*) Gutmann.—Vol. II., pp. 45, 53, 72, Troupenas et
77, 256, 258. Cie.

Nov., 1840. Op. 40. Deux Polonaises [A major and Breitkopf &
(Dec., C minor] pour le piano. Dediees a Hartel.
1840.*) Mr. J. Fontana.—Vol. II., pp. 45, Troupenas et
50, 51, 52, 54, 77, 87, 94, 213 (No. Cie.
1), 239-244, 246, 247.

Dec., 1840. Op. 41. Quatre Mazurkas [C sharp Breitkopf &
(Dec., minor, E minor, B major, and A flat Hartel.
1840.*) major] pour le piano. Dediees a Mr. Troupenas et
E. Witwicki.—Vol. II., pp. 46 (No. Cie.
1), 62, 77, 231-2, 234-9.

July, 1840. Op. 42. Valse [A flat major pour le Breitkopf &
piano,—Vol. II., pp. 77, 86, 248, Hartel.

249. Pacini.

(1841. An Op. 43. Tarantella [A flat major] Schuberth & Co.

nounced in pour le piano.—Vol. II., pp. 77, Troupenas et Cie.

Monatsbe-

82-86, 222.

richte on Jan.

1,1842. Paid

for by the

publisher on

July 7, 1841.]

(Oct., 1841.*)

(Nov. 28, Op.44. Polonaise [F sharp minor] Merchetti.

1841.) pour le piano. Dediee a Mme. la M. Schlesinger.

Princesse Charles de Beauvau.—Vol.

II., pp. 77,80, 81,86,239-244,246.

(Nov. 28, Op.45. Prelude [C sharp minor] pour Merchetti.

1841.) piano. Dediee a Mlle. la Prin-

M. Schlesinger.

cesse Elisabeth Czernicheff.—Vol.

II., pp. 77, 80, 81, 256

Jan., 1842. Op.46. Allegro de Concert [A major] Breitkopf & Hartel.

(Nov. 28, pour le piano. Dedie a Mlle. F. M. Schlesinger.

1841) Muller—Vol. I., p. 202; Vol.II.,

pp.77, 86, 87, 177, 223-5.

Jan. 1842 Op.47. Troisieme Ballade [A flat Breitkopf & Hartel.

(Nov. 28, major] pour le piano. Dediee a M. Schlesinger.

1841) Mlle. P. de Noailles.—Vol.II.,

pp.77,87, 92, 268, 269-70.

Jan., 1842 Op.48. Deux Nocturnes [C minor Breitkopf & Hartel.

(Nov. 28, and F sharp minor] pour le piano. M. Schlesinger.

1841) Dediees a Mlle. L. Duperre—Vol.II.,

pp. 77, 87, 88, 262, 265

Jan., 1842 Op.49. Fantaisie [F minor] pour Breitkopf & Hartel.

(Nov. 28, le piano Dediee a Mme. la Princesse M. Schlesinger.

1841) C. de Souzzo.—Vol. II., pp. 77,87,
230-1.

[Sept.,1842. Op.50. Trois Mazurkas [G major, Mechetti.
Announced A flat major, and C charp minor] M. Schlesinger.
in Monats-
pour le piano. Dediees a Mr. Leon
berichte.] Szmitkowski—Vol.II., p.77,231-2,
(Nov.28,1841 234-9.
[not again
advertised
till June 5,
1842,
although the
preceding
numbers
were.])
Feb.,1843. Op. 51. Allegro Vivace. Troisieme Hofmeister.
(July 9, Impromptu [G flat major] pour le M. Schlesinger.
1843.) piano. Dedie a Mme. la Comtesse
Esterhazy.—Vol.II.,pp.121,260.

Feb., 1843. Op. 52. Quatrieme Ballade [F minor] Breitkopf &
(Dec. 24, pour le piano. Dediee a Mme. la Hartel.
1843.) Baronne C. de Rothschild.—Vol. II., M. Schlesinger.
pp. 77, 121, 268, 270.
Dec., 1843. OP. 53. Huiticmc Polonaise [A flat Breitkopf &
(Dec. 24, major] pour le piano. Dediee a Mr. Hartel.
1843.) A. Leo.—Vol. II., pp. 77, 94, 97, M. Schlesinger.
121, 213, 239-244, 247.
Dec., 1843. Op. 54. Scherzo No. 4 [E major] pour Breitkopf &
(Dec. 24, le piano. Dedie a Mlle. J. de Hartel.
1843.) Caraman.—Vol. II-, pp. 121, 256, M. Schlesinger.
258-9.

Aug. 1844. Op. 55. Deux Nocturnes [F minor and Breitkopf &
(Sept. 22, E flat major] pour le piano. Dedies Hartel.
1844.) a Mlle. J. W. Stirling.—Vol. II., M. Schlesinger.
p. 118, 121,262, 265-6.

Aug., 1844. Op. 56. Trois Mazurkas [B major, C Breitkopf &
(Sept. 22, major, and C minor] pour le piano. Hartel.
1844.) Dediees a Mlle. C. Maberly.—Vol. M. Schlesinger.
II., pp. 118, 121-2, 231-2, 234-9.

May, 1845. Op. 57. Berceuse [D flat major] pour Breitkopf &
(June, le piano. Dediee & Mlle. Elise Hartel.
1845.*) Gavard.—Vol. I., p. 119; Vol. II., J. Meissonnier.
pp. 118, 122,267-8.

June, 1845. Op.58. Sonate [B minor] pour le Breitkopf & Hartel
(June, piano. Dediee a Mme.la Comtesse J. Meissonnier.
1845*) E. de Perthuis.—Vol. II., pp.
118, 122, 228-9.

[Jan., 1846, Op. 59. Trois Mazurkas [A minor, Stern et Cie.
announced A flat major, and F sharp minor] Brandus et Cie.
in Monats-
pour le piano.—Vol.II.,pp. 122,
berichte.] 231-2, 234-9.
(April,
1846.*)

Dec., 1846 Op.60 Barcarolle [F sharp major] Breitkopf & Hartel
(Sept., pour le piano. Dediee a Mme. la Brandus et Cie.
1846) Baronne de Stockhausen-Vol.II,
pp.77, 122 266-7.

Dec., 1846. Op.61 Polonaise-Fantaisie [A Breitkopf & Hartel
(Sept., flat major] pour le piano. Brandus et Cie.
1846.*) Dediee a Mme. A.Veyret.—
Vol.II., pp. 122, 239-244, 248

Dec., 1846. Op. 62. Deux Nocturnes [B major Breitkopf & Hartel.
(Sept., and E major] pour le piano. Dedies Brandus et Cie.
1846.*) a Mlle. R. de Konneritz.—Vol. II.,

pp. 122, 262, 266.

Sept., OP. 63. Trois Mazurkas [B major, F   Breitkopf &
1847. minor, and C sharp minor] pour le   Hartel.
(Oct. 17, piano. Dediees a. Mme. la Comtesse   Brandus et Cie.
1847) L. Czosnowska.—Vol. II., pp. 122,
205, 231-2, 234-9.

Sept., OP. 64. Trois Valses [D flat major,   Breitkopf &
1847. C sharp minor, and A flat major]   Hartel.
(Oct. 17, pour le piano. Dediees [No 1] a Mme. Brandus et Cie.
1847) la Comtesse Potocka; [No. 2] a Mme.
la Baronne de Rothschild;
[No. 3] a Mme. la Baronne Bronicka.—
Vol. II., pp. 95, 122, 142 (No. 1),
205, 248, 250-1, 387.

Sept., OP. 65. Sonate [G minor] pour piano   Breitkopf &
1847. et violoncelle. Dediee a Mr. A.   Hartel.
(Oct. 17, Franchomme.—Vol. II., pp. 122, 205, Brandus et Cie.
1847) 206, 207, 211, 229.

II—WORKS PUBLISHED WITHOUT OPUS NUMBERS DURING THE COMPOSER'S

LIFETIME.
[1833, in   Grand Duo concertant [E major] pour M.   Schlesinger.
print.]   piano et violoncelle sur des themes A. M.
(July 6,   de Robert le Diable, par F. Chopin   Schlesinger.
1833.)   et A. Franchomme.—Vol. II., p. 230.

Aug. or   Trois Nouvelles Etudes [F. minor, A   M. Schlesinger.
Sept., 1840   flat major, and D flat major]. Etudes A. M.
[this is   de Schlesinger. Perfection de la
the date of   Methode des Moscheles et Fetis.—Vol.
the   II., p. 252.
appearance
of the
Methode.]

(July 25, Variation VI. [Largo, E major, C] T. Haslinger.
1841.) from the Hexameron: Morceau de Troupenas et Cie.

Concert. Grandes Variations de
bravoure sur la Marche des
"Puritains" de Bellini, composees
pour le Concert de Mme. la Princesse
Belgiojoso au benefice des pauvres,
par MM. Liszt, Thalberg, Pixis, H.
Herz, Czerny, and Chopin.—Vol. II.,
pp. 14, 15.

[Feb., 1842, Mazurka [A minor] pour piano, No.2 B. Schott's Sohne.
announced of "Notre Temps."—Vol.II.,p.237
in Monats-berichte.

III—WORKS PUBLISHED WITH OPUS NUMBERS AFTER THE COMPOSER'S DEATH

[May, OP. 4. Sonate [C minor] pour le C. Haslinger.
1851.] piano. Dediee a Mr. Joseph Elsner. S. Richault.
(May, [This work was already in the hands
1851.*) of the German publisher, T. Haslinger,
in 1828.]—Vol. I., pp. 62,112,118;
Vol. II., p. 63.

1855. OP. 66-74 are the posthumous works A. M.
with opus numbers given to the world Schlesinger.
by Julius Fontana (publies sur fils. J. Meissonnier
manuscrits originaux avec
autorisation de sa famille).—Vol.
II., 270-1.

OP. 66. Fantaisie-Impromptu [C
sharp minor]. Composed about 1834.—
Vol. II.. p. 261, 271.

OP. 67. Quatre Mazurkas [G major

(1835), G minor (1849), C major (1835),
and A minor (1846).]—Vol. II.,
p. 271.

OP. 68. Quatre Mazurkas [C major
(1830), A minor (1827), F major (1830),
and F minor (1849).]—Vol. I., pp.
112, 122 (No. 2).

OP. 69. Deux Valses [F minor
(1836), and B minor (1829).]—
Vol. I., pp. 112, 122 (No. 2).

OP. 70. Trois Valses [G flat major
(1835), F minor (1843), and D flat major
(1830).]—Vol. I., pp. 128, 200
(No. 3).

Op. 71. Trois Polonaises [D minor
(1827), B flat major (1828), and F minor
(1829).]—Vol. I., pp. 62 (Nos. 1
and 2), 112, 121 (Nos. 1, 2, and 3),
129 (No. 3).

OP. 72. Nocturne [E minor (1827)];
Marche funebre [C minor (1829)];
et Trois Ecossaises [D major, G
major, and D flat major (1830)].—
Vol. I., pp. 62, 112, 121 (No. 1);
112, 123 (No. 2); 202 (No. 3).

OP. 73. Rondeau [C major] pour deux
pianos (1828).—Vol. I., pp. 62,
112, 116.

OP. 74. Seventeen Polish Songs by
Witwicki, Mickiewicz, Zaleski, &c.,
for voice with pianoforte
accompaniment. The German translation
by Ferd. Gumbert. [The
English translation of Stanley
Lucas, Weber & Co.'s English
edition is by the Rev. J.
Troutbeck.]—Vol. II., p. 271-272.

IV—WORKS PUBLISHED WITHOUT OPUS NUMBERS AFTER THE COMPOSER'S DEATH

[May, Variations [E major] pour le piano C. Haslinger.
1851.] stir un air allemand. (1824?) S. Richault.
[although not published till 1851,
this composition was already in 1830
in T. Haslinger's hands).—Vol. I.:
pp. 53, 55, 56.
Mazurka [G major]. (1825.)—Vol. I., J. Leitgeber.
p. 52; II., 236. Gebethner &
Wolff.
Mazurka [B flat major (1825)].—Vol.
I., p. 52; II., 236.

Mazurka [D major (1829-30)].—Vol.
I., PP—202-203; II., 236.

Mazurka [D major (1832.—A
remodelling of the preceding
Mazurka)].—Vol. I., pp.
202-203; II., 236.
Mazurka [C major (1833)].—Vol. II., Gebethner &
p. 236. Wolff.

Mazurka [A minor. Dediee a son ami Bote & Bock.
Emile Gail'ard.—Vol. II, p. 236.
1858. Valse [E minor].—Vol. II., p. 251. B. Schott's
Sohne.
Gebethner &
Wolff.
1864. Polonaise [G sharp minor]. Dediee B. Schott's
a Mme. Dupont.—Vol. I., p. 52 (see Sohne.
also Corrections and Additions, Vol. Gebethner &
I., p. VIII. Wolff.
1872. Polonaise [G flat major]. Nothing B. Schott's
but the composer's autograph could Sohne.
convince one of the genuineness of
this piece. There are here and there
passages which have the Chopin ring,
indeed, seem to be almost bodily
taken from some other of his works,
but there is also a great deal which
it is impossible to imagine to have
come at any time from his pen—the
very opening bars may be instanced.
Polonaise [B flat minor (1826)].—
Gebethner &
Vol. I., pp. 52-53. Wolff.
Valse [E major (1829)].—
Vol. I., Gebethner &
pp. 112, 122. Wolff.
W. Chaberski.

Souvenir de Paganini [A major].
This piece, which I do not know, is
mentioned in the list of the
master's works given by Karasowski

in the Polish edition of his life of Chopin. It was published in the supplement of the Warsaw Echo Muzyczne, where also the two preceding pieces first appeared. About a Mazurka in F sharp major, published under Chopin's name by J. P. Gotthard, of Vienna, see Vol. II., p. 237; and about Deux Valses melancoliques (F minor and B minor) ecrites sur l'Album de Mme. la Comtesse P. 1844, see Vol. II., p. 251.

La Reine des Songes, which appeared in the Paris Journal de Musique, No. 8, 1876, is No. 1 of the Seventeen Polish Songs (transposed to B flat major) with French words by George Sand, beginning:

"Quand la lune se leve
Dans un pale rayon
Elle vient comme un reve,
Comme une vision."

Besides this song, the letter-press, taken from George Sand's Histoire de ma Vie, is accompanied by two instrumental pieces, extracts from the last movement of the E minor Concerto and the Bolero, the latter being called Chanson de Zingara.
END OF VOLUME II.